HACKING EXPOSED™ J2EE & JAVA

"A well-presented analysis of J2EE security concerns and solutions with practical, real-world examples."

—John Ranta, Customer Training Instructor, Sun Services, Sun Microsystems

"By using a nice, clear sample project that focuses on actual code and discusses the strengths and weaknesses of design and coding decisions, this book provides a valuable reference for both the Java development community and security professionals."

—Dave Fautheree, CISSP, Systems Security Analyst, Southwest Airlines

"An essential guide for application developers of all levels, covering security across the spectrum of Java, J2EE, and web services technologies. Well-organized presentation of common security attacks and how to stop them cold, all demonstrated by working code in a realistic case study."

—Tim Seltzer, Enterprise Java Architect, Java Center, Sun Microsystems

HACKING EXPOSED™ J2EE & JAVA: DEVELOPING SECURE APPLICATIONS WITH JAVA TECHNOLOGY

BRIAN **BUEGE**
RANDY **LAYMAN**
ART **TAYLOR**

McGraw-Hill/Osborne
New York Chicago San Francisco
Lisbon London Madrid Mexico City Milan
New Delhi San Juan Seoul Singapore Sydney Toronto

The McGraw·Hill Companies

McGraw-Hill/Osborne
2600 Tenth Street
Berkeley, California 94710
U.S.A.

To arrange bulk purchase discounts for sales promotions, premiums, or fund-raisers, please contact **McGraw-Hill**/Osborne at the above address. For information on translations or book distributors outside the U.S.A., please see the International Contact Information page immediately following the index of this book.

Hacking Exposed™ J2EE & JAVA: Developing Secure Applications with Java Technology

1234567890 CUS CUS 0198765432

ISBN 0-07-222565-3

Publisher
Brandon A. Nordin
Vice President & Associate Publisher
Scott Rogers
Senior Acquisitions Editor
Jane Brownlow
Project Editor
Katie Conley
Technical Editor
Michael Judd
Copy Editors
Marilyn Smith, Bill McManus
Proofreader
Pat Mannion
Indexer
Irv Hershman
Computer Designers
Tara A. Davis, Kathleen Fay Edwards
Illustrators
Michael Mueller, Lyssa Wald
Series Design
Dick Schwartz, Peter F. Hancik
Cover Series Design
Dodie Shoemaker

This book was composed with Corel VENTURA™ Publisher.

To Virginia and Ethan, who remind me daily that perfect love
can exist in an imperfect world.
—Brian Buege

To Tracey for her many days and nights of understanding.
—Randy Layman

To the friends and family that have supported and advised me over the years;
you remind me constantly of what is truly valuable.
—Art Taylor

About the Authors

Brian Buege

Brian Buege is an information systems professional with over a decade of software development experience. An application developer and architect at heart, one of his dreams is to make Java application security accessible and understandable enough that it can be used by every developer, not just "security" specialists. Through his work on over 15 software projects, he's discovered that application security techniques need to be not just useful and effective, but also easy to implement.

In the five years he's worked with Java, he has architected and developed systems across a wide variety of business domains and with varying technologies that range from financial services to health care, and from standalone to N-tier.

In addition to his work with Fortune 500 clients as an independent consultant and application security analyst, he is a Sun Microsystems Certified Java Instructor, Developer, and Programmer. He has taught computer science and mathematics at the college level, and has also taught Java-related topics to business clients nationwide. He holds an M.S. in Computer Science from the University of Minnesota and a B.S. in Computer Science from Texas Christian University.

He used to have a life and some pretty interesting hobbies until he agreed to help write a book on J2EE application security.

—Brian Buege can be reached at brian@hackingexposedjava.com.

Randy Layman

Randy Layman is a software engineer with over five years of development experience. He has been involved in the design, development, and deployment of mission-critical financial and web publishing systems. Always concerned with developing the best possible system, he has worked diligently to secure computer systems from outside attack while still providing usable, responsive, and effective systems. Randy holds a B.S. in Computer Science from the Georgia Institute of Technology.

—Randy Layman can be reached at randy@hackingexposedjava.com.

Art Taylor

Art Taylor has over 17 years experience in the computer industry and can remember when a green screen character terminal with a 1200 baud connection was considered state-of-the-art. He spent some time in the database side of the industry working for a number of years at Informix Software, a relational database company, before making the switch to Java technologies in 1996.

Art has written several books on Java APIs and technologies and has taught Java courses for Sun Microsystems. He has performed a variety of project roles, including technical architect, project manager, database designer, and general Java guru.

Art likes to write (maybe even a little too much) and has published a number of technical books and articles over the years. He is currently focused on writing, teaching computer courses as an assistant professor at Rider University, consulting, and writing (some more).

—Art Taylor can be reached at taylorart@blast.net.

About the Technical Reviewer

Michael Judd is a Customer Training Specialist and Java expert with Sun Microsystems. Over the last five years, he has both taught and helped develop courses ranging from Java syntax, patterns, security, the J2EE environment, and object-oriented analysis and design. He is the lead instructor in North America for SUN's Java security and web component curriculum, and serves as the primary resource for training and certifying other Java instructors in the United States.

Prior to working for SUN, Judd worked at a Fortune 500 company where he specialized in web development. He was awarded the 1996 Technology Grant Award for a Java client/server project and served as the technical lead for the company's external website. He has been developing in Java since JSDK 1.0 and holds the Web Developer, Developer, and Programmer certifications.

Michael holds a B.S. in Computer Science from Southern Methodist University. He lives in Plano, Texas with his wife, three dogs, and a fish.

CONTENTS

ACKNOWLEDGMENTS

Writing a book is tougher than it looks! In fact, it's so tough that we weren't able to do it alone. We'd like to graciously acknowledge all of the people who contributed advice, assistance, and encouragement to us as we pursued this project.

First, we'd like to thank our families. Without their support, it would have been impossible to complete this project. They patiently tolerated our many late nights, weekends, and vacations spent working on this book. If "sacrifice is the measure of a hero," then they are truly heroes!

Also, we would like to thank all of our colleagues and friends who helped us with the development of the concepts in the book, especially Michael Judd for his precise, insightful technical editing. His skill in Java security topics is even greater than his prowess at Diablo II, Lord of Destruction (which is saying quite a bit). Nathan Paris, Java developer extraordinaire, also deserves credit for refactoring code written by three authors to make it look like it was written by one person. Additionally, we'd like to thank the many people who contributed time by listening to our ideas and giving us honest feedback, specifically John Ranta and Kevin Janise who freely traded their insight for Thai food (it was a bargain for us) and Jim Powell who taught at least one author how to see clearly with only a single eye…

We'd also like to thank all of the security architects and developers of the J2SE and J2EE platforms: You've given application developers a toolset which makes building secure applications (almost) easy. Nothing's perfect, but thanks for thinking about security first instead of last!

The McGraw-Hill/Osborne team also deserves a large measure of thanks, including our acquisitions editor Jane Brownlow, project editor Katie Conley, and copy editors Marilyn Smith and Bill McManus (trust us, we needed the last two!).

And finally, we'd like to thank nebulous and elusive Lester Goodwin for giving us a case study to work with. He's hard to stay in touch with because he's frequently on the move, but if you look closely enough, we think you might find that he's been working on your applications, too… Give him a shout at lester@javajockey.com. He just might respond…

INTRODUCTION

"So in the case of those who are skilled in attack, their opponents do not know where to defend. In the case of those skilled in defense, their opponents do not know where to attack." —Sun Tzu

In its short lifetime, Java has grown from an interesting side project started at a hardware company to the predominant language for server-side, middle-tier programming. This success has been no accident. The Java language has many features that make it the right choice for a variety of programming tasks, from the server to the palmtop. It is a platform-independent, type-safe, and compact language. It has a rich set of development libraries, provided in the Java Development Kit (JDK) itself and courtesy of open-source powerhouses like Apache's Jakarta project. But most important, the Java language has a level of strong, consistent, and extensible security that is sorely lacking in other languages and operating environments.

Java security was a key consideration in the development of the language. The developers knew that Java programs would be exposed to a broad set of unknown users, presenting distinct security risks. A number of security features were built into the language from the start, and these features have been augmented and extended with each new release. Unfortunately, many application developers and system architects seem to overlook

Java and J2EE security, even though it's a technology built into the fabric of the platform. In many instances, the authors have seen enterprises (and even vendors) build custom security solutions that almost exactly mirror the capabilities of the Java platform itself—simply because they didn't know that those particular security features already existed in Java.

Understanding the security tools available for Java and using these tools consistently are the foundation of a good Java security policy. The goal of this book is to help you select the appropriate security tools and use them correctly to protect your applications.

Know Thine Enemy

Exactly who are these people who want to attack our applications? Are they all 14-year-old kids sitting in their bedrooms with high-speed Internet connections? Are they all located outside our corporate firewalls? Most likely, that is not the case. Taking into account the fact that the majority of business applications in production today are not web-enabled and are not easily accessible from outside the corporate intranet, the demographics of our *application* attackers will be slightly different than what most people typically think of when they think of cyber-malfeasants. In fact, not many serious attackers of non-web-based business applications reside outside the organization.

Although some individuals attack systems applications from the outside, most of them are amateurs. (We use the term "amateur" in the true sense; some of these people are extremely skilled, but they are generally not paid for their services.) In most cases, these system attackers are not focused on pilfering or modifying information (the domain of corporate applications). Instead, external attackers are usually interested in gaining personal satisfaction through defeating system security, destroying data, demonstrating prowess by modifying publicly available information (like a public web page), or using the system as a springboard for an attack on another system.

Most sophisticated professional attackers know what government agencies around the world have known for centuries (and applied in the field of espionage): It's easier to convince someone with access to do your work for you than it is to try to break in and do it yourself. Compare the number of "Mission Impossible" style break-ins on U.S. Intelligence activities you've heard about in the last 15 years (few or none) with the number of employees of those same agencies who have willfully given away sensitive information for relatively small amounts of money. The same principle applies to corporate espionage: Why break in and risk getting caught when you can pay somebody who works there to get the information for you? This maxim was originally developed to defeat physical security measures, but the same principle applies to information system security measures. We must be aware that attacks on our application will not only come from outside, they also can originate within our organization.

Attackers generally fall into three groups: external attackers, deliberate internal attackers, and accidental internal attackers. External attackers include stereotypical hackers/crackers and corporate espionage specialists (competitors). Deliberate internal attackers might be disgruntled, malicious, or unethical employees; contractors; or very patient, dedicated espionage specialists who manage to infiltrate an organization. Then there is the biggest group of all: the accidental internal attackers, who can do a lot of damage unintentionally. This group includes novice or untrained application or system users, system administrators who don't always read the command line before pressing ENTER, and software developers who rush maintenance releases to production without proper regression testing.

Ideally, an application should attempt to defend itself against all three categories of people. In corporate computing today, internal attacks (both accidental and deliberate) on applications that are not web-enabled are more common than external attacks.

Therefore, in all but our web application chapters, the attacker we will be most concerned with will be a member of the organization where the application is used and a person against whom most system-level security measures will have a reduced effect (the attacker already possesses some degree of system access). We will let the operating-system and network-security specialists help us defend our applications against the external attackers. We won't ignore external attacks, but for non-web applications our primary focus will be attacks by internal users with knowledge of the system and existing security. We will also consider secondary threats presented by outsiders who have some knowledge of the technology, systems, or vendor software used within the enterprise.

What Makes this Book is Different

The philosophy behind this book is radically different from the majority of Java security-related books on the market today. Here are the main tenets we applied:

- **Focus on the whole application, not just one OS or one technology.** Instead of focusing on one technology, like EJB for example, we focus on *application* security and cover it over a wide variety of J2SE and J2EE application architectures that range from client-server to web-based, from standalone to web services, and from Java Web Start clients to EJBs in the middle tier. Our hope is that this will help you develop a comprehensive, integrated application security strategy that will transcend architectures and platforms.
- **Provide a toolkit for the application developer and system architect.** This book focuses on the use of security technologies in the context of a working Java/J2EE application. Instead of showing you code fragments out of context, we invite you to visit our website (www.hackingexposedjava.com) where you can download actual working sample applications, complete with installation instructions, which include the techniques that we outline in the book. In many cases, we show several different techniques for reaching the same security goal.
- **Focus on issues important to the application developer, not the security theorist.** We didn't rewrite the API specifications and documentation, and we don't discuss various cryptographic nuances, because we assume you can

find this information yourself by reading the documentation distributed with your system. Instead, we show you the issues and challenges that you might face when attempting to utilize these features in a real application.

- **Some security well implemented is better than perfect security not implemented.** The best security is security that is actually used. Therefore, we introduce mechanisms the typical overburdened developer can easily achieve, instead of "near perfect" yet overly complex mechanisms. It doesn't do any good to design the most comprehensive application security system in the world if the project manager cuts it from the project because there isn't time to implement it (we've seen this happen more than once).

Who Should Read This Book

This book is directed toward the Java developer familiar with the basics of the Java language and key language concepts such as object design, class inheritance, and the use of interfaces. The book also aims to serve as a reference for network administrators and security professionals who want to know how to keep J2EE and Java web applications secure.

A deep understanding of cryptography and the arcane math of ciphers is not a requirement. In fact, cryptography is only part of Java 2 Enterprise Edition (J2EE) security. The prevalence of Java Cryptography Extension (JCE) and the Java Secure Sockets Extension (JSSE) has made using these encryption mechanisms a relatively transparent, straightforward procedure.

Deep understanding of J2EE is also not required. While this book does not attempt to explain J2EE in detail, it does provide an explanation of the fundamentals of servlets and Enterprise JavaBeans (EJBs). Experienced Java programmers will be able to understand and follow the examples.

THE BASIC BUILDING BLOCKS: ATTACKS AND COUNTERMEASURES

As with the other titles in the *Hacking Exposed* series, the basic building blocks of this book are the attacks and countermeasures discussed in each chapter.

The attacks are highlighted here as they are throughout the *Hacking Exposed* series:

This Is an Attack Icon

Attacks or exploits are highlighted with this icon throughout the book. Our focus is application security issues, so many attacks covered in this book will relate to common attack strategies or techniques, not common tools that an attacker can use to conduct an attack. Because each application is unique, there are few "toolkits" built specifically to penetrate a particular application; there are plenty of toolkits built to penetrate a particular OS weakness, or a vulnerability of a particular web container, application server, or database, but because Java is platform independent, these toolkits may or may not apply to a particular Java business application in a particular environment.

For this reason, our attacks do not focus on vulnerabilities at the system or container/server level, but instead on vulnerabilities created (and correctable) by application developers. These are often the easiest vulnerabilities to exploit, but they require a skill set different from the typical system-level attacker's: An application-level attacker has to be able to think like an application developer.

Each attack is also accompanied by a Risk Rating, scored exactly as in the other titles in the *Hacking Exposed* series:

Popularity:	The frequency of use in the wild against live targets, 1 being most rare, 10 being widely used.
Simplicity:	The degree of skill necessary to execute the attack, 10 being little or no skill, 1 being seasoned Java programmer.
Impact:	The potential damage caused by successful execution of the attack, 1 being revelation of trivial business information, 10 being complete compromise of vital business information or loss of application availability.
Risk Rating:	The preceding three values are considered in the generation of the overall risk rating. In some cases we have subjectively adjusted the risk rating beyond a true average of the three criteria above if we feel that there are additional issues that contribute to an increase, or decrease, in the risk of a particular attack.

We have also followed the *Hacking Exposed* line when it comes to countermeasures, which follow each attack or series of related attacks.

This Is a Countermeasure Icon

This icon should draw your attention to critical fix information. Because many countermeasures for application security require development effort and programming, many of our countermeasures are quite extensive, detailing the exact steps that you need to take to implement the countermeasure in the context of your own application.

Other Visual Aids

We've also made prolific use of visually enhanced

icons to highlight those nagging little details that often get overlooked.

ONLINE RESOURCES AND TOOLS

Java and J2EE application security is a *big* topic. Because of this, there is a lot of information and many code examples that we simply did not have the space to include in this book.

To remedy this, we have implemented a website that tracks new information relevant to topics discussed in this book, errata, and, most important, the downloadable, fully-functional code examples from the text of the book. You'll also find several appendixes on Java technology posted to this site, too. The site address is:

```
http://www.hackingexposedjava.com
```

We suggest that you visit the website frequently to view any updated materials, gain easy access to the code mentioned in the book, and stay informed about developments in Java and J2EE security.

Additionally, to talk directly with the authors via email, we are reachable at the following addresses:

```
art@hackingexposedjava.com
brian@hackingexposedjava.com
randy@hackingexposedjava.com
```

QUICK START GUIDE: INSTRUCTIONS FOR THE READER

Before you dive in and start reading, we suggest you first familiarize yourself with the case study. A brief overview of the first version (a simple standalone application) is included following this introduction. Throughout the book, the case study is improved and re-implemented across a variety of common J2EE architectures. If you are familiar with its design from the beginning, you will better understand the context for the application of various application security techniques we discuss. So, for example, when we say, "... to fix this issue, we'll add the following lines of code to the `LocalPersistenceService` class..." you'll know what we are talking about.

Again, we also recommend that you download the working code examples from our website, www.hackingexposedjava.com. There are about 20 different iterations of our sample application, each with different application security techniques and idioms implemented across a variety of architectures. When you attempt to implement these strategies yourself, you'll find it incredibly helpful to have the full source code to look at.

HOW THIS BOOK IS ORGANIZED

The book is divided as follows:

- Chapter 1 reviews the overall Java architecture and basic security mechanisms.
- Chapter 2 focuses on the important new security packages included with J2SE 1.4: Java Authentication and Authorization Service (JAAS), Java Cryptography Extension (JCE), and the Java Secure Sockets Extension (JSSE).
- Chapter 3 focuses on J2EE architecture and security.
- Chapters 4-6 use a standalone version of the case study to study basic application security issues that are relevant in just about any Java application.
- Chapters 7 and 8 use a two-tier version of the case study to explore issues commonly faced when developing a system that needs to connect to either a database using JDBC or an object server using RMI.
- Chapters 9 and 10 use a web-based version of the case study to focus on security issues commonly encountered when deploying applications that use Servlet and JSP technology.
- Chapters 11 and 12 use both a web services and an EJB-based version of the case study to demonstrate securing the middle tier of your application.

CASE STUDY: THE RETIREMENT APPLICATION, A 401(K) DASHBOARD

Lester Goodwin, a fictitious person, is the owner of finalize(): Retirement Planning for Java Gurus, a fictitious company. An aspiring Java guru himself, Lester requires some automation support for his retirement planning endeavor, so he has written a small application to track the balance of his client's 401K accounts. This is the application that we will use as a case study throughout this book. As mentioned earlier, the complete documented code for all of the examples in this book is available on our website at www.hackingexposedjava.com.

.COM

Lester has tried his best to create a secure application, but despite the fact that he is quite the Java guru, he is not familiar enough with Java/J2EE security support to use many of those features correctly. Consequently, Lester's application is a bit naive and extremely vulnerable to attacks. As a Java guru, Lester is very interested in exploring various application architectures (despite the security issues), so there are several different versions of the Retirement Account 401K Application in circulation, including web-based, client-server, Java WebStart, J2EE Model 2 with Servlets and JSP, and others.

To understand Lester's application, however, we only need to examine the simple stand-alone application. As we explore Java security in more detail, we will examine specific architectures and the security issues associated with them.

The stand-alone version of the application can run on a single, stand-alone computer with no network connectivity whatsoever. The application is distributed as a set of Java class files, which the users unzip into a location within their Java system classpath.

The User Interface

To run the application, the user types the following on the command line:

```
C:\sec\book>java book.standalone.original.ClientFrame local orig.txt
```

The first argument is the string `local`, indicating that the application should run in stand-alone mode, using a data file on the local system. The second argument is the name of the file used to store the data—in this case, `orig.txt`. The system will automatically create this file with some sample data if it doesn't already exist. Two sample accounts will be added to the file: account 12345 and account 54321.

After entering this information on the command line, the user is presented with the User Login dialog box. The user enters the login information, which, in this case, is the username `lester` and the password `password`, as shown here.

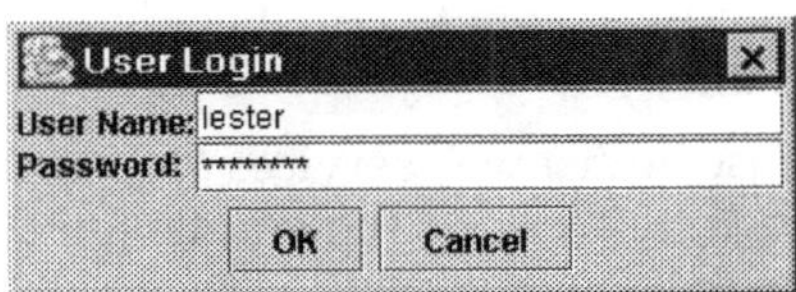

The system then proceeds with the login process. After authenticating the user (verifying Lester is who he says he is), the system displays the following highly intuitive main application screen:

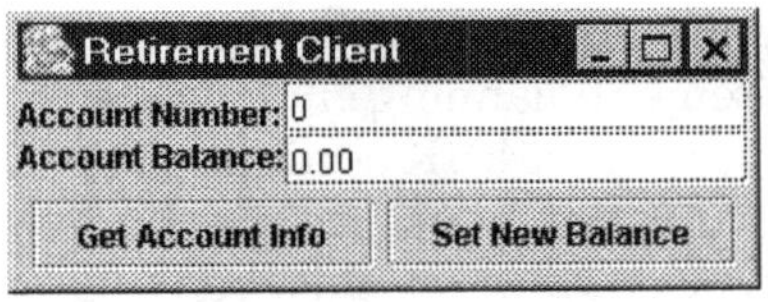

To use the system, a user enters an account number in the Account Number field and clicks the Get Account Info button. The balance for the account is then displayed in the Account Balance field. To set or change a balance for an account, the user fills in the relevant account number in the Account Number field, enters the balance in the Account Balance field, and clicks the Set New Balance button.

Currently, Lester has implemented programmatic authorization to enforce the business rule that Lester is the only user who can set the balance for any account (although all users can view the balances in any account). There are no current provisions in the system to add an account (Lester has only two clients).

The following is an example of what happens when user `brian` (whose password is `password`) tries to set an account balance for account 12345:

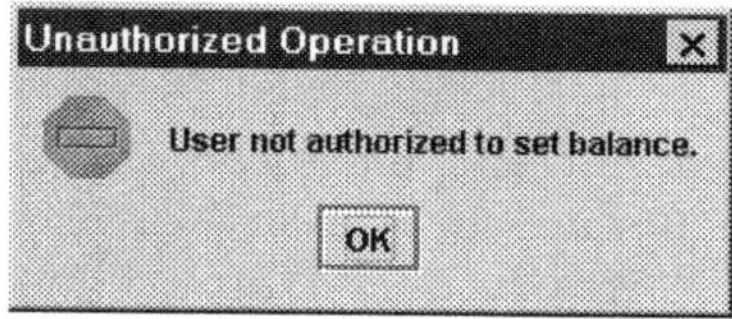

Closing the main application window exits the application and closes the data file.

The data for this system is currently stored in text format within a file specified by the user on the command line. Here's a listing of the contents of the application data file (`orig.txt`) after the user runs the application once and makes no changes to the data:

```
12345                              300.33
54321                            11111.22
```

Now that we've looked at how this application behaves, let's look at how it's designed and constructed.

The Application Design and Implementation

To develop security for this application, we need to understand its design and implementation.

Figure CS-1 shows the use cases realized by the retirement application. This appli cation allows any user to get the account balance for a retirement account, and only

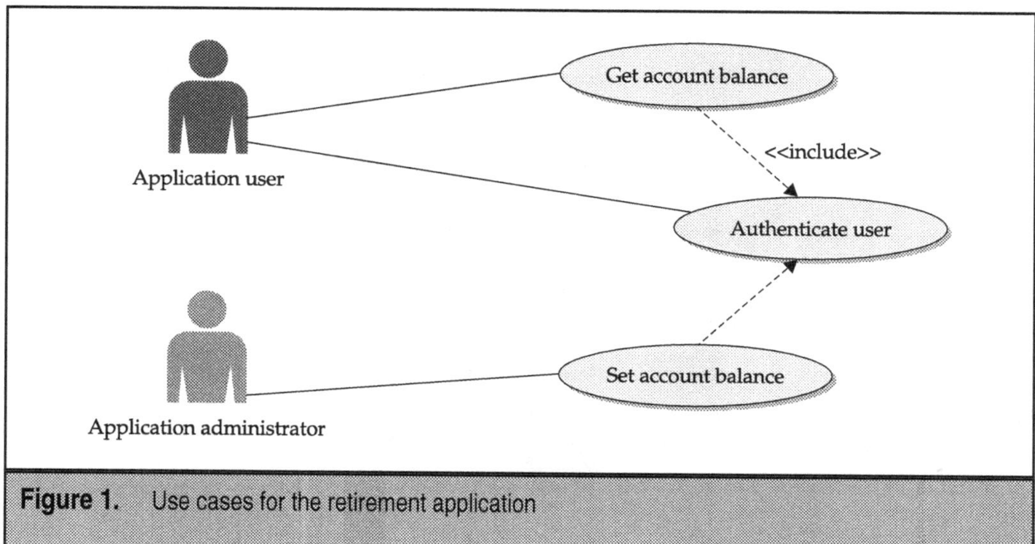

Figure 1. Use cases for the retirement application

administrators to set the account balance. All users must be authenticated as a part of either business use case (get the account balance or set the account balance).

Figure CS-2 illustrates the ultimate deployment for the stand-alone version of the application.

As you can see, the application is partitioned into two main pieces: the presentation layer, or user interface component, and the model or business and persistence layer, which is implemented by the `LocalPeristenceService` component. The user interface component communicates with the model through the `RetirementAccountInfo` interface.

The Presentation Layer

Figure CS-3 depicts the main classes in the user interface component and their associations with each other. The main driver for the application is the `ClientFrame` class, which contains the appropriate listeners to respond to the button clicks, as well as the ability to construct and show a login dialog box to prompt users for their credential information.

The username and password information is stored in an instance of the `RetirementCredential` object and initially authenticated by the `ClientFrame` to ensure that the user is authorized to use the application. Then, when a `setBalance` request is made, the `RetirementCredential` is passed, along with the account number and

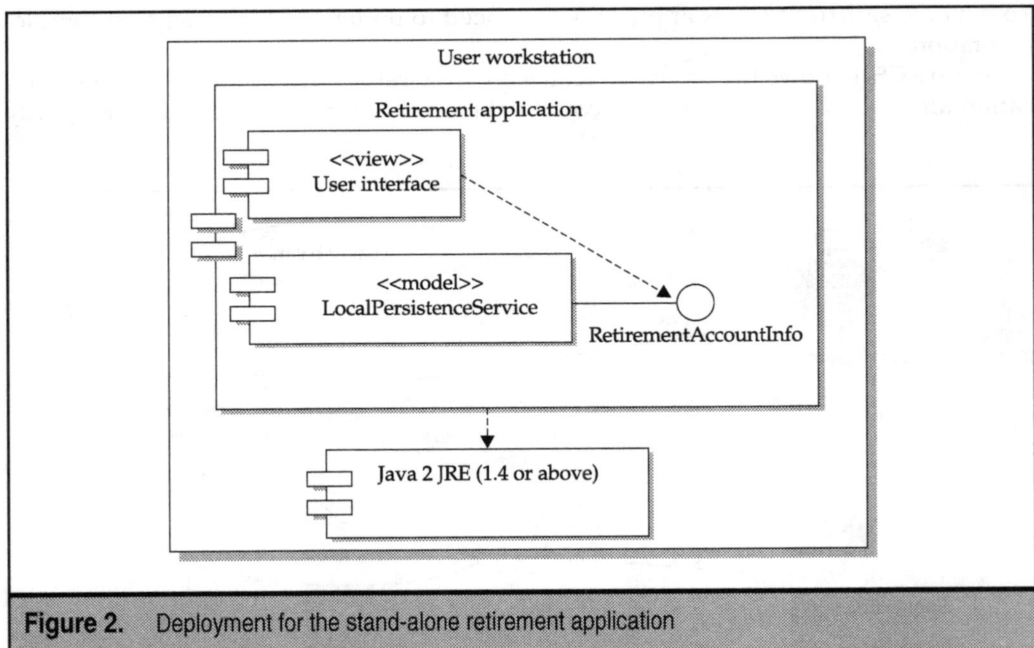

Figure 2. Deployment for the stand-alone retirement application

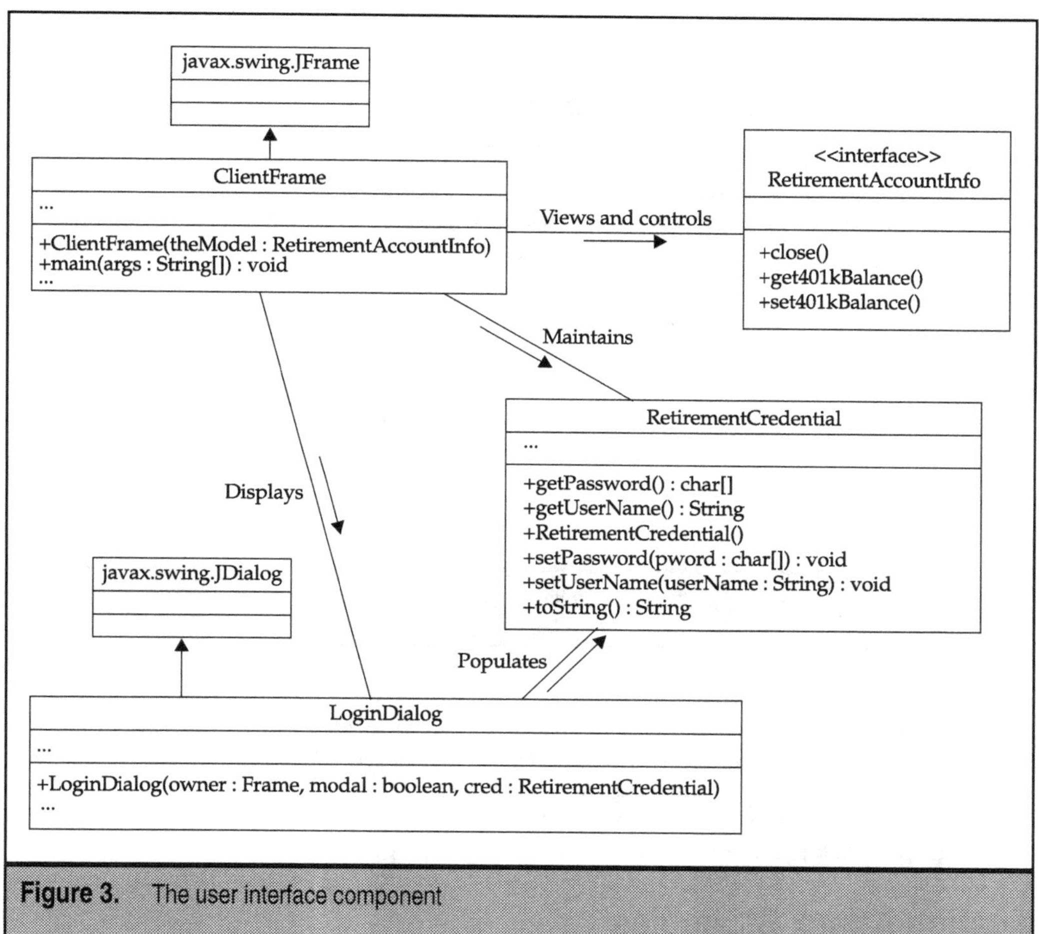

Figure 3. The user interface component

the requested new balance, to an implementation of the `RetirementAccountInfo` interface, which will actually perform the `setBalance` operation.

The Business and Persistence Layer

Figure CS-4 shows the model, which is the `LocalPersistenceService` class in this case. You can see that it implements the `RetirementAccountInfo` interface and provides both business validation and persistence services for its clients.

The `LocalPersistenceService` class is an implementation of the `RetirementAccountInfo` interface that uses a local file for its persistence. A single implementation of this service is shown in this example. In this book, you will see other

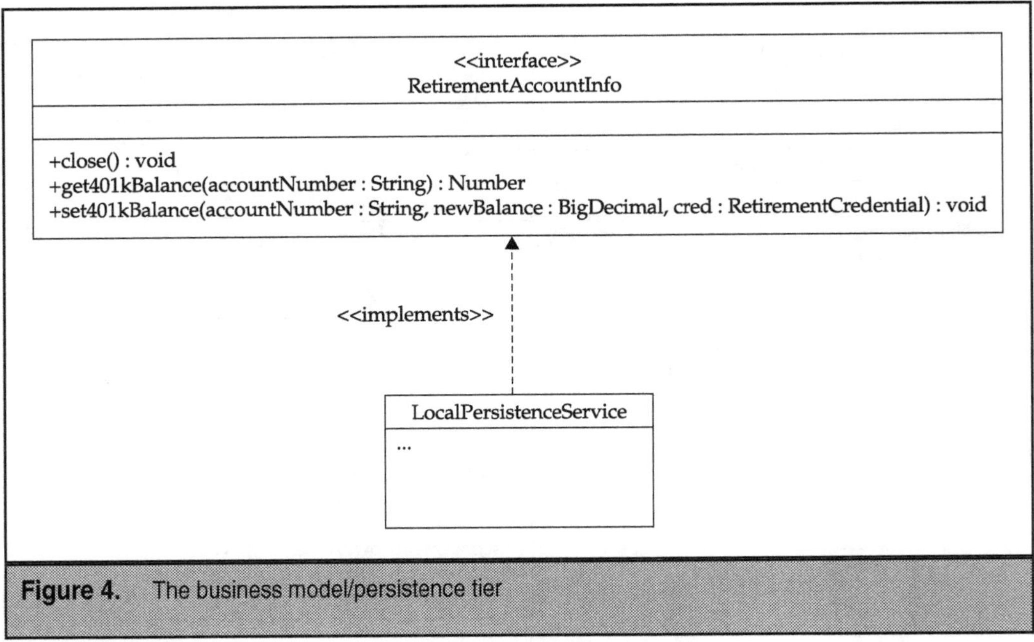

Figure 4. The business model/persistence tier

implementations of the `RetirementAccountInfo` interface that persist data to a SQL database, communicate using RMI, and serve as a proxy for an EJBs.

For more information regarding the implementation or low-level design of the sample application, consult the accompanying Javadoc HTML files (located in the downloadable example package available from www.hackingexposedjava.com).

Application Attack Strategies

To develop effective security for the retirement application, we need to know its vulnerabilities and how attackers might take advantage of those vulnerabilities. Given cursory knowledge of this application, a typical attacker may want to accomplish any one of the following tasks:

- Get an arbitrary account's balance anonymously.
- Change an arbitrary account's balance anonymously.
- Destroy or corrupt the application data.
- Destroy the application.

The first two tasks are much more attractive to a sophisticated application attacker than the last two. Destruction of data or code typically is nonproductive and only serves to alert authorities to the presence of an interloper. Furthermore, all but the most primitive organizations back up their data at regularly scheduled intervals.

Most corporate espionage is focused on the retrieval or modification of information without the knowledge of the owning party. Destroying all credit card information at an organization is much less disconcerting than reading all credit card information and posting it on the Internet (typical of more chaotic, destructive personalities) or selling it (typical of criminal/espionage specialists). So, the key to a good attack strategy for our malicious attacker would be to get in and get out undetected.

With a stand-alone application, the attack will necessarily require two phases. First, the attacker will need to gain physical or virtual access to the computer hosting the stand-alone application. Then the attacker will attack the application itself. This task focuses on surreptitiously invoking either of the business-related use cases. In the examples in this book, we will assume the worst: An attacker already has normal user access to the system hosting our stand-alone application.

NOTE This book focuses on Java security for applications, rather than system security. For more information on system security, consult one of the other titles in the *Hacking Exposed* series. You may also want to consult a text on physical security practices and techniques, like *Effective Physical Security* by Lawrence Fennelly, 2nd edition (Butterworth-Heinemann, 1997).

Generally, application attack strategies focus on the following areas:

- Attack the application's data outside the application in its storage medium.
- Attack the application itself by exploiting hidden, defective, or unintended functionality.
- Attack the application by modifying or altering the actual application code.
- Attack the application by convincing or coercing an authorized user to perform the attack for you.

In this book, we will address all of these strategies. We will look at the details of the application's various implementations and outline the vulnerabilities that are exposed. Then we will consider specific types of attacks and explore countermeasures to prevent or limit the damage from such attacks.

If you are already generally familiar with the security support built into the J2SE and J2EE architectures, feel free to skip to Chapter 4 to start learning about the application of those principles. If you'd like a quick refresher of the Java security model, just jump right into Chapter 1.

A FINAL WORD TO THE READER

We spent alot of time detailing techniques, building examples, and compiling references to make this book as comprehensive as possible. All of the techniques we include here are just that: techniques. It's up to you to apply your intelligence, experience, and domain knowledge to determine if these techniques are appropriate for your environment. Essentially, we're giving you a listing of hundreds of locks with installation instructions. You need to determine which of your doors need to be locked in the first place (we've never been to your house) and which locks are appropriate for each door. For example, you don't want to spend all of your time locking your linen closet if your front door is left wide open, and you don't want to try to put hundreds of locks on a single door. Very few applications will apply *all* of the techniques we're going to outline. We just want to show you what's possible; you decide what's practical.

Our example code has been written to demonstrate relevant Java security techniques in the most straightforward, expeditious manner possible. We're providing it to you as an adjunct to this text, to complement the contents of the book. It is intended to serve as a learning vehicle, not production-ready source code. Before you implement any security-related code in a production environment, make sure you understand all of its nuances and possible side effects. The code we provide is no exception.

Ultimately, the security of your application rests on your shoulders. We are giving you the tools and information to aid you in your decision making, but the final security decisions are yours. The best security approaches are integrated and consistent. Integrate your application security with existing OS and network security, and apply security principles consistently across your application. Regardless, when all else fails, rely on your personal judgment, intelligence, and diligence to guide you. At the application level, many more attacks are prevented through thoughtful analysis than are prevented by finding weaknesses with automated tools. As one of this book's authors often says: "It's better to have a sharp mind than a sharp sword… but it's best to have both!"

We're going to help you sharpen both your mind and your "security sword," but it's up to you to stay informed and aware of relevant security issues, exploits, and patches. The responsibility is yours.

PART I

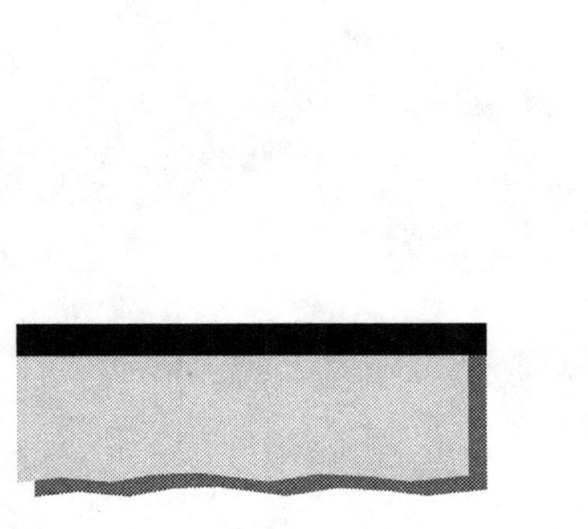

CHAPTER 1

THE JAVA BASICS: SECURITY FROM THE GROUND UP

Java security is not an afterthought; it is an integral part of the language. If used correctly, Java security can tightly control the operation of a Java application.

Java security does not run on automatic pilot. The security manager, which implements the security policy, is not automatically installed in an application. As with many of the Java security features, the developer must make the effort to implement the feature by installing a security manager in a running application and implementing a safe security policy.

As you will see in our case study, there is a learning curve involved in security implementation. In our case study, Lester the developer, over the course of many chapters, ultimately learns that Java security features can be implemented easily. The trick lies in knowing both how and when to use these features. This book will provide tips on creating secure, hack-resistant Java code.

In these first few chapters we will lay the foundation for the Java security discussions in the remainder of the book . In this chapter, you will learn how Java was designed to run as an embedded system, potentially operating in a networked environment. As you will see, security is part of the application infrastructure and is tightly integrated with the Java runtime environment.

JAVA THEN AND NOW

The story of the origins of Java has now settled into something of an urban myth. The language was developed as little more than a side project at a company that made money from selling hardware, not software. It was meant to be a language for embedded systems, running in a number of devices such as a car, a toaster, or a medical diagnostic device. Since it was probable that no operating system or environment would be available in such devices, the language needed to provide its own operating environment—a *virtual machine*.

In the years since its inception, the acceptance of the Java language has been both broad and deep. Over 2.5 million downloads of the Java language have been made. Java products run the gamut from embedded systems with Java 2 Micro Edition (J2ME) to applets, servlets, Java Server Pages, and middle-tier components such as Enterprise JavaBeans (EJB). The language itself has burgeoned with an API that now contains approximately 3,000 classes.

The success of the language can be attributed to its many features, most notably the cross-platform development capabilities provided by the virtual operating environment, allowing development efforts to easily straddle both Windows and Unix environments.

While cross-platform development is no doubt an important reason for using Java, it is the security of the language that has received the most notice in the past few years. The Java language was designed to run on a network, the medium of hackers everywhere, and so it was developed with security in mind.

The Java language and operating environment have been extended with Java 2 Enterprise Edition (J2EE) to include a set of APIs, tools, and servers to provide for the development of distributed applications with Java. This distributed, enterprise-wide environment presents a unique set of challenges for managing security. Developers must secure various resources, and control and monitor interfaces to external systems. Complex relationships between components are revealed as development proceeds. The integration of externally developed components into an existing environment can present difficulties and slow the pace of development.

The developers of J2EE were aware of the requirements of distributed software development and appended Java security mechanisms that take into account the object-oriented, component-based world of middle-tier programming. Using these J2EE security tools, security can become part of the basic design of the system. Integrating additional components, whether developed internally to the development group or from a third party, can be a relatively painless process.

JAVA LANGUAGE ARCHITECTURE

In order to understand the security architecture of the Java language we need to first understand the environment in which Java applications run. Central to this discussion is the Java Virtual Machine (JVM).

The Java Virtual Machine

As mentioned earlier, Java applications were designed to run in various operating environments, with or without a true operating system. One way to accomplish this would be to design numerous compilers to compile Java to local binary code (as is done with most third-generation programming languages such as C). But, instead, the Java designers chose to have the Java runtime environment shield the application code from the specifics of the operating environment.

The *Java Virtual Machine* (JVM) is a runtime architectural layer that manages the specifics of the operating environment, as illustrated in Figure 1-1. The JVM is effectively a virtual platform for the Java program. It is this architectural feature of Java that provides the platform independence of the language, and it is this runtime component that provides the first layer of security defense.

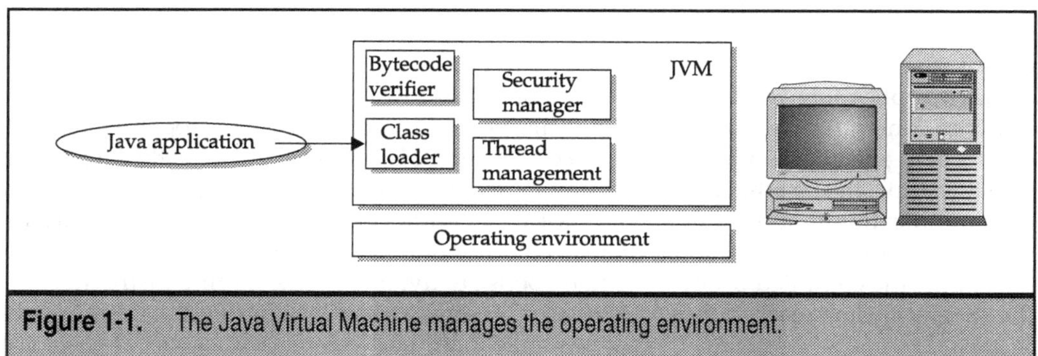

Figure 1-1. The Java Virtual Machine manages the operating environment.

The JVM provides various checks to determine that the code being executed is the code the developer meant to execute. This is done by carefully examining the bytecodes (the compiled representation of the Java language) and determining where they originated and what they are allowed to do. To understand how this security works, you need to understand how Java applications are structured in bytecodes.

An Interpreted Language: Java Bytecodes

Java programs are written as a collection of class definitions that represent the constituent parts of the Java program. A program in Java can be considered a collection of one or more classes that cooperate to provide a complete program.

These class files are compiled into a format known as *bytecodes* (also referred to as pseudo-code in other languages).

This format essentially creates a file where Java language statements—the flow-control statements and the declarations of class members and attributes—are converted into a more compact, concise, and optimized representation.

The compilation of Java programs into a bytecode representation is necessary for cross-platform execution of Java programs. If Java bytecodes were not available, the compilation process would need to be performed each time the program was executed, leading to an unacceptable performance penalty.

However, the use of a bytecode representation for Java programs also presents a potential security flaw: Java bytecodes can be decompiled into readable language format relatively easily. This allows potential hackers the opportunity to examine your code and develop strategies for circumventing your application security. Fortunately, there are techniques for dealing with this potential security breach. Code obfuscation, class file encryption, and other techniques are available as countermeasures to this potential attack and will be covered in more detail in upcoming chapters.

The Java Class Loader and Built-in Security

The Java runtime environment (JRE) executes a Java program by reading the bytecodes in a class file and executing program instructions as they are encountered.

A central element of Java program execution is the process of *class loading*. As you probably already know as an experienced Java developer, Java provides the ability to dynamically load classes at runtime. A Java class loader is responsible for loading the classes (the code) that compose the program.

Java applications may have more than one class loader. These class loaders are organized in a hierarchical tree, with the multiple class loaders working together to load classes as needed in the application. Java class loading is lazy and is done at the latest time possible; thus, the fact that a program has started and is waiting for some form of input is not an indication that it can load all classes needed to complete its task. Java programs first load a base set of classes, and then load additional class files as necessary (required as part of the the compiled program or in response to dynamic class loading instructions in the program). Since each of these class files represents a set of Java bytecodes, this presents a potential security breach, because hackers could intercept the class loading process and insert their own malicious version of a class. Fortunately, a number of features in the JRE work to prevent this "code spoofing" from occurring, as discussed in the "Security Controls for Java Class Loading" section later in this chapter.

As Java bytecodes are loaded and examined by the JRE, it makes a distinction between code loaded from the local environment (the platform on which it is running) and classes being loaded over the network (which is where we would expect class file spoofing to occur). The developer can control the extent of this checking through various mechanisms. You can also use signed Java archive (JAR) files and sealed packages as effective countermeasures to these and other attacks. Signed JAR files are covered in Chapter 2.

Other Language Features

A number of the other Java features enhance the safety of the language. The Java language is type-safe, manages the bounds of arrays, and performs its own memory management. In a pure Java application, a hacker cannot insert language instructions through an unbounded array (possible in the C language) or by manipulating memory storage. Programs (classes) also operate in a local namespace and are not able to interfere with the execution of other running programs.

Now that you understand the basics of the Java language architecture, you're ready to focus on its security architecture.

JAVA SECURITY ARCHITECTURE

The original Java security architecture was based on the concept of a *security sandbox*. This model made a distinction between local code (code loaded by the JVM from the local machine) and remote code loaded over the network. Local code was considered trusted and was granted access to local resources. Remote code was considered untrusted and was allowed to operate only in a security sandbox, with limited access to resources in that sandbox. In the original model, the remote code could not be given any additional permissions.

In Java Development Kit (JDK) 1.1, the untrusted remote code could be given access to other resources, but it needed to be granted explicit permissions to do so. If an applet were correctly signed, it would be provided access to all resources. A class loader and the security manager, as part of the JVM, ensured this compliance by making a distinction between local code and remote code, and managing each with a different class loader and security manager (see Figure 1-2). This model later evolved with the introduction of a *signed applet*, which is an applet that was digitally signed.

In an effort to simplify administration and improve the extensibility of the model, the Java designers appended a new security structure to the original security model. This new security model provides more fine-grained control over security and was built on the concept of the protection domain.

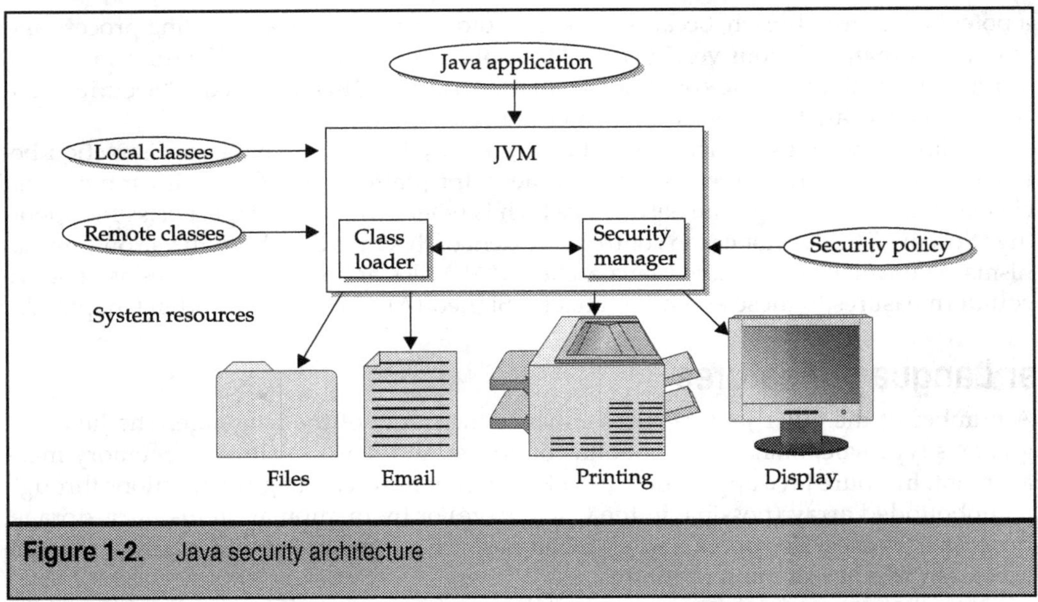

Figure 1-2. Java security architecture

Protection Domains

The Java security architecture draws a distinction between application security (who is allowed to execute what) and system security (what system resources can be accessed by the program). Central to the present Java security model is the concept of a *protection domain*, as illustrated in Figure 1-3. The term *domain* refers to a portion of the operating environment to which you will apply security. It is an abstract concept used to group components (such as groups of classes) or resources you would like to secure. The domain conceptually groups a set of classes that have all been granted the same permissions. A *security policy* defines the protection domain.

Some would consider the term "protection domain" a bit overworked in the Java vernacular. The term is constantly used to describe Java security. What is important to note is that there is no physical manifestation known as a protection domain in Java. The protection domain is in actuality a collection of technologies, APIs, and basic Java architecture which combine to provide a secure environment for the Java application.

How the Protection Domain Operates

A protection domain is similar to a security sandbox. Classes executing within the protection domain have specific permissions associated with them, just as classes executing in a security sandbox do. The security sandbox is effectively a protection domain with a fixed boundary. The current Java protection domain concept expands the security sandbox by

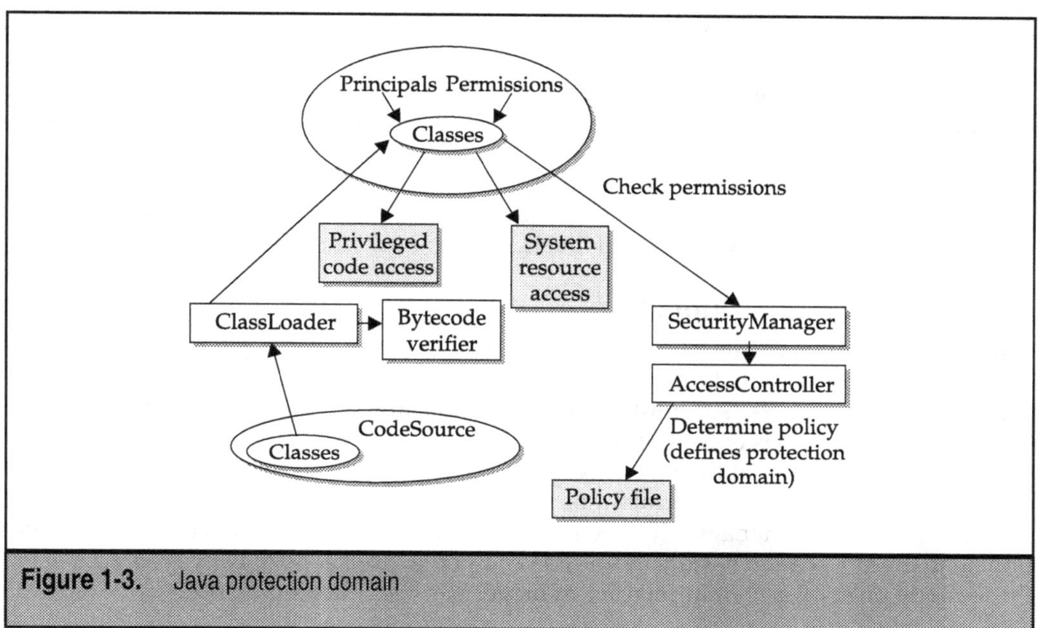

Figure 1-3. Java protection domain

associating with the protection domain an array of principals (users) and a collection of permissions. Similar to the sandbox model, the protection domain model requires that the actions of the classes executing within the protection domain have appropriate permissions to perform the actions they attempt, or an exception will be thrown.

A protection domain is provided using a code source (`CodeSource`) and associating permissions with that code source. The code being executed (the classes) is associated with a code source, which identifies where the code was loaded. This association between a code source and permissions is managed using a security policy. A code source is represented by a URL indicating the location of the code (either local or remote) and, optionally, a signature and key associated with the code source. Any classes originating from the same URL and, optionally, having the same signature and key will be placed in the same domain and will be granted the same permissions. As you can see from Figure 1-3, the process of implementing security domains is nontrivial. Classes are loaded from a code source by the class loader. The bytecode verifier is then called by the class loader to perform various validation operations (checking type, stack usage, class file format, and so on).

Associated with the loaded class are a static array of principals and a collection of permissions. These principals and permissions are not loaded with the class; they are defined through the security policy file currently in effect. A *codebase* represents the originating location of a loaded class and is referenced in the security policy file. The security policy file will be read to determine the principals and permissions for the codebase associated with the classes that have been loaded. You will learn more about the contents of the security policy file in the "Java Security Policies" section later in this chapter.

There is a great deal of flexibility built into this architecture. The security policy file that defines the protection domain may be passed to the application as a parameter, thus allowing you to use different protection domains with the application as needed. The code being loaded by the class loader can optionally be digitally signed, and these signatures can be used to verify that the code has come from the entity from which you expected it to come (meaning a network hacker has not substituted malicious code).

Types of Protection Domains

A protection domain can be either a *system protection domain* or an *application protection domain*. A system protection domain controls access to system resources such as the file system or network sockets. An application protection domain controls access to various components or portions of an application.

All code that is part of the Java Development Kit (JDK) is system code and is considered trusted and granted all permissions. All other application code, by default, does not run under a security manager. If a security manager is optionally loaded for an application, then the application has no permissions other than those specifically granted to it via the security policy which that security manager has been directed to use.

NOTE Applets, servlets, and EJBs are not stand-alone application code. They are *components* that run within a conceptual *container*, which provides a security manager for the code.

Protection domains and their associated security policies are flexible and can change as needed. Though they can be made a static part of a Java application, the binding between the security policy and the application does not need to be so direct. By keeping them flexible, the application can change and adapt as the requirements of the application change.

Application protection domains are specific to the application. They involve the execution of business logic to allow execution of sensitive sections of application code. These domains are often concerned with the application of business rules that apply to security. The case study used in this book demonstrates the use of application protection domains. Java provides some good tools to manage application protection domains (for example JAAS and J2EE security roles). These will be discussed in later chapters.

Security Controls for Java Class Loading

This process of class loading could potentially expose a program to security intrusions, so it is the subject of very specific, yet flexible, security controls in the Java language. An errant class, or one inserted by a malicious attacker, could severely compromise an application's security. Understanding the Java class loading process and how security plays a role in it is an important part of avoiding such an attack.

Java class loading uses a hierarchical structure. This structure can include multiple class loaders, which are class loaders themselves. This creates what appears to be a recursive relationship between a class and its class loader, leaving us with the "chicken or the egg" conundrum—which came first?

The problem of class loader relationships is resolved with a base class loader (also referred to as the *primordial class loader*) that is invisible and not accessible to the Java application. The primordial class loader loads the initial classes required by all Java programs (the base classes). Other class loaders—such as the `SecureClassLoader`, `URLClassLoader`, or some appropriate subclass of the `ClassLoader` class—are then started and begin the task of assembling the application from its constituent classes. As illustrated in Figure 1-4, the primordial class loader is the root of the hierarchy, and all of the other classes are loaded from the primordial class loader or one of its dependents.

A child class loader must delegate to the parent the task of loading a specific class. Only if the parent indicates it cannot load a class does it then allow the child to load the class. This prevents spoofing attacks, where hackers assume a certain identity on the network and attempt to load their malicious classes in your application, as illustrated in Figure 1-5. (Such a spoofing attack is not simple to implement, but it can be done by the more savvy hacker.) If not for this feature, hackers might be able to insert their own evil version of a common class, such as `java.lang.String`, into the application. But since the Java class loading architecture requires the child class loaders to delegate to the parent class loader, the parent in the local JVM will load a local version of `java.lang.String` (or some other important class), not the malicious version that a hacker is attempting to insert.

The delegation of class loading to parents is one architectural feature that helps to prevent spoofing attacks. Another important security mechanism is to severely limit the creation of class loaders. By default, a Java program using a security manager does not allow applications to create a class loader; explicit permission must be granted to allow a program to create class loaders. (This is done using the security policy file, as explained later in this chapter.)

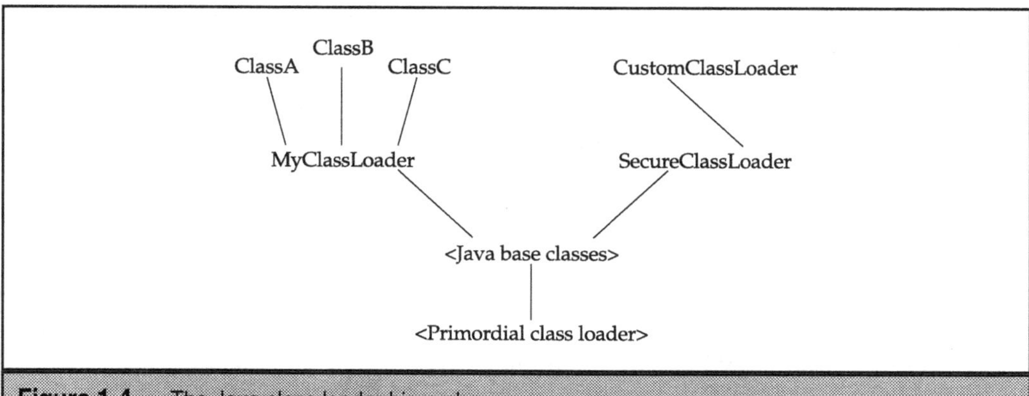

Figure 1-4. The Java class loader hierarchy

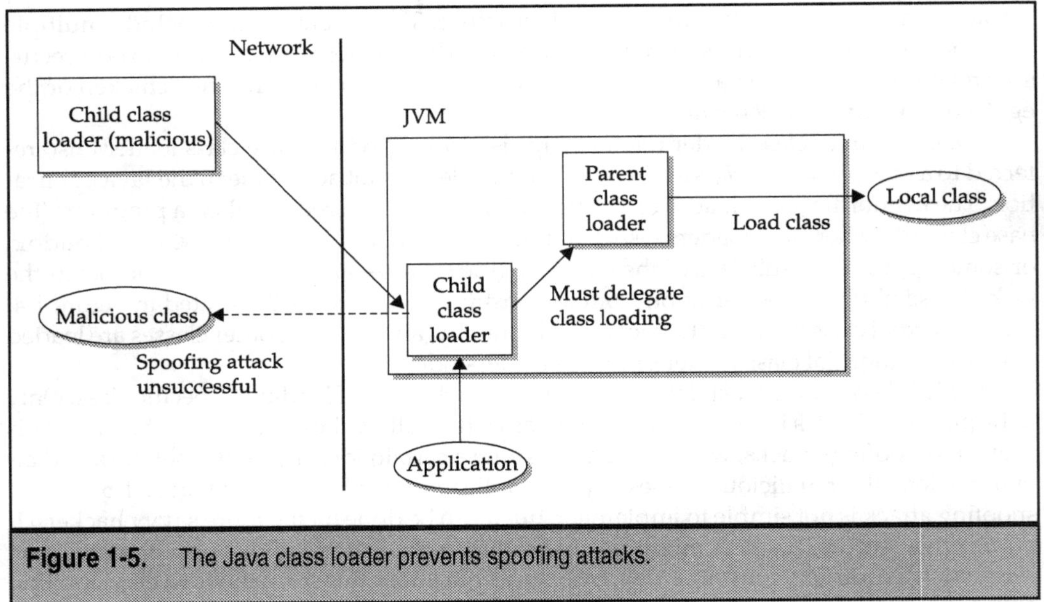

Figure 1-5. The Java class loader prevents spoofing attacks.

Java Permissions

As you learned earlier, a protection domain involves an association with a collection of permissions. A *permission* is basically a privilege granted to a principal. Access to system resources or privileged code is granted based on these permissions.

During program execution, an application may make a request to use a critical system resource, such as a file or network socket. Before this resource can be used, an `AccessController` evaluates the request and determines whether or not the current security policy in effect will allow the action. This evaluation of the request includes not only the class that requested the access, by also any other classes involved in the call that have method members on the call stack.

The `SecurityManager` (`java.lang.SecurityManager`) is called by most JDK code to determine whether or not code can access sensitive resources such as operating system files or network connections. The `AccessController` works with the `SecurityManager` to check permissions. By default, the `SecurityManager checkPermission` method will delegate the permissions check to the `AccessController` by calling its `checkPermission` method, as shown in Figure 1-6.

Java security uses the `Permission` class (`java.security.Permission`) to represent a permission. Java provides a number of subclasses for the `Permission` class to represent specific system permissions. Similarly, you can create application-specific permissions by subclassing this class or one of its subclasses. This interaction of the `SecurityManager`, the `AccessController`, and the `Permission` classes within the

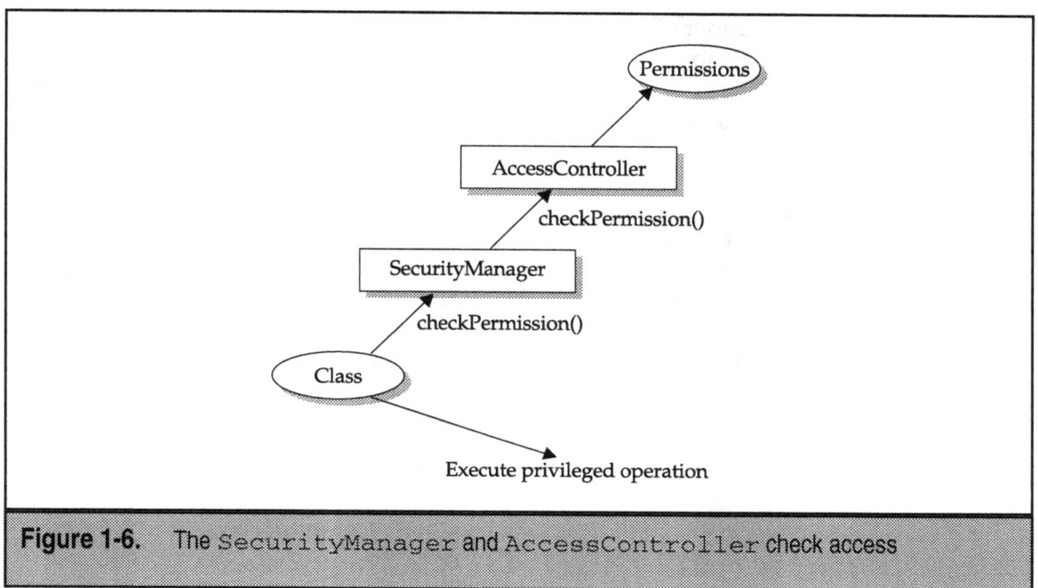

Figure 1-6. The `SecurityManager` and `AccessController` check access

JVM implements the security policy. The policy itself is defined in the Java security policy file, which is covered in the next section.

An application protection domain augments the current security policy with application security (for example, using the JAAS package or the container-managed security of J2EE). This application security commonly uses custom permissions to define access to privileged code. Creating these custom permissions requires subclassing the `BasicPermission` class. This combined set of custom permissions, along with the code that checks for the permissions, can be used to create an application protection domain.

An important aspect of permissions is that they may sometimes imply other permissions. For instance, the permission to read all files in the `/tmp` directory implies the permission to read the specific file `hello.txt` from the same directory. Developers need to be aware of this when constructing security policies which we will explain in more detail in the next section.

JAVA SECURITY POLICIES

One of the more important aspects of Java security is the flexibility. A great deal of the security for a Java application—the protection domain—can be described in the Java security policy file. If necessary, you can create different security policy files for different uses of an application. You can change various aspects of the protection domain by using the security policy file, without requiring any changes to the application code.

The security policy file contains the entries that define the security policy of the application. The JRE finds the security policy file based on entries in the *security properties* file.

You can prevent a number of system security incursions with proper configuration of the Java security policy file for an application. For this reason, and since it will be heavily referenced throughout this book, it is worthwhile at this point to gain a good understanding of how to configure system security using this file. But first, let's take a look at the security properties file.

The Java Security Properties File

The security properties file for the Java installation is named `java.security` and details where security policies will be loaded. It contains various entries that control how security policies are loaded and how security is implemented in the installed JRE. Several important entries in this file are shown in the listing that follows.

```
...
policy.url.1=file:${java.home}/lib/security/java.policy
policy.url.2=file:${user.home}/.java.policy


policy.expandProperties=true
```

The first two entries shown in this Java security properties file direct the JVM to use the security policy file at the designated URLs. This is the security policy file that will define the protection domain for the application. These entries typically point to a policy file in the user's home directory and a systemwide security policy file in the Java installation directory. As directed by the entries shown above, the applications running a security manager in this JRE will load the `JAVA_HOME/lib/security/java.policy` file, and will then search the user's home directory. If the `java.policy` file is located there, that security policy will be *appended* to the first security policy file already loaded. (The JAVA_HOME entry used here is the directory where the JRE is installed.)

You ultimately have three security policy files at your disposal for your Java application: the systemwide security policy file, the user policy file placed in the user's home directory, and any application security policy file the application may choose to load.

As you will see later, by setting system properties, it is possible to direct Java to a specific security policy file. The security properties file can be used in addition to the existing security policy, or it can be used in lieu of the existing security policy file. The latter feature, which effectively allows anyone running the program to change the Java security policy file to load, represents a security risk and can be turned off by turning off the `policy.AllowSystemProperty` in the security properties file. This will cause any attempts to set system properties on the Java command line to fail. The following is an example of that entry.

```
#policy.AllowSystemProperty=true
```

By commenting out this line, the JRE will not allow any system properties to be set on the command line, thus preventing security policy files loading from being changed by malicious users.

A number of system security incursions can be prevented with proper configuration of the Java security policy file for an application. For this reason, it is worthwhile at this point to gain a good understanding of how to configure system security using this file.

The Java Security Policy File

The Java security policy file is composed of a series of entries. The majority of entries in the security policy file are used to grant permissions, but optionally, the file may also indicate a *keystore* to use to find digitally signed certificates and associated keys.

Because of the sensitivity of the information in the security policy file, the access to this file should be limited. Since reading the information in this file can provide details of the program's operation and provide clues on how to compromise security, even read permissions on the file should be limited. In later chapters, you will learn how to digitally sign a policy file to prevent manipulation.

The keystore Entry

We will learn more about digital certificates and the keystore later, but for now just be aware that a keystore is a physical repository for the digital certificates that are used to verify that a file was sent by the entity you expected. In order for an X.509 digital certificate to be used to provide the principal identity, a `keystore` entry must be present in the security policy file. A single `keystore` entry in the security policy file indicates where the keystore will be found. This entry has the following syntax:

```
keystore "keystore_url", "keystore_type";
```

The URL for a keystore can be an absolute URL, or it can be a relative URL. If the URL is relative, it is relative to the URL of the security properties file being read. The keystore type provides some indication about how to understand the entries in the keystore. The default type is `JKS`, a proprietary Sun format.

The grant Entries

Following the single `keystore` entry, one or more `grant` entries may be used to indicate the permissions to be granted for the application. The syntax for these `grant` entries is as follows:

```
grant [SignedBy "signer"] [, CodeBase "<code_base_URL"]
      [, Principal [class_name] "principal_name"]
... {
    permission class_name [ "<target>" ]
               [, "action"] [, SignedBy "signer_names"];
    permission ...
};
```

The SignedBy Clause The `grant` entry is optionally followed by a `SignedBy` clause, which indicates the name used to sign the code. If this optional entry is used, code signed by this name will be granted the permission requested. You can use multiple names in the `SignedBy` clause, and they will be appended to the list of signers using a Boolean AND operation.

The CodeBase Clause The `CodeBase` clause indicates the codebase, or the location where the class files that will be subject to this grant entry will be loaded. Wildcards are allowed in this URL, as in this example:

```
grant CodeBase "file://general_apps/Java/*" { ...
```

This entry would provide all code loaded from the URL specified in the `CodeBase` entry, regardless of the specific class file name, with the permissions specified in the `grant` entry. A trailing asterisk (`*`) matches all files, both class and JAR files, in the directory. A codebase with a trailing - matches all files, both class and JAR files, in that directory and recursively in all subdirectories of that directory.

If the codebase entry is eliminated, the permission applies to all code, regardless of the location from which it was loaded. This is demonstrated in the following example.

```
keystore "k2", "JKS";

grant SignedBy "art" {
   permission java.io.FilePermission "test.out", "write";
   permission java.io.FilePermission "<<ALL FILES>>", "execute";
};
```

This entry uses a keystore named `k2` in the `JKS` format. Code must be signed by `art`. Since there is a keystore entry in the file, the Java `SecurityManager` will read the keystore and look for a certificate for the alias `art`. Permission is granted for any code signed by the alias `art` to write to the file `test.out` and to execute any file.

If the signer name and the codebase are eliminated from the entry, the permission is granted to all codebases. The name of the permission class in the `grant` entry must be a fully qualified class name and cannot be abbreviated. The name of the action class can be omitted if the permission class being used does not require it.

The Permissions Assignment The connection between the permission and the Java codebase or the principal is made in the security policy file. The permissions assigned using the `grant` statement are subclasses of the `java.security.Permission` class. Some of the more commonly set system resource permissions are listed in Table 1-1.

The most commonly used permissions are the `FilePermission` and `SocketPermission` classes. The `FilePermission` class allows fine-grained access to the file system. Using security policy file syntax, you can filter file permissions to the directory level, where access is granted to one or more files, or to the individual file level.

Permission	Description
`FilePermission`	Identifies which files and/or directories may be accessed using file i/o and what types of access are allowed.
`SocketPermission`	Identifies which sockets may be accessed and what actions may be taken on those sockets.
`RuntimePermission`	Base permission class for runtime operations. Provides the capability to restrict operations such as exiting the VM and loading specific libraries.
`AllPermission`	A class that indicates all permissions are allowed on all actions. Recommended for testing, not for runtime production usage.

Table 1-1. Common System Resource Permissions

The `SocketPermission` class provides the ability to grant fine-grained access for one or more Java applications. The action clause that follows the permission class indicates the actions allowed for this permission. Here is an example of a `grant` entry using `SocketPermission`:

```
grant {
     permission java.net.SocketPermission "127.0.0.1:1024-", "accept, listen, connect";
};
```

In the action clause, you can specify a network address as either an IP address or a hostname. The port is specified in the same string with the hostname, after the colon. The port specification may be either a single port number or a dash, indicating that all port numbers above the specified port number may be valid. This example allows socket connection on the local host on port number 1024 or higher (as indicated by the dash following the 124). Alternatively, and a safer alternative at that, you can specify a range of port numbers, as follows:

```
grant {
      permission java.net.SocketPermission "127.0.0.1:1024-1100",
"accept, listen, connect";
};
```

This entry is the same as the previous entry, except that it specifies a range of port numbers, starting at port 1024 and extending to port 1100. Any Java application using this security policy file would be limited to using only those ports.

The `AllPermission` class provides access to all permissions. This class is largely available for convenience. Any codebase granted `AllPermission` is free to use any system resource available. Using this permission entry is the same as turning off security for an application. Here is an example:

```
grant {
      permission java.security.AllPermission;
}
```

In this example, no codebase is specified, so the permission is applied to all code loaded by the program. The specific permission applied is `AllPermission`, which allows free, unfettered access to system resources.

It could be argued that it is never wise to use the `AllPermission` setting, although developers have a tendency to use it during development. In practice, applying some relatively liberal security with respect to network sockets and system directories would be more appropriate, even for development.

System Property Expansion

To provide some additional flexibility in the creation of a policy file, Java allows system properties to be expanded in the security policy file. This is a useful technique, as shown below.

```
grant codeBase "file:${java.home}/lib/ext/*" {
      permission java.security.AllPermission;
};
```

In this example, the runtime value of the `java.home` property is substituted in the URL for the `codebase`. Although useful, this feature does present a potential security hole. Hackers could change the various environment variables and direct an application to load code from another directory. Hackers could then substitute their code for system code, and with permissions set as shown above, could proceed to infiltrate the system. To avoid this security risk, do not use property substitution in policy files.

Security Manager Checking

With Web applications and J2EE applications, security policies are still significant but the location of the policy file and exactly how it is loaded and used will vary, depending on the application server vendor. Furthermore, most application servers run multiple threads with multiple JVMs and provide their own `ClassLoader` and `SecurityManager`, so behavior and configuration properties may vary.

Often, developers prefer not to load a `SecurityManager`. By default, no `SecurityManager` is loaded. It is good policy to check for the existence of a `SecurityManager` and, if the `SecurityManager` is not loaded, to load it in the application code. The code to do this is fairly simple:

```
...
SecurityManager security = System.getSecurityManager();
if ( security == null ) {
      System.setSecurityManager( new SecurityManager() );
...
```

JAVA PRINCIPALS AND SUBJECTS

At this point, you know how the Java security model works with protection domains and how to assign permissions to a codebase using the entries in the security policy file.

We now shift from what the code can do to what the authenticated user can do.

Determining who can do what is provided by the JAAS package. This package, which is covered in more detail in the next chapter, provides authentication and authorization services for Java applications. Authentication determines that an entity, an individual, is who they say they are. Authorization determines whether or not the authenticated user is allowed to do what they are requesting to do.

Java security previously centered around the concept of a principal, but has now expanded to includes the concept of a subject, which can encapsulate multiple principals.

A *principal* is an entity that is granted security rights. The entity could be an individual, a group of individuals, a corporation, or a login ID. The concept of a principal has been abstracted into the `java.security.Principal` interface. There are several concrete implementations of this interface provided in the Java 2 SDK (J2SDK), including `X500Principal`, `KerberosPrincipal`, `NTUserPrincipal`, and others.

Modern applications are often integrated masses of code, required to work extensively with legacy systems. Each of the various legacy systems that an application may need to work with may require a separate login and may have a separate set of security credentials. Users prefer a single sign-on (SSO) system, where they log in once and are authenticated for all or some of their assigned systems. A robust application should be able to manage all of these identities in a flexible manner, and this is precisely what a *subject* provides, as implemented in the `javax.security.auth.Subject` class.

The `Subject` class represents the source of the request and is what must be authenticated by the login process. A subject can represent multiple identities (as reflected by the `Principal` class), so there is a one-to-many relationship between a subject and principals. A `Subject` class may also contain security-related attributes known as *credentials.* Some credentials may require special access to be used and may be considered private; other credentials may be intended to be shared and would be considered public. The design of the subject allows both shared and public credentials to be associated with a subject, and it allows multiple credentials for both the shared and public credentials for a subject.

The Java runtime will continue to use the lists generated from the security policy file, which associate a `Principal` with a set of actions. But the runtime environment (through the `AccessController`) will check to determine whether or not the associated `Subject` has in its collection of `Principal` objects the principal required to perform the action. How the subject, principal, and credentials and a running Java application interact is shown in Figure 1-7.

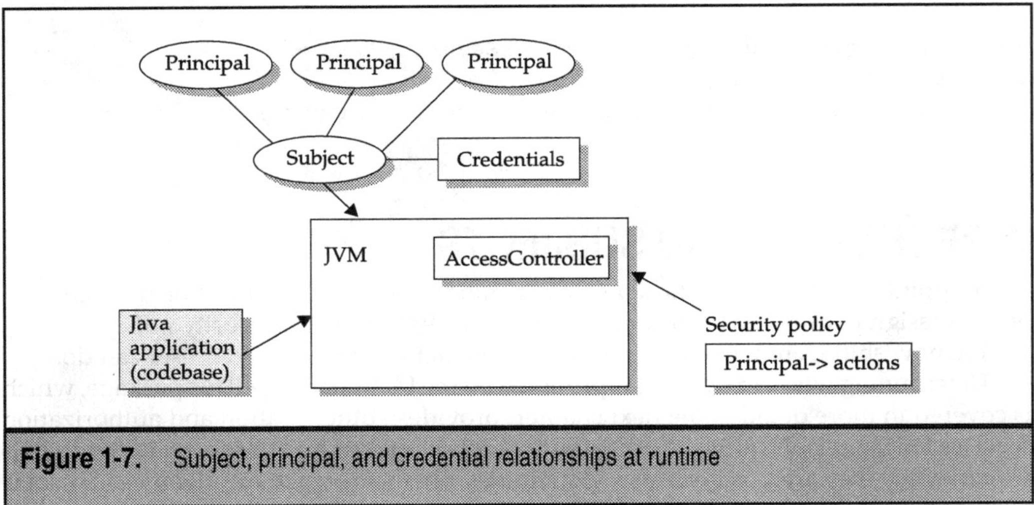

Figure 1-7. Subject, principal, and credential relationships at runtime

SUMMARY

The Java security architecture has been changed and expanded from its initial release. The original Java security sandbox now encompasses a more flexible architecture built on the concept of the protection domain. This protection domain uses components such as the security manager, the access controller, and the class loader to provide an operating environment that is both flexible and secure.

The security policy file describes the protection domain in effect and contains the entries granting the permissions to be implemented in the protection domain. You also learned that the Java security architecture includes the concept of principals, and that a subject can contain multiple principals. This security feature moves beyond the question of what the code can do to the question of who is running the code. You can grant permissions to the principals and create an application protection domain to encompass those permissions.

As you will see in the next chapter, the key security packages work with these security components to augment Java security. These packages provide authentication and authorization services for Java applications, as well as encryption services.

CHAPTER 2

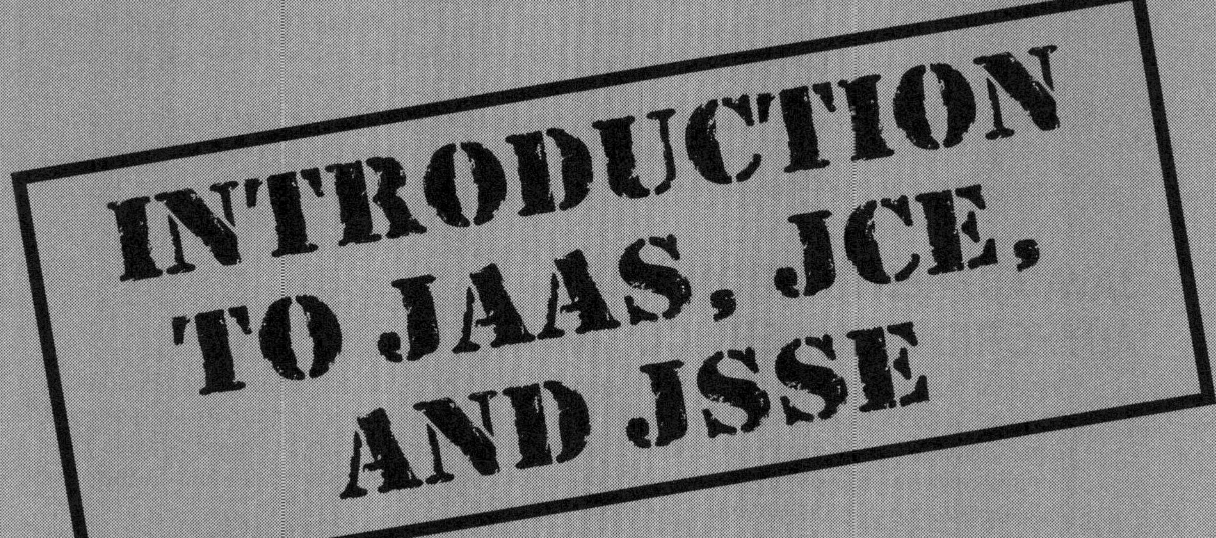
INTRODUCTION
TO JAAS, JCE,
AND JSSE

As developers, we need to perform a number of tasks in secure Java applications. Two important tasks are authentication, the process of verifying that a user is who they say they are, and authorization, the process of verifying that an authenticated user is allowed to perform a task is another process we must consistently develop.

Fortunately, Java provides a package, JAAS, that performs both of these functions. As you will see in this chapter, this package is tightly integrated into the Java security architecture.

Encryption is another important security tool that allows developers to hide information from malicious hackers. Java provides a consistent interface for a variety of encryption techniques in the JCE package. Since virtually all of the code in this book references these important Java security packages, this chapter introduces both the JAAS and JCE packages, with code examples.

The Secure Socket Layer (SSL) standard provides a network security protocol standard that combines two network encryption techniques into one extremely useful facility. In this chapter, we will introduce the JAAS package which provides access to this secure protocol.

Java security is not managed solely through program code. The JDK also includes a number of GUI and command-line tools that you can use to configure Java security. These include the `keytool` utility, which is used to manage security certificates, and the `jarsigner` utility, which is used to sign JAR files. Like the security packages, these tools are referenced throughout this book. This chapter introduces these utilities and their uses.

Later chapters will build on this introduction and, through our case study, demonstrate how to prevent the various security attacks that the determined hacker may engineer against your application.

JAVA AUTHENTICATION AND AUTHORIZATION SERVICES (JAAS)

The Java Authentication and Authorization Service (JAAS) package provides a Java security Application Program Interface (API) that works within the Java security architecture to perform authentication and authorization security services for Java applications. This package extends the security manager concept to include login services and authorization services for privileged blocks of code.

Introduced as an optional package in Java versions 1.2 and 1.3, JAAS is now part of the Java SDK version 1.4.

Prior to JAAS, Java security allowed code to be executed based on where the code originated (the code source) and who had signed the code. With JAAS, the Java security framework now provides the ability to verify *who* is running the code, which we refer to as authentication.

The JAAS API does not replace the previous Java security framework. Instead, JAAS augments Java security by providing additional functionality to authenticate a user and determine the authorization of the user. The definition of these two terms is important. *Authentication* means to determine with reliability and certainty who is running the code, regardless of how the code is running. *Authorization* means to determine that the user has permission (access control rights) to perform the actions attempted.

JAAS Architecture

JAAS is designed to be *pluggable*. Portions of a security implementation may be swapped without requiring changes to the Java code. Using the JAAS package interfaces, developers or third parties can create components to perform login authentication or to interact with a user or external system to access authentication information.

These additional components can be developed and integrated into an application as needed, merely by making changes in a JAAS configuration file.

For instance, an application may be required to perform authentication on the Windows NT platform by accessing NT credentials. The Java application could load a login context and read a configuration file that identifies an implementation of a JAAS component that accesses NT authentication information. The login context would then load the JAAS component and access the NT authentication information. You could move the application to another platform by making changes to the configuration file, and if necessary, by making entries in the code to recognize the new authentication information.

The JAAS package's design allows developers to apply changes in technology or the application environment to existing applications transparently. For instance, a login may be performed using a username and password, or potentially through fingerprint recognition or retinal scan. By abstracting the functionality of the login module, different login modules can be used for different purposes, and the controlling application need not change to accommodate a new login module.

JAAS Classes

The JAAS API is composed of a number of classes and interfaces that work together to provide the security features of the API. The following are the more commonly used classes:

- `LoginModule` performs the process of validating the user (either with a `CallbackHandler` or through some other means) and assigning principals to the subject.
- `CallbackHandler` is responsible for communicating with the user to validate the user's identity.
- `Subject` represents the target of the login process and can be associated with one or more principals.
- `Principal` represents an entity being granted access rights.

The `Subject` class represents the collective identity of the target of your authentication process. A subject is a collection of one or more principals or identities.

For many applications, the use of a single principal may be adequate. But the support for associating multiple principals with a single user (subject) provides an advantage. Consider that you are a potential user. You have more than one form of identification: a social security number, a driver's license number, a student ID number, and so on.

We can apply this analogy to the real world where, as mentioned in Chapter 1, it is not uncommon for a user to be required to access a number of legacy systems, each with their own separate password and set of credentials. A Java application could perform the authentication of the user and then assign multiple principals to the user (subject)—one for each of the legacy systems they are required to access.

The `Principal` class represents an identity for the entity you are authenticating. The principal is commonly a person (a user of a system), but a principal could also be a business or a group of users represented as one entity. If a subject and associated principals have been created for a JAAS session, it can be assumed that the subject has been authenticated.

Credentials

A *credential* represents a security-related attribute. Since there is a great deal of variation in the structure of security credentials, the JAAS package allows any class to represent a credential.

Credentials are stored as object references in two collections (`java.util.Set`), which are members of the `subject` class. To apply some structure to this representation, two interfaces are available that can optionally be implemented by the credential: `java.security.auth.Refreshable` and `java.security.auth.Destroyable`. The `Refreshable` interface details a set of methods for refreshing credentials, and the `Destroyable` interface identifies a set of methods for destroying a set of credentials.

JAAS Authentication

Using JAAS for authentication involves a set of processing steps to perform whatever actions are necessary to ensure that the identities being associated with an entity are valid. Since the steps necessary to make this determination may vary greatly, JAAS provides flexibility in how this processing is done.

The Authentication Process

Most of the work of JAAS authentication revolves around the login module, represented by an implementation of the `LoginModule` interface. The processing performed by JAAS can be summarized as follows:

1. One or more `LoginModule` (implementations of `javax.security.auth.spi.LoginModule`) are loaded based on the entries in the JAAS configuration file.
2. The constructor for the `LoginModule` is optionally provided with a callback handler (an instance of `javax.security.auth.callback.CallbackHandler`) to manage the process of communicating with the

user to obtain authentication (for instance, prompting the user for a name and password). If it is not provided in the constructor, the callback handler may be provided in a system property. If a callback handler is not provided at all, it is assumed the `LoginModule` will take responsibility for communicating with the user.

3. A `LoginContext` (`javax.security.auth.login.LoginContext`) is then instantiated and if successfully loaded, the `login` method of the `LoginContext` is called.
4. The `login` method of `LoginContext` will call the `login` method of the `LoginModule`, if provided, and determine the valid identity of the user. This method will populate the relevant callbacks and invoke the callback handler (`CallbackHandler`), if provided, to manage the login processing callbacks.
5. The `login` method of the `LoginModule` is responsible for evaluating the responses of the user in the login process. If the responses are not valid, the method returns a Boolean false. If the responses are valid, the method should populate the `Subject` object with the appropriate `Principal` objects and return a Boolean true.
6. The `LoginModule` may optionally delegate the process of obtaining user authentication information to a `CallbackHandler` implementation. The `CallbackHandler` will perform the interaction required to obtain the authentication information. (The `CallbackHandler` can perform other operations, but right now, we will only concern ourselves with the login operation.)

Figure 2-1 illustrates the interaction of these components. As you can see in Figure 2-1, the `LoginContext` acts as a controller, interacting with the other classes to perform the login process. The `LoginContext` can be constructed using parameters that specify the `LoginModule` name (as referenced in the JAAS configuration file) and the `CallbackHandler` instance to use.

The `LoginContext` instance begins by reading the JAAS configuration file to provide information about the login modules installed and whether or not they are required. It then calls the methods of the `LoginModule` to start the login process. The `initialize` method is used to provide the information the `LoginModule` needs to perform its work. The `LoginContext` instance has read the configuration file and knows which `LoginModule` instances are available.

The `initialize` method is called with a subject reference, along with a reference to the callback handler instance being used. Additional parameters are provided for collections to hold shared-state information and options; these are not always used.

Once the `initialize` method has been called, the `LoginContext` will call the `login` method of the `LoginModule`. The `LoginModule` instance may optionally delegate the capture of the login information to the `CallbackHandler` instance, or it may access the information on its own.

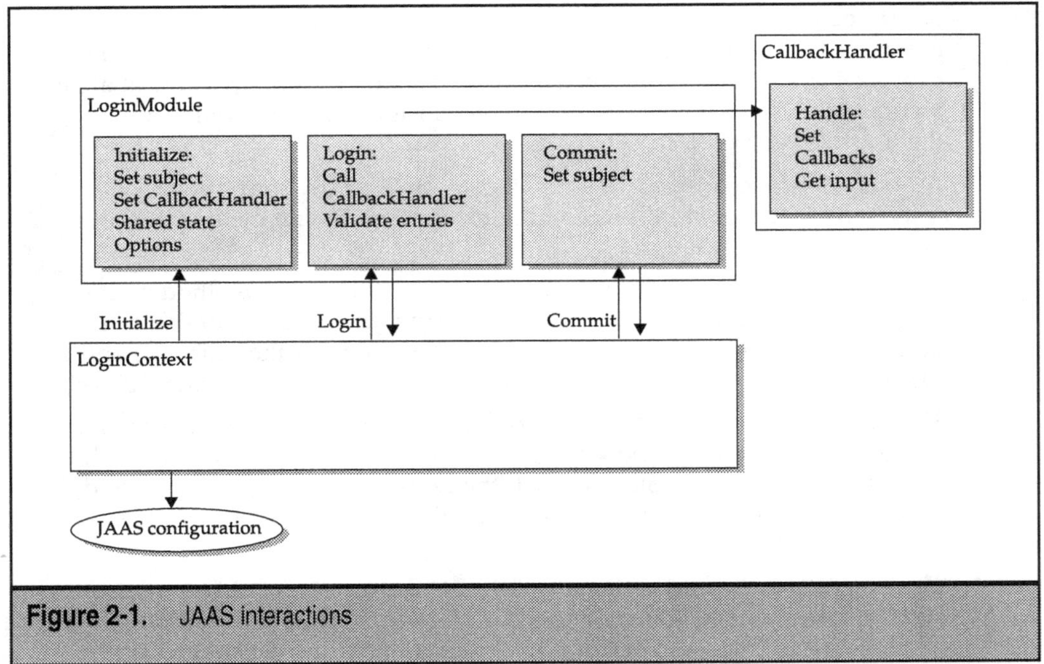

Figure 2-1. JAAS interactions

Once the `LoginModule` receives the results of the login process, it must validate those results. If the login was successful, this method should return a Boolean value of true. If the login was not successful, this method will return a Boolean value of false.

If the login was successful, the `LoginModule commit` method will be called by the `LoginContext` to commit the results to the internal state of the `LoginModule` instance. These results are generally a set of `Principal` objects stored as a collection with the `Subject` (which was provided by the `LoginContext` in the `initialize` method).

The `abort` and `logout` methods are also used by the `LoginModule` to manage the internal state of the `LoginContext`. The implementation for these methods must manage the information related to their principals and avoid impacting information entered by other modules.

Multiple Login Modules

Since the JAAS `LoginModule` interacts with a well-defined interface, it is relatively easy to provide the pluggability this package offers. The standard JAAS package provides some useful implementations of `LoginModule` and `CallbackHandler` that will be used later in this book. These include `LoginModule` implementations that access Windows NT and Unix login information from the user's environment.

An application using JAAS may use multiple `LoginModule` implementations together in one application, with each module authenticating and storing its own set of `Principal` objects in the `Subject` instance provided by the `LoginContext`. The JAAS configuration file allows these multiple `LoginModule` instances to be declared in a single location. Figure 2-2 illustrates the use of multiple login modules.

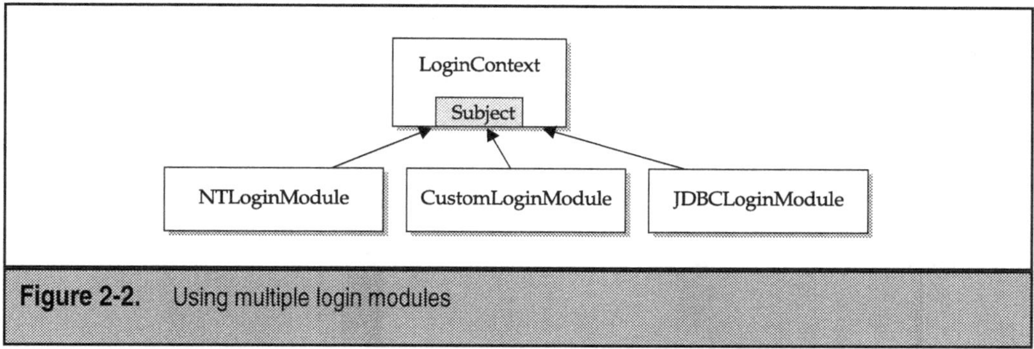

Figure 2-2. Using multiple login modules

As pointed out earlier, these multiple modules must take care not to impact the authentication information used by other modules. The process for avoiding conflicts is demonstrated in the sample application, presented next.

An Authentication Example

Despite what appears to be a complex relationship of objects, the process of using JAAS to provide authentication is fairly straightforward. The following code example provides a brief demonstration of this process.

```
import javax.security.auth.login.*;
import javax.security.auth.*;
import javax.security.auth.callback.*;

import java.security.Principal;
import java.security.AccessController;
import java.security.PrivilegedAction;
import java.io.*;
import java.util.*;

public class DemoJAAS {
String homeDirectory;
public static void main(String args[] ) {
LoginContext lc = null;
DemoJAAS demoJAAS = new DemoJAAS();

try {
      //
      // Create the login context.
      //
      lc = new LoginContext("TestJAAS",
               demoJAAS.new DemoCallbackHandler() );
}
catch (LoginException e) {
    System.err.println("Could not create login context." );
```

```
}
//
// Now perform the login. Give them 3 tries.
//
int tries=1;
boolean success=false;
for (;tries <= 3;tries++ ) {

    try {
       lc.login();
              success = true;
       break;  // we succeeded, so end the loop
    }
    //
    // If the login failed, the LoginContext will throw a
    // LoginException.
    //
    catch(LoginException e ) {
        System.err.println(
           "LoginException: authentication failed: " + e );
        e.printStackTrace();
    }
}

//
// If the login succeeded, print the information we collected.
//
if (  counter <=3  )  {
    Set principals = lc.getSubject().getPrincipals();
    Iterator i = principals.iterator();

    //
    // Output results
    //
    System.out.println("Login successful.");
    while ( i.hasNext() ) {
      success=true;
        System.out.println("\tPrincipal: " +
                  ((Principal) i.next()).getName() );
    }

}
else {
```

```
        System.out.println("Login failed.");
    }

}
// ==
```

The example works with a LoginModule and a LoginContext to authenticate a user through a login process. This code first instantiates a LoginContext object. The constructor for the LoginContext takes two arguments. The first argument to the constructor references the name of the JAAS configuration to use in the JAAS configuration file. This reference will, in turn, identify the LoginModule class to load to manage the login process. The entry for this example is as follows.

```
TestJAAS {
    DemoLoginModule required debug=false;
};
```

This entry specifies that the TestJAAS application name will use the DemoLoginModule module to manage the login process. (The code for that module is shown after the listing for the DemoJAAS class.)

The second argument to the constructor is a reference for the object that will handle callbacks generated by the login process. This example passes a reference for an inner class named DemoCallbackHandler.

Once the reference to the LoginContext has been instantiated, a loop is started to perform the login. As is customary, the user is given several tries to log in. During each iteration of the loop, the LoginContext login method is called. This method does not return a value indicating success or failure, so there is no return value to interrogate to determine the status of the login process. Instead, it throws a LoginException if the login fails. As this loop is written, the exception handler for the LoginException simply displays an error message and allows the loop to continue.

The threshold for the for loop will allow only three iterations. Alternatively, if the login is successful, the statement immediately following the login will be executed. We know that if we reach that statement, the login process did not throw an exception, so it succeeded. Based on this knowledge, there is no need to continue the loop, and we simply break out of the loop at that point.

If we have succeeded in logging in, then the counter from the for loop (which has scope beyond the loop and is therefore declared outside the for loop) will be a value less than or equal to three. Using that knowledge, we test the counter and display values that have been set by the LoginModule. The values displayed are the Principal objects that have been placed in the Subject object that is under control of the LoginContext. If the login has failed, a message indicating that is displayed.

An inner class is used to provide the CallbackHandler implementation and manage the callbacks from the LoginContext. (In this example, the callbacks are actually generated from the LoginModule, which is shown later in this section.) In this case, the callback handler will actually perform the task of prompting the user for a username and password. This work is performed in the `handle` method, which does not return a value.

```
//
// This inner class is responsible for getting the
// username and password. The name and password  are
// 'passed back' to the LoginModule using the callbacks[] array
//
class DemoCallbackHandler implements CallbackHandler {

public void handle( Callback[] callbacks )
            throws IOException, UnsupportedCallbackException {

boolean foundCallback=false;

for (int n=0;n < callbacks.length; n++ ) {

  if ( callbacks[n] instanceof NameCallback ) {
     foundCallback=true;
     NameCallback name = (NameCallback) callbacks[n];
     //
     // Prompt for the username.
     //
     System.out.print( name.getPrompt() + " " );
     //
     // Get the response.
     //
     name.setName((new BufferedReader
                  (new InputStreamReader(System.in))).readLine());
  }

  //
  // If we received the password callback, prompt for a
  // password.
  //
  if ( callbacks[n] instanceof PasswordCallback ) {
      foundCallback=true;
      PasswordCallback password = (PasswordCallback) callbacks[n];
      //
      // Prompt for password.
      //
      System.out.print( password.getPrompt() + " " );
      //
      // Get the response.
```

```
            //
            String pwd = (new BufferedReader (
                       new InputStreamReader(System.in))).readLine();
            password.setPassword(pwd.toCharArray() ); // need array of chars
        }

    }

    if ( !(foundCallback) ) {
        //
        // If we never processed a callback, throw an exception.
        //
        throw new UnsupportedCallbackException(
               callbacks[0], "No valid callback found." );
    }

    }

    }

    }
```

Since the `handle` method shown here does not return a value, it must use some other convention to return the results of its efforts. This is done by using the array of `Callback` objects, which are passed into the method. The `Callback` object array passed into the method represents a reference to an array managed by the `LoginContext` and passed to the various objects it manages. In the `handle` method shown here, elements of this array are set to the values entered by the user, and the `handle` method returns, thus making those entries visible to other objects that need to query the values.

We then test the contents of the `Callback` array for the `NameCallback` instance and `PasswordCallback`, which are two implementations of the `Callback` interface. If the value is determined to be a `NameCallback`, we display the prompt for the name and read the console input to obtain a name from the user. We store the value returned by the read operation in the `NameCallback` object using the `setName` method.

If the contents of the `Callback` array are determined to be a `PasswordCallback`, we retrieve and display the prompt string to prompt the user for the password. The value of the password is then read from the console. (For the sake of brevity, this example allows the password characters to be echoed back to the console and does not perform the extra work required in Java to make keystrokes invisible.) Once we have obtained the value of the password, we convert it to a byte array (as required by the `setPassword` method) and place it in the `PasswordCallback` object.

We use a flag to determine whether or not any callback has been processed by the `handle` method. If no callback has been processed (this is determined by the conditional statement at the end of the method) an exception is thrown indicating that no valid callback has been received.

The LoginModule Class for the DemoJAAS Example

Since JAAS allows multiple logins to be processed (although that is not shown in this example), there is a distinction between processing the login and committing the login. There is essentially a two-stage process to performing the login: validating the values provided to the module, and then if the `LoginContext` module indicates it is okay to do so, committing the values returned by the login process to the `Subject` object managed by the `LoginContext`. The `LoginModule` class is used by the `LoginContext` to process the user login. This module is responsible for determining whether the values provided by the user are valid for authentication.

The `LoginModule` class implements the `LoginModule` interface. This interface requires the implementation of several methods:

- The `initialize` method initializes the state of the object using object references provided by the `LoginContext` controlling this module.
- The `login` method performs the processing required to complete the authentication process.
- The `commit` method commits the results of the login process or, if login failed, clears the internal state.
- The `abort` method aborts the login process and clears the internal state.

As shown in this example below, the `initialize` method for this class is passed a reference for a `Subject` object, a `CallbackHandler` object, and two `Map` objects for shared state and options. These object references are managed by the `LoginContext` and passed into the `LoginModule` to retain and use to communicate with the other objects involved in authentication and authorization processing. The `initialize` method in this example stores these values in internal members, where they will later be retrieved and used.

```
import javax.security.auth.login.*;
import javax.security.auth.*;
import javax.security.auth.callback.*;

import java.util.*;
import java.io.*;
import javax.security.auth.spi.*;
import java.security.Principal;

public class DemoLoginModule implements LoginModule {

Subject subject;
CallbackHandler callbackHandler;
Map  sharedState;
Map  options;
```

```
boolean valid = false;
String name;     // username
String password; // user password
TestPrincipal  namePrincipal;
TestPrincipal  emailPrincipal;

public void initialize( Subject subject,
                        CallbackHandler callbackHandler,
                        Map sharedState, Map options) {

this.subject = subject;
this.callbackHandler = callbackHandler;
this.sharedState = sharedState;
this.options = options;

}
//
// Login
//
public boolean login() {

valid = false;

try {

Callback callbacks[] = new Callback[2];
callbacks[0] = new NameCallback( "name: " );
callbacks[1] = new PasswordCallback( "password: ", false );

//
// Let the callback handler get user input.
//
callbackHandler.handle(callbacks);

//
// If we have arrived here, we've been successful.
// Populate our state with the username and password.
//
name = ((NameCallback) callbacks[0]).getName();
password = new String(
           ((PasswordCallback) callbacks[1]).getPassword());

//
// Perform validation. Hardcoded here for sample.
```

```
//
if ( ( name.equals("art")) && ( password.equals("yes") ) ) {
   valid = true;
}
else {
   valid = false;
}

}
catch (IOException e) {
      System.err.println("IOException in login: " + e );
      e.printStackTrace();
}
catch (Exception e ) {
      System.err.println("Exception in login: " + e );
      e.printStackTrace();
}
catch (Throwable e ) {
      System.err.println("Exception in login: " + e );
      e.printStackTrace();
}

finally {
 return valid;
}
}
```

The `login` method shown here is called by the `LoginContext` object controlling the login process. In this implementation of the `LoginModule`, this method will, in turn, call the `CallbackHandler` to interact with the user, but this is not required behavior in JAAS; a developer could decide that the `LoginModule` should perform its own interaction with the user.

As shown in this example, the `login` method is passed no values and returns a Boolean value. This method first creates a `Callback` array and populates it with a `NameCallback` object and a `PasswordCallback` object, and then populates them with appropriate values. The method then calls the `CallbackHandler` `handle` method for the `CallbackHandler` member (that was provided by the `LoginContext` in the `initialize` method). This call to the `handle` method is passed the array of callbacks that has been populated on the previous lines.

On return from the `handle` method, we assume that the `handle` method has succeeded (or it would have thrown an exception). The `handle` method retrieves information from the user and populates the results into the `callbacks` array. We then retrieve these results from the `callbacks` array and use them to populate the values of our internal members. Although our goal is to ultimately populate the `Subject` object for the authenticated user, we do not do that at this point. But the method does perform a cursory test on the input values and sets a Boolean flag indicating whether the user has been authenticated. This Boolean flag is then returned by the method.

The `commit` method shown below is called by the `LoginContext` module to indicate that everything is okay and the `LoginModule` should commit the results of the login processing performed previously. The method shown here commits the results retrieved and validated previously by populating the `Subject` object with appropriate `Principal` objects. The method then clears its internal state and returns.

```
//
// Commit
//
public boolean commit() {

if ( valid ) {
  // Add this subject.
  namePrincipal = new TestPrincipal();
  namePrincipal.setName( name );
  subject.getPrincipals().add( namePrincipal );

  // Principal/user art also has an email account that is used as a login.
  emailPrincipal = new TestPrincipal();
  emailPrincipal.setName( "taylorart@zippy.net" );
  subject.getPrincipals().add( emailPrincipal );
}

//
// Clear state.
//
name     = null;
password = null;

return valid;

}

//
// Abort
//
public boolean abort() {
boolean retVal = false;
if ( !(valid) ) {
   //
   // Never committed, so only clear our state.
   //
    name = null;
    password=null;
   retVal = false;
}
else {
  //
```

```
    // Clear our committed state. Only clear our entries
    // in the subject.
    //
    subject.getPrincipals().remove( namePrincipal );
    subject.getPrincipals().remove( emailPrincipal);
    name     = null;
    password = null;

      retVal = true;
  }
  return retVal;

  }

  //
  // Logout
  //
  public boolean logout() {
    //
    // Clear our principals.
    //
      if ( valid )  {
      subject.getPrincipals().remove( namePrincipal );
      subject.getPrincipals().remove( emailPrincipal );
    }
    //
    // Clear state and reset flag.
    //
    name     = null;
    password = null;
    valid    = false;

    return true;
  }
  }
```

The `abort` method tests to determine whether the validation process succeeded. If the validation process did not succeed, the internal state has not been set and there is nothing to undo. Alternatively, if the validation process did succeed, the internal state must be reset. The method returns a Boolean value indicating true if it succeeded its abort operation or false if it should be ignored (for instance, if it failed to authenticate).

Since the `LoginModule` can expect to be part of a `LoginModule` set performing authentication, the entries in the subject member (received from the `LoginContext` instance during initialization) may belong to other `LoginModule` instances. For this reason, in the `abort` method, we clear out only the entries we have placed in the `Subject` object's collection of `Principal` instances. This is done using the `Set remove` method, passing in the `TestPrincipal` objects we have created. This method instructs the set to remove the object that matches the parameter passed in.

The logout method is used to clear the internal state of the LoginModule. This involves setting internal members for the username and password to null values and clearing the set of Principal objects in the Subject object. As with the abort method, the logout method also selectively removes only those Principal objects we have added. It returns a Boolean true value indicating that it succeeded.

The Security Policy File for DemoJAAS

When the DemoJAAS program is run, it performs a validation of the user, prompting the user for a name and password. To help secure this program, you should install a Java security manager and force restrictive security measures on the application. The following example is one possible implementation of a security policy file for DemoJAAS.

```
// Grant permissions to the JAAS lib code -
// not part of the standard JDK in 1.3.1.
grant codeBase "file:/lin/local/jdk/j2sdkee1.3.1/lib/jaas.jar" {
   permission java.security.AllPermission;
};

// Grant these permissions only to code in our package.
grant codebase "file:./-" {
permission javax.security.auth.AuthPermission "createLoginContext";
  permission javax.security.auth.AuthPermission "modifyPrincipals";
};
```

The security policy for the DemoJAAS program begins with a line to grant AllPermission to any code originating from the jaas.jar code source. In Java versions prior to 1.4, the JAAS API is not a part of the core JDK (which is granted AllPermission by default) and must be granted AllPermission explicitly. (In JDK versions after 1.3, this is not necessary.)

The next grant statement shown in the policy file grants a set of permissions to the package where the DemoJAAS program resides. These programs are explicitly allowed to create a LoginContext. Since any application that can create a LoginContext could be used by a hacker to potentially substitute a class to allow nonvalid users to authenticate, programs that use the LoginContext should have restrictive security. The same holds true for the modification of Principal classes, which can be used with JAAS (and J2EE) to identify users.

To run this program without a security manager from the command line, you would use this command:

```
java -Djava.security.auth.login.config=./demoJAAS.config DemoJAAS
```

To run the program with a security manager from the command line, you would use the following syntax:

```
java -Djava.security.manager  -Djava.security.policy=./security.policy \
-Djava.security.auth.login.config=./demoJAAS.config DemoJAAS
```

JAAS Authorization

As described in Chapter 1, Java security provides for code-based security, with permissions granted based on the signer of code. JAAS extends this security by allowing authorization to be granted based on who has authenticated and is currently running the code, not just on the digital signature of the code.

JAAS authorization uses a combination of security policy settings and custom class files for authorization. You create a `Permission` class for the actions to be executed and, optionally, a `Principal` class to reflect the principal (user) executing the privileged code. You can use JAAS authorization to authorize specific system security actions or to provide a form of programmatic code execution security.

NOTE There are several different approaches that can be used to execute privileged code. A complete code example is shown in Chapter 3.

The following steps are necessary to perform JAAS authorization:

1. Create appropriate security policy file entries.
2. Create a custom `Permission` class, a subclass of the `java.security.Permission` class.
3. Create a custom action class, an implementation of `java.security.PrivilegedAction`.
4. Execute the static `Subject doAsPrivileged` method, passing the `Subject` instance containing the principals required and the custom `PrivilegedAction`, along with an optional `AccessControlContext`.
5. Within the body of the `PriviledgedAction run` method, access the `SecurityManager` and call the `checkPermission` method using the custom `Permission` class.

An Authorization Example

An example of the code to perform a privileged action is shown next.

```
Object o =  Subject.doAsPrivileged( lc.getSubject(),
                new PrivilegedAction() {
                      public Object  run() {
                SecurityManager sm = System.getSecurityManager();
                   try {
                  sm.checkPermission(
                      new DemoPermission( "doIt" ) );
                      System.out.println("Did doIt." );
                 sm.checkPermission(
                     new DemoPermission( "doItAll" ) );
```

```
                    System.out.println("Did doItAll." );
            }
        catch (SecurityException e)   {
                System.out.println(
                  "You do not have permission to do that ... " );
                System.out.println("Exception: " + e );
        }
       finally {
                return null;
        }

        }
}
      , null );
```

In this example, we use the static doAsPrivileged method to execute some privileged code. The lc parameter passed in as the first argument is the JAAS LoginContext for the program. We call the getSubject method of this class to retrieve the Subject for that context. In the code prior to this call, the user has been authenticated, so we expect the Subject of the LoginContext to have been populated with the appropriate properties.

The second parameter creates an anonymous class, an implementation of the PriviledgedAction class. Within the implementation of the run method, we access a reference to our current security manager, and then proceed to call the SecurityManager checkPermission method to determine whether we are allowed to perform certain actions. Each call to checkPermission passes in an instance of our DemoPermission class. This parameter will be used to determine whether the permission has been granted in the security policy file.

The checkPermission call has no return value. If the checkPermission call fails, an exception is thrown and the line immediately following the checkPermission call is not executed. Therefore, we can assume that if the line immediately following the checkPermission call is executed, we have the permission being checked on the previous line.

The Custom Permission Class: DemoPermission

The DemoPermission class extends the BasicPermission class and and simply calls the superclass constructor for that class. The ultimate result of this inheritance is that calls to the getName method will return the name of the permission. The pertinent lines of this class file are shown next.

```
import java.security.BasicPermission;

public class DemoPermission extends BasicPermission {
String name;
```

```
public DemoPermission( String name ) {
    super(name);
    this.name=name;
}
```

The Java Security Policy File for JAAS Authorization

The Java security policy file shown below brings all of the JAAS authentication components together. The entries in this file create the association between the principals that have been assigned using authentication and the permissions they have been granted. These are the entries checked by the Java security manager when the `checkPermission` call is made.

```
// Grant these permissions only to code in our package.
grant  codebase "file:./-" {
  permission javax.security.auth.AuthPermission "createLoginContext";
  permission javax.security.auth.AuthPermission "modifyPrincipals";
  permission javax.security.auth.AuthPermission "doAsPrivileged";
  permission javax.security.auth.AuthPermission "getSubject";

grant  Principal com.sun.security.auth.UnixPrincipal "art"  {
  permission java.util.PropertyPermission "user.home", "read";
  permission examples.jaas.DemoPermission "doIt";
  permission examples.jaas.DemoPermission "doThat";
  permission examples.jaas.DemoPermission "doItAll";
};

grant  Principal examples.jaas.DemoPrincipal "art" {
  permission java.util.PropertyPermission "user.home", "read";
  permission examples.jaas.DemoPermission "doIt";
  permission examples.jaas.DemoPermission "doThat";
  permission examples.jaas.DemoPermission "doItAll";
};
```

First, we need to explicitly grant permissions to create the login context and modify principals. We also need to explicitly grant permission to make the `doAsPrivileged` call and the `getSubject` call, both of which are needed to access the privileged code.

Next, we see the principal entries specific to JAAS. These entries grant a principal named `art` the specific permissions needed to execute the privileged actions. We need to grant permissions for both the `UnixPrincipal` and the `DemoPrincipal`, even though the principal name is the same for both. The `SecurityManager` does not check for the common `Principal` superclass, but instead looks directly at the implemented class to find a match in the current security policy.

JAVA ENCRYPTION

Valuable data is only valuable to a malicious hacker if the data can be read. If malicious individuals manage to capture password or account information from an Internet site and download it to their personal site, only to find the information is encrypted and unreadable, they have been foiled by sound security practices.

One of the best techniques for securing valuable information is encryption. *Encryption* is the process of scrambling the encoding of information in such a way that it is meaningless and useless to someone who does not know how to unscramble it. The process of unscrambling the information is known as *decryption*.

Encryption Fundamentals

Encryption is performed using data known as *cleartext* and a short string, which is the *key*. The result of the encryption process using the cleartext and the key is the encrypted *ciphertext*, which is the scrambled, useless form of the data.

Decryption is performed using the ciphertext and the key to produce cleartext. Encryption is performed using a *cipher*, an object that performs the encryption and decryption of the target using a specific encryption scheme.

Password-based encryption is a variation of encryption that uses a password. To make the process of accessing the key more difficult, the password is often combined with a random number *salt* to produce the encryption key.

Both encryption and decryption of the same encrypted text involve using the same cryptographic key. The dispersal of this cryptographic key to multiple sites could become tedious. To make this process simpler, key-agreement protocols allow two or more parties to use the same cryptographic keys, without needing to exchange secret information.

Encryption Processing Techniques

There are two common encryption processing techniques in use today: secret key cryptography and public key cryptography. Both involve the exchange of an agreed-on key or pair of keys.

Secret Key Cryptography With *secret key cryptography*, also known as *symmetric encryption*, both parties performing encrypted communication use the same key, which is expected to be kept private and secure. The same secret key is used to both encrypt and decrypt the message. In order to communicate using this technique, both parties must agree to the algorithm to use for encryption. They use the same secret key either by exchanging the key before communicating or by exchanging it as a part of the communication process.

An obvious problem with secret key encryption is the dispersal of the secret key. If a malicious hacker gained access to the secret key, the encrypted conversations would be exposed to perusal by the hacker.

As you will learn in the "Java Secure Sockets Extension (JSSE)" section later in this chapter, Secure Sockets Layer (SSL) cleverly manages the problem of secret key dispersal and encrypts the majority of the data transferred using secret keys. Secret key algorithms are fast and efficient, and they are commonly used with encryption techniques such as Data Encryption Standard (DES), triple-strength DES (3DES), and Rivest Cipher 2 (RC2).

Public Key Cryptography *Public key cryptography* solves the problem of key dispersal that plagues secret key encryption. Public key cryptography, also known as *asymmetric cryptography,* involves using one public key, which is visible to everyone, and another key that is kept private. The public key is exchanged, and the private key is kept secret. The Rivest, Shamir, and Adleman (RSA) algorithm and the Rjindael algorithm are well-known public key algorithms.

In this case, the public and private keys are the inverse of each other. If the public key encrypts the data, the private key can be used to decrypt the data. The public key alone is not enough to decrypt the data; the private key of one of the communicating parties is required. As long as the private key is kept private, this technique offers a very effective means of encrypted communication. Although this technique solves the problem of key dispersal, it requires extensive computations and can be slow. For this reason, it is usually used for transmitting only small blocks of data.

Digital Signatures

If there is no issue with an unknown third party reading the data being sent over insecure channels, encryption of the data is not necessary. But to be sure the data is not tampered with by a third party, or that the third party does not try to become an impostor for the message originator, some form of *digital signature* should be provided with the message.

Digital signatures are commonly used with email messages, since the contents of an email may not represent secure material, but the sender and recipient would like to know that the contents have not been changed. A digital signature does not make any effort to conceal the contents of the message, but it does let the parties involved know whether the contents have been tampered with.

A digital signature is an encrypted digest or a checksum of the contents of a file. The signature is computed using an algorithm (checksum or one-way hash function) that scans the binary values of the data. The result is the digital signature, which is then usually encrypted and transmitted with the data. The recipient then decrypts the checksum and executes the same algorithm against the data. The result arrived at by the recipient should match the result arrived at by the sender. If not, this means that the message has been tampered with.

Message Authentication Code

Message authentication code (MAC) refers to the process of validating the integrity of data that has traveled through an insecure circuit (such as the Internet). This technique is similar to the process of computing a digital signature, except that a secret key (a key shared by both the sender and recipient) is used instead of a private key (where a different key is used by the sender and recipient).

To verify that the message has not been tampered with, a checksum is calculated based on the contents of the message and a secret key. The checksum is sent with the message, and the recipient uses the same secret key and checksum algorithm to arrive at a checksum value. If the checksum value arrived at by the recipient is the same as the checksum sent with the message, the recipient can be assured the message was not tampered with.

If the checksum computed by the recipient is different, the recipient is aware that the message was tampered with and can react accordingly. The mechanism for performing this validation is usually referred to as *hash MAC* (HMAC) and can be used in combination with a shared secret key.

Digital Certificates

A *digital certificate* is a technique for digitally signing a document. These certificates are usually in X.509 format and contain a digest, which is a number computed based on an algorithm used to scan the contents of the document. A digital certificate may also contain the digital signature of a certificate authority (CA), signed using the private key of the CA.

The public key of the CA is usually well known, and the recipient can use that key to decrypt the digest. If the decryption is successful, and the two digests match, you can be assured that the certificate has not been changed.

The recipient may verify the digest or hash by executing the algorithm on the contents of the document.

Java Cryptography Extension (JCE)

The Java Cryptography Extension (JCE) package provides a framework for encryption and decryption, key generation, key agreement, and MAC. Encryption allows symmetric, asymmetric, block, and stream ciphers, with additional support for secure streams and sealed objects.

JCE Architecture

The JCE API has been designed to support various encryption algorithms using a small set of classes. The specifics of the encryption algorithm being used are managed by the provider and are largely transparent to the developer. However, the developer does need to learn the specific properties required for the various forms of encryption, which unfortunately, given the complexity of the underlying math for encryption, is not a trivial matter.

The JCE API supports various providers that are identified in the security properties file for the Java runtime (usually named `JAVA_HOME/jre/lib/security/java.security`). Sun provides a number of useful implementations for common algorithms. You can also access implementations from third-party vendors and then add them to the Java installation by making the classes available and placing the provider entries into the security properties file.

Using JCE involves using a core set of classes consistently to perform encryption and decryption. This consistent use of classes shortens the learning curve for using the API. The most commonly used class is the `Cipher` class, which encapsulates the functionality of a cryptographic cipher. The process of encrypting or decrypting data is considered a *transformation*, which is the underlying algorithm used to perform the encryption. A `Cipher` object is created for a specific type of transformation.

The JCE API uses the factory design pattern to create `Cipher` objects. This design pattern precludes the using of a constructor to create the object (the constructor uses the protected access mode) and involves calling a `getInstance` method to return a reference to a `Cipher` object.

The `getInstance` factory method takes arguments for the transformation and optionally a provider, as shown below. If no provider is specified, the JCE runtime loads all providers specified for the installation, and then scans the providers to see which one can provide the transformation needed. If there is more than one provider for a transformation, JCE will try to determine which provider is the preferred provider.

```
...
// Use the blowfish algorithm.
Cipher cipher = Cipher.getInstance( "Blowfish" );
...
// Use the DESede algorithm.
Cipher cipher = Cipher.getInstance( "DESede/CBC/PKCS5Padding");
...
```

The transformation is specified using a string that includes the name of the transformation or algorithm to use and, optionally, a mode and a padding scheme. The specific values for this entry are provider-specific but should take the form of either *<algorithm_name>* or *<algorithm_name>/<mode>/<padding_scheme>*. If no specific mode or padding scheme is identified, then provider-specific default values will be used. When using a block cipher in stream mode (for example, DES in CFB or OFB mode), the developer may optionally specify the number of bits to be processed at a time by appending a number to the mode name.

When a `Cipher` object is returned by the `getInstance` method, it must be initialized before it can be used. The specifics of the initialization and the arguments to be provided to the initialization method are specific to the type of encryption being used. Initialization will set the `Cipher` object to one of four modes:

- The `ENCRYPT_MODE` mode encrypts data.
- The `DECRYPT_MODE` mode decrypts data.
- The `WRAP_MODE` mode wraps a key into bytes for secure transportation.
- The `UNWRAP_MODE` mode unwraps a previously wrapped key.

The initialize method takes a variety of forms, depending on the type of algorithm being used. If a particular encryption algorithm requires parameters that are not provided explicitly, the underlying implementation should attempt to provide those parameters with default values, either through random selection of keys or some other method. If the implementation cannot do that, the code will throw an exception.

An Encryption Example

The following example demonstrates the process of encrypting data using JCE. It creates a `Cipher` object for the Blowfish algorithm, creates a key, and then uses the key to encrypt data. The program then uses the same key to decrypt the data.

```
import java.security.*;
import javax.crypto.*;
import javax.crypto.spec.*;

public class DemoJCE {

public static void main( String args[] ){

try {
 //
 // Get the key generator and create the key.
 //
 System.out.println("Getting key generator ... ");
 KeyGenerator kgen = KeyGenerator.getInstance( "Blowfish" );

 System.out.println("Generating key ... ");
 SecretKey secretKey = kgen.generateKey();
 byte[] bytes = secretKey.getEncoded();
 SecretKeySpec specKey = new SecretKeySpec( bytes, "Blowfish" );

 //
 // Create the cipher object.
 //
 System.out.println("Creating cipher ... ");
 Cipher cipher = Cipher.getInstance( "Blowfish" );

 System.out.println("Encrypting ... ");
 cipher.init( Cipher.ENCRYPT_MODE, specKey );
 String target = "Encrypt this buddy.";
 byte[] encrypted = cipher.doFinal( target.getBytes() );

 System.out.println("before: " + target );
 System.out.println("after: " + new String( encrypted ) );

  // Decrypt
 cipher.init( Cipher.DECRYPT_MODE, specKey );
```

```
 byte[] decrypted = cipher.doFinal( encrypted );
 System.out.println("\nafter decrypt: " + new String( decrypted ) );
}
catch (Exception e) {
    System.out.println("Exception caught: " + e );
}

}

}
```

The program begins by creating a key generator to create a key to be used for the encryption process. It then generates a secret key and uses it to create a key for the encryption process. The `SecretKeySpec` class creates a secret key in a provider-independent, portable fashion.

Once the secret key has been created, we create the `Cipher` object to manage the encryption and decryption process. We then initialize the `Cipher` object and place it into encryption mode using the secret key that has been generated. Next, we call the `doFinal` method to encrypt the entire target string. The result is a byte array of encrypted data.

To reverse the process, the program places the `Cipher` object in decrypt mode using the same secret key and calls the `doFinal` method to decrypt the data. This also returns a byte array, which is converted to a string to output the results.

The keytool Utility

The `keytool` utility allows you to create and manage keys and security certificates. The authentication information managed by the tool involves a chain of X.509 certificates and an associated private key referenced by an alias.

The keys and certificates managed by `keytool` are stored in a database referred to as a keystore, the default implementation of which is a file. Certificates are structured as a chain and are generally provided by a CA, but `keytool` allows you to create and use a temporary certificate until a CA returns a permanent certificate chain.

Private keys are stored in the keystore database using encryption based on a password provided when the database is created. Passwords are provided for the keystore and for each private key added to the keystore. As the documentation for the `keytool` indicates, if you forget the password, you cannot reclaim the information in the keystore. For good security, the password should be several words long.

You invoke the `keytool` utility, which offers many options, from the command line. Some of the more common `keytool` options are covered here. In all cases, you will be prompted for the keystore password before the command will execute.

Generating a Key

To generate a key, use the -genkey option. The options usually provided with this command are -alias, which indicates the alias name to be associated with the key, and -keystore, which indicates the name of the keystore database where the key will be stored.

Listing a Key Certificate

Listing a certificate provides verification that the certificate was added as requested. To list a certificate, use the -list option. Once again, this option is usually combined with the -alias option to indicate the name of the key to print and the -keystore option to indicate the name of the keystore database to use. The following command lists the contents of the artskey certificate.

```
keytool -list -v -alias artskey -keystore teststore -keypass password
**
Alias name: artskey
Creation date: Thu May 09 20:07:27 EDT 2002
Entry type: keyEntry
Certificate chain length: 1
Certificate[1]:
Owner: CN=Art Taylor, OU=Books Inc., O=Books Inc., L=Unknown, ST=Unknown, C=US
Issuer: CN=Art Taylor, OU=Books Inc., O=Books Inc., L=Unknown, ST=Unknown, C=US
Serial number: 3cdb0f31
Valid from: Thu May 09 20:07:13 EDT 2002 until: Wed Aug 07 20:07:13 EDT 2002
Certificate fingerprints:
         MD5:  C2:C6:84:03:26:79:2F:A8:D1:F0:24:E5:4F:0D:04:F5
         SHA1: 6E:EE:8E:A7:96:24:1E:59:66:64:4E:A1:6C:1E:48:DC:67:C2:2E:76
```

If the alias name is omitted from the -list command, all the keys in the keystore are listed.

Exporting and Importing a Key

You can export a key from a keystore using the -export command in combination with the -alias command to identify the key being exported. Here is an example of using this command:

```
keytool -export -alias artskey -file artskey.cer -keystore teststore
```

A key that has been exported from a keystore can be imported into another keystore using the -import command, as in this example:

```
keytool -import -file artskey.cer -alias artskey -keystore newstore
```

Creating a Self-Certifying Certificate

A self-certifying certificate is certified as if it came from a CA. Although you wouldn't want to do this in a production system, it provides a convenient facility for testing secure applications. The following is the command line for self-certifying a key.

```
keytool -selfcert -alias artskey -keystore teststore
```

JAVA SECURE SOCKETS EXTENSION (JSSE)

The Java Secure Sockets Extension (JSSE) is a Java API that provides SSL connections over TCP/IP sockets. The SSL protocol was developed by Netscape in 1994 and, with input from the development community, has grown to become the most prevalent form of communication security on the Internet. SSL is the *de facto* standard for secure communications on the Web.

Part of the reason for the success of SSL is that it uses a combination of cryptographic strategies to provide security, making it exceedingly difficult to crack. The most commonly used form of SSL encryption is SSL with HTTP, or the HTTPS protocol. SSL encryption has also been applied to FTPs (File Transfer Protocols) and LDAPs (Lightweight Directory Access Protocols).

The specification for the SSL protocol is now under the control of the Internet Engineering Task Force (IETF), which has renamed it Transport Layer Security (TLS) and released a specification. There are only minor differences between TLS 1.0 and SSL 3.0, the commonly supported version of SSL.

SSL Fundamentals

Although it is somewhat transparent to the user, establishing SSL communications involves a number of steps executed through what is known as a *handshake* protocol. The handshake is used to perform the following tasks:

1. Determine the cipher suite to use for encryption.
2. Optionally, authenticate the server.
3. Agree on an encryption mechanism and exchange keys as needed.
4. Begin encrypted communication.

Since SSL is a protocol that has been widely used for a number of years, numerous applications support the protocol, but they may provide this support in different ways. For this reason, the cipher suites available from these implementations vary. The ability to negotiate an appropriate cipher suite provides a great deal of flexibility to the protocol.

The process of authenticating the server is optional, but the ability to perform this authentication provides an additional layer of trust for e-commerce applications. Since it is possible for a clever hacker to pretend to be another site, the ability for the client to validate the server is a big plus. The authentication is performed using a public key certificate presented to the client. If the certificate can be validated using a CA, the client can assume the server is valid.

As part of the exchange of information between the client and the server, a secret key is agreed on. To avoid the intervention of a malicious hacker, this secret key is exchanged using public key encryption. The public key certificate provided by the server is used as the public key to encrypt a secret key selected by the client and sent to the server. Since the server has the corresponding private key for the public key encrypted document, the server can decrypt the secret key.

At this point, both the client and the server hold a secret key that can be used to encrypt data using symmetric encryption. The SSL protocol avoids the overhead of asymmetric, public key encryption and uses symmetric secret key encryption with the secret key the client has selected. This secret key encryption is augmented with an HMAC, which is appended to the message.

Library and Certificate Installation

JSSE requires several steps be taken before it can operate in a JRE. These steps involve installation of class libraries and certificates.

Class Libraries

If you are working with a JDK prior to JDK 1.4.0, or using an SSL provider other than Sun, you must install the class libraries to support JSSE. Additionally, you must configure the Java security properties to recognize the SSL providers for the installation. While Sun does provide a very complete SSL implementation, other providers may also be installed if needed.

Required Certificates

The public and private keys used by SSL are created using security certificates. JSSE uses the X.509 certificate by default, but it supports other certificate types. The certificate used by SSL must be trusted by the client. This requires that the certificate either be signed by a CA or self-signed and installed in the client's keystore of trusted certificates.

You can create a self-signed certificate with the `keytool` utility provided by the JDK, as described in the "The keytool Utility" section earlier in this chapter. You need to create and install this certificate in the keystore for the server, and then export it from the server's keystore and import it into the client's keystore of trusted certificates.

Alternatively, you can create the server certificate and then send it to a trusted CA. The CA will sign it and return it. Then you can install the certificate in the server's keystore. Using this strategy, if your client is a web browser (which has the CA's public key), you will not need to install a certificate with the client, because it will trust a certificate signed by a CA. This eliminates the need to distribute certificates to numerous clients. (This is not the case with nonbrowser clients, which will need to have access to the CA's public key, most likely through a local certificate.)

JSSE Demonstration Program

The program presented in this section provides a minimal implementation of an SSL server and client program written with JSSE. As this program demonstrates, the work necessary to create an SSL application is not much different from working with Java sockets in general. What can be tricky, however, is creating the environment for JSSE to use.

A production application would be structured differently (and would probably not complete all of its work in the main program block) than the program shown here. Our goal is to demonstrate the actions necessary to create an SSL socket, not to show the process of merging SSL into a business application.

The SSL Server Program

An SSL socket is an extension of a Java socket (and, in fact, `javax.net.ssl.SSLServerSocket` class subclasses `java.net.ServerSocket`). But before you can create an SSL socket, you must establish various properties of the SSL connection.

The following program creates an SSL socket server, which creates a socket and then listens for a connection. When a connection is made, it reads a UTF string from the connection and outputs the string to the console. It then writes a UTF string as a response and closes the socket connection.

```
import java.net.*;
import javax.net.*;
import javax.net.ssl.*;
import java.security.*;
import java.security.cert.*;

import java.io.*;

import java.security.KeyStore;
import javax.security.cert.X509Certificate;


public class SSLServer {

public static void main( String[] args ) {

try {

SSLContext context;
KeyManagerFactory keyManagerFactory;
KeyStore keyStore;

  //
  // Our keystore password as a byte array
  //
  char[] passphrase = "password".toCharArray();
```

```
//
// Get an instance of an SSLContext.
//
context = SSLContext.getInstance("TLS");

//
// Get an instance of our X509 key manager.
//
keyManagerFactory = KeyManagerFactory.getInstance("SunX509");

//
// Get an instance of our keystore.
//
keyStore = KeyStore.getInstance("JKS");

//
// Load our keystore and initialize.
//
keyStore.load(new FileInputStream("keystore"), passphrase);
keyManagerFactory.init(keyStore, passphrase);

//
// Initialize our SSL context using our key managers.
//
context.init(keyManagerFactory.getKeyManagers(), null, null);

//
// Create a server socket factory.
//
ServerSocketFactory ssf = context.getServerSocketFactory();

//
// Create a server socket on port 1500.
//
ServerSocket ss = ssf.createServerSocket( 1500 );

System.out.println("Secure socket created. Listening ... " );

//
// Listen for connections.
//
Socket socket = ss.accept();

//
// Connection received. Get an input and output stream.
//
DataInputStream in = new DataInputStream( socket.getInputStream()  );
DataOutputStream out = new DataOutputStream( socket.getOutputStream()  );
```

```
    //
    // Read from the stream.
    //
    System.out.println("read: " + in.readUTF() );

    //
    // Send a response.
    //
    out.writeUTF( "Secure is as secure does ... " );

    //
    // Now go away.
    //
    socket.close();
  }
  catch ( IOException e) {
   System.err.println("IOException in main: " + e );
  }
  catch ( KeyStoreException e) {
   System.err.println("KeyStoreException in main: " + e );
  }
  catch ( KeyManagementException e) {
   System.err.println("KeyManagementException in main: " + e );
  }
  catch ( NoSuchAlgorithmException e) {
   System.err.println("NoSuchAlgorithmException in main: " + e );
  }
  catch ( CertificateException e) {
   System.err.println("CertificateException in main: " + e );
  }
  catch ( UnrecoverableKeyException e) {
   System.err.println("UnrecoverableKeyException in main: " + e );
  }
  }
  }
```

This program begins by creating an `SSLContext` that encapsulates many of the characteristics of the SSL connection and can be used to create both client sockets and server sockets. As part of initializing the `SSLContext`, we must identify a keystore for certificates, along with the password for that keystore. We do this by creating a `KeyManagerFactory`, which will manage the keys and identify the SSL provider implementation to use for managing the keys (in this example, SunX509), and a `KeyStore` class, which is passed the `InputStream` for the keystore file in the local directory.

We then use this `KeyManager` instance to initialize the `SSLContext`.

The initialization method for the `SSLContext` takes three arguments for the keystore manager, the truststore manager, and secure random generator to use for all secure sockets created by the context. (A truststore is simply a term for a keystore containing the public keys of certificates we trust; this is usually used on the JSSE client as we will see shortly.)

In this example, only the keystore value is used. This is adequate for the example, since only server sockets will be created in this program.

Once the SSLContext has been initialized, we create a ServerSocketFactory object, and then from that object, a ServerSocket. (Note that the SSLContext did not create an SSLServerSocket, but the underlying SSL implementation is still present.)

We then make an accept call on the ServerSocket to listen for connections. When a connection is made on the socket, the program creates an InputStream and OutputStream on the socket. It reads a UTF string on the socket, writes a UTF string as a response, and then closes the connection.

The SSL Client Program

The SSL client program opens a connection to the SSL server socket and then writes and reads a UTF string from the socket. As with the server program, this is essentially a socket client that adds SSL security to socket communications (the SSLSocket class is a subclass of java.net.Socket).

The program begins by doing much of the preparation that the SSL server socket program did, but, in this case, we make a point of identifying a keystore of trusted certificates. By identifying trusted certificates, we can ensure that the server with which the client is communicating is who it says it is.

```
import java.io.*;
import javax.net.*;
import javax.net.ssl.*;
import java.security.KeyStore;

import java.security.*;
import java.security.cert.CertificateException;


public class SSLClient {

public static void main( String[] args ) {

try {
    SSLContext context;
    KeyManagerFactory keyManagerFactory;
    KeyStore keyStore;

    //
    // Our password as a byte array
    //
    char[] password = "password".toCharArray();

    //
```

```
// Assign our trustStore. These are certificates we trust.
//
keyStore = KeyStore.getInstance( "JKS" );
keyStore.load( new FileInputStream( "truststore"), password  );
TrustManagerFactory trustManagerFactory =
    TrustManagerFactory.getInstance(
                        TrustManagerFactory.getDefaultAlgorithm() );
trustManagerFactory.init ( keyStore );
TrustManager[] trustManagers =
             trustManagerFactory.getTrustManagers();

//
// create an SSLContext
//
context = SSLContext.getInstance("TLS");

//
// Create a key manager.
//
keyManagerFactory = KeyManagerFactory.getInstance("SunX509");

//
// Get a keystore instance.
//
keyStore = KeyStore.getInstance("JKS");

//
// Load our keystore. If we need to authenticate, we can use these.
//
keyStore.load(new FileInputStream("keystore"), password);

//
// Initialize our key manager.
//
keyManagerFactory.init(keyStore, password);
KeyManager[] keyManagers = keyManagerFactory.getKeyManagers();

//
// Initialize our context using the key managers.
//
context.init( keyManagers, trustManagers, null);

//
// Create an SSL socket factory from our context.
```

```
    //
    SSLSocketFactory factory = context.getSocketFactory();

    //
    // Create an SSL socket connection to our server.
    //
    SSLSocket socket =
      (SSLSocket)factory.createSocket("localhost", 1500);

    //
    // Start an SSL handshake to achieve secure communications.
    //
    System.out.println("Starting handshake ... " );
    socket.startHandshake();

    //
    // We are secure. Send our secure message.
    //
    DataOutputStream out = new DataOutputStream(
socket.getOutputStream()  );
    out.writeUTF( "This is secure  ... " );
    System.out.println("Wrote string ... " );

    //
    // Read a response.
    //
    BufferedReader in = new BufferedReader(
              new InputStreamReader(  socket.getInputStream() ));
    System.out.println( "received: " + in.readLine() );

    //
    // Now go away.
    //
    socket.close();
}

catch ( IOException e) {
 System.err.println("IOException in main: " + e );
}
catch ( NoSuchAlgorithmException e) {
 System.err.println("NoSuchAlgorithmException in main: " + e );
}
catch ( KeyStoreException e) {
 System.err.println("KeyStoreException in main: " + e );
```

```
}
catch ( UnrecoverableKeyException e) {
 System.err.println("UnrecoverableKeyException in main: " + e );
}
catch ( CertificateException e) {
 System.err.println("CertificateException in main: " + e );
}
catch ( KeyManagementException e) {
 System.err.println("KeyManagementException in main: " + e );
}
}
// ==

}
```

The program begins by creating a keystore for the `trustStore`, the collection of trusted certificates, and loading the contents of the truststore file in the current directory as the `trustStore` to be used by the program. We create a `TrustManagerFactory` to manage the `trustStore` using the default algorithm for the SSL security provider.

Next, we create an `SSLContext` based on the SSL protocol, as well as a `KeyStoreManager` and an associated `KeyStore` to load the keystore for the client program using the keystore file in the current directory.

Both the `KeyManager` and `TrustManager` arrays are used to initialize the `SSLContext`. The third argument to the initialization method is an instance of `SecureRandom`, which is passed as a null, informing the SSL installation to use the default implementation.

We then use the context to create a `SocketFactory`, which we use to create a `Socket` for the local host server on port 1500. Once the socket has been obtained, we call the `startHandshake` method to initiate the SSL security on the socket.

If the SSL handshake is successful, the next step is to write a UTF string to the socket. We then obtain an `InputStream` on the socket and read a UTF string as a response from the server. Finally, when all the work is complete, we close the socket connection.

SECURING JAR FILES

Java archive (JAR) files are the common means of packaging Java applications. Java classes, property files, XML data, images, HTML, and JavaServer Pages (JSP) files can all be packaged together in a single, compressed format, which is easy to distribute.

But JAR files also present a security risk: As they are distributed, they may become available to would-be attackers, who can manipulate the contents of the archive in order to launch an attack on some resource available to the application. For instance, consider an archive that contains a number of classes that extract and update accounting information. Clever hackers could insert their class (through manipulation of the program's class path or by deleting it from the archive) for one of the accounting classes in the archive. Using their class, they could potentially manipulate accounting data to suit their needs. You can protect JAR files by signing them and by sealing them. Signing JAR files can provide assurance that the contents of a JAR file have not been manipulated by a third party. By sealing JAR files, you can ensure that a package of classes within the archive is kept intact.

The jarsigner Utility

To associate a digital signature with a JAR file, and to later verify the signature versus an entry in a keystore, you can use the `jarsigner` utility. The signature in a signed JAR file is created using a private key from the keystore. The signature can be verified later using the public key for the private key used to create the signature.

To digitally sign a JAR file, use the `-keystore` option. Here is an example of a command to digitally sign a JAR file:

```
jarsigner -keystore acctKeyStore accounting.jar artskey
```

This command associates the alias `artskey` with the contents of the JAR file.

To verify the signature of a JAR file, use the `-verify` option. Here is an example of a command to verify the signature of a JAR file:

```
jarsigner -verify -keystore acctKeyStore accounting.jar artskey
```

If any of the components of the JAR file have not been signed, the output of the `verify` command will indicate this.

The Sealed Directive

You can seal packages in a JAR file by using a set of entries in the manifest of the archive. Sealing a JAR file ensures that all classes from the package come from that JAR file. When the practice of sealing JAR files is combined with signing JAR files, it becomes exceedingly difficult to insert malicious code into an application.

The `Sealed` directive in the archive can indicate that the entire archive is sealed or that the previously named package is sealed. Here is an example of using the `Sealed` directive:

```
...
Name: /com/taylor/accounting/
Sealed: true
```

Appearing in a manifest, the entry above would indicate that the contents of the `com.taylor.accounting` package are sealed, and all classes from the package must come from this JAR file.

If the `Sealed` directive is placed on the first line of a manifest entry, the entire contents of the archive are considered. You can seal an entire archive but exclude particular packages in the archive, as shown next.

```
Sealed: true
Name: com/taylor/misc
```

```
Sealed: false
...
```

These entries indicate that the entire archive, except the com.taylor.misc package, is sealed. These entries could be placed in a manifest. The manifest could then be included in an archive using the following syntax.

```
jar -cvmf acctgManifest extensions
```

When executed, this command will include the acctgManifest into an archive of the extensions directory (and all of its subdirectories).

SUMMARY

This chapter covered the JAAS, JCE, and the JSSE Java APIs. These APIs augment the basic security of the Java language. We also discussed the keytool and jarsigner utilities, along with the Sealed directive.

The JAAS API provides authentication and authorization capabilities, providing a plug-in architecture that allows different security modules to be substituted or added to an application. You learned that JAAS also allows you to use the security policy file to describe a set of authorization rules for principals. We demonstrated how you can use custom permissions to describe an allowable set of actions for an application. Later chapters will demonstrate the use of custom permissions again with the case study.

The JCE API provides the ability to encrypt data using Java programs. Using this API, you can effectively hide critical data "in plain sight." This allows you to protect the integrity of your data by enciphering the information and to use message digests to verify the proof of sender. The keytool utility allows you to manage security certificates. Later chapters will provide more detailed JCE examples with the case study.

The Java Secure Sockets Extension (JSSE) is a Java API that provides SSL connections over TCP/IP sockets. This chapter presented an implementation of an SSL server and client program written with JSSE.

Finally, you learned how to protect JAR files by signing them and by sealing them. By using the jarsigner utility to sign JAR files, you can ensure that the contents of a JAR file have not been manipulated by a third party. By sealing JAR files with the Sealed directive, you can ensure that a package of classes within the archive is kept intact.

Java security forms the foundation for J2EE security. Next we will take a look at specific multi-tiered J2EE technology such as the web tier Java servlets and Java Server Pages (JSP), and the business tier components provided by Enterprise Java Beans. Through all of these technologies Sun has developed a consistent security architecture as we will see in the next chapter and throughout the remainder of the text.

CHAPTER 3

Java is a flexible language used to create applications running in a variety of environments. At one time, most applications were monolithic in structure; a single application provided the user interface, executed the business logic, and communicated with a database server. Applications developed in this fashion were overloaded, having put on too many pounds of business logic and control structures. They were the proverbial *fat clients*.

The many problems of the fat client were addressed by distributed application development. J2EE represents a blueprint of distributed Java technologies that are used to create distributed applications. Exactly what the J2EE standard provides, the technologies involved, and how its security architecture is implemented will be covered in this chapter. The remainder of the book will build on this material, providing more detailed examples of potential security attacks and how they can be managed using sound J2EE security practices.

MIDDLEWARE AND DISTRIBUTED SOFTWARE COMPONENTS

In the early 1990s, client-server software dominated. This software provided a consistent, robust user interface to users who had struggled with the primitive user interfaces provided by character-based applications. But client-server applications exacted their toll on the IT organizations that supported these applications. The same client-server application would run on one machine but not the other (for dubious reasons), and the size of application binaries would grow without bounds with each successive release. In short, deployment and support of the client side of the client-server application was exceedingly difficult.

Security was also an issue, as client-server applications usually contained all of the business logic of the organization. Many applications would place critical information, such as server names and passwords, in configuration files on the machine. Connections to critical servers were made by each installation of the client-server software, so the number of server connections could be high. Since it was not possible to determine who was connected but inactive (out to lunch), connections would often be retained for a long period of time—a security risk, as well as a resource consumption nightmare for the server. Middleware addressed many of the issues of client-server software.

Middleware Development

Middleware is software that resides "in the middle" between the client application and the server that contains the resources (databases or other systems) of the enterprise (see Figure 3-1). Middleware was designed to encapsulate the various business services, to execute the business logic of the enterprise. This frees clients of the responsibility of managing the details of business logic (which often changes) and allows them to focus on managing the user interface. The middleware manages the specifics of business processing and exposes a simple, concise interface to the clients.

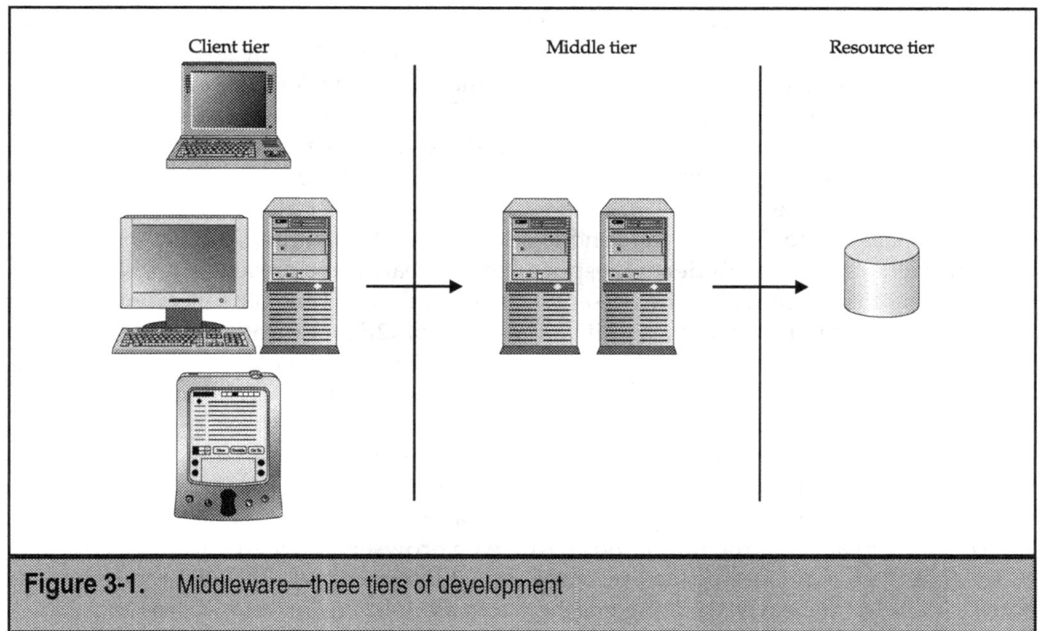

Figure 3-1. Middleware—three tiers of development

The common approach to developing middleware involved using object-oriented software. Developers would create components as objects, for example using CORBA, and then deploy them on servers, which would provide various services for the objects. These middleware servers would provide life-cycle management, security, transaction management, failover and fault tolerance, load balancing, and other services for the components. With the servers providing these value-added services, developers could avoid needing to develop these services on their own.

Middleware met with some success during the heady days of client-server software, but the development process for these distributed components was very specialized and involved knowledge of object-oriented languages such as C++ and the nontrivial task of programming using CORBA and IDL. The actual components were also developed using a platform-specific language, which required porting to move to a different hardware/operating system (OS) platform.

Multitiered Application Development

As part of the middleware development effort, developers were restructuring applications using a *multi-tiered* model. In its simplest form, this model involved three tiers: a client tier, which was focused on delivering a user interface to the end user of the application, a middle tier that delivered business services, and a back-end tier that provided the resources of the application. The distributed software components would be delivered on the middle tier using application servers, and the back-end would be provided using relational databases or possibly a legacy system.

This three-tiered model (and programming design patterns such as Model-View-Controller) quickly evolved based on changing technology. With the advent of web technologies, a simplified model for what had become a bloated client tier quickly emerged. The web browser provides a simple, lightweight, and adequate user interface (though it trailed the capabilities of more robust client-server software). But to address some of the shortcomings of the user interface for the web browser, additional processing needed to be done on another tier.

The logical tier to describe the functionality of this tier is the presentation tier. The components running on this tier are responsible for creating the presentation, which is ultimately sent to the client tier. The presentation tier is also responsible for communicating with the business tier. Because a significant portion of J2EE applications are built for the Web, this tier is also commonly referred to as the *web tier*, but we will use the term *presentation tier* in this text to more clearly describe the full spectrum of J2EE applications, including those that are not web-based.

The initial Sun entry for the presentation tier was the applet that ran inside a web browser and provided access to a GUI. But applets were problematic for a number of reasons, and the focus for delivering dynamic web content quickly moved to the web server.

The need to address the limitations of the web browser spawned various web server technologies to create interesting and more robust interfaces for the web browser. These entries included the early scripting engines such as Cold Fusion and Microsoft's Active Server Pages (ASP), as well as the functional, but not very efficient, Common Gateway Interface (CGI).

Sun's initial Java entry for creating dynamic content in the web server was the Java servlet. This provided a set of classes to operate within a web server (the container), which would provide basic services such as life cycle management and security for the servlet component. The servlet would receive an HTTP request and provide an HTTP response.

Though this approach was functional and efficient, creating a servlet involved Java coding—a skill many web developers did not have (a good number were not even familiar with basic programming constructs). Technologies such as Cold Fusion and Microsoft's ASP did not require such coding, so they offered a shorter learning curve and less expensive development alternative to working with servlets.

Sun later added JSP to round out the Java offering for the web tier. JSP uses a scripting language that conceal the details of the Java code. As with Microsoft's ASP, JSP provides a shorter learning curve and is easier to maintain than Java servlets. Later revisions even provided scripting extensibility through tag libraries.

The Multitiered Environment

Client-server applications were by definition two tiers: the client application and the back-end database server. Using middleware implied the use of at least a third tier, and with the birth of the Web, the concept of a multitiered application model became dominant. There are commonly five tiers that are identified with a multitiered environment, as shown in Table 3-1.

Tier	Technologies	Description
Client	Web browser, client application	Interacts with the user and the presentation tier.
Presentation	Web server (Tomcat, BEA, Apache, IIS, IPlanet)	The web server. Creates the presentation and interacts with the business tier.
Business	Application servers (WebLogic, Websphere, JBoss, IPlanet)	Executes the business logic of the organization. Interacts with the integration tier.
Integration	Application servers	Responsible for interacting with the various back-end (data) resources of the application.
Resource	Relational databases, legacy databases/systems (Oracle, PostgreSQL, SQL Server, mainframe), enterprise messaging systems (MQ Series)	Represents the data—the information used by the application.

Table 3-1. Multitiered Application Tiers

Not every tier identified in this table will appear in every multitiered application. With web applications, the client tier, web tier, and resource tier are very common, and many applications are developed using just the technology from these three tiers (web browsers, JSPs, servlets, and relational databases). More complex and transaction-intensive applications with more varied system-integration requirements add business and integration tiers to handle higher transaction loads and assist in the integration of disparate systems.

J2EE Multitiered Technologies

Many of the major features of Java made it a particularly adept technology to use for middleware development. It is platform independent, so components could be developed on Windows NT and deployed on Unix and Windows platforms without requiring porting. It is multithreaded, so it is relatively easy to develop efficient multithreaded servers using Java. Its extensible security model also provides a safe operating environment for components that can be exposed to the world at large.

The J2EE release reorganizes and refocuses development efforts for some existing Java tools (such as servlets) and packages them with middleware tools (such as EJB). It also provides a consistent, useful standard for server vendors and developers.

Remote Method Invocation (RMI) allows Java applications to use Java objects remotely by invoking methods on the objects. This package was part of an early Java release and had originally used a proprietary protocol, the Java Remote Method Protocol (JRMP). This package has since been extended to support other protocols, such as the Internet Inter-ORB Protocol (IIOP).

As part of the J2EE release, Sun also provided a specification for a middleware component known as Enterprise JavaBeans (EJB). EJB provides a standard for creating a middleware component that builds on existing technologies such as RMI and IIOP and can easily be made to run within the existing application servers. Combined with JSPs and servlets, these packages represent the core of the J2EE component technologies, as shown in Figure 3-2.

The key technology in the business tier and integration tier is the J2EE compliant application server. The J2EE application server provides the scalability features (resource pooling and component pooling) and the integration services (distributed transactions and JDBC connectivity) that reduce the difficulty of system integration and extracting sufficient performance from a distributed application. These features are a required part

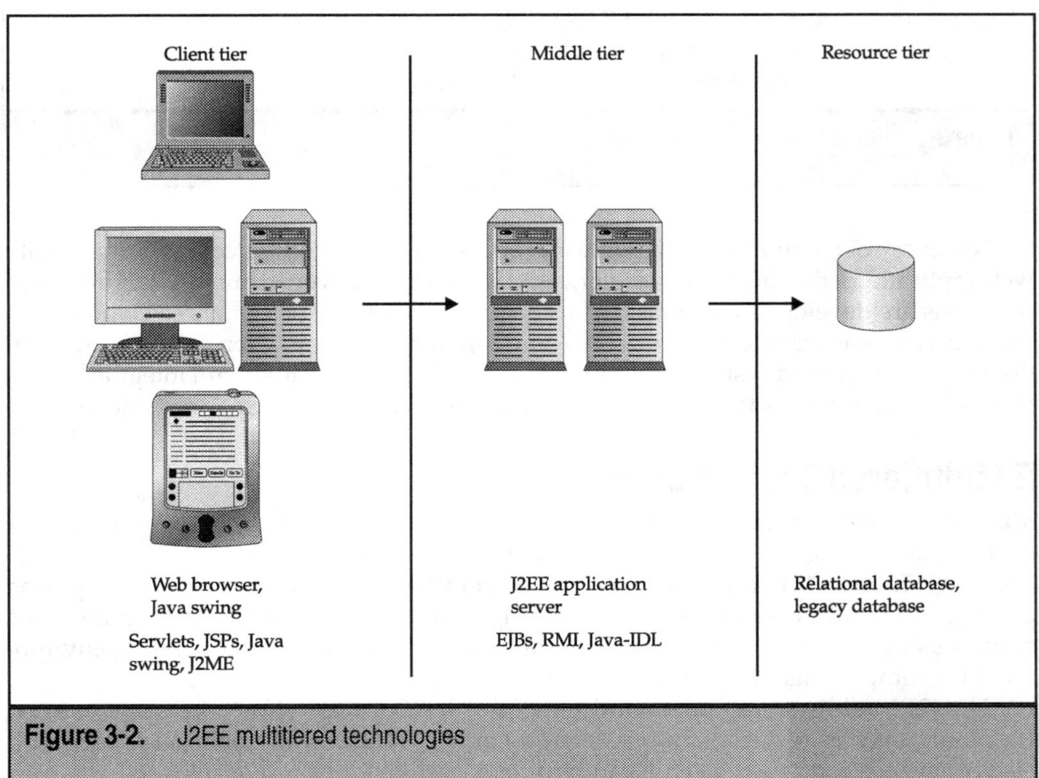

Figure 3-2. J2EE multitiered technologies

of J2EE compliance, and most vendors will provide other features in addition to those required by the J2EE specification. The primary technologies in J2EE are web tier components such as servlets and JSPs, and the business tier component of EJBs. The next sections will provide a brief introduction to JSPs and servlets and demonstrate how these two technologies are related, what security mechanisms are available, and how these mechanisms work with the business tier EJB components.

WEB TIER COMPONENTS: SERVLETS AND JSP

The Java web tier components of servlets and JSPs perform the task of processing and responding to HTTP requests. These components operate within a web server container that provides a basic set of services for the component, such as mapping requests to the component, life cycle management for the component, and security.

Servlets

Java web components are all related to the original web component: the servlet. The servlet defines a component that receives HTTP requests and provides HTTP responses. A servlet is defined as a Java class and is compiled with a Java compiler; then the resulting class file is deployed onto a web server. Deployment makes the web server aware of the web component and assigns various properties to the component using an XML configuration file named `web.xml`.

Internet or intranet applications may potentially serve a large number of users. The basic technology for the Internet, the HTTP server, was designed to handle a large number of requests efficiently. Web servers providing servlet invocation can also expect a large number of potential users.

To provide efficient servlet life cycle management, servlet components are inherently shared among incoming requests. A request for a servlet will most likely use an existing instance of a servlet, instead of creating a new instance of the servlet component.

But this creates an environment where instance members of a servlet may not retain the values of instance members from one page invocation to the next. Java servlet class instance members, if used at all, should either contain information or a resource that can be shared among multiple users of an application and should be declared final, or should be reset to new values each call (which would make local variables the more sensible alternative).

Java Servlet Creation

The process of creating a servlet is little more than creating a class that extends one of the servlet classes. The developer then prepares the servlet response by retrieving an I/O stream or writer from a response object. But a servlet must be deployed into a servlet container before it can be used. This process, though not complex, does require the developer to make some decisions and does present the opportunity to add some security to the application.

The following example demonstrates the process of creating a Java servlet. This example handles an HTTP GET request. It receives a request (`HttpServletRequest`) and a response (`HttpServletResponse`) as parameters to the `doGet` method, which is called by the container when a request for the servlet is received.

```
import javax.servlet.*;
import javax.servlet.http.*;
import javax.net.*;
import java.io.*;
public class ServletExample1 extends HttpServlet {

 public void doGet( HttpServletRequest request, HttpServletResponse response )
          throws IOException, ServletException {
    PrintWriter out = response.getWriter();
    String name = request.getParameter( "name" );
    String anotherName = getInitParameter( "anotherName" );
    if ( name == null ) {
         name = "NoName";
     }
    out.println("</html>");
    out.println("</body>");
    out.println("<p> Hello there: " + name );
    out.println("<p>Another name: " + anotherName );
    out.println("</body>");
    out.println("</html>");
   // --
}
   public void init( ) {

     //
    // Could put initialization code here
    //    }
}
```

This class begins by importing the servlet, network, and I/O classes needed for operation. We then provide an implementation for the `doGet` method to process an HTTP GET request. The first line of this method retrieves a `PrintWriter` object from the response object. This effectively provides the ability to write to the output stream of the response. (A Java `OutputStream` could be retrieved to provide binary output.)

We then attempt to retrieve the `name` parameter from the request. If this `getParameter` call returns a null reference, we can assume the parameter was not passed and a default value is substituted.

We retrieve an initialization parameter, a parameter stored in the `web.xml` deployment file for the servlet, and store it in a local string. We then write both strings to the output, along with some HTML closing tags.

The `init` method of a servlet is called when the servlet is first loaded by the servlet container. This method is called only once, so overriding the `init` method is a good way to perform initialization in a servlet.

Figure 3-3 shows the output from this servlet when it is executed.

Java Servlet Deployment

The `web.xml` file contains the information that describes how to deploy the servlet class into the web server. The minimal file provides an entry for a context parameter, a value that can be retrieved by servlets running in a container. In the previous example, we retrieved this parameter through the `ServletContext`. Using the `web.xml` file allows servlets to retrieve various configuration parameters. This is a better, easier, and more

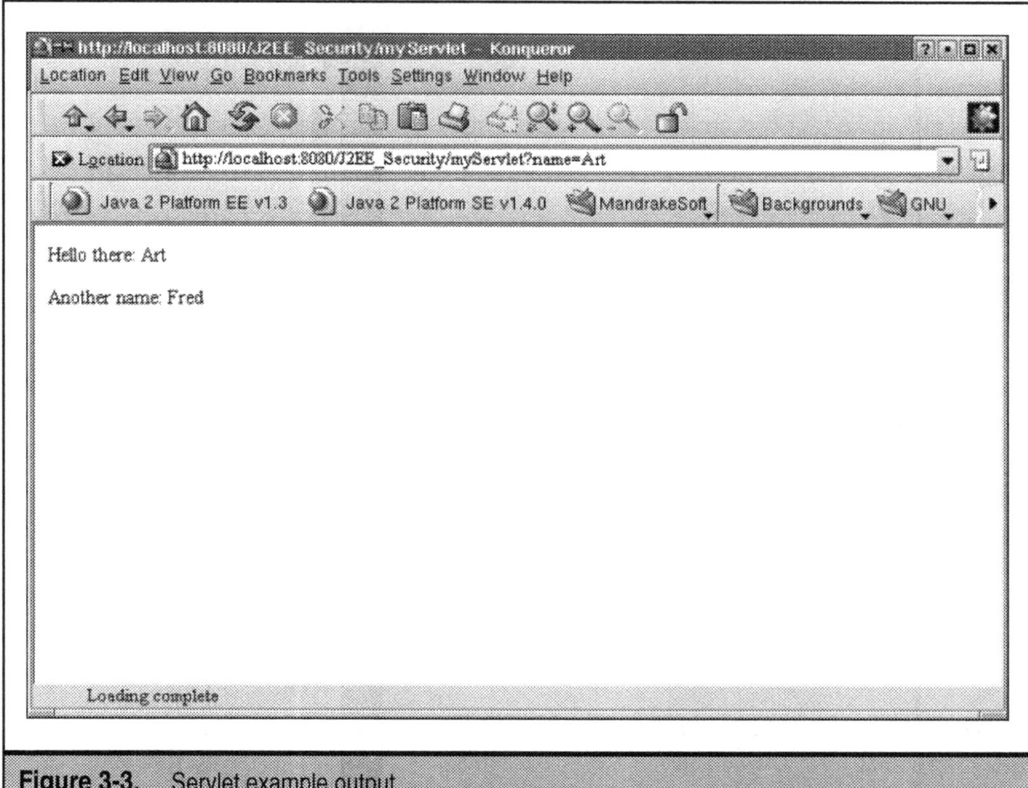

Figure 3-3. Servlet example output

standards-based approach for web components than trying to open and retrieve the contents of a property file. The web.xml file is also guaranteed to be hidden from prying eyes, since it must be stored in the ./WEB-INF directory, which cannot be accessed through the web server implementing the servlet container.

In the web.xml file, the servlet tag defines the servlet name and maps the name to a class name. This is the class that the servlet container will attempt to load at runtime. A servlet mapping class is then used to map the servlet name to a URL. This provides an opportunity to further obscure the true location of the servlet (which hackers may want to substitute with their own servlet class). In this example, we substitute the name myServlet for the servlet that has been named servlet1. Since the servlet has been deployed into the context /J2EE_Security on the local host, it could now be invoked using the URL http://localhost:8080/J2EE_Security/myServlet.

The partial contents of the web.xml file are shown below.

```
...
<servlet>
    <servlet-name>
      servlet1
    </servlet-name>
    <servlet-class>
        ServletExample1
    </servlet-class>
  <load-on-startup>
    1
  </load-on-startup>
</servlet>

<servlet-mapping>
    <servlet-name>
         servlet1
    </servlet-name>
    <url-pattern>
        /myServlet
    </url-pattern>
</servlet-mapping>
...
```

The deployment process for a servlet or JSP involves placing the component into a specific directory. The name of the root directory for the installation is usually configurable and dependent on the container implementation. Alternatively, it is possible to create an archive of the components and their support elements (such as graphics and HTML pages) combined with the appropriate directory structure and web.xml file. This archive, dubbed a WAR (for Web ARchive) file can be placed into an appropriate directory, where the web server will read the file and automatically deploy its contents.

JSP

A JSP is a scripted "page" that is compiled into a servlet, so a JSP can be considered a servlet. The web server that handles JSPs and servlets maintains a cache of compiled JSPs and can make intelligent decisions on when a page needs to be compiled.

JSP Composition

A JSP is composed of static content, scripting elements, directives, and actions. These elements may be mixed throughout the JSP and do not need to appear in any particular order.

Static Content The static content of a JSP is the HTML content or comments that will not be processed by the JSP compiler. This content will not be altered when the page is invoked and will be delivered as-is to the response stream.

Scripting Elements The scripting elements are the elements that contain Java code. Since the structure of the Java code appearing in the JSP has been relaxed, this code is sometimes referred to as a *scriptlet*. Unlike Java program code, a scriptlet does not need to be within a method block that is, in turn, declared within a class. A scriptlet appears virtually anywhere in the JSP and is generally used to make method calls or execute Java flow-control statements to generate HTML output. The entire Java syntax is available, though good web programming style recommends limiting the Java code in the JSP as much as possible. Any scriptlet code should be focused on maintaining the view. Any business logic should be processed in another component, such as a JavaBeans or EJB component, not in the page script.

Directives The directives of a JSP are instructions for the compiler. As such, they are executed at compile time, when the JSP is converted into a servlet and then compiled (a process that is usually executed in sequence). Directives are used to include files into the page, to import classes, and to provide instructions on how the page should be handled when invoked.

The expressions of a JSP allow a shortcut for outputting a value of an expression to the output stream for a page. This shortcut uses the syntax `<%=`, followed by the expression to be evaluated and terminating with the syntax `%>`. Using this syntax, and assuming that `firstName` and `lastName` are strings, the expression `Full Name: <%= firstName + lastName %>` outputs the concatenation of the `firstName` and `lastName` strings to the response page.

JSP Actions The JSP actions are converted into servlet code and then executed when the page is invoked, so they have a runtime impact on the behavior of the JSP. These actions can be used to identify and use JavaBeans, include files into the JSP at runtime when the page is invoked, forward execution to another JSP, and perform other actions.

JSP Taglibs JSPs also provides the capability to create custom tags for a JSP. These custom tags are known as *taglibs* and are composed of XML-like tags that may optionally contain attributes and bodies. Their content is processed when the page is invoked, and the processing performed by the tags is Java code.

JSP taglibs allow complex Java processing to be moved off the JSP. This provides a clean separation of roles and also increases security, since the business logic of the organization and potentially important information is further obscured from the potential hacker.

When a request is received for a Java web component, the web server must first determine which web component will manage the request. The web server will ultimately map the component referenced by the URL to a servlet class. If the reference is to a JSP that has been updated after its associated servlet was created, then the JSP will be compiled into a servlet. Invoking the servlet may not mean the class that represents the servlet needs to be instantiated. Instead, a currently instantiated instance of the servlet class may be used to process a request.

JSPs and servlets provide a session object that can be used to track information about a session. They also provide the ability to create filter chains, manipulate cookies on the client machine, and forward requests to other HTTP resources, including servlets and JSPs.

JSP Use

The Java servlet provides a functionally rich and efficient means of responding to HTTP requests. But to create even a simple servlet requires fairly sophisticated programming knowledge.

The JSP was designed to provide a more natural means of programming a web page. By design, the JSP was meant to be maintainable by nonprogrammers. It is even possible, with the use of JSP taglibs or JavaBeans, to create an environment in which a nonprogrammer could produce fairly sophisticated, dynamic web pages, without requiring constant programmer intervention.

A JSP is an HTML page with JSP script interspersed into the document. The JSP is transformed into a Java servlet, which is then compiled and executed. Since this is obviously a process that should not be occurring each time a page is accessed, the JSP-enabled web server will track the date the JSP was created versus the date the corresponding servlet was created. Only when the JSP is newer than the associated servlet will the JSP transformation and compilation process be executed.

The following example demonstrates the process of using a JSP. Mixed in with the normal HTML tags such as `<html>` and `<center>` are tags that begin with `<%`. These tags introduce JSP elements and are interpreted and converted by the JSP compiler.

The code listing shown below also demonstrates the use of Java language syntax within the JSP. The Java code within the web page, known as a scriptlet, can include any valid Java language element and can reference any API that is visible to the JVM of the container. This provides a powerful tool for web development.

```
<html>
<body bgcolor="#FFFFFF" background="/JavaWeb/img/bg2_grey.jpg">
```

```
<%@ page errorPage="Failure.jsp" %>

<center>
<p>Hello There: <%= request.getParameter( "name" ) %>
</center>
<ol>
<% for (int n=0; n < 3; n++) { %>
   <li>Hello again ...
<% } %>
</ol>
<br>
<br>
<br>

<%@ include file="footer.txt" %>
</body>
</html>
```

The result of processing this file will be a servlet that includes a number of output statements to output the HTML elements. The resulting servlet will contain Java code for portions of the JSP script that contain Java statements. For instance, in the page, the statement

```
<p>Hello There: <%= request.getParameter( "name" ) %>
```

will map into servlet code similar to the following:

```
PrintWriter out = response.getWriter();
...
out.println("<p>Hello There: " + request.getParameter( "name" ) );
...
```

BUSINESS TIER COMPONENTS: EJBS

The EJB is a business tier component, a distributed component that runs in a container that is provided by an application server. EJBs are the core distributed component for J2EE. There are other methods for working with remote objects with Java, but EJBs provide the most functionality, courtesy of the container in which they operate.

Services Provided by the EJB Container

The container provides a number of core services for the EJB component, including life cycle management, security, transactions, persistence, and naming.

Life Cycle Management

The life cycle management provided by the EJB container essentially manages the creation and potentially the sharing of the EJB remote object. The container will make decisions about creating any EJB objects needed and will manage the sharing of objects among clients, if that is allowed.

Most application servers that provide EJB containers use *bean pools*, where multiple instances of a bean are created when the application server is started and are then provided to client sessions as they are requested. When a bean is no longer needed, it can be returned to the pool. This movement of a bean from an active state to a passive state is known as *passivation*, and the movement of the bean from a passive state to an active state is known as *activation*. The EJB classes used to implement beans provide callback methods for passivation and activation.

Life cycle management also includes the general management of memory resources by the container. The container can destroy components, effectively freeing the resources used by those components. When a bean should be destroyed is not part of the specification and is left to the container provider to implement. Most EJB vendors will provide a timeout parameter for destruction of components as part of the configuration parameters for the server. Any component that is idle for a period of time greater than the timeout parameter will be destroyed.

Security Mechanisms

The container provides security mechanisms to identify principals and the user, and allows roles to be assigned to principals. The application server must provide a mechanism allowing principals to be mapped to roles and roles assigned to components, so that only principals in specific roles are allowed to execute certain components. This security mechanism will be discussed in more detail later in this chapter, in the "EJB Security Architecture" section.

Transaction Handling

The container allows transactions to be run over multiple data sources, thus providing for distributed transactions. By necessity, J2EE servers come bundled with a transaction server, which allows distributed transactions to be executed across multiple data sources.

Persistence Mechanism

The J2EE specification provides for persistence, which allows component state to persist in a database. This persistence mechanism applies to the entity type of bean, which synchronizes its state with an underlying datastore. The various bean types are descibed in the next section, and the persistence mechanism is described in the discussion of entity beans.

Naming Service

A J2EE compliant server provides a naming service, which allows resources and EJB components to be found and retrieved and provides access to stored application parameters. This convenience mechanism greatly simplifies the process of providing access to distributed components.

Types of EJBs

The design for the EJBs acknowledges that one simple type of remote component does not meet the needs of all applications. For this reason, the designers of EJBs have provided several different types of components. As of version J2EE version 1.3, there are three primary types of components: session beans, entity beans, and message-driven beans. These components and their variations are detailed in the following sections.

Session Beans

The EJB session bean represents a client conversation. This is a conversation between the client application that is using the remote component and the remote component. The client application invokes the remote component requesting a service, and the remote component—the session bean—replies.

A session bean may retain state (the values of its instance members) between invocations, or it may operate on a simple request/response cycle, where all work is performed during the invocation and results are immediately returned to the client. These distinctions are reflected in the stateful and stateless session beans.

Stateful Session Beans The stateful session bean retains state information between invocations. When a client obtains a reference to a stateful session bean, it can then begin to make calls on the exposed methods of the bean. Between the time the client makes one call on a bean method and the time it makes another call, the actual remote component represented by the bean may have changed, so that the first call to the bean was made to a different remote object instance than the object instance of the second call.

It is the responsibility of the container to maintain the state information for a stateful session bean. The container does this by using various techniques, such as Java serialization and Java reflection. As beans are moved to and from the pool of available beans, the state of the stateful session bean must be maintained, as shown in Figure 3-4.

Stateless Session Beans A stateless session bean does not require state to be maintained. A remote reference to the bean is obtained, and methods are invoked on the bean. Between the time one method is invoked and the time a second method is invoked, there is no guarantee that the internal state of the remote object will be maintained. This implies

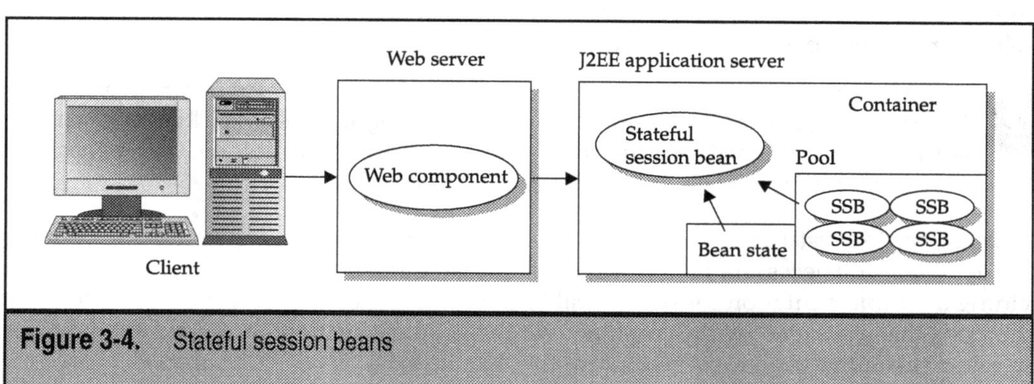

Figure 3-4. Stateful session beans

that all of the bean's work must be performed within the confines of a single method call, or if state is required, it is maintained in the client and passed into the methods of the stateless session bean on each invocation.

The question of whether to use stateful or stateless session beans is not easy to answer. Using stateless session beans provides a more efficient component for the business tier where speed and efficiency are important, but such an approach requires state information to be retained elsewhere, most likely on the presentation tier in a servlet's session information. This could ultimately lead to added complexity and possibly even the inclusion of business logic on the presentation tier, which would be undesirable.

In practice, current application servers now provide very efficient mechanisms for managing stateful session beans, so performance is usually not an issue. J2EE business tier components provide an operating environment which provides a number of services, including security. As we will see throughout this book, maintaining the separation of roles that places business logic in the business tier (even if it requires state) and presentation logic in the presentation tier allows for a more cohesive implementation of the J2EE security architecture.

Entity Beans

The entity bean is a distributed component whose state is synchronized with a persistent datastore by the container. Entity beans are also required to be transactional, so that any interaction with an entity bean is a participant in a transaction.

The persistence mechanism for an entity bean can be managed by either the container or program code in the bean. If the container manages persistence, no code is written to perform the synchronization with the database; this is referred to as *container-managed persistence*. If the definition for the entity bean contains code to perform the database update, the bean is said to have *bean-managed persistence*.

Container-Managed Persistence With container-managed persistence, the application server vendor provides tools that allow the developer to describe the object-relational mapping, which is the mapping from the entity bean component (a Java object with instance members) to the corresponding relational database table or tables. With simple tables and relationships, the process of performing this object-relational mapping is not difficult. However, with more complex relationships (for example, the recursive/self-join relationship of a parts table), object-relational mapping becomes extremely difficult.

NOTE The EJB specification does not describe how container-managed persistence will be implemented. It just specifies that the vendor will provide the object-relational mapping facility and that the container will support container-managed persistence for entity beans.

Bean-Managed Persistence An alternative to container-managed persistence is to provide the detailed code necessary to perform the database synchronization. This is done by providing an implementation for several callback methods in the class definition. These are methods that are called by the container when the entity bean must update the database or when the entity bean must read from the database.

For more complex database relationships, this type of entity bean may be the only solution. Given a database mapping that requires a bean to represent some complex relational structure such as a parts assembly, or to access database-stored procedures, the use of bean-managed persistence may be the only choice.

Message-Driven Beans

The message-driven bean provides an EJB component model for a messaging service. These beans are the message-oriented middleware (MOM) equivalent of a message queue or topic. A callback method provided in the implementation is executed on receipt of the message. The developer only needs to provide the implementation to process the message. The container automatically provides multiple threads for execution for each message received, so there is no need to provide a multithreaded processing loop (which is a common technique in message processing).

EJB Deployment

Since EJBs operate within a container, the container environment must be made aware of their existence. This is accomplished through a deployment process. Deployment not only makes the container aware of the classes used to implement the remote components, but also provides instruction on how the components will be made available, what resources the components will use, and what properties the components will exhibit.

Deployment of EJBs involves creating a JAR file, which includes a configuration file known as the *deployment descriptor*. This XML file contains entries that describe the deployment process for the set of components contained in the JAR file. Deployment of the EJB components cannot take place without appropriate entries in the deployment descriptor file.

The EJB specification was intended to provide flexibility, portability, interoperability, and plug-and-play type functionality for distributed components. In order to meet that goal, a number of the properties for the distributed components are not managed programmatically; instead, they are configured during the deployment process. This is referred to as *declarative programming* and provides a new dimension to the development process that can ultimately provide additional opportunities. Declarative programming is discussed in the "EJB Security Architecture" section later in this chapter.

The developer can manage various bean properties—such as transaction behavior, security, and references to the bean's resources—through entries in the deployment descriptor. This allows developers to develop components in a generic fashion and reduces the amount of specific coding for security or transaction behavior, making the process of integration into one or more distributed applications an easier task. The transaction security behavior of the component is defined when the component is integrated into the application, at deployment time, as illustrated in Figure 3-5.

Development Roles with J2EE

The development of J2EE applications involves a markedly different development paradigm than that of client-server and legacy application development. There are several

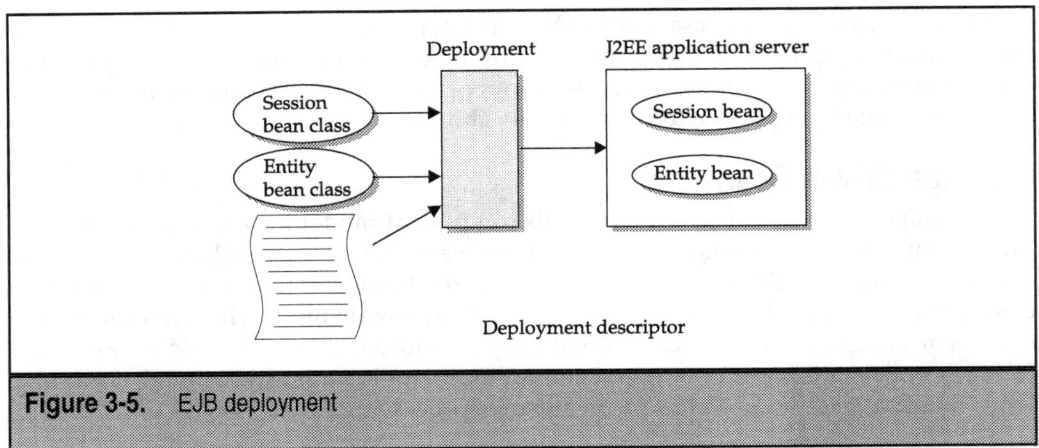

Figure 3-5. EJB deployment

distinct roles involved in the creation of a distributed component application with J2EE: provider or developer, assembler, deployer, and administrator.

Provider

The bean provider may be the developer (an individual or group), a third-party vendor, or an outside group (perhaps an open-source development group) who created the component. This distinction is made with J2EE because bean components are intended to be pluggable (to be able to be integrated into an existing application without requiring changes to the components being inserted).

Assembler

The assembler is the individual who gathers the components to be used in the application. For a moderately complex application, this could involve a large number of components. The assembler decides how to package the components, taking into account the interaction of the components. The assembler may also play a role in architecting or developing the client application, which may in part drive the process of assembling the components for deployment.

The EJB specification dictates that each deployable JAR contain a deployment descriptor. It is reasonable to expect then that the assembler, working with the provider and the deployer, will participate in writing the deployment descriptor.

Deployer

The deployer will perform the process of deploying the assembled and grouped components onto the system. This process involves resolving any problems that may occur and working with the provider and assembler to ensure that the deployment descriptor has been written correctly, that resources are mapped correctly, and that declarative security roles and transactions have been established correctly. With the more robust application servers supporting clustered environments, the deployer may need to decide where specific components will run on the server cluster.

The deployer, working with the provider and the assembler, will complete the transaction and security entries in the deployment descriptor. This is a very critical step that must be managed carefully. Entries could be made in the deployment descriptor that run counter to the design of a bean component and could lead to indeterminate results at runtime. For instance, a stateful session bean could be deployed with a deployment descriptor setting of "stateless." Since there is no difference between the class declaration of the stateful and stateless session bean (they both implement the `SessionBean` interface), the deployment would proceed without error, but runtime results could be disastrous.

Incorrect security and transaction entries could also run counter to the development of the component. These mistakes would not be caught by the deployment and may not immediately reveal themselves at runtime. Carefully documenting components and their behaviors could help avoid this problem.

Administrator

The administrator is responsible for the operational health of the system. In large, complex, clustered environments this could involve reviewing and maintaining various logs, and monitoring load-balancing techniques to determine whether the current deployment of components is performing efficiently.

The administrator should also monitor logs to determine that current security protocols are being met.

Project Roles

While this discussion has centered on separate development roles, this does not imply that separate individuals will always be involved in these tasks. In practice, on small to medium-size projects, the same individual will play many of these roles (most commonly, the overworked developer of the component). Fortunately, most robust application servers provide deployment tools that simplify this process by assembling the components and making the XML entries in the deployment descriptor.

The ability to easily manipulate declarative security in the EJB deployment descriptor is a powerful feature that opens potential security holes if not implemented correctly. Unlike programmatic security, where the programmer has defined the security in the application code, with declarative security, it is the assembler and deployer who will ultimately define the implementation of the security policy for the application.

Deployment descriptor entries for security and transactions must carefully consider the expectations of the developer or provider of the component before making pertinent entries for the bean in the deployment descriptor. It is important that the staff performing these operations be aware of the proper security role assignments and be employees who are qualified to perform what could be sensitive security tasks.

Each of the development roles mentioned previously plays a part in the overall security of the application. The bean provider enforces programmatic authorization, and the bean assembler provides the declarative authorization and the type of authentication.

The deployer then maps component roles to principals. The assignment of security across these various roles and the individual performing these tasks must be carefully considered.

The important point to remember here is that J2EE application security is not controlled with a single configuration file entry by a single person. Security is designed to be flexible, which tends to add some complexity to the operation. Coordination of the various entries in the deployment descriptor is an important part of maintaining an appropriate level of system security. EJB security is discussed in more detail in the "EJB Security Architecture" section later in this chapter.

EJB Development

In order to create an EJB, you must write the bean component and determine the methods that the component will expose. You must then write a set of interfaces that define how to interact with the component remotely. In all, you need to create three files for each component: the home interface, the remote interface, and the bean (the component) implementation.

The Home Interface

The *home interface* identifies the methods that can be used to create an instance of the bean. The `create` method returns a remote reference to the bean component, not the actual bean component. Since entity beans represent a persistent component, they are not created each time they are used (since they have persisted); instead, they are found using a finder method.

The `create` method does not imply instantiation of the component, since the EJB container is able to make intelligent decisions about pooling components. In fact, the container may be retrieving the component from a pool instead of creating a new instance of the component.

The developer writes the home interface to extend the `EJBHome` interface. This interface should declare one or more signatures for potentially overloaded versions of the `create` method. These `create` methods will return a reference to the remote interface for the bean component.

The following example is a home interface declaration for a simple session bean. The interface extends the `EJBHome` interface and declares a single `create` method signature, which is the `EJBHelloRemote` interface in this example. The method throws a `RemoteException` and a `CreateException` as required.

```
package examples.ejbs;
import javax.ejb.*;

import java.rmi.*;

public interface EJBHelloHome extends EJBHome {
```

```
    public EJBHelloRemote create() throws RemoteException, CreateException;

}
```

The Remote Interface

The *remote interface* defines the methods that the EJB will expose to its clients. The EJB class may contain a number of methods, but not all methods need to be accessible to clients. It is a good policy, and one that meets our goal of limiting the information available to the potential hacker, to limit the number of methods the bean exposes to a concise set of methods that performs the tasks required by the client.

In the listing below, two method signatures are declared. The methods return a string result and both throw a `RemoteException`. These method signatures relate to implementations of the methods in the bean component. Any parameters passed to the method or values returned from the method must be `Serializable`. (The `java.lang.String` parameter and return value shown here are, of course, `Serializable`.)

```
package examples.ejbs;

import javax.ejb.*;

import java.rmi.*;

public interface EJBHelloRemote extends EJBObject {

  public String helloYou( String name ) throws RemoteException;
  public String helloSomeoneElse( ) throws RemoteException;

}
```

The Bean Implementation

The bean implementation provides the actual implementation of the distributed component. This is the code that will run in the EJB container and will perform the services requested by the client. The code for the implementation must implement the appropriate interface from the `javax.ejb` package, currently one of `SessionBean`, `EntityBean`, or `MessageDrivenBean`. These interfaces define a set of methods, referred to as callback methods, that are invoked by the container during various life cycle events for the bean.

Actually, the client will never communicate directly with this component; instead, it will interact with it by proxy using the remote interface. The method signatures identified in the remote interface must match the method declarations in this file. Any problems with methods and signatures that do not match will usually be identified in the deployment process (not the Java compilation process, since there is no Java language relationship between the remote interface and the bean implementation of the methods in the interface).

The code example below demonstrates the minimal code needed to create a session bean implementation. The class is declared to provide an implementation of the `SessionBean` interface. The `SessionBean` interface requires the implementation of several methods, including the `ejbCreate` method, which relates directly to the `create` method defined in the home interface.

```
package examples.ejbs;

import javax.ejb.*;
import java.io.Serializable;
import java.rmi.*;
import javax.naming.*;

public class EJBHelloBean implements SessionBean {

InitialContext init;
SessionContext context;

public String helloYou( String name ) {

     //
     // Simply return the name that was passed in.
     //
     return "Hello " + name;
}

//
// Generate a hello message using an environment entry.
//
public String helloSomeoneElse( ) {
String name  = null;
try {
     //
     // Look up the name and return it. We defined the entry as a
     // String.
     //
     name = (String) init.lookup( "java:comp/env/anotherName" );
}
catch (NamingException e) {
      System.err.println("NamingException : " + e );
}
finally {
     return "Hello " + name;
}
```

```
}
// --

public void ejbCreate() {
try  {

   //
   // Store the initial naming service context. We will use it
   // later.
   //
   init = new InitialContext();
}
catch (NamingException e) {
    System.err.println( "NamingException : " + e );
}

}
// --

public void setSessionContext( SessionContext sc ) {

   //
   // Store the session context.
   //
   context = sc;
}

//
// Don't need to implement these right now.
//
public void ebjPostCreate() {};
public void ejbRemove() {};
public void ejbActivate() {};
public void ejbPassivate() {};

}
```

The class defined in this example implements the `SessionBean` interface as expected. Two methods that were referenced in the remote interface are defined: `helloYou` and `helloSomeoneElse`. The `helloYou` method demonstrates parameter passing with EJBs. It simply takes a single string parameter and appends the string with a value, and then returns the result. The `helloSomeoneElse` method demonstrates the retrieval of environment entries with EJBs. This method takes no parameters and instead performs a lookup for a specific entry in the naming service provided by the container.

The value for the `anotherName` entry is retrieved and cast as a `java.lang.String` (as it was defined in the naming service entry). This value is then appended with another value and returned by the method.

The only other methods declared in this file are the `ejbCreate` method and the `setSessionContext` method. The `ejbCreate` method is called by the container when the bean component is created. In this example, the method is used to create the initial context for the naming service (which is used by the `helloSomeoneElse` method). The `setSessionContext` method is used to preserve the session context in an instance member for the bean. This `SessionContext` reference will allow us to access security information about the user of the bean.

The Client Application

The `EJBClient` application shown in the listing below demonstrates the process of a remote client (known as a *rich client*) connecting to an EJB server and obtaining a remote reference. In order to be able to do this, the client application must have access to a number of specific classes relating to the EJB it would like to access, including (but not limited to) the home and remote interface and the stub class generated for the remote object. In this example, the program calls the two methods exposed by the `EJBHello` bean and displays the results of those calls to the console.

```
package examples.ejbs;

import java.rmi.*;
import javax.naming.*;
import javax.rmi.*;
import javax.ejb.*;

import java.util.*;

public class EJBClient {

public static void main( String args[] ) {

//
// Our remote reference
//
EJBHelloRemote ejbHello = null;

try {

     //
     // Specify our initial naming context.
     // (This would probably be stored in jndi.properties in the environment.)
     //
```

```
        Hashtable env = new Hashtable();
        env.put( "java.naming.factory.initial", "org.jnp.interfaces.NamingContextFactory");
        env.put( "java.naming.provider.url", "jnp://localhost:1099");
        env.put( "java.naming.factory.url.pkgs", "org.jboss.naming:org.jnp.interfaces");

        //
        // Obtain the initial naming service context.
        //
        Context init = new InitialContext( env );

System.out.println("Initial context found ... ");

       //
       // Look up our home interface.
       //
       EJBHelloHome home = (EJBHelloHome) PortableRemoteObject.narrow( init.lookup("EJBHello"),
EJBHelloHome.class );

System.out.println("EJBHelloHome found ... ");

        //
        // Create (obtain) a reference to our remote interface.
        //
        ejbHello = home.create();

System.out.println("EJBHello created  ... ");

        //
        // Make some method calls using our remote reference.
        //
        System.out.println("A hello message: " +
                      ejbHello.helloYou( "Art" ));
        System.out.println("Another hello message: " +
                      ejbHello.helloSomeoneElse( ));
}
 catch (RemoteException e) {

     System.out.println("RemoteException: " + e.getMessage() );
     e.printStackTrace();
}
catch(CreateException e ) {

   System.out.println("CreateException: " + e.getMessage() );
   e.printStackTrace();
```

```
}
catch (NamingException e) {

   System.out.println("NamingException: " + e.getMessage() );
   e.printStackTrace();

}

} // End main

}
```

The programmatic process of accessing the remote resource is not difficult. The naming service for the application server must be obtained. In this example, we place the parameters to access the naming service in a `Hashtable` and pass them to the constructor for the `InitialContext`. These parameters could have easily been placed in a `jndi.properties` file, but are shown here to highlight the fact that the specific naming service for the application server should be used to access the EJB references.

Once we have obtained the `InitialContext`, we use it to retrieve the bean named `EJBHello` in the naming service (and described in the previous sections). The process for accessing an EJB is to first retrieve a reference to the home interface for a bean, and to then use the `create` method in the home interface (which may have optionally been overridden to include parameters) to obtain a reference to the remote interface. We then use the remote interface to make the calls on the methods that have been made available to clients in the remote interface.

The Deployment Descriptor

The deployment descriptor for the code in the previous sections is shown below.

```
<?xml version="1.0" encoding="ISO8859_1"?>
<!DOCTYPE application PUBLIC '-//Sun Microsystems, Inc.//DTD J2EE Application 1.2//
EN' 'http://java.sun.com/j2ee/dtds/application_1_2.dtd'>

<application>
  <display-name>J2EE_Security</display-name>
  <description>Demonstration EJBs for J2EE Security Book</description>
  <enterprise-beans>
    <session>
      <ejb-name>EJBHello</ejb-name>
      <ejb-class>examples.ejbs.EJBHelloBean</ejb-class>
      <home>examples.ejbs.EJBHelloHome</home>
      <remote>examples.ejbs.EJBHelloRemote</remote>
      <session-type>Stateful</session-type>
      <transaction-type>Bean</transaction-type>

      <env-entry>
            <env-entry-name>anotherName</env-entry-name>
```

```
        <env-entry-value>Fred</env-entry-value>
     <env-entry-type>java.lang.String</env-entry-type>
    </env-entry>
   </session>
  </enterprise-beans>
</application>
```

In the deployment descriptor, we declare a session bean named `EJBHello` using the `ejb-name` tag. The class for this session bean is identified with the fully qualified class name as `examples.ejbs.EJBHelloBean` (the bean component implementation). The `home` and `remote` tags are used to identify the classes for the home and remote interfaces for the bean. The `session-type` tag is used to identify the type of session bean being declared, which is a stateful session bean in this case (since we have declared instance members in the implementation class and we use them without checking their state). The `transaction-type` entry indicates that we allow the bean to control its own transactions (not an issue in this example).

The `env-entry` tag is used to identify a set of environment variable entries that can be declared in the deployment descriptor. These entries are visible to the bean components (as shown in the previous example) and are read-only (their value cannot be changed by the component).

The name of the environment entry is identified with the `env-entry-name` tag, and the value is identified with the `env-entry-value` tag. The `env-entry-type` tag identifies the type of object that will store the environment entry. (Java language primitives cannot be declared as environment entries; a Java language data type wrapper class must be used.)

This example provided a minimal description of an EJB. More complex examples are provided in Chapter 12.

OTHER J2EE APIS

Technically speaking, J2EE is a superset of the J2SE, so that all of the various APIs in the SDK are part of J2EE. However, a number of APIs are particularly important when working with enterprise applications. Table 3-2 lists the APIs that are currently an official part

API	Description
JDBC	Java Database Connectivity. This is the most commonly used API, which provides for connecting to and manipulating data in relational databases. As the container-managed persistence mechanism of EJBs becomes more reliable, this API is used less and less.

Table 3-2. J2EE APIs

API	Description
JavaMail	Provides access to standard mail protocols such as POP3 and IMAP.
RMI	Remote Method Invocation. This provides access to remote Java objects. J2EE components such as EJBs use RMI transparently, since RMI is the enabling technology for EJBs. But J2EE components may also use RMI to provide access to RMI remote objects. This usage is most common to provide integration with some existing RMI-based system.
JAXM	Java for XML Messaging. This API is used to create peer-to-peer or asynchronous XML messaging applications using protocols such as SOAP. Currently, JAXM is used to provide web services using J2EE. The next release of J2EE (version 1.4) should integrate this capability into EJBs, which to a large extent should preclude the use of this API.
JMS	Java Messaging Service. This API provides access to message queues and is used to create applications that use asynchronous messaging. With the latest release of J2EE, message-driven beans provide messaging server implementation for EJBs, but JMS is still needed to provide client access.
JAXP	XML Parsing. This API is used for parsing/transforming or creating XML documents. JAXP allows Java applications to manipulate XML documents. XML has become the *de facto* standard for moving data between applications, an important part of the system integration required of enterprise applications.
JAAS	Java Authentication and Authorization. This API is used to provide login (authentication) and permission validation (authorization) for Java applications. This is not heavily used on the business tier, since EJBs provide a built-in security mechanism.
JCE	Java Cryptography Extension. This API is used for developing private key and public key encryption programs in Java. (This is J2SE.)
JSSE	Java Secure Sockets Extension. This API is used for creating secure socket connections with Java applications. This is not heavily used, since an alternative is to simply create a servlet that uses a HTTPS connection created by the web server container.
JAX-RPC	Java for XML over RPC. This API provides the capability to move XML documents over RPC connections. This offers an XML messaging alternative to using the SOAP protocol.
JTA	Java Transaction API. This API provides access to transaction managers, which are applications that interact with multiple database servers to allow transactions to span multiple databases from different vendors. Transaction managers are usually integrated into the J2EE server.

Table 3-2. J2EE APIs *(continued)*

API	Description
JNDI	Java Naming and Directory Interface. This API is used to access virtually all resources in J2EE. EJBs are retrieved using JNDI, as are JDBC DataSource objects and messaging queues and topics. JNDI access is usually limited to performing lookups to find the resource in the naming service and return the object reference.
Java-IDL	Used to allow Java objects to act as distributed CORBA components. (This is part of J2SE, but extended in J2EE.)

Table 3-2. J2EE APIs *(continued)*

of J2EE and others (primarily web-service-related APIs) that are expected to be added to J2EE soon.

The security APIs—JSSE, JCE, and JAAS (described in the previous chapter)—are used as needed in J2EE. Since EJBs provide a number of security features implemented as required by the EJB specification, the use of these APIs is generally relegated to the web tier.

EJB SECURITY ARCHITECTURE

The security architecture for EJBs is focused on application security, not system or resource security. The basic security architecture of the language still exists, but it is augmented and largely controlled by the application server. (Developers and application server administrators should nevertheless be aware of the security policy settings of their server and set them accordingly.)

Principals and Roles

EJB security architecture uses the concept of a principal, and once again, a principal is considered a realized identity. This realization of the identity assumes the principal has been authenticated.

How the principal is authenticated is not defined by the EJB specification. Any mapping from a user to principal is not provided by the EJB specification.

This is not surprising, since the EJB component is not expected to interact directly with the end user. Instead, the web tier should interact with the user and perform the user validation. This information should then be made available to the EJB component as part of the bean's context.

A security *role* represents a grouping of principals and is associated with permissions, or authorization within the application. Permissions are associated with roles, and roles are associated with principals. Thus, a principal is assigned a role, and a role is granted permission to execute specific methods.

Note that, unlike the grouping of principals into subjects with JAAS, the use of security roles with EJBs can be (and often is) representative of a group of people. Since you are working with business-tier components that are implementing business logic, your concern is not so much exactly who has made the request but whether or not they are in the group of people who are allowed to make the request. Therefore, this security is focused on roles or groups of users.

Declarative Security and Programmatic Security

EJBs have two options for managing security: declarative security and programmatic security.

With *declarative security*, declarations made in the deployment descriptor dictate the security of the components. Security boundaries are based on the beans and the methods provided by the beans. Security is based on what can and cannot be done—essentially, which roles are allowed to use which beans and which methods they are allowed to execute within the beans. Within the deployment descriptor, you can assign a role to one, several, or all methods within a component.

With *programmatic security*, Java code within the component controls the execution of application security. The EJB API provides several methods that indicate the role of the caller and the principal of the caller.

The authorization check can be performed programmatically using specific methods defined in the `EJBContext` interface:

- `getCallerPrincipal` returns the principal of the caller as identified by the `java.security.Principal` object reference returned. Since the security architecture of EJBs is intended to use the security role for authorization, the principal of the caller alone is not enough to perform authorization. The role or roles to which the principal has been assigned are needed to authorize the user to perform some operation.
- `isCallerInRole` returns a Boolean true if the caller is assigned to the role passed as a parameter. The role is a string with the name of the role, as defined in the deployment descriptor for the component.

Using these methods, though not the preferred approach for managing security, does provide a more fine-grained control over the execution of an application security policy. This programmatic approach, as compared to the declarative approach to security control, is more prone to the occasional programmer error. As components become more complex and business logic becomes more complicated, the chance of programmer error becomes more likely.

Both security approaches work with principals and roles. As noted earlier, the API does detail how the security will be implemented using the principals and the roles they are assigned, but it does not dictate how authentication will be performed. Essentially, the EJB developer (or assembler or deployer) works with authorization and must rely on others to perform authentication correctly. The implication of this is that there must be careful coordination between the authentication (most likely done on the web tier or client tier) and the authorization to be performed on the business tier. The "Security on the Business Tier" section provides examples of using declarative security, the preferred method.

System-Level Security

According to the EJB specification, it is up to each application server vendor to implement system-level security as the vendor sees fit. For many of the application servers based on Java technology, the system-level security is Java security (with some possible customization of the various security classes such as `SecurityManager`).

Application servers such as JBoss and WebLogic use Java security policy files. These files do not necessarily have restrictive security in place. For example, some JBoss implementations set all code to `AllPermissions` in the security policy file, allowing all JBoss code unfettered access to system resources.

An insider could manage to manipulate these security files to allow remotely loaded code to perform sensitive operations on local resources or to allow connections on numerous ports. These could be the start of a security exploitation that could allow the application and the application data to be manipulated remotely.

It is important to check the default permissions on these servers to determine whether or not the correct level of security is being maintained. Staff must be monitored to see that only qualified and trusted personnel are allowed to manipulate the application server security file. File access permissions on the file or files should also be set to restrictive settings that allow only the application server administrator to alter the files.

SECURITY ON THE PRESENTATION TIER

Web components are the most likely candidates to perform authentication. With web applications, these components perform the bulk of user interaction. Once again, the servlet specification does not specify how the authentication and principal assignment will be performed; it just indicates that the container (and associated web server) must support it.

The current servlet specification also indicates that certain types of authentication must be supported. There are methods within the servlet API that allow the type of authentication to be discerned. The common types of authentication are listed in Table 3-3 and are identified in the servlet 2.2 specification. Only digest authentication is optional for servlet containers.

Basic authentication and form-based authentication are common login facilities on the web, but alone they cannot provide a secure environment. Both are used fairly frequently in combination with SSL security with HTTPS. The HTTPS protocol provides strong security and is widely supported in web browsers and web servers, and is now commonly used to provide secure logins.

Authentication Type	Description
Basic authentication	Performs authentication by sending an `'authenticate'` response to the client browser. Not particularly secure, since the password is returned unencrypted using base 64 encoding.
Digest authentication	Similar to basic authentication, except that the password is scrambled and is used to return the user password. Since this is not widely supported by web browsers, servlet containers are not required to support this.
HTTPS client authentication	Uses HTTP with SSL encryption to secure the communication channel before requesting the username and password.
Form-based authentication	Uses HTML forms to request the password from the user. The password is sent in plain text unless the network channel is secured using a virtual private network (VPN) or HTTPS before the login form is transmitted.

Table 3-3. Common Types of Servlet Authentication

The servlet 2.2 specification also provides several methods that allow the current security state to be examined. These methods, part of the `HttpServletRequest` class, are as follows:

- `getRemoteUser` returns the login name of the user, if the user has been authenticated. It will return a null if the user has not been authenticated.
- `isUserInRole` returns true if the user is in the role passed as a parameter. The role is a string that resolves to the role name.
- `getUserPrincipal` returns the `java.security.Principal` object associated with the current session.

A web application may optionally use role-based security to control access to resources. The servlet specification provides for a set of entries in the web application configuration file (`web.xml`) that detail the security policy for accessing the web components. The following code listing shows how security roles and corresponding security role links are defined in the `web.xml` file.

```
<security-role>
   <role-name>admin-user</role-name>
</security-role>

<security-role-ref>
   <role-name>admin-user</role-name>
   <role-link>manager-login</role-link>
</security-role-ref>

<servlet>
 ....
<security-constraint>
   <web-resource-collection>
      <web-resource-name>SalesMgmt</web-resource-name>
       <url-pattern>/sales/manage/*<url-pattern>
       <http-method>GET</http-method>
       <http-method>POST</http-method>
            <auth-constraint>
                    <role-name>admin-user</role-name>
            </auth-constraint>
   </web-resource-collection>
</security-constraint>
...
</servlet>
```

Within the body of the `security-role` element, we use a `role-name` element to identify the name of the security role. This is the name that will be used in the `web.xml` file to associate roles with specific security components.

We use the `security-role-ref` element to associate the `role-name` defined with a different set of roles. This allows programmatic roles used by other servlet providers, for instance from a software vendor, to be mapped to a different role. A servlet may have code that checks for an `admin` role (`isUserInRole("admin")`). The `security-role-ref` element effectively allows the `admin` role to be mapped to an application-specific role, a role that has been designated for the application being assembled, of `accounting-admin`. This facility allows the final implementation of security to be defined at a later (and more sensible) point in time, when the application is being assembled and deployed.

Then we use the `security-constraint` element to map roles to web resources. Within the `auth-constraint` element, we identify the `role-name`. This `role-name` will be required by the servlet container in order to access the resource specified in the `url-pattern` element. The example demonstrates the use of this element.

Once again, the manipulation of the role references by a hacker intent on infiltrating a system could have a subtle, yet devastating, effect. A hacker could take a simple user role, such as `general-user`, and could map it to a very secure role such as `admin`. Once the system is deployed, the hacker could use a `general-user` login to execute the `admin` user functions.

The countermeasure to this type of attack is to control the access to these files and ensure that only qualified, trusted users are allowed to manipulate their contents. At most sites, only a senior administrator or developer should be manipulating the deployment descriptors for an assembled application.

SECURITY ON THE BUSINESS TIER

As mentioned in the previous sections, EJB components do not concern themselves with authentication, which is presumed to have been managed by other tiers. Security is relative to the component and is related to the methods within a component. For authorization, permissions are checked to determine whether or not a principal assigned to a role has permission to execute a particular method. This means that components must be aware of the current role assigned to the caller. The authorization check can be performed by the container (declarative security), or it can be performed programmatically.

The declarative approach, based on the bean component, provides a more natural and intuitive way to manage the application security policy. Applications grow and change, and the programmer doesn't know how the components will be used in the future. Using declarative programming provides a flexible facility for managing unforeseen change. The following sections provide examples of using declarative security.

Defining Security Roles

As part of the application assembly process, the developer defines a set of security roles through a series of entries in the deployment descriptor. (Most J2EE application server providers will provide tools to help perform this process.) These entries are associated with the components collected in the JAR file that contains the deployment descriptor and do not apply to other components deployed within the application server instance. This means that their scope is limited to their constituent JAR file.

The following example demonstrates the creation of a security role for a general user and an administrative user of a J2EE application. The administrative user will be allowed to perform administrative functions plus general user functions. The example creates two security roles within the `security-role` element: the `general-user` role and the `admin-user` role.

In the `assembly-descriptor` element of a deployment descriptor file, we can enter a series of `security-role` elements. The `security-role` element identifies a security role that will be used in the deployment descriptor. Within the `security-role` element, a `role-name` subelement assigns a name to the role to be used in the deployment descriptor. Optionally, we can use a `description` element to provide a text description for the assignments to be made in the file.

```
...

<assembly-descriptor>
```

```
    <security-role>
          <description>
               Define the general user.
        </description>
        <role-name>general-user</role-name>
     </security-role>

      <security-role>
          <description>
               Define the administrative user.
         </description>
     <role-name>admin-user</role-name>
 </security-role>

 </assembly-descriptor>
```

Mapping Roles

Now that we've defined security roles, we need to map them to one or more methods to establish the application security policy. We accomplish this by using the `method-permission` block within the deployment descriptor. The `method-permission` element identifies a block of method permissions and associates a method signature with one or more roles. This block would contain one or more `role-name` elements and one or more `method` elements. The association indicates that the roles listed are allowed to execute the named method. Any method not assigned to a security role is considered not callable (through the EJB call mechanism in the container, either locally or remotely). Optionally, you can use the `description` element to explain the `method-role` assignments. The following listing shows the use of this element in a deployment descriptor.

```
...
<method-permission>
    <role-name>general-user</role-name>
    <method>
           <ejb-name>SystemLogin</ejb-name>
           <method-name>*</method-name>
     </method>
</method-permission>

<method-permission>
    <role-name>general-user</role-name>
    <method>
           <ejb-name>GeneralServices</ejb-name>
           <method-name>*</method-name>
     </method>
```

```
</method-permission>

<method-permission>
    <role-name>general-user</role-name>
    <method>
           <ejb-name>LoginMaintenance</ejb-name>
           <method-name>modifyPersonalInfo</method-name>
     </method>
</method-permission>

<method-permission>
    <role-name>admin-user</role-name>
    <method>
           <ejb-name>LoginMaintenance</ejb-name>
           <method-name>*</method-name>
     </method>
</method-permission>
....
```

Within the method element, the ejb-name, method-name, and method-params subelements denote one or more methods of a bean's home and remote interfaces. Certain wildcard characters are supported for the method-name element. An asterisk (*) indicates all the methods in the home and remote interface for an EJB are allowed.

Using the method-name element with a specific name refers to all overloaded implementations of the method, regardless of the signature. Using the method-name element with the method-parms element, you may define a set of parameters to identify a single overloaded version of a method. You can use the optional method-intf element to distinguish between interfaces (the home and remote interfaces) for methods with the same signature that may appear in both interfaces.

Within the body of the method-permission element, specific methods to be secured are identified. For the SystemLogin EJB, the general-user role is granted permission to access all methods. The same broad set of permissions is granted to the general-user for the GeneralServices EJB. But for the LoginMaintenance module, only the modifyPersonalInfo method is available to the general-user. Alternatively, for the same LoginModule, the admin-user is granted permission to execute all methods.

Assigning Principals to Roles

The role-link element allows role names used with programmatic security (hardcoded into the text) to be mapped to security roles. The role-link is a required element that provides a link between one role and another role. Since we want the admin-login to be able to perform the actions of a general-user, we will provide a mapping of the admin-login to the general user.

In the following listing, a `standard-login` link is mapped to the `general-user` role used in the previous listing. The `admin-login` link is then mapped to both the `general-user` role plus the `admin-user`. This will allow the `admin-user` to execute the methods that have been made accessible to the `general-user` role plus the `admin-user` role.

```
<session-bean>
      ...
       <security-role-ref>
                <description> A security role reference </description>
                <role-name>general-user</role-name>
                <role-link>standard-login</role-link>
        </security-role-ref>

       <security-role-ref>
                <description>
                  Admins are given general user permissions.
                 </description>
                <role-name>general-user</role-name>
                <role-link>admin-login</role-link>
        </security-role-ref>
      <security-role-ref>
                <description> Admin login is also provided with
                     admin-user permissions
                </description>
                <role-name>admin-user</role-name>
                <role-link>admin-login</role-link>
        </security-role-ref>
```

Security for Resources

The resources for a bean are declared in the deployment descriptor and describe the name and security for a resource. The resource is made available through environment entries of the naming service using the `java:comp/env/` namespace, though the name of the resource is not explicitly bound there in the deployment descriptor (EJB specification compliance requires the container to place it there implicitly).

The resource is declared in the deployment descriptor using the `resource-ref` element. Within the body of the `resource-ref` element, the `res-auth` indicates whether the container will perform the sign-on to the resource using the principal mapping information or the EJB component will perform the login programmatically. A sample `resource-ref` entry is shown below.

```
<session>
....
<description>The JDBC driver of choice</description>
```

```
    <res-ref-name>SalesDB</res-ref-name>
    <res-type>javax.sql.DataSource</res-type>
    <res-auth>Container</res-auth>
    <res-sharing-scope>Shareable</res-sharing-scope>
</resource-ref>
</session>
```

In this example, we identify the `SalesDB` resource as a JDBC `DataSource` and make it available in the `java:comp/env/jdbc/SalesDB` namespace of the J2EE naming service. The `res-auth` entry identifies the EJB container as controlling access to the resource. Exactly how the container will authenticate the access to the resource is not defined in the EJB specification and is left to the container provider to implement.

Passing Authentication Information from the Web Tier

If authentication is being performed on the web tier and the web-tier components will be using business-tier components (EJBs) to provide business services, you must be able to pass authentication information to the business tier. The specifics of this process are left to the application server provider and are not defined in the EJB specification.

For example, the WebLogic server passes authentication information from the web tier into the business tier (passing the information to the WebLogic application server) using the `InitialContext`, as shown in the code fragment below.

```
...
env = new Hashtable();
env.put( Context.INITIAL_CONTEXT_FACTORY,
              "weblogic.jndi.WLInitialContextFactory" );
env.put(WLContext.PROVIDER_URL, "t3://aserver.com:7001" );
env.put( WLContext.SECURITY_AUTHENTICATION, "simple" );
env.put( WLContext.SECURITY_PRINCIPALS, "fred" );
env.put( WLContext.SECURITY_CREDENTIALS, "secretePassword23323" );
IntialContext context = new InitialContext( env );
...
```

This code passes the authentication information to the WebLogic application server. The WebLogic application server will compare the principal against its configured access control list (ACL) to determine which roles the principal has been assigned. It will then use this information to manage its declarative role-based security.

Setting the Caller Identity

The `security-identity` is an optional deployment descriptor element that allows the identity of a bean to assume that of its caller, or to assume another identity. This is a convenience mechanism, also known as *impersonation*, which is similar to the `Subject doAs` method. It is useful for components such as message-driven beans, which have no specific caller and thus no identity unless one is provided.

To implement this identity mapping, the `security-identity` tag can take two values: `use-caller-identity` or the `run-as-specified-identity` element. Within the `run-as-specified-identity` element, a `role-name` is defined. This `role-name` is then linked at some other point to a principal or group of principals. The following listing provides an example of using this element.

```
<session>
<ejb-name>LoginServices</ejb-name>
<security-identity>
   <run-as-specified-identity>
          <role-name>admin-user</role-name>
   </run-as-specified-identity>
</security-identity>
</session>
....
```

SUMMARY

Assuming that not all readers are familiar with J2EE technologies, we used this chapter to provide an overview of the J2EE architecture. Since our focus in this book is security features, we drilled down and provided additional detail on those features of J2EE components.

You saw that J2EE technology is essentially Java for distributed applications. Java components can be developed for client applications (Swing and applets), web servers (JSPs and servlets), and application servers (EJBs). These are identified as multiple application tiers: the client tier, the presentation tier and the business tier, the integration tier and the resource tier. Java security for the client tier involves using much of the technology discussed in Chapters 1 and 2. Java security for the web tier involves using servlet programmatic security or the declarative security that provides for security roles. Business tier security—security with EJBs—can be handled through either programmatic or declarative security.

PART II

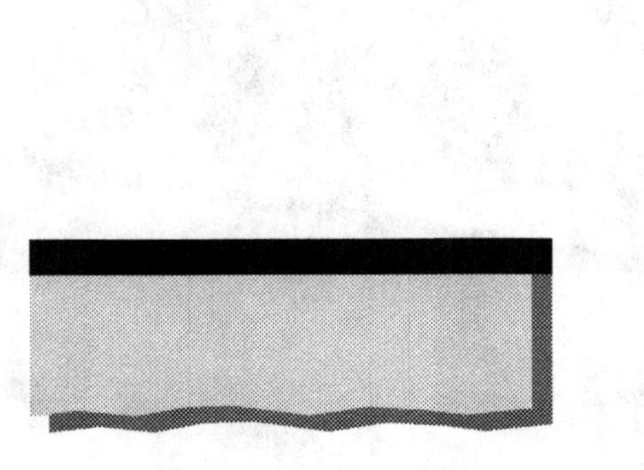

CHAPTER 4

USING ENCRYPTION AND AUTHENTICATION TO PROTECT AN APPLICATION

Now that we have covered the basics of Java security, it's time to focus on the types of attacks directed at Java applications and how to prevent or detect them. As explained earlier in the book, as our example, we use a simple and naively implemented Java application developed by Lester, a fictitious administrator at a fictitious company.

Looking at Lester's application, you may think that no one could write a sample application quite as insecure as the one presented here. But all of the weaknesses we outline have been spotted in actual code, and, in many cases, in actual production code running in enterprise computing environments around the world. Lester's application is a consolidation of these common, yet insecure Java coding techniques.

As we progress through the rest of the book, we will incrementally improve Lester's application across a variety of architectures, before finally arriving at a relatively secure application that should be resistant to all but the most determined attacker. In this chapter, we begin by adding encryption and authentication to the application.

APPLICATION SECURITY: THE PROCESS

Application security is not just technology; it's a process. Likewise, planning to defeat an application's security is also a process. In many cases, it's a process without "toolkits" and other resources that are available to the operating-system–level attacker.

System-level versus Application-level Security

In some areas, application security is remarkably different from system-level security, but in many areas, the two types of security are similar. With a mostly platform-independent environment such as Java, defeating system-level security may not provide attackers with appropriate access to the application-level data, logic, or methods that they seek. In fact, after discovering a compromise, the Java application developer can move the application not just to another system, but to an entirely different platform. This technique is not used commonly, but the fact that application developers have this option should illustrate the difference between system and application security.

Additionally, since Java applications run on multiple platforms, many times it is more efficient to push some security responsibilities up to the application level instead of handling them at the operating-system level on two or three separate physical operating systems. The following diagram illustrates the differences in focus between typical system-level and application-level security.

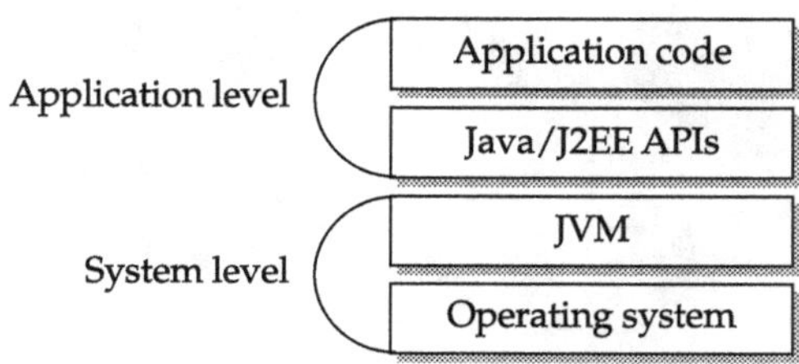

Most commonly, system and application security specialists work together to build a secure system/application combination. An individual who hopes to have any success attacking a secure application needs to have an understanding of both of these domains.

In many cases, good application security can compensate for poor system security and vice versa. As an example, an application may encrypt its data files so that, even if the underlying operating system is breached, attackers would be unable to recover the valuable, business-sensitive data that they desire. Conversely, many applications in production environments make no effort to hide sensitive data, choosing to rely instead on the diligence and skill of operating-system security experts to protect that data from prying eyes.

The most effective approach is one that combines operating system and application security and coordinates efforts so that "the right tool for the job" is used wherever and whenever possible. The attacker must be able to look across both of these domains to find the weakest link in an application's security. The following chapters will detail common weak links in the application layer.

TIP To discover common weaknesses at the operating-system level, consult a reference that focuses for system-level security attacks, such as *Hacking Exposed: Network Security* (McGraw-Hill/Osborne).

Application Security Techniques

Building from the assumption that our attacker has user-level access to the system on which our application resides and has the programming and application-specific knowledge to do damage, is there any possibility our application can survive intact? Is the game over already? Fortunately, no, because we have the tools to circumvent many types of attacks.

There are many techniques we can use at the Java application level that can help protect our system from all but the most determined attackers. But the sample application shown, as developed by the inexperienced Lester Goodwin, is not using any of these mechanisms. As the application is written, physical access alone will allow attackers to compromise the application extremely easily.

It is important to be aware of the fact that there is *no* perfect way to secure a stand-alone system against a concerted attack. If a skilled, diligent attacker has access to your system and unlimited access to the machine on which it resides, there is *nothing* that can be done to prevent that attacker from breaching your security. But there are techniques available that, if implemented with the proper controls over personnel, can severely limit what the attacker can do.

That said, there is a strong analogy between home security and information system security: The most attractive targets are usually the first victims of attacks. By investing a little effort in basic application security, you can make your application a tough target, which should deter or prevent all but the most resilient, determined attackers.

In the course of the following chapters, you will see how the following techniques can be applied to the sample stand-alone application in order to improve its security stature:

- Encryption and secure digesting of sensitive data using the JCE
- Logging and auditing using the Java Logging API

- User authentication using JAAS
- Programmatic principal-based authorization using JAAS with custom application permissions
- Digitally signing a file to verify its integrity
- Programmatic verification of a digital signature
- Programmatic access to a Java keystore
- Use of an asymmetric algorithm to wrap a secret key for key-storage purposes
- Techniques to defeat decompilation, including a custom class loader that loads encrypted Java class files

We will apply all of these techniques to our sample application. In practice, you will most likely use a subset of these techniques, based on your risk assessment of your application, its environment, and its users. However, to provide working examples of how these techniques can be used to counter possible attacks on your application code, we show an application with all of the techniques applied.

Additionally, the code we present is geared toward demonstrating the relevant security principles; it is not meant to be used in a production environment. For example, to counter one attack, we describe how to digitally sign a JMS message. This is meant to be first and foremost a demonstration of digital signature technology and secondarily a demonstration of a possible mechanism to verify the integrity of JMS messages. Is it appropriate for your application? Only you can be the judge of that. Our examples are intended to provide you with ideas on which you can build your own Java application security strategy.

THE DANGERS OF STORING DATA LOCALLY

Lester, being the naive developer he is, is very happy with his Retirement Account 401K application. He is unaware of the dangerous situation he has created for his users.

The Retirement Account 401K application is very user friendly and does not require a big, expensive server to operate. In fact, it even allows data files to be stored locally on the client's machine. Little does Lester know that by writing his application this way, he has created a huge security hole. A stand-alone application that stores its data locally has a big problem: The users who run the application generally need to have access to read and write the data files. This means that they can read, and potentially modify, the data without using the application to do it. On some operating systems, this can be alleviated by running `setuid` code (or code that can run with the identity of a different user), but generally, the problem remains. Our sample system is no exception.

Reading or Modifying Application Data Files

Popularity:	*10*
Simplicity:	*8*
Impact:	*10*
Risk rating:	***9***

The retirement application stores its information in plaintext format in a file provided by the person who invokes the application. Using a text editor, anyone can easily see the contents of the file and modify its data. Even if this data were in binary (nontextual) format, it would be a relatively easy task, given a good hex editor, to find information and modify it.

So, let's modify the information and see if the application detects the change. First, we open the data file with a text editor.

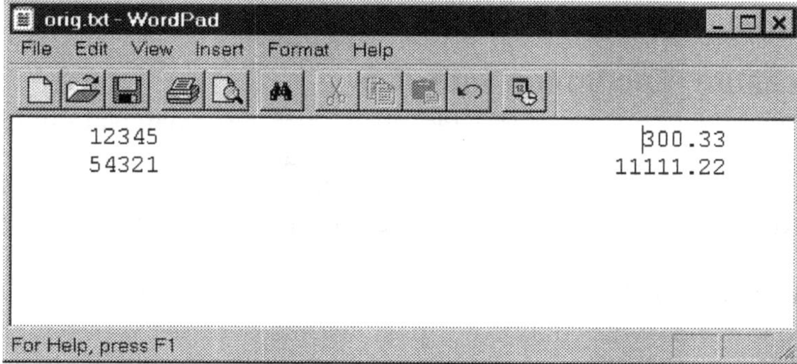

Then we change the balance for account 12345 in the data file.

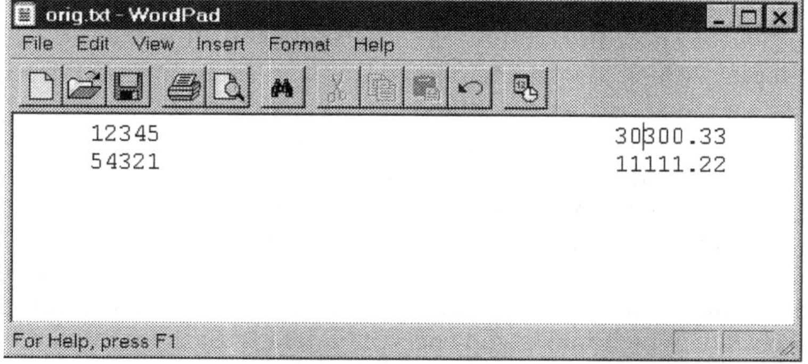

Now we view the data by invoking the application with the following command line, logging in:

```
C:\sec\book>java book.standalone.original.ClientFrame local orig.txt
```

And lo and behold, we just increased the account's balance by $30,000!

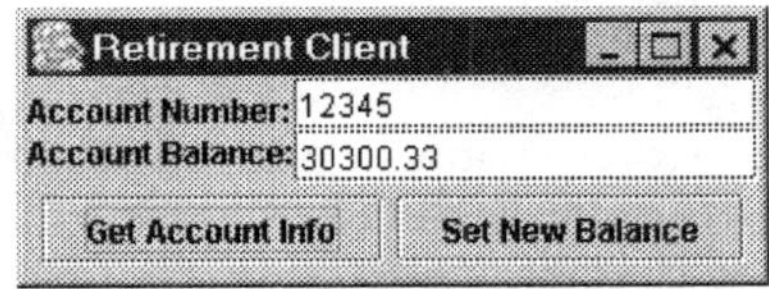

How can we prevent an attack like this? The easy answer is to store the information somewhere more secure, like a relational database on some faraway server. But what if we don't have that option? What if we must store the information locally, as is usually the case for nonnetworked applications? Fortunately, Java provides a solution.

Countermeasure: Encryption with JCE

Java gives us some extremely powerful technology to hide data in plain sight of potential attackers. It's easy to encipher the data before we put it into the file by using JCE combined with a suitable provider. If we can encipher the account balance data before we put it in the local data file, we'll be able to defeat a casual unauthorized read or write attempt.

Deciding What to Encipher and Which Algorithm to Use

First, we need to decide which data to encipher. Because we use the account number field to search our file (and right now, we use a slow, sequential search), it would really slow us down if we encrypted all of our account numbers. A search (using our suboptimal algorithm) would, on average, need to decipher half of the account numbers in our file. Therefore, we will leave the account numbers in cleartext and encipher only the account balances. This leaves one vulnerability, called account switching, which we will discuss later in the "Replay Attack: Use of Enciphered Data for Unauthorized Purposes" section. However, this is a much smaller risk than what we are currently facing.

We must also decide which type of algorithm to use for our encryption. When dealing with encryption of sensitive data, there are two main concerns that drive selection of an appropriate algorithm: level of security (strength) and performance (speed).

Typically, symmetric, or secret key, algorithms execute many times faster than asymmetric algorithms. However, when data must be shared between two users, symmetric algorithms lack the security of a private/public key combination (both parties must know the secret key, which makes the encrypted data itself more vulnerable). Furthermore, algorithms come in various flavors, with various key sizes and numerous other parameters, many of which affect both cipher speed and strength. Here, we will focus on using Java to access the JCE, and leave algorithm and parameter selection up to you and your security team.

TIP For details on cryptography techniques, refer to a book on that subject. A great one is *Applied Cryptography: Protocols, Algorithms, and Source Code in C, 2nd edition*, by Bruce Schneier (John Wiley & Sons).

For the sample application, we will be enciphering every balance we write to the data file and deciphering each balance we read; therefore, we will make the conscious decision to relax algorithm strength in favor of speed. This is a realistic tradeoff for us, because we are not expecting to defend our data from a coordinated assault by an organization with the computing resources of a small nation. Instead, we want to add a high degree of security to our data without compromising the runtime performance of our system unnecessarily. Based on these criteria, we will select the triple-strength DES (3DES) algorithm for our cipher. This algorithm is moderately strong, yet also relatively quick. For our application, normal 56-bit DES would probably be adequate also, but with future advances in computing in mind, we'll go with the stronger version. The 3DES algorithm is also known as DESede, and this is how we must refer to it in our code when we request it from our JCE provider.

For most of the exercises in this book, we will use the Bouncy Castle JCE provider (available from www.bouncycastle.org). This is a free, extremely comprehensive implementation of a JCE provider, which supports many algorithms not available with the Sun JCE provider distributed with the 1.4 version of the JDK. Additionally, some algorithms in the Sun JCE provider are limited or disabled based on U.S. export restrictions applying to cryptography. The Bouncy Castle provider does not have these restrictions, so it is a good tool to use to demonstrate the many facets of the JCE. References to complete installation instructions for the Bouncy Castle provider, along with download information can be found at www.hackingexposedjava.com.

As you learned in Chapter 2, there are several steps involved in using the JCE to encipher data with a symmetric algorithm:

1. Generate a byte array containing the data to encipher.
2. Build an instance of a `Cipher` by calling `Cipher.getInstance`.
3. Initialize the `Cipher` in encrypt mode by calling the `init` method and passing in the secret key.
4. Call the `doFinal` method, passing in the byte array representing the data to encipher.

The cipher will generate as output an array of bytes. Since we will be writing these bytes to a text file, we need to be somewhat concerned. After all, some of the bytes generated by our cipher could correspond to ASCII end-of-line characters or end-of-file characters. This could corrupt our text file and make it unreadable to the rest of our application. To prevent this, we will use a process called base 64 encoding. This process converts a group of three bytes to a group of four printable characters. Essentially, it maps every six bits to an eight-bit ASCII character (it's called base 64 because six bits can represent numbers between 0 and 63, for 64 possible values). This allows us to write binary data to a text file in a well-behaved manner.

Sun provides a set of classes with the JDK to perform this encoding process for us. The classes are called `BASE64Encoder` and `BASE64Decoder` and appear in the `sun.misc` package.

All classes in the `sun.misc` package are not guaranteed to be available in future versions of the JDK, but for our purposes, these classes will work just fine. If you are concerned about using classes from the `sun.misc` package, feel free to write your own encoder / decoder. The algorithm is publicly available (RFC 2045, Section 6.8 – `www.faqs.org/rfcs/rfc2045.html`) and is relatively simple to implement.

Generating a Secret Key

The last item that we need before we can perform symmetric encryption is a secret key. Generating a secret key using the JCE is quite simple and, once you have selected an algorithm to use, can be done with only a few lines of code. Once the key is generated, the security of your encryption depends on the security of your secret key. If attackers are able to get access to your secret key, they will be able to decrypt anything that you have encrypted. Figuring out how to store your key securely is a common issue referred to as *key storage*. We will address this topic in more detail in Chapter 5. For now, we handle key storage simply, but we will progressively make our key-storage mechanism stronger to defend against possible attacks.

We will use our cipher in Cipher Block Chaining (CBC) mode, which modifies the encryption slightly based on the previous block that has been enciphered. This is somewhat stronger than ECB (Electronic Cook Book) mode, for which DESede enciphers each 64-bit block separately and independently from all other blocks. However, to use CBC mode, we need to "prime the pump" of the cipher with some initialization data, so that the cipher always starts at the same reference point; this is called the *initialization vector* (IV).

The following is the code that we will use to generate a secret key and initialization vector to be used in our application:

```
  // Get a key generator for the DESede cipher.
  // The "BC" specifies that we want to use the
  // BouncyCastle provider.
KeyGenerator kg = KeyGenerator.getInstance("DESede", "BC");
// Generate a secret key and print it.
SecretKey key = kg.generateKey();
byte[] ba = key.getEncoded();
System.out.println("Key is: ["
    + new sun.misc.BASE64Encoder().encode(ba) + "]");

// Generate a valid initialization vector for our cipher and print it.
```

```
Cipher c = Cipher.getInstance("DESede/CBC/PKCS5Padding", "BC");
c.init(Cipher.ENCRYPT_MODE,key);
System.out.println("IV is: ["
    + new sun.misc.BASE64Encoder().encode(c.getIV()) + "]");
```

This code is located in the `main` method of the class `KeyBuilder.java` in the `book.standalone.filecrypt` package. Running this code produces the following output:

```
C:\sec\book>java book.standalone.filecrypt.KeyBuilder
Key is: [AccTO5GktvcLuq0H8tZdjwHHEzuRpLb3]
IV is: [MAIfMwm/T9Q=]
```

You may notice that the key is displayed in base 64 format. This makes it easier for us to cut and paste into our application.

Adding the Encryption Code

Now that we have our secret key, let's add the appropriate code to the sample application to encrypt the contents of the account balance fields in the data file. We will make most of the necessary changes in the `LocalPersistenceService` class, so that they will be transparent to the user interface. The only addition will be a modification of the constructor of the `LocalPersistenceService` to accept a `SecretKey` as a parameter.

First, we will modify the constructor of `LocalPersistenceService` to receive the `SecretKey` and store it in a private, final member variable.

```
public LocalPersistenceService(String localFileName, SecretKey key)
throws PersistenceException {
    myKey = key;
    ...
}
```

We will store the initialization vector for our cipher internally as a private, final member of our class:

```
private final String myIVBASE64 = "MA1fMwm/T9Q=";
```

Then, in our `writeLine` method, which actually writes data to the text file, we will call the `encryptToBASE64` method, which will encipher the balance and encode it in base 64 format before returning it to us. By using the same initialization vector each time, we guarantee that future attempts to decipher the enciphered data given the same secret key will succeed.

```
  /**
   * Encrypts the input string and returns the ciphertext encoded in
   * BASE64 encoding.
   * @param inputString The string to be encrypted
```

```
   * @return The BASE64 representation of the ciphertext
   */
  private String encryptToBase64(String inputString) {
    try {
      // Build the cipher and initialize it.
      Cipher c = Cipher.getInstance("DESede/CBC/PKCS5Padding", "BC");

      // Because we are operating in CBC mode,
      // we need to reseed the algorithm
      // with the proper initialization vector.
      AlgorithmParameters ap =
AlgorithmParameters.getInstance("DESede","BC");
      ap.init(decoder.decodeBuffer(myIVBASE64));

      c.init(Cipher.ENCRYPT_MODE,myKey,ap);

      byte[] plainText = inputString.getBytes("UTF-8");

      // Do the encryption.
      byte[] cipherText = c.doFinal(plainText);

      // Do the encoding and return the proper value.
      return encoder.encode(cipherText);

    } catch (GeneralSecurityException e) {
      e.printStackTrace();
    } catch (IOException e) {
      e.printStackTrace();
    }
    return null;
  }
```

The enciphered data will then be written to the file by the `writeLine` method.

Adding Salt to the Encrypted Data

So far, so good, but our mechanism is still somewhat weak. First of all, one weakness of any cipher is that the same plaintext data will always generate identical ciphertext, as long as the cipher is using the same key and the same (for feedback-based algorithms) initialization vector. For example, the balance $100.00 will always encipher to the same string, perhaps `ABC@#$`, if the same secret key and initialization vector are used.

This is a weakness because attackers with access to the system could look for identical encrypted entries in the account balance field of the data file. This would allow them to know that the accounts with identical entries had the same balance. Now if they gained access to just one account and set its balance to a certain number, they could spot other accounts with the same balance. If attackers can set the balance for one account, they can create a hash table of every possible encrypted account balance and reverse-engineer the encryption. This may sound time-consuming, but it is much less time-consuming than defeating the encryption itself.

Fortunately, we can counter this technique by doing something extremely simple during the encryption process: We can add something called *salt* to the encrypted data. Salt is just a sequence of unrelated data that is added to the data that will be encrypted. In our application, we will prepend the integer value of a random number, followed by a colon, to the balance we want to encrypt. For example, to encrypt the balance $100.00, we would create a plaintext string that looks like this: `1021490625840:100.00`, representing *<a random number: the balance>*. We would then encipher that plaintext string. That way, the balance $100.00 will encipher to different ciphertext each time, because each value will have been salted differently. When we decipher, we can easily remove the salt from the plaintext by dropping everything before the colon. With salt, each ciphered balance will be radically different from the next.

We are using a random number from a nonsecure random number generator (the `java.util.Random` class) for this example. This means that if attackers were somehow able to figure out the seed we use to initialize our generator (in this case, the system time in milliseconds at the point the generator is instantiated), they could generate the same sequence of random numbers. To be extremely secure, we might want to use the `java.security.SecureRandom` class to generate our random salt values. However, the `SecureRandom` class has a disadvantage: It takes a long time to instantiate a new generator. In this case, we will sacrifice performance for more security, but you should be aware that there are many more options for generating salt for encrypted business data.

The following code outlines our `getSalt` method and its use during encryption:

```
  /**
 * Gets the value that will be used to salt the encrypted data (so we
 * won't have duplication of the same ciphertext for the same plaintext data).
 * This particular method uses an integer from our nonsecure random
 * number generator (randomGenerator).
 * @return The salt
 */
private String getSalt() {
  return String.valueOf(randomGenerator.nextInt());
}
```

The `getSalt` method is called from within the `writeLine` method, immediately before the balance string is passed to `encryptToBASE64`:

```
/**
 * Writes a line of information to the file.
 * @param position The absolute position in the file to begin the write
 * @param acctNum The information to place in the AccountNumber (first) field
 * @param balance The information to put in the Balance (second) field
 * @throws IOException If there is a problem with the write attempt
 */
private void writeLine(long position, String acctNum, String balance)
     throws IOException {

   // Build a space-padded array to be used for right justification.
   char[] fillChars = new char[RECORD_LENGTH];
   Arrays.fill(fillChars,' ');

   acctFile.seek(position);
   // Read the line into a StringBuffer and replace the balance with first spaces,
   // then the proper balance (right justified).
   StringBuffer currentLine = new StringBuffer(String.valueOf(fillChars));
   currentLine.replace((ACCOUNT_NUM_LENGTH-1) - acctNum.length(),
                       (ACCOUNT_NUM_LENGTH-1), acctNum);

   // Build the salted balance string to encrypt.
   String salt = getSalt();
   balance = salt + ":" + balance;
   String encBalance = encryptToBase64(balance);
...
   currentLine.append("\n");

   // Seek back to the beginning of the line, then write the data.
   acctFile.seek(position);
   acctFile.write(currentLine.toString().getBytes("UTF-8"));
 }
```

Now our data file looks something like this:

```
12345          aKzPqNWggRXRZRt7lkgTXg6cqnn6+1T4
54321          aKzPqNWggRUQs2enladl3dYEIdBgDlLP
```

This is much better. Our account balances are now essentially unreadable, and the same balance will encipher to different ciphertext based on our addition of salt.

While this may appear to be secure and bulletproof, that is not quite the case. As you probably have noticed, we have chosen to leave our account numbers in the clear for performance reasons, but our balances are securely encrypted. This still leaves us vulnerable to a particular attack: *account switching*.

Replay Attack: Use of Enciphered Data for Unauthorized Purposes

Popularity:	*4*
Simplicity:	*10*
Impact:	*10*
Risk rating:	***6***

Even though attackers can't read an individual balance (because of the encryption), they could still cut and paste a balance from one account to another. For example, if an attacker knows that Scott McNealy's account number is 12345 and his account number is 54321, even though he can't see or change Scott's exact balance, he can be reasonably sure that Scott's balance is greater than his. The attacker can then merely use an editor and copy Scott's encrypted balance to his account (overwriting his previous balance). Then both Scott and the attacker would have the same balance—whatever it was.

How can we defend ourselves against this attack? We can use message digests to ensure that data has not changed.

Countermeasure: Data Verification with Message Digests

The JCE gives us implementations of several algorithms to produce *message digests*, which are secure hashes based on a given sequence of bytes. As discussed in Chapter 2, for a given input sequence of bytes, a message digest algorithm will return a fixed-size sequence of bytes that represents a hash of that input data. The sender can generate the digest and send it with the data. If we are the recipient, we can recompute the hash on the data and compare it to the stored hash value included with the data to determine whether the data has changed. If the input data is changed, the digest generated will not match the stored value.

So, to counter this potential assault, when we write a record, we generate a digest of the account number combined with the *unencrypted* balance and salt. Then we store that digest along with the record. When we read a record, we read the balance, decipher it, remove the salt we added, and recompute the digest using the plaintext balance *and* the account number. If the digest we compute matches the one we stored, the balance and account number pair hasn't been changed. If the digests don't match, somehow some of our data has been modified.

Attackers can't know what the encrypted balance is, so they can't regenerate the proper message digest, even if they have the account number and knowledge of the message digest algorithm we are using. They would need to guess our balance and our random salt value to successfully modify the information.

This method demonstrates the computation of a digest during the encryption phase. It is called from the `writeLine` method in the `LocalPersistenceService` class and uses the SHA-1 message digest algorithm to compute the hash:

```
/**
   * Hashes the line contained in the string buffer and returns the string
   * corresponding to the hash.
   * @param accountNumber The account number to hash
   * @param balanceWithSalt The balance to be written ALONG WITH the salt
   * value (before encryption)
   * @return A string representing the SHA-1 hash
   */
  private String hashData(String accountNumber, String balanceWithSalt)  {
    try {
      MessageDigest md = MessageDigest.getInstance("SHA-1");
      md.update((accountNumber + balanceWithSalt).getBytes("UTF-8"));
      byte[] lineHash = md.digest();

      return encoder.encode(lineHash);

    } catch (Exception e) {
     // Handle the exception
    }
    return "";
  }
```

After adding the message digest, our data file now looks like this :

```
12345        aKzPqNWggRXRZRt7lkgTXg6cqnn6+1T4 QEm4OTjj/0AuY41QjtsFBW+t23I=
54321        aKzPqNWggRUQs2enladl3dYEIdBgDlLP t4EiKv5yjYNmRcCB5+dKClMXJw0=
```

Notice the addition of the digest (shown in bold) at the end of each line.

An alternate technique to prevent modification is to compute a digest of our entire data file each time our application is closed or stopped and store it in a secure location. This technique is faster at runtime for small data files, but introduces the additional risk of not having a valid digest for the data file if the application terminates unexpectedly (due to a power failure, VM crash, and so on). This could be dangerous for many types of sensitive data, because we wouldn't be able to tell if our file had been changed or if we merely crashed before we had a chance to compute a new digest.

Now that we've made it more difficult for someone to read or modify our data outside our application, how can we keep track of what's going on *inside* our application?

There are several types of common attacks that we cannot prevent. However, even though we can't prevent them, we can *detect* them and take appropriate actions.

Modification of Data by an Unauthorized User with an Authorized User's Credentials

Popularity:	5
Simplicity:	9
Impact:	10
Risk rating:	*8*

Imagine this situation: A nefarious individual looks over Lester's shoulder as he is entering his application username and password. Now the attacker has the administrator's application credentials and can log in to the system as the administrator. This attack is equivalent to unauthorized users paying or coercing an authorized user to use the system on their behalf.

For obvious reasons, we have no way to prevent an attack like this with certainty. If the system believes that the administrator is using the application, no amount of code we write will allow us to prevent the attacker from doing anything that the administrator is authorized to do.

There are two ways that we can address this issue: We can introduce an auditing system, or we can introduce a more secure authentication mechanism. For now, we will focus on auditing, the first option. We will cover authentication later in this chapter, in the "Countermeasure: System Authentication with JAAS" section.

Countermeasure: Logging and Auditing with the Java Logging API

JDK 1.4 provides a great, integrated technique to help us track and trace users who are exhibiting suspicious patterns of behavior: The Java Logging API. By using the Logging API, described in JDK documentation for the package `java.util.logging`, we have a simple way to log security-related messages. Furthermore, we can direct these log messages to a file, a database, a network socket, or even the console.

Other logging frameworks, such as Log4J (available from http://jakarta.apache.org), are available and will work just as well for logging and auditing. We use the Java Logging API because it is included with the JDK, but any mechanism that will allow a developer to write messages to a secure log repository is acceptable.

To add these features into our code, we need to create a special logging subsystem that we will use for security purposes only (not normal debugging or application events). It is important that we segregate our application log from our security log. Not only does this make it easier to read our security log (because we don't need to wade through application exceptions and other debugging messages), but it also allows us to potentially direct the log to a different destination.

Adding Security Logging

To introduce security logging to the `LocalPersistenceService` class, first we create an instance of the `Logger` class that is designated as the security logger. To provide more fine-grained control and improve the readability of output, loggers are given names that can be referenced in the logger configuration and included in output messages. We will give our logger a name of `RetirementApp.Security`. This will allow us to log security-related messages separately from application messages. As shown in the code fragment below, after the creation of the security logger, we create an application logger, thus keeping the output for these two loggers separate.

```
/**
   * The logger that will be used for security-related messages
   */
  private static Logger secLogger = Logger.getLogger("RetirementApp.Security");
/**
   * The logger to be used for application-related messages
   */
  private static Logger appLogger = Logger.getLogger("RetirementApp.Application");
```

We will use the security logger to write messages to our security log. We do this by calling the `log` method on the appropriate logger, providing the severity level, a message, and optionally an exception or other object that we would like to log with the log entry.

Here are some examples of how we can use this technique in our code. Specifically, we can use it to add security logging to the `set401KBalance` method in the `LocalPersistenceService` class:

```
  public void set401kBalance(String accountNumber, BigDecimal newBalance,
                             RetirementCredential cred)
      throws AccountNotFoundException, OperationNotAllowedException,
      PersistenceException {

    if (cred == null || !cred.getUserName().equals("lester")) {
      // Log the failed attempt.
      String uName = cred == null ? "Null User" : cred.getUserName();
      secLogger.log(Level.WARNING,"Unsuccessful setBalance attempt UID: " +
                   uName, cred);
      throw new OperationNotAllowedException("User not authorized to set balance.");
    }
    String newNumber = newBalance.toString();
    try {
```

```
    long position = findAccount(accountNumber);
    if (position >= 0) {
      writeLine(position, accountNumber, newNumber);
    } else {
      throw new AccountNotFoundException("Account not in database");
    }
  } catch (IOException e) {
    appLogger.log(Level.SEVERE,"IOException in setBalance", e);
    throw new PersistenceException("Unable to write new balance", e);
  }
// Log the successful attempt.
 secLogger.log(Level.INFO,"Balance for account " + accountNumber
               + " changed to " + newBalance + " by "
               + cred.getUserName());
```

Notice that we are logging both successful and unsuccessful attempts to set the balance, but at different severity levels. Successful balance changes are logged at a level of INFO, which is the lowest nondebugging logging level. Unsuccessful attempts are logged with a level of WARNING.

Why do we want to log successful balance changes? Precisely for the reason we stated earlier: We want to know what our *authorized* users are doing as well as what any unauthorized users are attempting.

Deciding What to Log

Now that we know how to log, we face the problem of what to log. In a general sense, we should log anything that interests us from a security perspective. In a more practical sense, these are some events that are commonly logged at the application level in security logs:

- Successful and unsuccessful login attempts
- Logouts and application shutdowns
- Successfully accessing sensitive functionality
- Unsuccessfully attempting to access *any* functionality
- Severe application exceptions that could affect the integrity of application data or functionality

With the listing above in hand, we can modify the application appropriately.

Configuring Logging

Our final task is to tell the Java Logging Framework exactly how to log the data. This can be done in one of four ways:

- By setting the system property `java.util.logging.config.file` to read the configuration from a file

- By setting the system property `java.util.logging.config.class` to read the configuration using a class that we provide (this allows us to read the configuration from a database, web server, or any other location we choose)
- By modifying the default logging configuration file (`logging.properties`, located in the `lib` directory of the JRE)
- By specifying the properties programmatically in our code

For our purposes, we will use the simple approach, the first one listed above, and set the options in a file that we will specify on the command line. In a typical production application, it may be better to opt for the second or fourth option in the list. Those approaches give the application developer more control over the logging, which is good for security purposes, but generally is not as desirable for typical application-level debugging logs, where control may need to be delegated to the client for debugging or technical-support purposes.

The following is a listing of the logging configuration file (`logging.properties`) that we will use for our retirement client application:

```
# This line will direct logging to both a file and the console.
handlers= java.util.logging.FileHandler, java.util.logging.ConsoleHandler

# The default logging level will be informational messages and above.
# Essentially, this means all nondebugging messages
.level= INFO

# Write the output to a file in the current working directory named:
# RetirementApp.log
java.util.logging.FileHandler.pattern = RetirementApp.log

# Limit the file to 50 KBytes of information.
java.util.logging.FileHandler.limit = 50000
# Refrain from rotating the files.
java.util.logging.FileHandler.count = 1
# Write the data to the file in XML format.
java.util.logging.FileHandler.formatter = java.util.logging.XMLFormatter
# Append to the file instead of rewriting it each time.
java.util.logging.FileHandler.append = true

# Format the messages directed to the console in human-readable format.
java.util.logging.ConsoleHandler.formatter = java.util.logging.SimpleFormatter

# Only log SEVERE application messages
# and log security messages at the INFO and above level.
RetirementApp.Application.level = SEVERE
RetirementApp.Security.level = INFO
```

As you can see, we are logging information to both a file and the console, and we are interested in all security-related messages, but only application exceptions with a classification of SEVERE.

Let's run our application twice—once as Lester (who is authorized to change balances) and once as Brian, who is not authorized to change balances. We will log in and attempt to change the balance for account number 12345. Here are the results for a user who logs in as Lester, the administrator:

```
C:\sec\book>java
-Djava.util.logging.config.file=src/book/standalone/filecrypt
/logging.properties
book.standalone.filecrypt.ClientFrame local filecrypt.data
May 15, 2002 5:16:42 PM book.standalone.filecrypt.ClientFrame
authenticateUser
INFO: Successful login for UID: lester
May 15, 2002 5:16:56 PM book.standalone.
filecrypt.LocalPersistenceService set401kBalance
INFO: Balance for account 12345 changed to 100.50 by lester
May 15, 2002 5:17:06 PM book.standalone.filecrypt.ClientFrame shutdown
INFO: App shutdown. UID: lester Code: 0
```

Here are the results for a user who logs in as Brian, a normal user:

```
C:\sec\book>java
-Djava.util.logging.config.file=src/book/standalone/filecrypt
/logging.properties book.standalone.filecrypt.ClientFrame local
filecrypt.data
May 15, 2002 5:17:17 PM book.standalone.filecrypt.ClientFrame
authenticateUser
INFO: Successful login for UID: brian
May 15, 2002 5:17:30 PM book.standalone.
filecrypt.LocalPersistenceService set401kBalance
WARNING: Unsuccessful setBalance attempt UID: brian
May 15, 2002 5:17:33 PM book.standalone.filecrypt.ClientFrame shutdown
INFO: App shutdown. UID: brian Code: 0
```

If we look at the log file (`RetirementApp.log`) that we specified in the `logging.properties` file, we can see that the log entries look somewhat different:

```
<log>
<record>
  <date>2002-05-15T17:22:04</date>
```

```
  <millis>1021501324214</millis>
  <sequence>0</sequence>
  <logger>RetirementApp.Security</logger>
  <level>INFO</level>
  <class>book.standalone.filecrypt.ClientFrame</class>
  <method>authenticateUser</method>
  <thread>10</thread>
  <message>Successful login for UID: lester</message>
</record>
```

In fact, they're in XML format. This makes it incredibly easy to view the logs using a variety of tools, such as a simple XML editor or a custom application.

The complete source code representing the application at this state, with file encryption, record digests, and auditing, can be found in the `book.standalone.filecrypt` package and can be downloaded from www.hackingexposedjava.com.

Use of an Application with a Compromised or Revoked Password

Popularity:	4
Simplicity:	9
Impact:	8
Risk rating:	7

After looking at the following fragment of code from the retirement application's `authenticateUser` method in the `ClientFrame` class, we can see that our options are somewhat limited if we want to revoke a user's access to our system. We are also extremely hampered if we become aware of a password compromise and need to change a user's password immediately.

Currently, the `main` method of the `ClientFrame` builds an instance of a `RetirementCredential` object and uses it to store the username and password provided by the user via the `LoginDialog`:

```
public static void main(String[] args) {

ClientFrame cf = null;
currentUser = new RetirementCredential();

// Perform the login (fill up the currentUser credential with
// authentication tokens...
```

```
    LoginDialog ld = new LoginDialog(null,true,currentUser);
    ld.show();

    if (authenticateUser(currentUser)) {
...
```

After the application gets the `RetirementCredential`, it passes it to the `authenticateUser` method to be validated, as shown below.

```
  /**
   * Authenticate the current user based on the given RetirementCredential
   * @param rc The credential to authenticate
   * @return true if the user is authenticated and authorized to use
   * the system, false otherwise.
   */
  private static boolean authenticateUser(RetirementCredential rc) {

    if (rc != null) {
      if (rc.getUserName().equalsIgnoreCase("lester") &&
          String.valueOf(rc.getPassword()).equals("password")) {
        secLogger.log(Level.INFO, "Successful login for UID: "
          + rc.getUserName());
        return true;
      } else if (rc.getUserName().equalsIgnoreCase("brian") &&
          String.valueOf(rc.getPassword()).equals("password")) {
        secLogger.log(Level.INFO, "Successful login for UID: "
          + rc.getUserName());
        return true;
      }
    }
    // Log the unsuccessful attempt as a warning.
    secLogger.log(Level.WARNING, "Unsuccessful0 login attempt UID: "
                      + rc.getUserName());
    return false;
  }
```

All authentication is done in the `authenticateUser` method by comparing the username and password entered by the user to hardcoded usernames and passwords that have been built into the application. (Granted, this is an extremely simple authentication strategy, but there are actually numerous instances of "homegrown" authentication strategies only a little more refined than this one used in production applications.)

The largest weaknesses of the current strategy are that it is not integrated with the operating system and it is inherently static; it can't be modified easily. In our current application, if we need to revoke the access of user Brian, our only recourse is to change the application code—not a pretty solution. Even if we managed to build our own password file, and encrypt or digest the entries, we would have a more dynamic, but still nonintegrated solution. We would need to write our own tools to administer users, change passwords, revoke access, and so on. This static, nonstandard nature of our authentication mechanism is a large weakness that exposes us to attacks by users with revoked access or through compromised passwords, along with many other types of attacks.

Countermeasure: System Authentication with JAAS

Again, we're fortunate to be using Java! JDK 1.4 ships with technology that will help us integrate our authentication with the system on which our application resides. JAAS, described in Chapter 2, provides us with exactly the assistance we need.

In Chapter 2 you saw how to write a basic `LoginModule` implementation for JAAS and a simple callback handler. In this section, we will use `LoginModule` and `CallbackHandler` classes that are provided with the JDK to help with authentication. Later in the book, we will write a more complex `LoginModule` from scratch. For now, though, we're going to use the tools that Sun provides with the JDK to try to enhance the application's authentication scheme.

The first mechanism that we will attempt to add is integration with the existing operating system's authentication scheme. There are two implementations of `LoginModules` provided with the JDK that will aid us in this endeavor: `com.sun.security.auth.module.UnixLoginModule` and `com.sun.security.auth.module.NTLoginModule`. These two modules provide integration with operating-system–level authentication on various Unix platforms and Windows NT and 2000, respectively.

By using these modules, our Java application can determine the host operating system's identity for the user running the application. If the administrator is logged in to the Windows 2000 workstation hosting the retirement application, we will assume that it is the administrator who is using our application. If another user, such as Brian, is logged in to the Windows 2000 workstation, we will assume that it is Brian running our application. With this scheme, in order for one user to use our application if another was logged in, the first user will need to log out of Windows 2000 and the new user will need to log in, which is a good idea anyway.

Populating the LoginContext Class

The first step in integrating JAAS into the application is to insert the code to build and populate an instance of the `LoginContext` class. We will use this object throughout our application any time we need information about who is running our code.

First, we will add a static variable in the `ClientFrame` class to keep track of the context:

```
/**
 * A static variable to hold onto the login context generated by the user
 * during the login process
 */
private static LoginContext loginContext;
```

Then we will remove all references to our homemade `RetirementCredential` object, and instead rewrite the `authenticateUser` method as follows:

```
/**
 * Authenticate the current user based on the governing JAAS configuration
 * file.
 * @return true if the user is authenticated and authorized to use the system,
 * false otherwise.
 */
private static boolean authenticateUser() {

  try {
    // Build a new loginContext using the basic DialogCallbackHandler
    // provided with the JDK.  It won't even be used if the NTLoginModule
    // is the only one we specify in our configuration file.
    loginContext = new LoginContext("RetirementClient",
                                    new DialogCallbackHandler());
  } catch (LoginException loginException) {
    secLogger.log(Level.WARNING,"Unsuccessful Login.",loginException);
    return false;
  } catch (SecurityException secException) {
    // This means there's a problem with our JAAS infrastructure.
    secLogger.log(Level.SEVERE,"Security Exception.",secException);
    appLogger.log(Level.SEVERE,"Security Exception.",secException);
    return false;
  }
```

Notice that we use a class called `DialogCallbackHandler` as our callback handler when building a new `LoginContext`. This class is provided in the `com.sun.security.auth.callback` package. It is a simple implementation of a callback handler, which uses Swing `JDialogs` and other components to gather information from the user.

NOTE There is also a class called `TextCallbackHandler` in the `com.sun.security.auth.callback` package, which uses the console for I/O instead of dialog boxes. In this example, we have a GUI-based application, so we'll use the GUI callback handler.

As you'll see, the `NTLoginModule` will never use our callback handler to prompt the user for information. Instead, it will read all of the necessary information from the host operating system. But in the future, we're going to be using multiple login modules, so we include the callback handler here for completeness. Also, it's much safer to give *every* `LoginModule` a callback handler, because we, as the users of the module, should not assume that a module will never need to use our handler to get input.

After we've built the `LoginContext`, we can attempt a login by calling its `login` method.

```
    try {
      // Attempt the login.  After we do this, the LoginContext will have
      // valid Principal and Credential information.
      loginContext.login();
    } catch (LoginException loginException) {
      secLogger.log(Level.WARNING,"Unsuccessful Login.",loginException);
      return false;
    }
    secLogger.log(Level.INFO, "Successful Login: " + loginContext.getSubject());
    return true;
  }
```

After this method completes successfully, the `LoginContext` will be populated with a `Subject` containing valid principal and credential information from whatever `LoginModules` were specified in the JAAS configuration file.

Creating the Configuration File

To get the authentication working with the `NTLoginModule`, which is the one that we want to use for now, we must add one more component: a JAAS configuration file. The configuration file, as you learned in Chapter 2, needs to contain the name of our application as it appears in our call to the `LoginContext` constructor (`"RetirementClient"` in our code shown earlier), as well as the `LoginModules` that should be used and how they should be used to authenticate the user. For this example, we will create a simple configuration file that indicates that as long as Windows NT/2000 has authenticated the user, that's fine with us. The contents of this configuration file (named `jaas.conf` for our application) are as follows:

```
RetirementClient {
  com.sun.security.auth.module.NTLoginModule required debug=false;
};
```

Usually, there is only one JAAS configuration file per system, and it contains entries for all JAAS-enabled applications on that system. For this example, the configuration file contains only one entry for the `RetirementClient` application. The one line in the application section indicates that the `NTLoginModule` is required for the application to run. If, for some reason, the `NTLoginModule` cannot authenticate the user, the login attempt will be aborted, and the `login` method will throw a `LoginException`.

When we run the application, we must specify which configuration file should be used. We can do this via a system property called `java.security.auth.login.config`. Alternatively, we can specify the default URL for the configuration file in the `java.security` file in the JRE's `/lib/security` directory, by setting the `login.config.url` property to the URL of the appropriate configuration file.

When we run the retirement application with this JAAS configuration, and include one extra line of code to print the contents of the `Subject` returned from the `LoginContext` for demonstration purposes, something interesting happens:

```
C:\sec\book>java
-Djava.util.logging.config.file=src/book/standalone/ntauthenticate/logg
ing.properties
-Djava.security.auth.login.config=src/book/standalone/ntauthenticate/ja
as.conf book.standalone.ntauthenticate.ClientFrame local ex2.data
May 15, 2002 9:08:01 PM book.standalone. ntauthenticate.ClientFrame
authenticateUser
INFO: Successful Login: Subject:
        Principal: NTUserPrincipal: Lester
        Principal: NTDomainPrincipal: LestersDomain
        Principal: NTSidUserPrincipal:
S-1-5-21-1275210071-1682326488-1343024091
-1001
        Principal: NTSidPrimaryGroupPrincipal:
S-1-5-21-1275810071-1682526488-13
43024091-513
        Principal: NTSidGroupPrincipal:
S-1-5-21-1275210071-1682521488-134302409
1-513
        Principal: NTSidGroupPrincipal: S-1-1-0
        Principal: NTSidGroupPrincipal:
S-1-5-21-1275210071-1282526488-134302409
1-1002
        Principal: NTSidGroupPrincipal:
S-1-5-21-1275210071-1682526488-134302409
1-1003
        Principal: NTSidGroupPrincipal: S-1-5-32-544
        Principal: NTSidGroupPrincipal: S-1-5-32-545
        Principal: NTSidGroupPrincipal: S-1-5-5-0-47620
        Principal: NTSidGroupPrincipal: S-1-2-0
        Principal: NTSidGroupPrincipal: S-1-5-4
        Principal: NTSidGroupPrincipal: S-1-5-11
```

NOTE There's currently a bug in the `NTLoginModule` distributed with JDK 1.4 that causes it to fail if it is used to authenticate a user running without local administrator access on a Windows 2000 machine. This could present a problem during deployment if your users don't have local administrator access to the computer on which they are running your application. According to the JAAS team at Sun, this deficiency should be corrected in a future release of the JDK.

No login dialog box appears! Instead, the information associated with our NT login is silently added to the `Subject` available from the `getSubject` method of the `LoginContext`, which the application dutifully writes to its security log. This makes sense, because there is no need for JAAS to force users to log in again when they have already logged in to Windows.

If we look more closely at the information now associated with the subject, we can see that there is an instance of `NTUserPrincipal` holding the value `'Lester'`. This indicates the username of the current NT user. There is also an `NTDomainPrincipal` returned that indicates which NT domain (or workgroup) the user is currently a member of. Then there are many `NTSid`*`XXX`*`Principals` indicating the numeric values of the user and groups the user belongs to in the NT system registry. So, by merely adding an entry to a JAAS configuration file, we are able to silently discover much information about the user running our application.

We can use this information in lieu of our proprietary `RetirementCredential` object to perform authorization in the `set401KBalance` method of our `LocalPersistenceService`.

Checking Users and Group Membership

Let's modify the interface, so that instead of passing a `RetirementCredential`, we instead pass the `Subject` that we get from the `getSubject` method of the `LoginContext`.

This following is the code listing from the `RetirementAccountInfo` interface.

```
/**
 * Sets the 401kBalance for the appropriate account
 * @param accountNumber The number of the user account (no more than 8 characters)
 * @param newBalance The new balance to attach to the account
 * @param subject The JAAS subject associated with this request
 * @throws AccountNotFoundException If the account number does not exist in the
 * database.
 * @throws OperationNotAllowedException If the user is not authorized to perform
 * the operation.
 * @throws PersistenceException If there is a problem writing the data to the
 * backing store.
 */

public void set401kBalance(String accountNumber, BigDecimal newBalance,
                           Subject subject)
    throws AccountNotFoundException, OperationNotAllowedException,
           PersistenceException;
```

Again, notice that instead of using a RetirementCredential object (which Lester, the application developer, constructed), we are passing an implementation of the Subject interface (from the javax.security.auth package).

Once we have the Subject within our set401KBalance method, we can manually iterate through the Principal objects, find all of the NTUserPrincipal objects, and check to see if one of them is Lester, the administrator.

```
    if (subject == null) {
      throw new OperationNotAllowedException("User not authorized to set balance.");
    }

    // Only get instances of NTUserPrincipal.
    // Notice that this is platform specific (MSWin platforms only)
    Set principals =
        subject.getPrincipals(com.sun.security.auth.NTUserPrincipal.class);

    Iterator i = principals.iterator();
    Principal ourPrincipal = null;

    // Walk through the set of Principals associated with this subject
    while (i.hasNext()) {
      Object o = i.next();

      // This is the user...
      ourPrincipal = (Principal) o;
      // If it's not our administrator, throw an exception.
      if (ourPrincipal.getName().equalsIgnoreCase("Lester")) {
        break;
      }
      ourPrincipal = null;
    }

    if (ourPrincipal == null) {
      // We weren't able to find the correct principal
      secLogger.log(Level.WARNING,"Unsuccessful setBalance attempt UID:
                   " + subject);
      throw new OperationNotAllowedException("User not authorized to set balance.");
    }

    String newNumber = newBalance.toString();
...
```

Now we are able to not only look for a particular user, but also to authenticate based on group membership by using the NTGroupPrincipal object attached to the Subject. We could create an NT group called RetirementAppAdmins and add to that group all users who should have administrative access. Then we could write our code to check for membership in that particular group. However, to prevent group overlap, we need to do all group-based matching on the NT SID for the group, not on the group name.

This can be somewhat cumbersome and requires us to recompile the code each time we install it on a machine in a new NT domain, so even though this is possible, it is not an approach that we will pursue.

On the bright side, after applying this countermeasure, we have eliminated the login dialog box from our application and are still enforcing a somewhat solid level of programmatic authorization in our code. We have solved the problem of password compromise or user revocation. If a password is compromised, we merely need to change the user's password in the operating system. If we wish to revoke a user's access completely, we can disable that user's account in Windows. This is good, but still not as dynamic as we might like.

You have probably noticed that there still is one weakness to our programmatic authorization scheme: We currently have no way of dynamically configuring exactly *who* can perform the `set401KBalance` operation. That is still hardcoded within the application, and furthermore, we have written code within our application that specifically references a platform-specific object (the `NTUserPrincipal`). Let's see how we can solve that problem.

Use of an Application by a User with Partially Revoked Access

Popularity:	3
Simplicity:	5
Impact:	8
Risk rating:	**5**

What if Lester, the administrator of our application, needs to go on vacation? He has several choices regarding how to arrange for other staff members to perform their role in the retirement application:

- Give another person, perhaps Brian, the administrator password.
- Rewrite the application to give another user access to set 401K balances by changing the appropriate code in the `set401KBalance` method. Then, when Lester returns, he can remove the code granting access and rebuild the application again.

Neither of these two options is very good. For obvious reasons, Lester should be hesitant to give someone else his system password. Additionally, modifying and rebuilding code just to change someone's level of access is cumbersome and adds the risk of injecting bugs into the system.

A possible solution would be to write our own access-control file, which would list each user along with their respective application-level permissions. Again, JAAS comes to our rescue. The functionality we need, new in JDK 1.4, is already provided in the form of the Java security policy file, which was introduced in Chapter 1. The huge advance in the JDK 1.4 is that permissions can now be granted not just to code from a certain codebase or signed with a particular key, but also to a specific principal. And, interestingly enough, we are already able to get the current principal quite easily by using various JAAS `LoginModule` implementations, as shown in the previous section.

Countermeasure: Custom Permissions with Principal-based Access

Our solution to this quandary is to remove explicit authorization from the program and move it to the security policy file. This will make our authorization scheme much more dynamic. We will be able to grant or revoke access to specific functionality by merely changing the security policy file, either with a text editor or with a tool such as `policytool`—a graphical tool, distributed with the JDK, used to administer policy files. To do this, we must perform several tasks:

- Build our own custom permission class to represent the access that we wish to regulate.
- Build a suitable security policy file to grant the proper levels of access to appropriate users.
- Ensure that a Java `SecurityManager` is installed and in force while our code is running.
- Programmatically use the `SecurityManager` to check the permission in question at the appropriate points in our application.

Creating a Custom Permission Class

Our first task will be to write a custom permission to represent the ability to perform various actions in the application. Fortunately, there is a nice, easy starting point in the form of the `BasicPermission` class, found in the `java.security` package. The `BasicPermission` class implements all of the functionality necessary to fulfill the contract of the `Permission` abstract class. We will extend `BasicPermission` to create our own `RetirementAppPermission` class, which we can use to embody capabilities of our application to which we would like to restrict access. The code for our `RetirementAppPermission` class is as follows:

```
import java.security.BasicPermission;

/**
 * This class represents a particular application-level permission for the
 * Retirement Application.
 */
public class RetirementAppPermission extends BasicPermission {
```

```
    /**
     * Basic constructor that takes the name of the permission to build
     * @param name The permission name
     */
    public RetirementAppPermission(String name) {
      super(name);
    }
    /**
     * More advanced constructor that takes the name and some actions.
     * @param name The name of the permission
     * @param actions Actions associated with the permissions
     */
    public RetirementAppPermission(String name, String actions) {
      super(name,actions);
    }
}
```

Notice that the implementation of this class is extremely simple. We merely extend the `BasicPermission` class and delegate all functionality to our superclass.

Creating a Security Policy File

The next step we will follow will be to create a security policy file that grants a `RetirementAppPermission` to a principal or group of principals. At first, since we are only going to receive `NTPrincipal` objects with our `NTLoginModule`, we will write a `grant` statement that grants our `Permission` to specific `NTUserPrincipals`. In the next chapter, you will see how to grant permissions in a more independent, less operating-system–specific way.

Within the context of a security policy file, the `grant` statement looks like this:

```
// This will also work for a NT-only based solution
grant      principal com.sun.security.auth.NTUserPrincipal "Lester" {
  permission book.standalone.common.RetirementAppPermission "setBalance";
};
```

Here, we need to specify not only the name of the principal, but also the type of the principal in the form of a fully qualified class name. Then we list the fully qualified class name of our permission, followed by a *permission name*. This name is arbitrary (we made it up), but it will need to exactly match the name that we will verify programmatically in the next steps.

Ensuring a Security Manager Is Running

Next, we need to modify our program to guarantee that we will be running with a `SecurityManager` installed. If a `SecurityManager` is not installed, any user will effectively run with unrestricted access. The following code will accomplish this:

```
public static void main(String[] args) {

  ClientFrame cf = null;

  // Guarantee that there's a security manager installed.
  // If we don't do this, none of our application-based policies
  // will be enforced.
  if (System.getSecurityManager() == null) {
    System.setSecurityManager(new SecurityManager());
  }
```

In a Java application, a program usually is allowed to set a security manager only once, unless someone (usually unwisely) has granted the `RuntimePermission setSecurityManager` to the code. In addition to adding a security manager programmatically, you can also request that a `SecurityManager` be installed for your application by setting the `java.security.manager` system property on the Java command line.

Additionally, to be really thorough, we could add code to the application at this point that calls `System.getSecurityManager`, and then checks the class name to make sure that it is the default security manager and not a customized one written by a nefarious user, to always approve our application's requests for `setBalance` access. However, that level of security isn't necessary for Lester's application, so we do not show it explicitly in our code.

Checking for the Permission

Once we guarantee that a `SecurityManager` is in force, we have the job of inserting the check for the permission in question into our code. In our case, we will place the check into the `set401KBalance` method in our `LocalPersistenceService` class:

```
 /**
  * Sets the 401kBalance for the appropriate account
  * @param accountNumber The number of the user account (no more than
  * 8 characters)
  * @param newBalance The new balance to attach to the account
  * @throws AccountNotFoundException If the account number does not
  * exist in the database.
  * @throws OperationNotAllowedException If the user is not authorized
  * to perform the operation.
  * @throws PersistenceException If there is a problem writing the
  * data to the backing store.
  */

 public void set401kBalance(String accountNumber, BigDecimal newBalance)
     throws AccountNotFoundException, OperationNotAllowedException,
            PersistenceException {

   // Use the built-in Java security manager to enforce our permissions.
```

```
    SecurityManager sm = System.getSecurityManager();
    if (sm != null) {
      try {
        // Check the appropriate permission
        sm.checkPermission(new RetirementAppPermission("setBalance"));
      } catch (SecurityException e) {
        secLogger.log(Level.WARNING,"Unsuccessful setBalance attempt Subject: "
                     + Subject.getSubject(AccessController.getContext()));
        throw new OperationNotAllowedException(
            "User not authorized to set the balance");
      }
    }

    String newNumber = newBalance.toString();
...
```

As you can see, we no longer need to pass the Subject into our method as a parameter. All we need to do is get the current SecurityManager and call its checkPermission method, passing it an instance of the permission that we want to check. The SecurityManager consults the PermissionCollection attached to the current AccessControlContext (the set of all principals and codebases, under whose auspices the current thread is executing) and lets us know if the permission we are checking should be allowed or denied. Every thread has an AccessControlContext, and we can always ask the context (somewhat indirectly) who our current subject is, by executing the following line of code:

```
Subject ourSubj = Subject.getSubject(AccessController.getContext());
```

We have one last hurdle to overcome. We need a way to add the subject that our LoginContext gets to the current AccessControlContext, so that the checkPermission method will be aware that our Principal is the one executing the code. For good reason, this attachment does not happen automatically. To perform this step, we will use a static method in the Subject class called doAsPrivileged (rather than Subject.doAs, as explained after the code listing).

The doAsPrivileged method allows us to specify a Subject and a block of code to run as that Subject. This will add the specified subject to the AccessControlContext for the running thread at that point. Essentially, it says: "Run this code as this person." Here's what the call looks like in the setBalance button event handler in our code:

```
} else if (ev.getSource() == setInfoButton) {
  // Handle the SetButton click.
  try {
    // Run the set401kBalance with the credentials of the authenticated
    // subject.  Notice we are using the doAsPrivileged() method
    // instead of doAs(). This is because this will be invoked from
    // the AWT thread, so the inherited AccessControlContext will be
    // too stringent for our tastes.
```

```
      Subject.doAsPrivileged(loginContext.getSubject(),
          new PrivilegedExceptionAction() {
            public Object run() throws Exception {
              model.set401kBalance(acctNumberField.getText(),
                                   new BigDecimal(balanceField.getText()));
              return null;
            }
          }, null);
    } catch (PrivilegedActionException e) {
      if (e.getException() instanceof AccountNotFoundException) {
        JOptionPane.showMessageDialog(ClientFrame.this, "Account [" +
            acctNumberField.getText() + "] was not found in the database.",
            "Account Not Found", JOptionPane.ERROR_MESSAGE);
      } else if (e.getException() instanceof OperationNotAllowedException) {
        JOptionPane.showMessageDialog(ClientFrame.this,
            e.getException().getMessage(),
            "Unauthorized Operation", JOptionPane.ERROR_MESSAGE);

      } else if (e.getException() instanceof PersistenceException) {
        appLogger.log(Level.SEVERE,"Persistence Exception", e);
        JOptionPane.showMessageDialog(ClientFrame.this,
                                      e.getException().getMessage(),
                                      "Persistence Error",
                                      JOptionPane.ERROR_MESSAGE);
      }else {
        appLogger.log(Level.SEVERE," Exception setting balance.", e);
      }
    }
  }
```

There is a simpler version of the `doAsPrivileged` method called `Subject.doAs`, but the `doAsPrivileged` method provides a capability that we need here: It allows us to specify as a last parameter (which we set to `null`) the `AccessControlContext` under which to run our code. The `doAs` method does not allow us to do this.

If we used the normal `doAs` method, our subject's permissions would be added to the permissions already in force for the AWT thread and the codebase from which our `ActionListener` for our button was loaded. Then (as it should) the `SecurityManager` would enforce the *most stringent* of those permissions. Because the codebase containing our `ActionListener` has not been granted the `setBalance` permission explicitly and because the `ActionListener` is invoked by the AWT Thread, so there is no subject associated with it, adding our permission through our subject would have no effect. The `SecurityManager`, in effect, says to itself, "Code that doesn't have that permission (the AWT Thread calling the `actionPerformed` method in our listener) is trying to circumvent my authority by calling code that does have the permission." This is not allowed.

The `doAsPrivileged` method, on the other hand, allows the code in the event handler to tell the `SecurityManager`, "I take full responsibility for my actions. Even though code calling me may not have the right permissions, let me do this action anyway because I *do* have the proper permissions."

Executing privileged code, either via `doAsPrivileged` in the `Subject` class or `doPrivileged` in the `AccessController` class, is somewhat dangerous, but in some cases it is necessary. A good way to make the decision is to ask yourself, "Do I care who is calling the current method when I do this action?" If the answer is "No," feel free to use privileged code. If the answer is "Yes," or "I'm not sure," you may want to look for other alternatives.

In this case, we don't care who calls our method—it could be the AWT event handler, or it could be some block of code from another class. We want to execute the `set401KBalance` method as the `Subject` in our current `LoginContext`, so it doesn't matter which code is invoking our `set401KBalance` method, it only matters which person (or subject) is using our application. Using a privileged block in this case is acceptable. Passing `null` into the `doAsPrivileged` method as the last argument effectively runs the code specified with the permissions of the specified `Subject` added to an *empty* `AccessControlContext`.

Now if we run the code as a Windows NT user logged in as `Lester`, we will be allowed to set the balance. If we run the code as `Brian`, the following happens when that user tries to set the balance on any account:

```
C:\sec\book>java
-Djava.security.auth.login.config=src/book.standalone/authorization/jaa
s.conf
-Djava.security.policy=src/book/standalone/authorization/retirement.pol
icy book.standalone.authorization.ClientFrame local ex3.data May 16,
2002 10:31:44 AM book.standalone.authorization.LocalPersistenceService
set401kBalance
WARNING: Unsuccessful setBalance attempt Subject: Subject:
        Principal: NTUserPrincipal: Brian
```

As you can see, Brian's attempt to set the balance was rightfully denied by the security manager. Integrating application authorization with Java's built-in access control scheme is an extremely powerful, yet underutilized technique. The small, working example above should be enough to get you started, but you can find more complete information regarding writing and asserting custom permissions in the documentation distributed with JDK 1.4.

SUMMARY

This chapter examined some of the basic Java security mechanisms that can be used to protect against the security intrusions of the determined hacker. Using cryptography, we can encipher any data that needs to be stored locally, thus hiding the data in plain sight.

Secret key cryptography requires us to protect our key, since any individual with that key could decipher our data.

Authentication—determining that the user who is attempting to use our system is who they actually say they are—is requisite for a secure system.

Fortunately, as you have seen in this chapter, Java provides packages for both encryption and authentication. You saw how the JCE package can be used to encipher data using a variety of encryption mechanisms. JAAS can be used to provide both authentication and authorization services, which can be used to dramatically increase the security of our system.

CHAPTER 5

SOFTWARE
PIRACY AND
CODE LICENSING
SCHEMES

Though Lester is somewhat confident that he has managed to plug various security holes in his application, it is still vulnerable. (Lester has nevertheless gone on vacation, leaving us to our own resources.) In this chapter, we will address the application's vulnerability to software piracy through the use of a software licensing scheme.

Software licensing is generally a good way to keep honest people honest. However, it shouldn't be counted on to defend your application against a commercial software piracy operation in a rogue nation that pays no attention to international copyright laws. As with all security measures, with licensing, there is a point of diminishing returns. At a certain level, you need to exert an inordinate amount of effort to gain a small improvement in your application's security stature. Only the application architects and designers can define this point of diminishing returns for a particular system.

THE DANGERS OF CODE MISUSE

Even without application source code, in the hands of a knowledgeable technical person, an application can be used in ways that the developer never intended. What mechanisms are available to us to help us prevent people from pirating our software—copying our application and using it in an unauthorized and unlicensed manner?

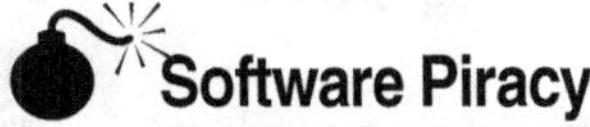

Software Piracy

Popularity:	10
Simplicity:	5
Impact:	7
Risk rating:	7

Unfortunately, there is no perfect defense against software piracy. Any time an attacker has access to all of the application code and unfettered administrative access to a machine to run it on, a stand-alone application has limited defenses. However, by using the JCE intelligently, we can make the attackers' job difficult enough that they may be dissuaded from attempting to "crack" our application.

Countermeasure: Develop a Licensing Strategy

One way to deter would-be pirates is to develop a comprehensive software licensing strategy. In the past, most licensing mechanisms have focused on using a hash code or simple encryption scheme to transport or validate licensing information. These techniques are still possible in a Java application. However, we will demonstrate how using the JCE to facilitate our licensing plan is also feasible and relatively simple. We will assume that we can deliver a specialized license "key" to all authorized users of our application. The license key will be a string of base 64-encoded ciphertext which, when decrypted, contains all of the information necessary to enforce our licensing approach.

To get this mechanism working, we will need to perform the following steps:

1. Build a Java interface that represents all of the information that we might need to retrieve from a license.
2. Implement the interface with a class that uses a simple symmetric algorithm to decrypt a user license key and extract the relevant information.
3. Implement a mechanism for storing the license key on the client machine so that users don't need to reenter it every time they run the application.

Building the Interface

The following is a simple implementation of an interface that exposes license-like functionality. It allows an application to get the name of the organization for whom the license is approved, a license number, the number of simultaneous clients allowed, and the internal application modules that are enabled. It also includes a field that contains the application keystore password. We can then use the application keystore password to open our application keystore. This alleviates the need to hardcode that password in our application and gives us the latitude to distribute different keystores, each potentially having a different password, to different clients.

NOTE We developed the properties (expiration date, which modules, and so on) for this `License` object in an arbitrary manner to demonstrate some of the many possibilities that you have when developing an object of this type. To use this object in the context of your own application, you may want to change some or all of the public properties presented by this particular interface to match your licensing requirements.

```
import java.util.Date;

/**
 * This interface represents a application-specific license. Once constructed
 * it is considered to be immutable.
 */
public interface License {

  /**
   * Gets the license expiration date
   * @return The expiration date of the license
   */
  Date getExpireDate();

  /**
   * Gets a list of modules that have been enabled for the software
   * @return An array of integers with each integer corresponding to a
   * particular module in the software
   */
  int[] getWhichModules();

  /**
```

```
     * Gets the license number
     * @return The vendor-generated license number
     */
    String getLicenseNumber();

    /**
     *
     * @return The name of the individual (or organization) to which this
     * license applies
     */
    String getClientName();

    /**
     *
     * @return  The maximum number of simultaneous clients allowed under this
     * license
     */
    int getMaxClients();

    /**
     *
     * @return The password for the application-based keystore
     */
    char[]  getAppKeyStorePassword();

    /**
     * Helper method to determine if the license is expired today. Uses the
     * system date.
     * @return true if the expiration date has not elapsed, false if the license is
     * expired.
     */
    public boolean isValid();

}
```

To make it easier to develop new types of licenses, we'll create an abstract class called `AbstractLicense`, which implements the `License` interface. This class will take care of all license-based functionality, except for the decryption of a particular license string. Here's the code for the `AbstractLicense` class:

```
import java.util.Date;
import java.util.StringTokenizer;
import java.text.SimpleDateFormat;
import java.text.ParseException;

/**
 * This is an abstract helper class for quickly creating new license
 * implementations. When extended, the decipherLicense() method
 * must be implemented.
 */
public abstract class AbstractLicense implements License {
```

```
// Instance-specific variables
private Date     expireDate;
private int[]    whichModules = { };
private String   licenseNumber;
private String   clientName;
private int      maxClients;
private char[]   appKeyStorePassword;

/**
 * Represents the initialization state of the data in the object.
 * It's false as long as the license string has not been deciphered.
 */
private boolean isDataLoaded = false;

private String encipheredLicenseString;

/**
 * Builds an abstract license from the provided encrypted string.
 * Calls the abstract decipherLicense to actually decipher the license.
 * @param encLicenseString The license string, encrypted and in
 * BASE64 format... When deciphered, must be of the following format:
 * <BR><CODE> [License Expire Date (MMDDYY)]:[# of enabled modules]:[enabled
module #1]:...:[enabled module #n]:[license number]:[client name]:[max num
clients]:[app key store password]</CODE>
 */
protected AbstractLicense(String encLicenseString)
    throws InvalidLicenseException {

  encipheredLicenseString = encLicenseString;

}
```

Notice that the constructor takes an enciphered, then base 64-encoded, license string as an argument. The license string must be enciphered using the same cipher (and compatible key) as appears in the `decipherLicense` method. Also, when deciphered, the license string should be a colon-delimited string in the exact format outlined in the Java documentation for the constructor.

```
/**
 * Deciphers the license key and loads the data values in the private
 * members of the class. The load will happen lazily unless a subclass
 * specifically requests that it happen earlier.
 * @throws InvalidLicenseException If the license string does not decrypt properly
 */
protected final void loadData() throws InvalidLicenseException {

  // NOTE: Handling of NumberFormatExceptions and other miscellaneous parsing
  // exceptions has been omitted for clarity.

  // Get the license information in the clear.
  String clearLicense = decipherLicense(encipheredLicenseString);
```

```
    // Parse the string.
    StringTokenizer tok = new StringTokenizer(clearLicense, ":");
    String dateString = tok.nextToken();

    // Initialize the instance variables.
    SimpleDateFormat sdf = new SimpleDateFormat("MMddyy");
    try {
      expireDate = sdf.parse(dateString);
    } catch (ParseException pe) {
      throw new InvalidLicenseException("Invalid date in license key");
    }

    int numModules = Integer.parseInt(tok.nextToken());
    whichModules = new int[numModules];
    for (int i=0; i < numModules; i++) {
      whichModules[i] = Integer.parseInt(tok.nextToken());
    }

    licenseNumber = tok.nextToken();
    clientName = tok.nextToken();

    maxClients = Integer.parseInt(tok.nextToken());
    appKeyStorePassword = tok.nextToken().toCharArray();

    isDataLoaded = true;
  }

… << Removed all accessor methods >> …

  /**
   * Helper method to determine if the license is expired today. Uses the
   * local system date. Could add a time server for more security
   * @return true if the expiration date has elapsed, false if the license is
   * still good.
   */
  public final boolean isValid() {
    if (!isDataLoaded) {
      return false;
    }
    return expireDate.getTime() >= new Date().getTime();
  }

  /**
   * This method must be implemented by any subclasses and should take a
   * BASE64 encoded version of the encrypted license string and return
   * a plaintext version of the same string.
   * @param origLicense The encrypted license string (BASE64)
   * @return The plaintext license string
   * @throws InvalidLicenseException If the license string is invalid.
   */
```

```
  protected abstract String decipherLicense(String origLicense)
      throws InvalidLicenseException;

}
```

Implementing the SimpleSymmetricLicense Class

Using the `AbstractLicense` as a base, we can easily implement our own license based on a symmetric cipher:

```
import javax.crypto.spec.DESKeySpec;
import javax.crypto.SecretKeyFactory;
import javax.crypto.Cipher;
import javax.crypto.SecretKey;
import java.security.Key;
import sun.misc.BASE64Decoder;
import sun.misc.BASE64Encoder;

/**
 * This class is a simple implementation of the license interface, which uses
 * a symmetric algorithm with a predefined key to decipher the license string.
 */
public class SimpleSymmetricLicense extends AbstractLicense {

  /**
   * The secret key (in BASE64 format)
   */
  private static final String mySecretKeyBASE64 = "Q2inPZQBjxo=";

  // The license key, when decrypted should be of the following format:
  // <LicenseExpirationDate (MMDDYY)>:<# of enabled modules>:<enabled module #1> :
  // <enabled module #n>: <licenseNumber> : <clientName> : <maxClients> :
<appKeyStorePassword>

  /**
   * The constructor for the license. Expects an encrypted license string
   * encoded using BASE64 of the following format:
   * <BR><CODE> [License Expire Date (MMDDYY)]:[# of enabled modules]:[enabled
module #1]:...:[enabled module #n]:[license number]:[client name]:[max num
clients]:[app key store password]</CODE>
   * @param licenseKeyString An BASE64 encoded, encrypted string of the format
mentioned above
   * @throws InvalidLicenseException If the license key is invalid.
   */
  public SimpleSymmetricLicense(String licenseKeyString)
                                   throws InvalidLicenseException {

    super(licenseKeyString);
    loadData();

  }
```

```
    /**
     * Deciphers the license key using a symmetric algorithm
     * @param origLicense
     * @return
     * @throws InvalidLicenseException
     */
    protected String decipherLicense(String origLicense)  throws
InvalidLicenseException {
        String retval = "";

        try {
          sun.misc.BASE64Decoder decoder = new sun.misc.BASE64Decoder();
          byte[] decodedKey = decoder.decodeBuffer(mySecretKeyBASE64);

          // Generate the DES key from our static data.
          SecretKeyFactory skf = SecretKeyFactory.getInstance("DES");
          SecretKey myKey = skf.generateSecret(new DESKeySpec(decodedKey));

          Cipher cipher = Cipher.getInstance("DES");

          // Initialize Cipher with key.
          cipher.init(Cipher.DECRYPT_MODE,myKey );

          byte[] ciphertext = decoder.decodeBuffer(origLicense);

          // Decrypt the ciphertext.
          byte[] cleartext = cipher.doFinal(ciphertext);

          retval = new String(cleartext);

        } catch (Exception e) {
         throw new InvalidLicenseException("Decryption of license key failed");
        }
        return retval;
    }

    /*****************************************************************
    **** This is a utility method and can be removed from this class *******
    ***************************************************************/

    /**
     * This method will help the user build a new license key if needed.
     * It's meant to be for vendor use only and SHOULD BE REMOVED (or moved
     * to another class) before the app is distributed.  It's here for
     * demonstration purposes only.
     * @param licenseString The string containing the license key in plaintext
     * @return The enciphered, encoded license key.
     */
```

```
  private static String encipherLicense(String licenseString) {

      try {
        sun.misc.BASE64Decoder decoder = new sun.misc.BASE64Decoder();
        SecretKeyFactory skf = SecretKeyFactory.getInstance("DES","BC");
        Key myKey = skf.generateSecret(new
DESKeySpec(decoder.decodeBuffer(mySecretKeyBASE64)));

        Cipher cipher = Cipher.getInstance("DES","BC");

        // Initialize Cipher with key and parameters.
        cipher.init(Cipher.ENCRYPT_MODE,myKey );

       // Our cleartext
       byte[] cleartext = licenseString.getBytes();

       // Encrypt the cleartext.
       byte[] ciphertext = cipher.doFinal(cleartext);

       // BASE64 encode it.
       BASE64Encoder enc = new BASE64Encoder();
       return enc.encodeBuffer(ciphertext);

     } catch (Exception e) {
        e.printStackTrace();
     }
     return "";
  }

  /**
   * A short, simple regression test for the class
   * @param args None needed
   */
  public static void main(String[] args) {
     try {

     // Test the class...
        String licString = "062603:2:12:15:12345abc:Brian:15:keystore";
        String encLic = encipherLicense(licString);
        System.out.println("Encrypted License Key:\n" + encLic);
        License l = new SimpleSymmetricLicense(encLic);
        System.out.println("License constructed from key:\n" + l);

     } catch (Exception e) {
        e.printStackTrace();
     }
  }

}
```

Notice that for this license, we are using the plain DES algorithm and embedding the secret key in the class file itself. We also include a static encipherLicense method, which can be used to generate a license key. For production use, this method would most likely be moved to another class and not distributed with our license class. It is included here for demonstration purposes only. Additionally, the main method of this class contains some simple test code that exercises both the encipherLicense and decipherLicense methods.

Integrating Licensing into the Application

Our last task is to integrate the licensing mechanism into our application. We will do this in the ClientFrame class and use the new Preferences mechanism from JDK 1.4 to store the license key locally on the user's system. On Windows NT/2000 platforms, the Preferences class will store our data in the user portion of the Windows registry. Therefore, if users are using NT roaming profiles, their application license key will roam with them.

To integrate the license into our application, we add the following private method to our ClientFrame class:

```
/**
 * Validate the user's license information.  This particular implementation
 * first looks in the root node of the Preferences object (for NT this
 * is an entry in the registry) for the enciphered license key string.
 * If it is found, it is deciphered, checked and validated. If it is not
 * found, the user is prompted to enter the license information. This method
 * still has some slight weaknesses: It relies on the system's local date and
 * it stores the license key in the registry.
 * @return true if the license information is valid on the local system's
 * current date.
 */
private static boolean checkLicense() {
  // We will look for the license key under the user registry.
  // Could also put it under the system reg, but this way it will move
  // with the user.
  Preferences p = Preferences.userRoot();
  // Read the registry for the license key.
  String licenseString = p.get(LICENSE_REGISTRY_KEY,"NONE");

  if (licenseString.equals("NONE")) {
    // Prompt the user for their license key -- we don't have it in the reg.
    licenseString = JOptionPane.showInputDialog("Enter License Key:");
    try {
      currentLicense = new SimpleSymmetricLicense(licenseString);
      // Put the key in the registry.
      p.put(LICENSE_REGISTRY_KEY,licenseString);
    } catch (InvalidLicenseException e) {
      // They entered a bad key.
      secLogger.log(Level.WARNING, "Invalid license key entered.",e);
      return false;
```

```
      }
    } else {
      try {
        currentLicense = new SimpleSymmetricLicense(licenseString);
      } catch (InvalidLicenseException e) {
        // There's a bad key in the registry... remove it.
        secLogger.log(Level.WARNING, "Invalid license key in registry.",e);
        p.remove(LICENSE_REGISTRY_KEY);
        return false;
      }
    }

    return currentLicense.isValid();
  }
```

This code will check to see if the license exists in the registry. If the key already exists, the application will load it. If the license can't be found in the registry, the application will prompt the user to enter a key. Once the key is received, it is passed to the constructor of the `License` class. If the `License` class constructs properly, it is checked to determine if it is valid on the current system date.

After we run the application and enter our license key when prompted, we notice that there has been some information added under the `JavaSoft` key in our Windows user registry:

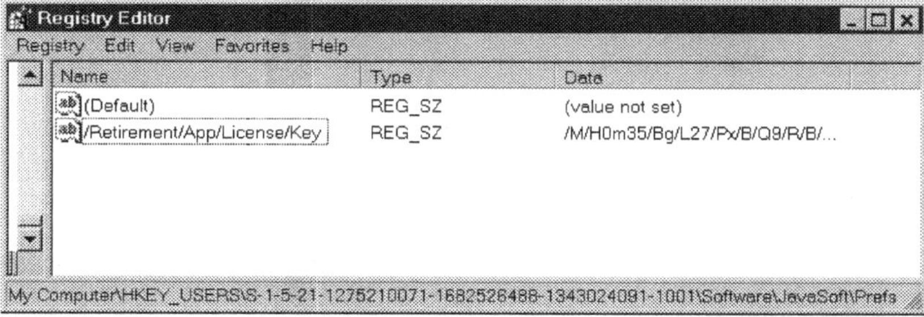

Like other software-licensing methods, this scheme is not foolproof. Users could roll back their system date to trick the code into running. To counter this, we could add an encrypted entry in the registry detailing the date the license was installed and the date the code last ran. If we ever noticed that the current date was "behind" the last-run date, we would know that someone changed the clock and could react accordingly.

Also, an attacker could give their license key string to another individual. To counter this, we could add code to validate the username stored in the license key against the current `Subject` maintained by our `LoginContext`.

Another Licensing Strategy

Along with the sample code, we also include an implementation of the `License` interface called `AsymmetricLicense`. This implementation uses the RSA asymmetric cipher to decipher a license key. With the `AsymmetricLicense` class, the application developer enciphers the license using a *particular* user's public key. That license can be deciphered only with the same user's private key. This is one possible way to accomplish "one-to-one" licensing.

This asymmetric mechanism is only as strong as the users' desire to keep their private key private. Consider that if each user generates a special public/private key pair, only to be used for this application, it would be a relatively small issue for a user to sacrifice that private key to give a friend or associate a copy of the application. However, if you encipher the license key using the same public/private key pair used by other applications to secure the user's online transactions, credit card information, and identity, you have raised the stakes. Now if users give away your application, they are essentially giving away their entire online identity to their associates. Many people would hesitate to divulge such information, and this fact raises the security of your application code.

Essentially, a public key infrastructure becomes more robust as users assign more value to their private keys. It's the difference between giving a friend a $5 bill and giving her the keys to your house, telling her where your wallet is, and asking her to get the $5 herself. You *really* must trust a person to take the second course of action.

For this asymmetric mechanism to be effective, each user must have a different license key, enciphered using that particular user's public key. The value of this approach is that users cannot give another user their application license without also giving that other person their private key, and that's generally not a good idea.

This method consumes more overhead and adds more complexity (a different license must be generated for each system user), but it also adds slightly more security. In the next section, we will see how to use a hybrid approach, which strikes a good balance between security and complexity.

▼ We mention both approaches because they are both valid, but each addresses a different set of needs. You can decide which strategy to use for your licensing (symmetric or asymmetric cipher) by applying the following criteria:

Use an asymmetric cipher if:	Use a symmetric cipher with an embedded key if:
Unauthorized use of your application is tantamount to a system compromise.	You want to deter unauthorized distribution, but you can accept a certain level of piracy.
You have a Public Key Infrastructure (PKI) in place, where each potential user of your system has a public/private key pair.	You want to distribute a single license key per site.
You don't mind generating a new license key for every potential user of your system.	You want to simplify client key management and installation issues.

Secret Key Storage

Up to this point, our application has been storing its secret keys used for file encryption in private member variables in the relevant classes. This mechanism is relatively secure, but an attacker could potentially gain access to our secret key value by reverse engineering our code through a technique called *decompilation* or by gaining access to our source code in some other way.

Compromise of a Secret Key

Popularity:	*1*
Simplicity:	*2*
Impact:	*10*
Risk rating:	***3***

We will discuss decompilation in the next chapter, but for now, we would like to store our key data outside our application so that even if an attacker has access to our source code, our application data will remain secure. In fact, as developers of a secure system, even we should be unable to access a user's data without their permission. This mechanism will help us accomplish this.

Countermeasure: Key Wrapping

One way to securely store key data is to encrypt the secret key using an asymmetric algorithm. The JCE gives us a simple way to encrypt the secret key, called *key wrapping*. Key wrapping allows us to "wrap" a key for one cipher by encrypting it with another cipher.

NOTE An alternative for key storage is to store the secret key in a keystore. The normal Java JKS keystore is not able to store secret keys. It will store only public certificates and private keys for asymmetric ciphers and signature algorithms. However, the JCEKS (available in JDK 1.4) is capable of storing keys for both symmetric and asymmetric ciphers. To store the key in a JCEKS keystore, you must write the secret key to the keystore programmatically using the `setKeyEntry` method in the `Keystore` class.

The most common way to use key wrapping is to wrap a symmetric key with an asymmetric algorithm. This means that the symmetric secret key is enciphered using an asymmetric algorithm and the intended recipient's public key. The recipient then uses the private key to decipher the symmetric key, which the recipient then uses for all further encryption. Figure 5-1 illustrates how key wrapping works.

This approach helps us solve the key-transport problem by providing a secure way for two parties to exchange a secret key, without passing it unencrypted over some communication medium. This mechanism will also help us solve the key-storage problem for our application. We will store our secret key that we use for file encryption (and perhaps licensing also) on the user's local disk, but we will encrypt it with the user's public key. Then only someone who possesses the user's private key will be able to decrypt the secret key, and thus read the data file for our application or validate the license key.

You may wonder why we are going through this complex key-storage process instead of just using asymmetric encryption for all of our encryption needs. As explained in Chapter 4, asymmetric encryption is much slower than symmetric encryption. Thus, by

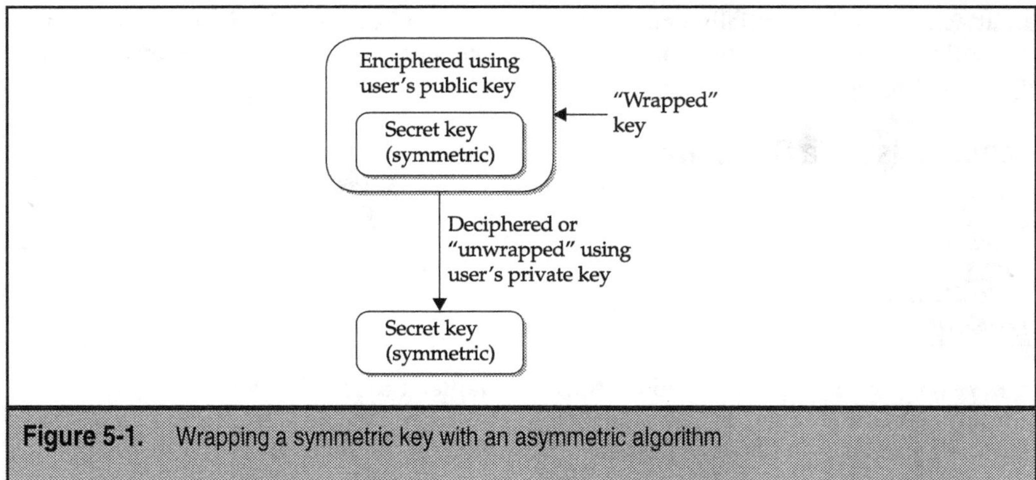

Figure 5-1. Wrapping a symmetric key with an asymmetric algorithm

wrapping a symmetric key with an asymmetric algorithm, we gain the speed of symmetric encryption with the security and flexibility of asymmetric encryption. Additionally, if we used asymmetric encryption on our data file, we would need to use the public key of the user who enciphered any data in the file to decipher it! As the number of users of our application grew, this could make file maintenance extremely complex. With key wrapping, we can wrap the same symmetric key with each user's asymmetric key pair. That way, only authorized users can unwrap the symmetric key, but once that is done, all users will be using the same key to read from and write to the data file. To implement this feature, we take advantage of another powerful, but underutilized, JAAS `LoginModule` that comes with JDK 1.4: `KeyStoreLoginModule`. This `LoginModule` will prompt the user for a key alias and keystore password. It will then read that key from the specified keystore and add its principal and credential information to the appropriate subject.

Once a user logs in via the `KeystoreLoginModule`, that user's *private key* for the alias the user provided is associated with the `Subject` associated with the user's `LoginContext` and is available to us programmatically (if we have the proper permission), without requiring us to open the user's keystore ourselves. In effect, this will allow us to store our secret key in such a way that there is no way to tell, even with complete access to our source code and the local file system, how to decrypt our data files or defeat our licensing mechanism. To defeat this mechanism, the user must relinquish the private key or the keystore itself must be compromised.

To implement this mechanism, we will perform the following tasks:

1. Wrap the secret key that we will use in our application with the RSA cipher and store the wrapped key in a file.
2. Add the `KeyStoreLoginModule` to the JAAS configuration file for our application.

3. Add code to our application to interrogate the JAAS `Subject` and get the user's private key.
4. Use the private key to unwrap the key for the symmetric algorithm.
5. Use the secret key gained in the previous step for all other encryption.

Generating and Wrapping the Secret Key

To generate and wrap the secret key, we will write a small helper class called `SecretKeyWrapper`. This class will generate a DESede key and wrap it with the RSA public key in the specified keystore with the specified alias.

```
package book.standalone.keywrap;

import sun.misc.BASE64Encoder;
import sun.misc.BASE64Decoder;

import javax.crypto.Cipher;
import javax.crypto.SecretKey;
import javax.crypto.KeyGenerator;
import java.io.FileInputStream;
import java.io.FileOutputStream;
import java.security.KeyStore;
import java.security.PublicKey;

/**
 * This utility class will wrap a symmetric DES key using the RSA asymmetric
 * algorithm.
 */
public class SecretKeyWrapper {

  /**
   * The driver method for the KeyWrapper
   * @param args <BR>arg0 - The keystore file name
   * <BR> arg1 - The keystore password
   * <BR> arg2 - The alias of the public key to wrap with
   * <BR> arg3 - The filename for the output file (BASE64 encoded, wrapped key)
   */
  public static void main(String[] args) {

    // Some really thorough argument checking (not!)
    if (args.length != 4) {
      System.out.println("Usage: java SecretKeyWrapper <Keystore file name>
<keystore password> <public key alias> <output file name>");
    }

    try {
      FileInputStream keystoreFile = new FileInputStream(args[0]);
```

```
      KeyStore ks = KeyStore.getInstance("JCEKS");
      ks.load(keystoreFile, args[1].toCharArray());
      keystoreFile.close();

      // Get the certificate from the keystore.
      java.security.cert.Certificate cert  = ks.getCertificate(args[2]);

      PublicKey thePublicKey = cert.getPublicKey();

      // Generate the DES key from our static data.
      KeyGenerator kg = KeyGenerator.getInstance("DESede","BC");
      SecretKey secretKey = kg.generateKey();

      Cipher cipher = Cipher.getInstance("RSA/ECB/OAEPPadding", "BC");

      // Initialize the Cipher with the key and parameters.
      cipher.init(Cipher.WRAP_MODE, thePublicKey );

      // Wrap the key.
      byte[] ciphertext = cipher.wrap(secretKey);

      // BASE64 encode it.
      BASE64Encoder enc = new BASE64Encoder();

      FileOutputStream wrappedKeyFile = new FileOutputStream(args[3]);
      enc.encodeBuffer(ciphertext, wrappedKeyFile);

      System.out.println("Key wrapped to file: " + args[3]);
    } catch (Exception e) {
      e.printStackTrace();
    }
  }
}
```

We then run this code and point it at the intended user's public key, most likely in the form of a signed certificate that we have imported into our keystore. It will generate a file that contains the wrapped key. We will distribute this file with our application. In this example, the file will be called `wrappedkey.fil`.

```
C:\sec\book>java book.standalone.keywrap.SecretKeyWrapper user.ks
password userkey wrappedkey.fil
Key wrapped to file: wrappedkey.fil
```

Using the JAAS KeyStoreLoginModule

With the key wrapped, we will add code to our application to retrieve it. First, we will modify the JAAS configuration file for our application to introduce the `KeystoreLoginModule`, as follows:

```
RetirementClient {
  com.sun.security.auth.module.NTLoginModule required;
  com.sun.security.auth.module.KeyStoreLoginModule required
keyStoreType=JCEKS
      keyStoreURL="file:///${user.dir}/user.ks";
};
```

We add the entry to our JAAS configuration file to require the user to log in to a keystore of type JCEKS located in the user's home directory with the filename user.ks. This module will automatically log in the user, using the callback handler we provide, without our intervention. The dialog box presented to the user by the default DialogCallbackHandler looks like this:

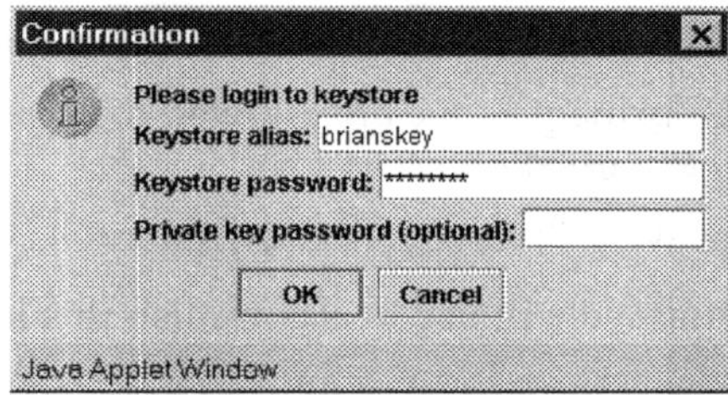

The following is a partial listing of the Subject object returned from the getSubject method of our application's LoginContext.

```
Principal: NTUserPrincipal: Brian
<< More NT Principal Information Removed >>
Principal: CN=Brian, OU=Operations, O="Lester's Retirement Planning, Inc.",
L=Anywhere, ST=AK, C=US
Public Credential: NTNumericCredential: 952
Public Credential:
X.509 Cert Path: length = 1.
=========================================================Certificate 1 start.
  Version: V1
  Subject: CN=Brian, OU=Operations, O="Lester's Retirement Planning, Inc.",
L=Anywhere, ST=AK, C=US
  Signature Algorithm: MD5withRSA, OID = 1.2.840.113549.1.1.4

  Key:  com.sun.net.ssl.internal.ssl.JSA_RSAPublicKey@5fc40c
  Validity: [From: Sun Jun 02 16:45:36 CDT 2002,
               To: Mon Jun 02 16:45:36 CDT 2003]
  Issuer: CN=Brian, OU=Operations, O="Lester's Retirement Planning, Inc.",
L=Anywhere, ST=AK, C=US
. . .
Private Credential: javax.security.auth.x500.X500PrivateCredential@61736e
```

Notice the addition of a new Principal, a new PublicCredential, and a new PrivateCredential to our Subject. These are produced by the KeyStoreLogin-

Module and are instances of X500Principal, X500PublicCredential, and X500PrivateCredential, respectively. The X500Principal acts like an NTUserPrincipal (or any other principal, for that matter) and gives us the ability to write grant statements in our security policy file for that particular principal.

Private credential information—which usually takes the form of a secret key, a private key, or a password—is extremely sensitive, and for good reason—we don't want an application to be able to access our private key without giving it specific permission. Fortunately, the default SecurityManager agrees with us. A private credential cannot be accessed from any Subject unless permission to do so is granted in the prevailing security policy. The permission that needs to be granted is the javax.security.auth.PrivateCredentialPermission. When we grant this permission, we must specify several things:

- The type of private credential we are authorizing the code to access
- The type and which principals we are allowed to access (in other words, whose private credentials we are allowed to see)
- What type of access we will have to those credentials (read, write, or both)

The grant statement that we will use to accomplish this looks like this:

```
grant principal javax.security.auth.x500.X500Principal
  "CN=Brian,OU=Operations,O=Lester's Retirement Planning\\,
Inc.,L=Anywhere,ST=AK,C=US" {
    permission javax.security.auth.PrivateCredentialPermission
            "javax.security.auth.x500.X500PrivateCredential
                          javax.security.auth.x500.X500Principal
\"CN=Brian,OU=Operations,O=Lester's Retirement Planning\\,
Inc.,L=Anywhere,ST=AK,C=US\"", "read";
};
```

Note that lines of code above wrap to fit the printed page. The actual policy file can be downloaded from www.hackingexposedjava.com.

The grant statement above gives code running with the Subject containing the X500Principal matching the string above access to the private credentials for that principal only. This means that the user Brian can access only Brian's private credentials.

CAUTION When matching X500Principals, there can be no spaces between the elements of the distinguished name (DN). Even one space, such as CN=Brian, OU=XXXX..., will cause the name not to match. The parser uses a strict interpretation of RFC 2253. The easiest way to get a DN for a X500Principal that the policy file parser will accept is to actually print the RFC 2253 representation by making a call such as yourPrincipal.getName("RFC2253").

Reading and Unwrapping the Secret Key

Once we have granted the proper permissions to our application, the most appealing thing about our Subject is that it has an instance of PrivateCredential attached, and that instance corresponds to the Principal's RSA private key. We will use this private key, read from the keystore for us by the KeyStoreLoginModule, to unwrap our secret key, which currently resides in the wrappedkey.fil file. The following addition to our ClientFrame class makes this possible:

```
public static SecretKey getPersistenceKey() {
  SecretKey retVal = null;
  Subject ourSubject = loginContext.getSubject();
  InputStream wrappedKeyStream = null;
  try {
    // Get the private credentials from the logged-in subject.
    // Use a privileged block to make sure that we try to read the private
    // credential acting as the logged-in user.
    final Set creds = new HashSet();
    Subject.doAsPrivileged(ourSubject, new PrivilegedAction() {
      public Object run() { creds.addAll(ourSubject.getPrivateCredentials(
        javax.security.auth.x500.X500PrivateCredential.class)); return null; }
    }, null);
    PrivateKey usersPrivateKey = null;

    // We're expecting RSA keys to be here.
    // Grab the first X500PrivateCredential for the Subject.
    Iterator i = creds.iterator();
    while (i.hasNext()) {
      X500PrivateCredential pc = (X500PrivateCredential) i.next();
      usersPrivateKey = pc.getPrivateKey();
      break;
    }
```

We add a method called getPersistenceKey, which allows us to read the wrapped key from our file, unwrap it, and return it to our caller. When this method runs, it will be using our new policy file. Because of this, the call to getPrivateCredentials must be contained in a privileged code block. This will allow the SecurityManager to rightfully grant Brian access to his own private credential, as we specified in our security policy file. If we left off the doAsPrivileged block, the request to getPrivateCredentials would run as the null Subject, and the request would be denied by the SecurityManager.

At this point, we have extracted the private key from the Subject. We now use that key to unwrap the secret key stored in the wrappedkey.fil file.

```
      // Init the cipher
      Cipher c = Cipher.getInstance("RSA/ECB/OAEPPadding", "BC");
      c.init(Cipher.UNWRAP_MODE, usersPrivateKey);

      // Get the stream to read the wrapped key.
      ClassLoader myCL = ClientFrame.class.getClassLoader();
      wrappedKeyStream = myCL.getResourceAsStream(WRAPPED_KEY_RESOURCE);

      // Handle the BASE64 encoding.
```

```
      sun.misc.BASE64Decoder decoder = new sun.misc.BASE64Decoder();
      byte[] wrappedKeyBytes = decoder.decodeBuffer(wrappedKeyStream);

      // Unwrap the key -- notice that we need to specify the algorithm
      // for the *secret* key.

      retVal = (SecretKey) c.unwrap(wrappedKeyBytes,"DESede",Cipher.SECRET_KEY);

    } catch (Exception e) {
      // Handle the exceptions that could possibly occur.
    } finally {
      try { wrappedKeyStream.close(); } catch(Exception exp) { }
    }
    return retVal;
  }
```

The following addition to the `main` method of the `ClientFrame` class calls our new method:

```
// Get the file key from the wrappedkey on disk.
 SecretKey fileKey = getPersistenceKey();

 // Instantiate our model.
 model = new LocalPersistenceService(args[1], fileKey);
```

This nontrivial code has created a mechanism that will allow us to distribute a secret key to one particular individual. If we wanted to have many individuals using the same application, we would send each individual the *same* symmetric key, but the key would be custom wrapped for each user using that particular user's public key.

Though extremely complex, this mechanism is just about as secure as you can get for a stand-alone application.

SUMMARY

In this chapter, we examined how we can prevent software pirates from using our software in ways we never intended for it to be used. As you saw, Java provides a number of techniques for preventing this code misuse, all of which center around the use of the JCE and JAAS packages.

In the next chapter, you will learn how to extend these techniques to defend your application's source code against reverse engineering through decompilation.

CHAPTER 6

THE EXPOSURE
OF BYTECODES

Lester, our fictional Java guru, is feeling more confident now that we have strengthened his retirement application. But Lester must be informed that his application is still vulnerable.

In all of our examples so far, we have been failing to recognize the proverbial elephant standing in the corner. The strength of Java is that it gains platform independence by compiling source code to a collection of bytecodes that can be transported to any platform and interpreted by a JVM running on that platform.

But what if an attacker could simulate a JVM, read our application's bytecodes, and determine exactly how our application worked by reverse-engineering our actual Java source code from the generated bytecodes? Unfortunately, tools that can do just that are readily available. But, fortunately, there are also techniques we can use to disrupt any effort to apply these tools.

THE DANGERS OF REVERSE-ENGINEERING

It is important to recognize that *any* code can be reverse-engineered. In order for a CPU to execute the code, it must be able to read opcodes that it can understand. An opcode, or operation code, is a code which instructs the CPU to execute a particular operation or task, like adding the contents of two CPU registers. If the CPU can read the opcodes, a person can also read these codes. Given enough time, a person can "hand run" the opcodes and figure out what the application code looks like. To take things one step further, this process can be automated and done in a matter of seconds. The same technique can be applied programmatically to Java bytecodes. This process is known as *decompilation*.

Decompilation provides access to the source code of your application. Another potential risk is access to your application's debugging information.

Viewing Debugging Information

Popularity:	3
Simplicity:	8
Impact:	5
Risk rating:	**5**

Most integrated development environments (IDEs) are configured to automatically build Java code with debugging information included. In fact, many production applications are shipped with debugging information; this is what allows a stack trace to be generated with line numbers.

By default, the Java compiler `javac` includes line number and source file information, and many IDEs add the option to include local variable debugging information. When our code is compiled with debugging information, attackers can potentially attach a debugger to our application and watch the code as it runs. They won't have the benefit of source code (unless they decompile it), but they will be able to potentially modify local variables, trace program execution, and determine program flow.

Countermeasure: Turn Off Debugging Information during Compilation

To turn off debugging information, include the `-g:none` option on your `javac` command line:

```
javac -g:none Test.java
```

This simple technique will help eliminate one approach to reverse-engineering or defeating the security mechanisms included in our code.

Decompilation

Popularity:	*8*
Simplicity:	*8*
Impact:	*8*
Risk rating:	*8*

Using decompilation, an attacker could, in the worst case, gain access to all of our source code. If we don't store sensitive data in our code (for example, by using key wrapping or externalizing key information in a Java keystore, as described in the previous chapter), having our source code available to anyone may not bother us too much. However, if our code contains proprietary methods, algorithms, or other technology, having that code exposed to the general public could mean a huge boost for any of our competitors in the marketplace.

Many tools that support decompilation are available. JODE, a popular decompiler freely available from http://jode.sourceforge.net, is the one that we will use as an example. To use JODE, you need to download the JAR file (in this case, `jode-1.1.1.jar`), place it in an appropriate directory, and run it using this command:

```
C:\> java -cp .\jode-1.1.1.jar jode.swingui.Main
```

After we execute this command, we see a screen that looks like Figure 6-1.

Next, we want to add our target application to JODE's classpath. To do this, we do *not* need the `.java` files for the application; we need only the `.class` files. We can do this by

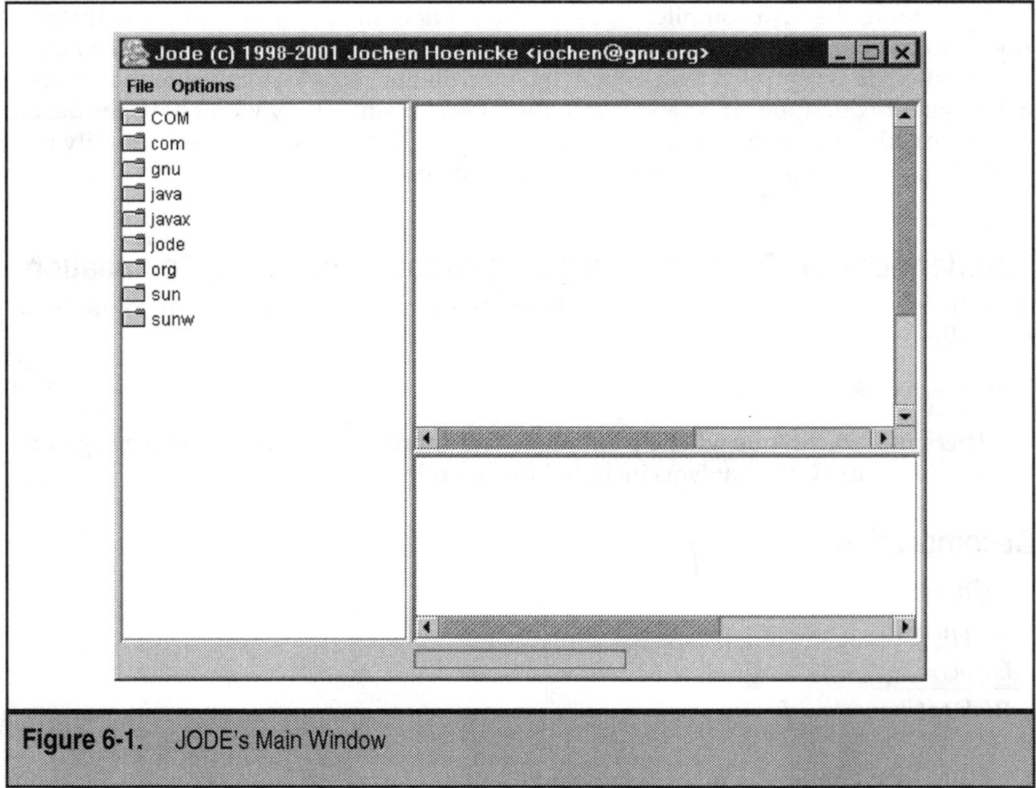

Figure 6-1. JODE's Main Window

selecting the Set Classpath option from JODE's Options menu and filling in the dialog box that appears, like this:

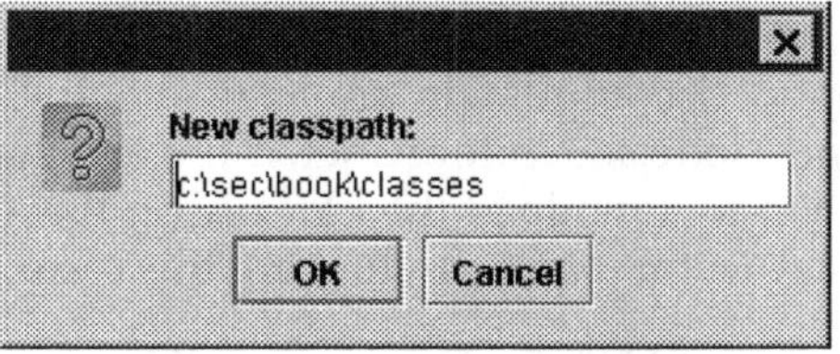

After we set the classpath, we see a tree view of the package structure of our application appear in the JODE window's left pane. Let's see what JODE can tell us about the `SimpleSymmetricLicense` class. We click on the class in the tree view, and we see the display shown in Figure 6-2.

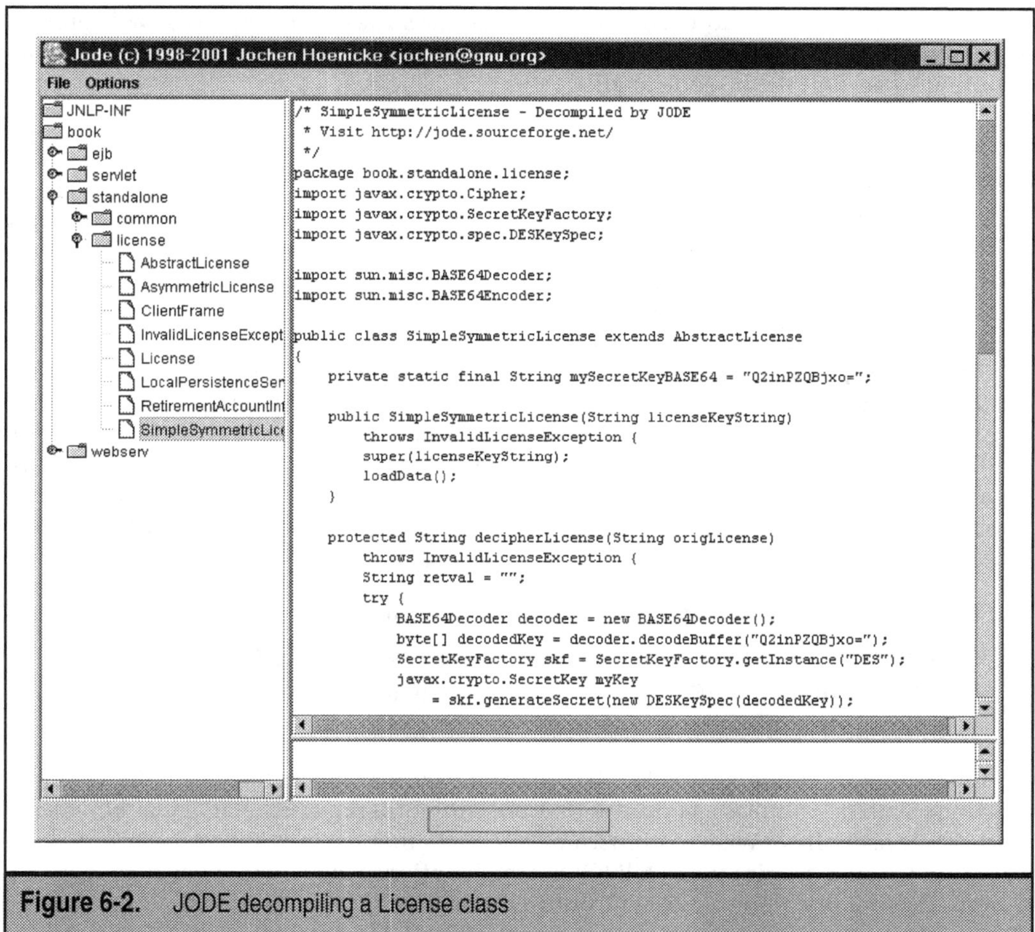

Jode (c) 1998-2001 Jochen Hoenicke <jochen@gnu.org>
File Options
JNLP-INF
book
ejb
servlet
standalone
common
license
AbstractLicense
AsymmetricLicense
ClientFrame
InvalidLicenseExcept
License
LocalPersistenceSer
RetirementAccountInf
SimpleSymmetricLic
webserv
/* SimpleSymmetricLicense - Decompiled by JODE
* Visit http://jode.sourceforge.net/
*/
package book.standalone.license;
import javax.crypto.Cipher;
import javax.crypto.SecretKeyFactory;
import javax.crypto.spec.DESKeySpec;
import sun.misc.BASE64Decoder;
import sun.misc.BASE64Encoder;
public class SimpleSymmetricLicense extends AbstractLicense
{
private static final String mySecretKeyBASE64 = "Q2inPZQBjxo=";
public SimpleSymmetricLicense(String licenseKeyString)
throws InvalidLicenseException {
super(licenseKeyString);
loadData();
}
protected String decipherLicense(String origLicense)
throws InvalidLicenseException {
String retval = "";
try {
BASE64Decoder decoder = new BASE64Decoder();
byte[] decodedKey = decoder.decodeBuffer("Q2inPZQBjxo=");
SecretKeyFactory skf = SecretKeyFactory.getInstance("DES");
javax.crypto.SecretKey myKey
= skf.generateSecret(new DESKeySpec(decodedKey));

Figure 6-2. JODE decompiling a License class

It should be immediately apparent that this is not good. An attacker can see the full source code of our class, including the embedded secret key for our symmetric license cipher. Our comments in the source code are gone, but just about everything else has been faithfully reconstructed from the class bytecode.

Luckily, there are several techniques we can use to thwart decompilation. One method, obfuscation, works like a virtual paper shredder for our bytecode. It will still be possible for an attacker to reverse-engineer our "shredded" code, but it will require an equivalent amount of effort as would be expended trying to paste together a shredded sheet of paper. Unless the information on the piece of paper was really valuable, or the attacker had a lot of time on his or her hands, it wouldn't be worth the time or effort to attempt to paste it together.

Another technique is to encode or encipher class files. This approach will prevent anyone, with the exception of an authorized application user, from decompiling or attempting to decompile the code at all.

Countermeasure: Obfuscation

An *obfuscator* is a program that is built specifically to defeat decompilers. The principle upon which an obfuscator depends is simple: The more obscure something is, the fewer people will be able to understand it. This doesn't mean that nobody will be able to understand your code; it just means that most people, with average tools, won't be able to understand it. Obfuscators for Java apply this principle to Java class files.

The main purpose of an obfuscator is to make a class file that will confuse a decompiler but still be understood by the VM. To do this, obfuscators take advantage of the fact that a computer is the reader of the bytecodes in the VM, and a human is the reader of the output from a decompiler. Therefore, if the class file can be transformed so that it will be hard for a human to read but still easy for a computer to read, that will add a degree of security to our distribution. Obfuscators accomplish this using many techniques, including the following:

- Renaming variables to cryptic, nonintuitive values
- Renaming and repackaging class files to destroy logical groupings
- Making slight modifications in program flow to confuse a decompiler as to the control structures embedded in the code

Interestingly enough, JODE, the decompiler we used to view the `SimpleSymmetricLicense` class, comes with a built-in obfuscator. So, JODE can be used to help defeat itself. If we wish to obfuscate the classes that we previously decompiled, we first need to build a script file to tell JODE which options we want it to use during obfuscation. To simplify things, we will obfuscate only our `SimpleSymmetricLicense` class, along with its related dependent classes. The JODE configuration file, along with instructions concerning how to run the obfuscator, can be found at our website, www.hackingexposedjava.com.

With our configuration file stored in the file `jode.obf`, the following command will obfuscate our code:

```
C:\sec\book\tools>java -cp ./jode-1.1.1.jar jode.obfuscator.Main jode.obf
Jode (c) 1998-2001 Jochen Hoenicke <jochen@gnu.org>
used before: 645320
Loading and preserving classes
preserving: MethodIdentifier book.standalone.license.SimpleSymmetricLicense.main.([Ljava/la
ng/String;)V
Time used: 430
Computing reachability
Time used: 60
used after analyze: 1931016
Renaming methods
```

```
Time used: 41
Transforming the classes
Time used: 20
used after transform: 1918816
Writing new classes
Time used: 80
```

After we run the obfuscator, if we try to decompile the obfuscated code, we notice something extremely interesting, as shown in Figure 6-3. The `SimpleSymmetricLicense` class still exists, but it is accompanied by three other classes: `a`, `b`, and `c`. These are the obfuscated versions of `AbstractLicense`, `License`, and `InvalidLicenseException`, respectively. Notice that the name of `SimpleSymmetricLicense` was not changed, because we instructed the obfuscator to leave it alone, so that we could still use the same command-line arguments for our program. Furthermore, if we look at class `book.standalone.license.b` (formerly the interface `License.java`) in Figure 6-3, we see that the interface is still intact, but there is almost no

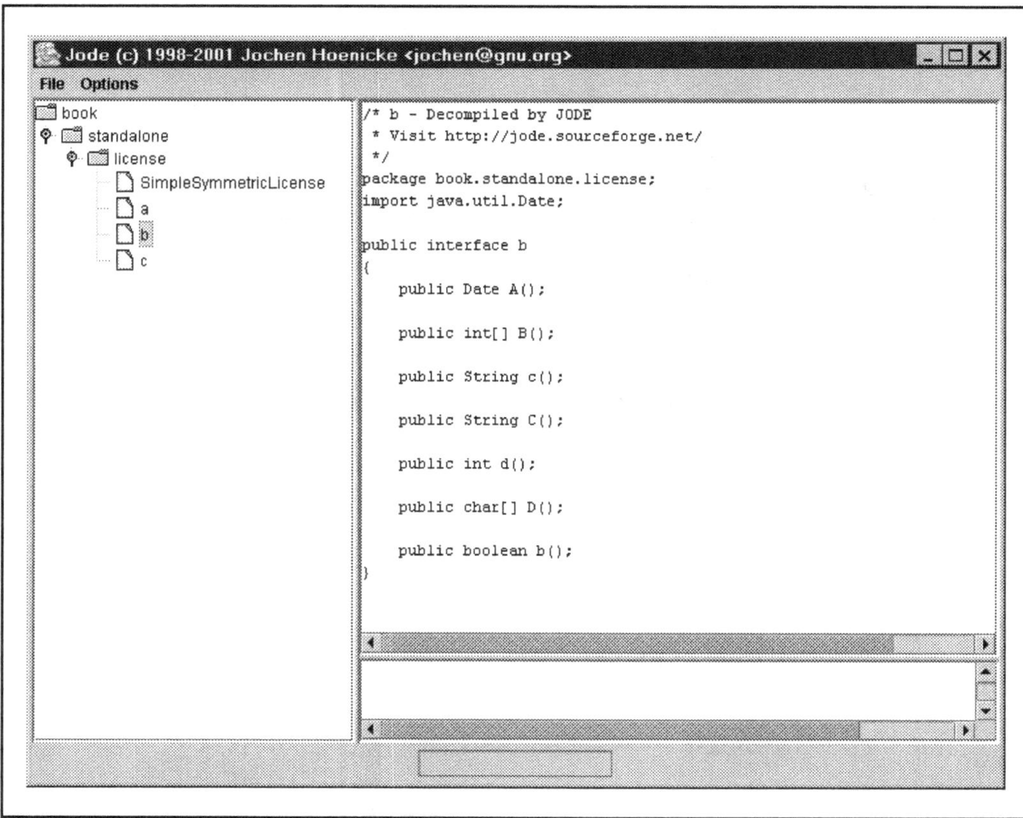

Figure 6-3. Decompilation of obfuscated files

information available to the would-be attacker. It is still a syntactically valid Java file, but all of the names have been mangled to the point that useful information has been lost.

If we decompile the `AbstractLicense` class, we get the partial results, as shown next.

```
public abstract class a implements b
{
    private Date a;
    private int[] A = new int[0];
    private String b;
    private String B;
    private int c;
    private char[] C;
    private boolean d = false;
    private String D;

    protected a(String string) throws c {
       D = string;
    }

    protected final void a() throws c {
      String string = a(D);
      StringTokenizer stringtokenizer = new StringTokenizer(string, ":");
      String string_0_ = stringtokenizer.nextToken();
      SimpleDateFormat simpledateformat = new SimpleDateFormat("MMddyy");
      try {
          a = simpledateformat.parse(string_0_);
      } catch (ParseException parseexception) {
        throw new c("Invalid date in license key");
      }
      int i = Integer.parseInt(stringtokenizer.nextToken());
      A = new int[i];
      for (int i_1_ = 0; i_1_ < i; i_1_++)
          A[i_1_] = Integer.parseInt(stringtokenizer.nextToken());
      b = stringtokenizer.nextToken();
      B = stringtokenizer.nextToken();
      c = Integer.parseInt(stringtokenizer.nextToken());
      C = stringtokenizer.nextToken().toCharArray();
      d = true;
    }

    public final Date A() {
```

```
        if (!d)
            return null;
        return a;
    }
. . .
```

Again, this is readable, but attackers would need to spend more time trying to determine what this code was doing than they would spend if it were not obfuscated.

This code looks very convoluted. We should probably check to make sure that it will still run. If we invoke it, using the following command line, we find that it does run correctly:

```
C:\sec\book\tools>java -cp obfuscated book.standalone.license.SimpleSymmetricLicense
Encrypted License Key:
MH0m35BgL27PxBQ9RBKv00NbMJ6rY/PKHXsNjZFWwe1uoK1IxWTsGAq+DYjURTCi

License constructed from key:
Wed Jun 26 00:00:00 CDT 2002 : [12,15] : 12345abc : BrianBuege : 15 : keystore
```

So, the obfuscator has done its job. The true value in obfuscation comes when a large project is obfuscated, not just three or four classes. In a typical project with between 500 and 1,000 application classes, the obfuscated code is nearly impossible for all but the most diligent attacker to unravel.

But there is a downside to all of this. Obfuscating code does affect your ability to log errors and print stack traces, because all of your classes and methods will now have new names. This can make trying to track down bugs in a production system extremely difficult. To help with this problem, JODE generates a translation table when it obfuscates code. This table will allow you to cross-reference the original class, method, or variable names to the obfuscated values. The following is an extract from the translation table generated during our obfuscation of our license files, focusing on the translation that occurred with the `License` interface:

```
book.standalone.license.b=License
book.standalone.license.b.A.()Ljava/util/Date;=getExpireDate
book.standalone.license.b.B.()[I=getWhichModules
book.standalone.license.b.C.()Ljava/lang/String;=getClientName
book.standalone.license.b.D.()[C=getAppKeyStorePassword
book.standalone.license.b.b.()Z=isValid
book.standalone.license.b.c.()Ljava/lang/String;=getLicenseNumber
book.standalone.license.b.d.()I=getMaxClients
```

We can see that `book.standalone.license.b` actually equals `License` and that the `B` method within that interface originally was the `getWhichModules` method. This is somewhat helpful, but again, in a large project, wading through a stack trace of obfuscated code can be quite tedious.

Countermeasure: Modify, Encode, or Encipher Class Files

What if we want to be absolutely sure that an unauthorized individual can't decompile our classes? It would be nice if there were some way to encrypt or encode our class files. But, if we change the format of our class files, then the VM won't be able to read them; in other words, we won't be able to run them.

Fortunately, Java gives us a mechanism that allows us to decode or decrypt the data in a class file before the VM gets a chance to look at it. To do this, we need to write a custom class loader. By using our custom class loader, we can read an encrypted class file, decrypt it, then pass it to the VM. That way, when the class files reside on the disk, they are almost totally unreadable. However, at runtime, our class loader will decrypt them and hand them to the VM to run.

Java class loading, which we introduced in Chapter 1, is an important but often overlooked subject. The security mechanisms in many application servers, web containers, and stand-alone programs are based on the concept of using different class loaders to partition the namespace of a particular application to ensure that classes loaded from a certain source can access only other classes loaded from that same source, and cannot access other classes to which they're not entitled access. We will take advantage of this powerful mechanism to ensure that our encrypted classes are loaded by our custom class loader.

Here is the strategy we will use to build our custom class loader, specifically designed to load nonstandard `.class` files:

1. Write a utility to encipher, encode, or modify a normal class file so that it is unintelligible to the JVM or any decompilers.
2. Extend the `URLClassLoader` class and override the `findClass` method to find and decrypt the class files we encrypted in the first step.
3. Write a test harness that will load a particular class using our custom class loader.

Writing a Utility to Encode Class Files

Let's first write a simple utility to encode class files. For this utility, we will use an extremely simple encoding scheme: We will encode each byte in an input file by XORing it with a static key. This is not secure and can be easily broken, and it is not the fastest mechanism, since every byte in the target class file must be processed by the decoding class loader every time the class is loaded. However, it will be sufficient for our purposes.

It should be clear that this mechanism could be extended to support any form of encryption. If we wanted more security than the XOR method, we could use the JCE to encipher/decipher the class file using a secret key. This is much more secure, but also much slower. If we wanted more speed than the method presented here, we could modify only several bytes in the file, at predetermined locations. For example, we could XOR the ninth byte with `0f` and the fourtheenth byte with `d0`. Doing this in several locations would make the class file extremely confusing to a decompiler and probably not runnable. Or we could generate a hash of some segment of the class file and insert it in the data at a predetermined point.

The disadvantage to these "modification" approaches is that segments of the file still would exist with plaintext bytecode that potentially could be decompiled. The advantage of these approaches is that they are fast and will hardly slow down class loading.

As with most design decisions, this one involves compromises. We will present a "middle-of-the-road" approach (encoding the entire class file using the XOR operation), but you can use any mechanism you would like to encode, encrypt, or modify the target class files.

We will do our encoding using two files: a utility class called `EncryptionHelper`, which will implement our encoding algorithm in a method called `simpleEncode`, and a class called `FileMangler`, which will apply the encoding in `simpleEncode` to a target file.

```
public class EncryptionHelper {

  /**
   * The key that is used for our encoding and decoding
   */
  private static final byte simpleEncodeKey = 0x1F;
  private EncryptionHelper() {
  }


  /**
   * Encode an array of bytes by XORing them with a one byte key...
   * This is just about as simple as encoding can get.
   * @param cleartext The byte array to be encoded
   * @return An array containing the encoded bytes
   */
  public static byte[] simpleEncode(byte[] cleartext) {
    byte[] retVal = new byte[cleartext.length];
    for (int i=0; i < cleartext.length; i++) {
      retVal[i] = (byte) (cleartext[i] ^ simpleEncodeKey);
    }
    return retVal;
...
```

The following is the listing for the `FileMangler` class.

```
package book.standalone.classloader;

import java.io.*;
```

```
/**
 * This is a simple utility to read an input file and apply the given
 * transformation to it. In this case, it will encode the file using the
 * simpleEncode() method in the EncryptionHelper class.
 */
public class FileMangler {

  /**
   * Take a file and apply the appropriate transformation to it.
   * @param args java FileMangler <Input-File> <Output-File> <Transformation>
   */
  public static void main(String[] args) {
    if (args.length != 3) {
      printUsageMessage();
      System.exit(1);
    }

    try {
      if (args[2].equalsIgnoreCase("simple_encode")) {
        byte[] dataToProcess = FileUtilities.readFileToBuffer(new File(args[0]));
        byte[] encData = EncryptionHelper.simpleEncode(dataToProcess);
        FileUtilities.writeBufferToFile(new File(args[1]),encData);
      } else if (args[2].equalsIgnoreCase("simple_decode")) {
        byte[] dataToProcess = FileUtilities.readFileToBuffer(new File(args[0]));
        byte[] decData = EncryptionHelper.simpleDecode(dataToProcess);
        FileUtilities.writeBufferToFile(new File(args[1]),decData);
      } else {
        System.out.println("Invalid transformation: " + args[2]);
        printUsageMessage();
      }
    } catch (IOException e) {
      e.printStackTrace();
      System.exit(1);
    }

  }

  private static void printUsageMessage() {
    System.out.println("Usage: java FileMangler <Input-File> <Output-File>
[simple_encode | simple_decode]");
  }

}
```

For the sake of utility, the `FileMangler` class will encode or decode a target file, depending on the command-line arguments.

We will use two simple classes to test this mechanism: ASimpleClass and ASimpleReferencedClass. Here is the ASimpleClass (notice that it implements the Runnable interface):

```
/*
 * File: ASimpleClass.java
 * Author: Lester Goodwin
 */

package book.standalone.classloader;

/**
 * A simple class used for demonstration purposes
 */
public class ASimpleClass implements Runnable {

  /**
   * Method that is invoked by the ProgramLauncher
   */
  public void run() {
    System.out.println("This is a really simple class..");
    // Make an instance of a referenced class to show the class loader at
    // work in an indirect sense.
    ASimpleReferencedClass asrc = new ASimpleReferencedClass();
    System.out.println(asrc.sayHello("Lester"));
  }

  public static void main(String[] args) {
    new ASimpleClass().run();
  }
}
```

The ASimpleReferencedClass, shown below, is used by ASimpleClass to generate a greeting message.

```
/*
 * File: ASimpleReferencedClass.java
 * Author: Lester Goodwin
 */

package book.standalone.classloader;
```

```
/**
 * This is a class that has no real purpose other than to sayHello().
 */
public class ASimpleReferencedClass {
  /**
   * Returns a personalized greeting
   * @param name The name of the person to whom the greeting should be directed
   * @return The greeting
   */
  public String sayHello(String name) {
    return "Hello there, " + name;
  }
}
```

When we run `ASimpleClass`, we get the following results.

```
C:\sec\book>java book.standalone.classloader.ASimpleClass
This is a really simple class..
Hello there, Lester
```

Now, to encode these two files with our file mangler, we execute the following command lines:

```
C:\sec\book>java book.standalone.classloader.FileMangler
classes/book/standalone/classloader/ASimpleClass.class
classes/book/standalone/classloader/ASimpleClass.class simple_encode
Read 921 bytes.

C:\sec\book>java book.standalone.classloader.FileMangler
classes/book/standalone/classloader /ASimpleReferenced
Class.class classes/book/standalone/classloader
/ASimpleReferencedClass.class simple_encode
Read 645 bytes.
```

If we now try to run `ASimpleClass`, we see the following results.

```
 C:\sec\book>java book.standalone.classloader.ASimpleClass Exception in
thread "main" java.lang.ClassFormatError:
book/standalone/classloader/ASimpleClass (Bad magic number)
        at java.lang.ClassLoader.defineClass0(Native Method)
. . . <body of stack trace eliminated> . . .
        at java.lang.ClassLoader.loadClassInternal(ClassLoader.java:322)
```

The Java application class loader cannot read the class file because it is in an unknown format. This is what we want. Similarly, if we try to decompile the class, we see the results shown in Figure 6-4.

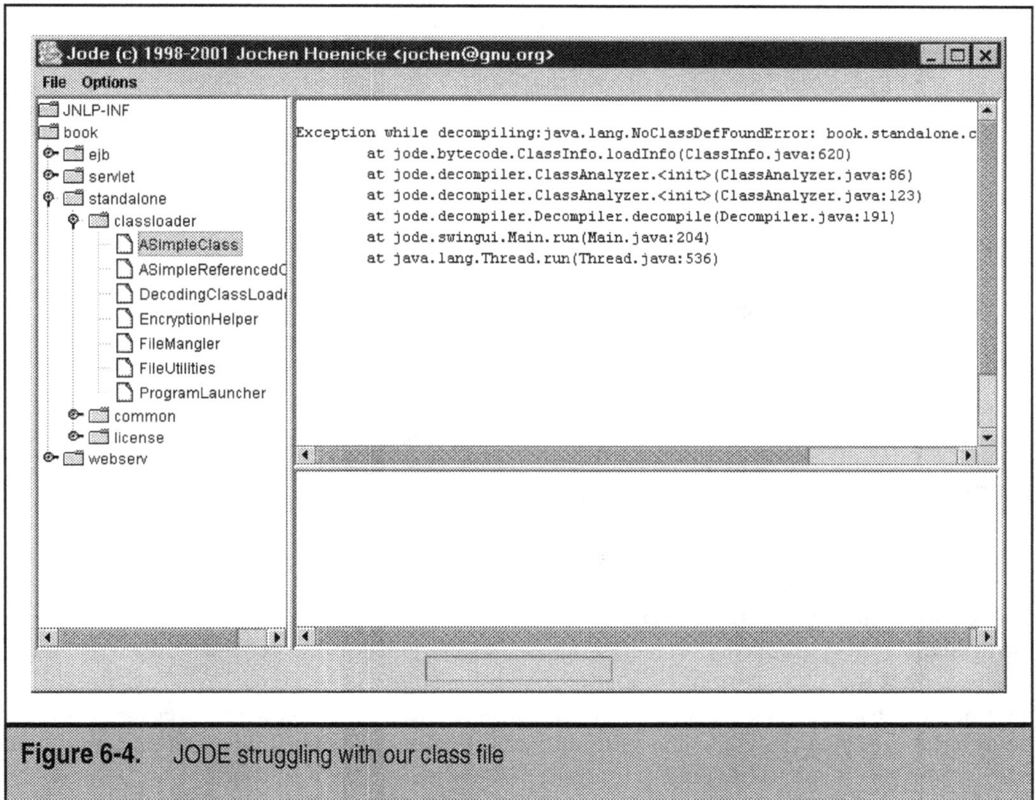

Figure 6-4. JODE struggling with our class file

This part is really good. Any decompiler someone tries to use on this class file will not be able to read it. We still have a pretty large problem though: The code won't run. To fix this, we need to build our own class loader to decode the class files that we just encoded.

Building a Class Loader

When a class loader is requested to load a class, it should perform the following process:

1. Delegate the call to load the class to its parent class loader. This will automatically search the system classes, as well as any other classpaths supported by the parent class loader *before* we even get a chance to load it. If the class has already been loaded, the parent is also responsible for returning it to us. This is incredibly important because, by delegating the request to load to our parent first, it stops a potential attacker from spoofing a system class.
2. If the parent cannot find the class in question, the class loader should traverse its classpath, looking for the appropriate class file.

3. Once the class file is found, the class loader is responsible for creating a `ProtectionDomain` for the loaded class, based on the `CodeSource` and the `PermissionCollection` involved. This is necessary because the `AccessController` will compare the codebases from the `grant` statements in the current security policy file to the `ProtectionDomain` for the current class. Additionally, it will automatically grant the class any permissions specified in the `PermissionCollection` for the class, regardless of what the policy file contains.
4. The class loader should then define the class by calling the `defineClass` method in the abstract `ClassLoader` superclass. This method will validate the bytecode for the class, attach the relevant `ProtectionDomain`, and return an instance of the `java.lang.Class` class corresponding to the class in question.
5. The class loader should return the defined class to its caller.

There are some additional steps that need to be implemented if a class loader is built from scratch instead of built by extending an existing one. However, for our purposes, we will extend an existing `ClassLoader` class, so the steps above will be sufficient for us.

To build our own class loader, we will extend the `URLClassLoader` class in the `java.net` package and override the `findClass` method. There is much additional complexity that is embodied in a class loader. However, for our purposes, all we need to know is that if a class cannot be loaded by the system class loader or is not already in memory, the `findClass` method in our class loader will be called to request that we search the classpath, load the class file, and pass the bytes corresponding to its contents to our superclass's `defineClass` method. The `defineClass` method will read the bytecode, verify it, and return an instance of the `java.lang.Class` class, which represents the class that has been loaded.

Here is the code for our simple decoding class loader. Notice that it uses the `EncryptionHelper` class to decode the actual bytes in the class file:

```
/*
 * File: DecodingClassLoader.java
 * Author: Lester Goodwin
 */
package book.standalone.classloader;

import java.net.URLClassLoader;
import java.net.URL;
import java.io.IOException;
import java.io.InputStream;
import java.security.ProtectionDomain;
import java.security.CodeSource;
import java.security.PermissionCollection;
import java.util.jar.Manifest;
```

```
/**
 * This is a special class loader, which will read .class files that have
 * been either enciphered or encoded and, at runtime, decipher or decode them
 * before returning them to the Java runtime environment. This class loader
 * DOES NOT support loading classes from JAR files.
 */
public class DecodingClassLoader extends URLClassLoader {

  public DecodingClassLoader(URL[] urls, ClassLoader parent) {
    super(urls, parent);
  }

  /**
   * Finds and loads the class with the specified name from the URL search
   * path.
   *
   * @param name The name of the class
   * @return The resulting class
   * @exception ClassNotFoundException if the class could not be found
   */
  protected Class findClass(String name)
      throws ClassNotFoundException {
    Class retVal = null;

    // A debugging message so we know what our class loader is up to...
    System.out.println("   Loader: Finding class: " + name);
```

The following sequence of code gets the classpath from our parent, creates a relative path to the class file we are trying to load, and then traverses the classpath looking for that file.

```
    URL[] urls = super.getURLs();

    // Convert the fully qualified package name to a relative path.
    String endOfPath = name.replace('.', '/');

    byte[] classBytes = null;

    for (int i=0; i < urls.length; i++) {
      try {
        // Try to find the class at URL[i] in our classpath.
        URL tmpURL = new URL(urls[i].toExternalForm() + endOfPath + ".class");
        // Another status message for those people who are interested
        System.out.println("   Loader: Searching: " + tmpURL);

        // Try to open the URL.
        InputStream is = tmpURL.openStream();
```

If we can find the class file, we then read it into a byte array. Once we have the bytes, we need to tell our superclass (through the `defineClass` method) exactly where we found the class, so that it can be associated with the proper codebase. We do this by constructing an instance of the `CodeSource` class and passing in the URL from which we loaded the class file. We then ask our superclass for the set of permissions that have been granted to code originating at our `CodeSource` (`super.getPermissions`), and then use the `CodeSource` and the `Permissions` to construct a new `ProtectionDomain`.

CAUTION You may have noticed that you have a lot of power here. You could lie to your superclass about the URL you have loaded a particular class from, or you could add extra permissions to the `PermissionCollection` you generate. For this reason, installing a new class loader is constrained by the `RuntimePermission createClassLoader`. This is an extremely dangerous permission to grant any application that originates from an unknown source. In the next chapter, you will see how you can use digital signatures and the `jarsigner` utility to guarantee that you grant this permission only to code that a trusted entity has signed.

```
// Read the class file into a byte[].
classBytes = FileUtilities.readStreamToBuffer(is);
is.close();

// Assign the protection domain for the class -- no static permissions.
CodeSource currentCodeSource = new CodeSource(tmpURL,null);
// Defer the permission collection build to our superclass.
PermissionCollection permCollection =
     super.getPermissions(currentCodeSource);

ProtectionDomain protDomain =
    new ProtectionDomain(currentCodeSource, permCollection);

// Define the package -- New in JDK 1.4.
definePackage(name,new Manifest(),null);
```

The following code decodes the bytes corresponding to the class file and then calls the `defineClass` method, passing the decoded bytes and the `ProtectionDomain` we built above. If the class verifies successfully, we then return the `Class` object to our caller. If it doesn't verify, we assume the class was actually in normal class file format (and consequently was corrupted when we attempted to "decode" it) and delegate the loading of the class to the `findClass` method in our superclass to load the unencoded class file.

```
// Decode the bytes.
classBytes = EncryptionHelper.simpleDecode(classBytes);

try {
  // This is the call that actually builds the instance of the Class
```

```
          // object.
          retVal = defineClass(name,classBytes,0,classBytes.length,protDomain);
          return retVal;
        } catch (ClassFormatError e) {
          // It's not encoded in our format... Must be a real class file.
          // Let our superclass handle it.
          System.out.println("   Loader: Non-encoded class found: " + name);
          break;
        }
      } catch (IOException e) {
        // Do nothing.. we couldn't open the URL (could be 'cause it didn't exist).
      }
    }
    if (retVal == null) {
      // Delegate to our superclass.
      System.out.println("   Loader: Letting parent find: " + name);
      retVal = super.findClass(name);
    }

    return retVal;
  }
}
```

Writing a Test Harness

Our last step is to write a driver program that will actually replace the default application class loader with our class loader. To do this, we need to construct a new instance of our class loader, use it to load the top-level class in our application (in this case, the `ASimpleClass`), and then call the `run` method. Because of Java's sophisticated class loading semantics, all classes that the `run` method in `ASimpleClass` references or uses will be loaded using the same class loader as the loader that loaded `ASimpleClass`. In other words, from this point on, all classes will be loaded using our `DecodingClassLoader`.

Here's a look at what a sample test harness might look like. Notice that we implement the `Runnable` interface in `ASimpleClass` and make sure it has a default, no-argument constructor. This will help us construct an instance of the class and call the `run` method without referencing the class directly by name (`ASimpleClass`). If we hardcoded a reference to `ASimpleClass` in our driver code—for example, a call to the constructor—it would force the default application class loader to try to load `ASimpleClass`, which would fail because we have changed the format of the class file. Therefore, we need to write our code in such a way that `ASimpleClass` will not load until our `DecodingClassLoader` is in force. The following code accomplishes this.

```
/*
 * File: ProgramLauncher.java
 */
```

```
package book.standalone.classloader;

import java.net.URL;
import java.net.URLClassLoader;

public class ProgramLauncher {


  /**
   * This program will launch the run() method of a class (which must implement
   * the Runnable interface) using the DecodingClassLoader.
   * @param args arg0 - The fully qualified name of the class to run
   */
  public static void main(String[] args) {
    Class target = null;
    try {

      // The default appclassloader is a URL classloader.
      URLClassLoader myCL = (URLClassLoader) ProgramLauncher.class.getClassLoader();
      // Transfer our current working classpath to our own classloader.
      URL[] urls = myCL.getURLs();
      ClassLoader newLoader = new DecodingClassLoader(urls,null);
      target = newLoader.loadClass(args[0]);

      // Notice that we ARE NOT multi-threading here...
      // We are just using the Runnable interface as a vehicle to start
      // code in our loaded class.
      Runnable r = (Runnable) target.newInstance();
      r.run();
      System.out.println("Finished run...");
    } catch (Exception e) {
      e.printStackTrace();
    }
  }
}
```

When we use this launcher to run our encoded class files, we get the results shown next.

We can see the results of the class loader searching through the classpath, finding the proper class files, loading them, decoding them, and then handing them off to the Java runtime, where they execute successfully. Again, if we try to run `ASimpleClass` directly without our `ProgramLauncher`, we get the following result:

```
   Loader: Finding class: book.standalone.classloader.ASimpleClass
   Loader: Searching:
file:/C:/sec/book/book/standalone/classloader/ASimpleClass.class
   Loader: Searching:
file:/C:/java/j2sdkee1.3/lib/j2ee.jarbook/standalone/classloader/ASimple
Class.class
```

```
   Loader: Searching:
file:/C:/sec/book/classes/book/standalone/classloader/ASimpleClass.class
Read 908 bytes.
This is a really simple class..
   Loader: Finding class: book.standalone.classloader.ASimpleReferencedClass
   Loader: Searching:
file:/C:/sec/book/book/standalone/classloader/ASimpleReferencedClass.class
   Loader: Searching: file:/C:/java/j2sdkee1.3/lib/j2ee.jar
book/standalone/classloader /ASimpleReferencedClass.class
   Loader: Searching: file:/C:/sec/book/classes/ book/standalone/classloader
/ASimpleReferencedClass.class
Read 645 bytes.
Hello there, Lester
Finished run...
```

There is one weakness in this approach that needs to be addressed before it is production-ready: The `ProgramLauncher` and the `DecodingClassLoader` cannot be encoded or encrypted. The normal Java application class loader needs to be able to read those classes. This means that both of these classes potentially could be decompiled.

To correct this weakness, we can obfuscate the `ProgramLauncher` and the `DecodingClassLoader`, or we can use a more secure approach. It won't matter if an attacker can see our launcher and class loader if we are using a mechanism for decryption that requires a key and the key data is not stored in our class files.

Key wrapping, as described in the previous chapter, is an excellent solution for this issue. We could, instead of encoding using the XOR operation, encrypt all of our class files using a secret key and a symmetric algorithm. Then we could wrap that secret key with an asymmetric algorithm combined with the user's public key and deliver the wrapped key to the user with our application. When our `ProgramLauncher` ran, it could use the `KeystoreLoginModule` to get the user's private key, unwrap the secret key, and give it to the class loader to decrypt the class files. Using this technique, the only way the code could be decompiled would be to somehow get the private key of a licensed user, unwrap the secret key used to encrypt the class files, and then use that key to decrypt and decompile the files in question. This would require a compromise of a particular user's private key, which is much less likely to happen. The value of this technique is that it makes our code highly resistant to attacks by people outside any organization licensed to have our code.

What have we accomplished with this effort? As we discussed previously, regardless of what we do, anyone who is authorized to run the code can decompile the code, given enough time and sophistication. What this scheme does is prevent people who can't run the code from decompiling it to figure out how it works.

Is this overhead worthwhile? For most applications, probably not. But if your business hinges on trade secrets contained in your algorithms, it might be worthwhile to pursue a path such as this.

THE DANGERS OF EMBEDDED STRINGS

Lately, in many tutorials, books, and articles, there has been much discussion regarding the use of the `java.lang.String` class to store password or other sensitive information. The risk associated with the `String` class is that, since `String` objects are immutable, and since garbage collection in Java is not controllable by the user, there could be `String` objects containing user passwords floating around in memory, long after they've been used for authentication. An attacker could scan an application's memory to extract this password information.

The recommended solution to this dilemma is to store all sensitive information in arrays of `chars` (`char[]`). The advantage to this approach is that after the password is checked, it can be removed by overwriting the array with some other data, perhaps using the `Arrays.fill` method. This way, the password information is in memory only long enough to check, and then it's deleted and cannot be scanned.

Although theoretically this is a great idea, it's almost impossible to implement in a real-world application. This is because many of the classes commonly used in Java enterprise computing *require* passwords to be passed as `String` objects. So even if you store the password in a `char[]` array, usually you must convert it to a `String` object to pass it to anything else. This is just as bad as you storing it in a `String` yourself, since the `String` you pass as an argument could potentially float around in memory for quite awhile.

For example, the JDBC `DriverManager` and `DataSource` classes both take `String` objects for passwords, not `char` arrays. Additionally, most JNDI implementations will take only `String` objects as passwords (usually passed as `String` entries in a hash table). Most proprietary LDAP libraries for Java require `String` objects to be passed as passwords. The JMS `QueueConnectionFactory` and `TopicConnectionFactory` classes require passwords as `String` objects. Also, the JavaMail API requires `String` objects as passwords in the `javax.mail.PasswordAuthentication` class.

So, as a rule, you should try to minimize your use of `String` objects in your application, but it will be very difficult for you to totally eliminate them. Additionally, you need to make the decision whether the use of `char[]` arrays could potentially make your code more error prone. Remember that such arrays *are* mutable, unlike `String` objects. If an array is passed to another method, the called method can freely modify the array (perhaps prematurely clearing its values), thus making the array unusable for the calling method. In large applications, this can introduce many issues regarding "Who clears out the array?" If you abide by the solid design principle that "Whoever makes it, must clean it up…," you'll find yourself making copies of the `char[]`s all of the time. This is because whenever you ask for a password from a system class that returns a `char[]`, in many cases, you'll want to make a copy of it to be sure that it won't be deleted.

For this reason, the authors remain agnostic about this topic and use both methods interchangeably. However, if you are striving for the highest level of security in your applications, you should be using arrays of characters to store your sensitive information, not `String` objects.

String Parsing

Popularity:	3
Simplicity:	9
Impact:	4
Risk rating:	**5**

One technique that an attacker could use to glean information from your class files without decompilation is scanning the files for string literals embedded within. As you probably already know, whenever you write a line of code that looks like this:

```
String password = "shhhhhhhh!";
```

The string literal `"shhhhhhhh!"` is stored in the constant pool within the generated class file.

Attackers can use various utilities, such as the popular Unix `strings` utility, to scan your class files for embedded strings. Then they could potentially use the strings they found to discover likely password strings. As you will see in the next chapter, although it isn't a good idea, it is very common for user ID and password information (especially for databases) to be hardcoded in application clients. Doing this makes the client extremely vulnerable to an attack using `strings` or a similar utility.

Countermeasure: Eliminate String Literals with Sensitive Information

Wherever possible, you should eliminate string literals containing sensitive information from your application, preferring instead to accept them from a user as input, or load them from another secure source.

You may have noticed that in Lester's original application, he was storing his secret key information as an embedded string in a class file. So, his application was vulnerable to a string parsing attack. To eliminate this weakness, he should use either a keystore or wrapped key for storage of his key material instead. You saw an example of this technique in the previous chapter on code licensing.

The main point is this: The longer you hold onto credential information, the more vulnerable it is to exploitation. Your goal should be to keep credentials within your application for the minimum amount of time necessary to use them for authentication, and then release them. If you hardcode credentials into your application as string literals, then these credentials are with you forever. And forever is a very long time to try to keep a secret.

SUMMARY

In this chapter, we saw how to protect our application from the attacker who would like to decompile our code. We saw that code obfuscation makes the relatively simple process of decompiling Java bytecodes a much more difficult task for the attacker. By encrypting class files and using a custom class loader we can make our application code even more secure. We also saw some simple steps that you can take to defend against an attacker attaching a debugger to your application, or conducting a string parsing attack.

In the next chapter, you will see how to extend these techniques to attack and subsequently secure a client-server application accessing a relational database, deployed as both an applet and via Java WebStart.

CHAPTER 7

HACKING JAVA CLIENT-SERVER APPLICATIONS: ANOTHER TIER TO ATTACK

The arrival of low-cost, prolific, networking technology introduced the advent of, debatably, the simplest form of networked application: the two-tier, client-server architecture. In most cases, a traditional client-server application is implemented with what is commonly referred to as a *fat client*, meaning that the majority of processing work is done on the client workstation, while the server is used primarily as a data repository. In this configuration, the server is usually running some type of relational database management system (RDBMS).

Another form of two-tier application is a *thin client*, in which most of the processing load is located on the server, not the client. Simple web applications that use HTML content for their presentation fall under this category. In this chapter, we will focus on how to attack and consequently secure two-tier, fat client applications. We will cover thin-client applications, along with more sophisticated architectures, in future chapters.

In a typical corporate enterprise computing environment, two-tier, fat-client applications are still commonly used. The two-tier architecture lends itself well to small or medium-sized departmental applications that don't require the full enterprise scalability or reliability that a mutitier architecture offers. Unfortunately, many fat-client applications have the poorest security.

In the previous chapter, you saw many techniques for strengthening a typical stand-alone Java application. In this chapter, we will modify our sample application to conform to a client-server architecture. The techniques for securing a stand-alone application are still valid in a client-server application. However, we will need to extend those techniques to support the new threats to our application in a networked environment.

THE CLIENT-SERVER IMPLEMENTATION

To change our sample application to accommodate a two-tier architecture, we will use the `RetirementAccountInfo` interface developed in previous chapters and write a new persistence service to replace the `LocalPersistenceService` we were using in the `book.standalone` examples. This new persistence service will store and retrieve information from a relational database using a JDBC Type IV (thin) driver. We will use MySQL as our relational database (www.mysql.org) and configure it with two users in addition to the administrator: Lester and Brian. Each user has all of the necessary database privileges to successfully run the application and read from and write to the application tables. Figure 7-1 illustrates the client-server deployment for the retirement application. See the website www.hackingexposedjava.com for instructions regarding how to install and configure the working client-server version of Lester's test application.

This implementation is, much like the stand-alone implementation in the previous chapter, representative of security-related vulnerabilities typically found in two-tier, client- server business applications. We have modified the code in the client to use the database server for authentication by attempting to establish a JDBC connection with the provided username and password. Additional authentication and authorization are still

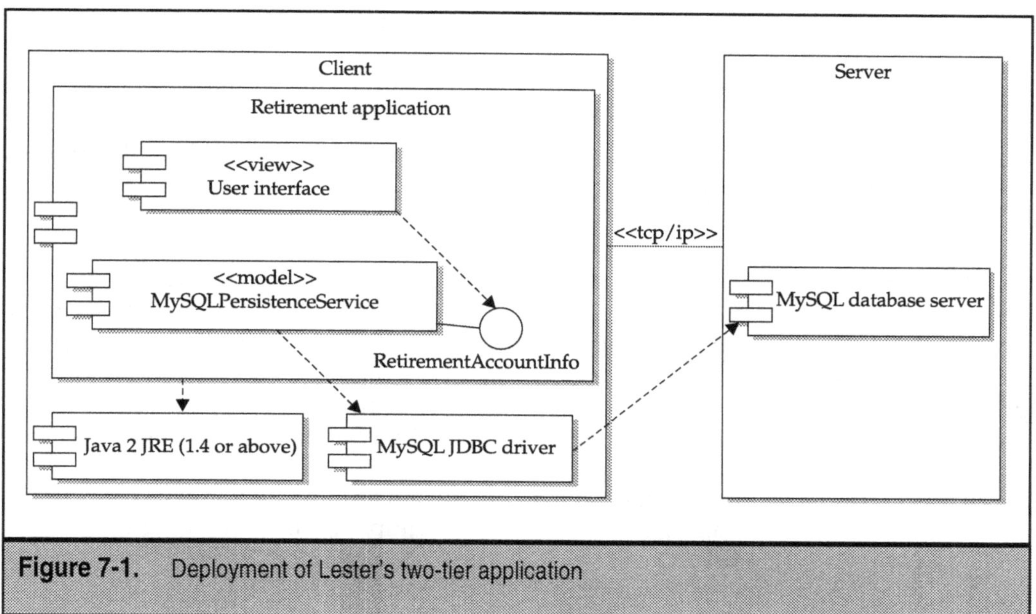

Figure 7-1. Deployment of Lester's two-tier application

done via JAAS using the `NTUserPrincipal` mechanism introduced in Chapter 5. All data is persisted in the database using JDBC `PreparedStatements`. The database schema for the application is extremely similar to the flat-file schema used for our `LocalPersistenceService`, as shown here:

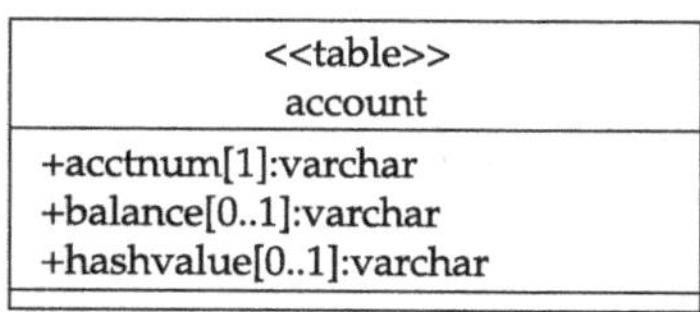

THE DANGERS OF A CLIENT-SERVER ARCHITECTURE

Attacking a client-server application is, in some ways, easier than attacking a stand-alone application. A client-server application necessarily has one additional component that makes it much more attractive to the prospective attacker: the network. The client in a client-server application must have the ability to communicate with the server over a network of some type. This removes the previous restriction of physical access that we had with a stand-alone application. Attackers no longer need to be physically at the workstation in question. They can attack the client workstation by using a combination of operating-system–level attack techniques.

A two-tier application can typically be attacked in the following ways:

- Attack the database server itself. Gain access to the data within and read or change it outside the application.
- Attack the data as it transits the network between the client and the database server via network monitoring, or in sophisticated attacks, IP spoofing.
- Attack the application itself on the client side.

We will mainly focus on client-side attacks in this chapter, although we will cover the other attack categories briefly from the perspective of what the application developer can do to aid the system security specialist in these areas. We will assume that a potential attacker can gain access to the workstation client or the database server with typical user privileges. In other words, we will assume that our system security has been partially breached (user-level access has been compromised), but that the attacker cannot gain administrative access to the database server.

In the course of the following chapters, we will cover how the following techniques can be applied to the sample application in order to improve its security stature:

- Sealing packages to prevent class file spoofing
- Using remotely loaded JAAS configuration files, policy files and keystores
- Building a custom JAAS `LoginModule` to perform authentication with a RDBMS via JDBC
- Building custom principals and credentials to track application-level access
- Implementing security with an applet-based client
- Implementing security with a Java WebStart client

We will also provide a brief overview of high-level techniques for database security, as well as applying secure SSL tunneling technology to our JDBC connection to encrypt traffic with the database.

NOTE If you are following along in the full code examples downloaded from www.hackingexposedjava.com, you will notice that we have undone some of the changes that we implemented in the last two chapters, most notably the use of the `KeystoreLoginModule`, `X500Credential`, and `Principal` information in the sample application client. We have done this purely for instructional purposes, to keep our code clear and focused. The fact that we removed these technologies does not mean that they do not apply to client-server applications, or that they wouldn't work with the techniques we present in this chapter.

Watching the Basket: Application Database Security

It is common for most applications to store data in some sort of relational database. Provisions for security in these databases differ somewhat by vendor, and they are typically the domain of the database administrator (DBA). However, there are some database attacks that a typical application developer can help degrade or prevent.

The key point to remember is that securing the database is a separate job that needs to be done in concert with system-level and application-level security planning. The application developer should be aware of these techniques and should try to build the application to be "database-security friendly," but the expertise and knowledge to successfully design a database security strategy lies with the DBA.

Compromise of Application-level Database Credentials

Popularity:	*5*
Simplicity:	*3*
Impact:	*10*
Risk rating:	***6***

Many two-tier applications use special application credentials to access the database. For example, instead of granting individual users access to read and update the application's tables in the database, the application itself authenticates the user using a different method, then authenticates itself with the database using a predefined application ID and password. This raises the issue of where to store the application user ID and password.

Many times, the application credentials are either hardcoded into the client-side application code or specified in a property file on the client workstation or a network file system. This saves the DBA the time and effort of setting up database privileges for each user, and protects against the perceived threat of a particular user accessing a native SQL interface to the database in question (using the user's own database credentials) and modifying application data.

This seems like a good idea in general, but these credentials are usually highly vulnerable to compromise. When they are compromised, they give the attacker *carte-blanche* access to the application data, without the benefit of any database-level auditing or logging that might have tracked the changes of users logged in using their own credentials. Now all we can see in our database audit trail are changes by a semi-anonymous "application" account. We're not sure whether these changes were made by an authorized user or by a rogue individual using a direct SQL interface to update our application data. Furthermore, once a compromise is detected, updating the credentials—specifically the new password—on all of the clients is usually a time-consuming, arduous task. There are several countermeasures we can use to defend ourselves against an attack such as this.

Countermeasure: JDBC Data Sources with JNDI Authentication and Embedded Credentials

One way to help handle application-level credential compromise is to place the database credentials in a single, secure location: a JDBC `DataSource` object. Changing the credentials on compromise is relatively easy and can be done in one place: the `DataSource` configuration. With this solution, there is no need to store application database credentials on client workstations. Access to the `DataSource` itself is then protected by another enterprise-level authentication mechanism, such as a JNDI/LDAP-based scheme, which could authenticate a particular user's access to the DataSource with *that user's credentials*. Once the application retrieves the DataSource using the user's credentials, it can then get connections from the DataSource that connect with the necessary application credentials.

In many cases, this is a preferred countermeasure for this particular attack, but sometimes the infrastructure to support it does not exist. It usually requires a distributed naming service and `DataSource` support from the database vendor, or at the very least, the installation of a JDBC Type II (thick) driver on the client workstation, which makes applet and Java WebStart deployments more difficult. However, this technique is still valuable and should be considered as a valid option in many enterprise environments.

Countermeasure: User-level Database Passwords and JCE for Encryption

Another way to protect data is to use the JCE, much as we did in Chapter 4, to encrypt sensitive data, write it to the database, and also generate a message digest for each data record. This will prevent a person from changing the information in the database, outside our application, without our knowledge. In fact, our sample program starts out using this approach.

This countermeasure has some big advantages, but also comes with some serious liabilities. Its primary advantage is that *any* user of the database with access to the application tables, including the DBA, cannot read or change the data residing in those tables without us knowing about it (the message digest will be invalidated). Additionally, sensitive data is secure as it transits the network, because it is encrypted and decrypted on the client side, before being passed over the network to the database server.

The major weakness of this approach is that the encrypted data is not very amenable to ad-hoc queries. All data that the developer wants to use as either search criteria or index values must be left unencrypted. In many cases, this places excessively unrealistic constraints on the application developer and makes this approach unfeasible.

Countermeasure: User-level Database Passwords and Stored Procedures or Callable Statements for Access Control

An extremely common approach to securing the database-tier of the application focuses on allowing no user or application-level access to the application tables at all, but instead controlling access through stored procedures or callable statements on the database server. Individual users or applications are then granted access to these procedures or statements by the DBA, rather than being granted access to the actual tables. The procedures are maintained by the DBA, and as such, modify the database in a controlled manner. With this approach, an attacker with normal user-level database access can access application data only by using these stored procedures and will find it much more difficult to modify data in an ad-hoc manner. Additionally, we are virtually guaranteed that all attempts to modify information can be logged and audited in a clear, easily accessible manner.

This approach also comes with some weaknesses. One weakness is that portions of the application logic must reside in the database server, usually written in a database-scripting language. This can hinder application maintenance and support. Also, this is usually a database-specific solution. Moving the application to another DMBS would require rewriting all stored procedures.

NOTE In the authors' opinion, the amount of effort expended by developers to build "database-independent" JDBC code is grossly out of proportion to the number of times business applications are actually moved to a different relational database. Usually, from an application design standpoint, reuse efforts are much better spent building a common, shared, "persistence" layer, rather than attempting to write database independent JDBC-level code to guard against the unlikely event the application is ever ported to another RDBMS.

In some cases, there is so much business knowledge required to check the validity of information entering the database that it becomes unfeasible to write stored procedures without placing the entire application on the database server. In cases such as this, it is usually a much better idea to pursue an architecture involving an application server. (See Chapter 12 for more details on security issues involved in this approach.)

Securing the Database Connection

Whenever data is passed across a network, the possibility for eavesdropping exists. The easy availability of packet sniffers and other network-monitoring utilities, coupled with the sensitivity level of enterprise data bound for a repository such as an RDMBS, make the client-server database connection an attractive target.

Generally, securing a connection to the database is considered to be a system security or DBA-level task. However, as application developers, we need to be aware of the risks, so that we can help the other security specialists to implement a defense in depth with several levels of protection to guard our sensitive data.

Illicit Monitoring of Database Connections—Packet Sniffing

Popularity:	3
Simplicity:	1
Impact:	8
Risk rating:	**4**

If we use Ethereal, a common packet sniffer for Windows (www.ethereal.com), to look at the packets sent between our sample client application and the MySQL database, we see somewhat disconcerting information. First, we can identify the login packet that is sent to our database by monitoring inbound TCP traffic to port 3306 (the MySQL port) on our database server. If we look at the login packet, we see the information shown in Figure 7-2.

We can see in the highlighted packet payload that the username (lester) we are using to log in to the database is sent in the clear. The bytes following the username are the encrypted password (in this case, the string `password`). Unfortunately, things get worse. If we continue to monitor the packets corresponding to our database session, we can gain even more information, as shown in Figure 7-3.

We can see here that the entire text of our SQL request is sent over the network in the clear. Anyone with a packet sniffer can see that our application is performing a `SELECT ACCTNUM FROM ACCOUNT` SQL statement on the database. The database response to the query is similarly unencrypted, as shown in Figure 7-4.

We can clearly read the two account numbers that are the response to our query: 12345 and 54321. Obviously, information like this could be extremely valuable to an attacker. Note that even though we are using MySQL as an example here, the majority of other JDBC/RDBMS combinations, when run in their default mode, behave exactly like this.

How likely is an attack like this? If your application is performing a direct JDBC connection over the Internet (which is almost never a good idea), you are incurring an extremely high risk of compromise. If, however, your application runs on an internal network or a VPN, your risk is somewhat less. But remember, to exploit a technique like this, an attacker only needs access to *any* network segment that your packets traverse on their way to the database server.

System security specialists typically provide internal networks with a much higher level of security than the Internet has, but passive attacks like this are extremely difficult to defend against at a system level. Once an attacker has access to one of the segments

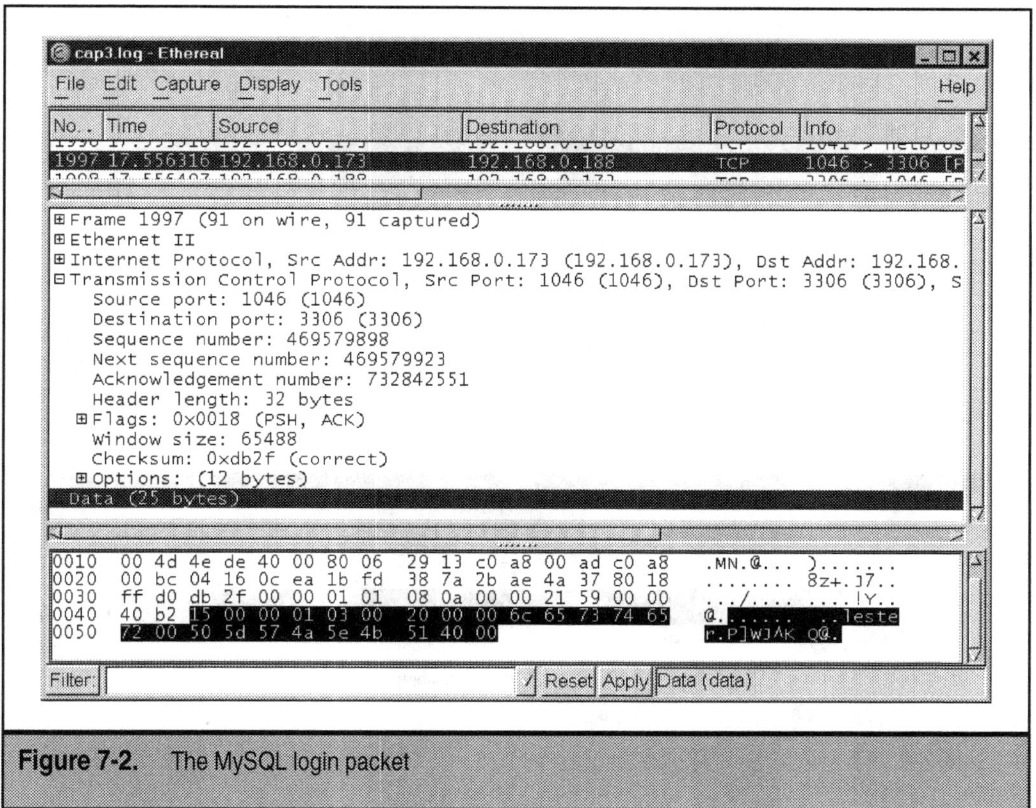

Figure 7-2. The MySQL login packet

our packets are routed over, passive monitoring can yield the information we saw in Figures 7-2, 7-3, and 7-4.

The best defense is to help the system-level security specialists and make sure that, even if attackers can see our packets traversing the network, they can't gain any useful information.

Countermeasure: Use a Secure JDBC Driver

The easiest, and usually best, solution to this quandary is to use a secure JDBC driver to connect to your database. Many database vendors provide technology that will allow a DBA to configure the database in such a way that all connections must be encrypted, usually using SSL. The vendors then provide JDBC drivers that can act as clients of the newly secured database server. This technology is generally vendor-specific though and not available for all RDMBSs. MySQL, for example, does not have a secure JDBC driver.

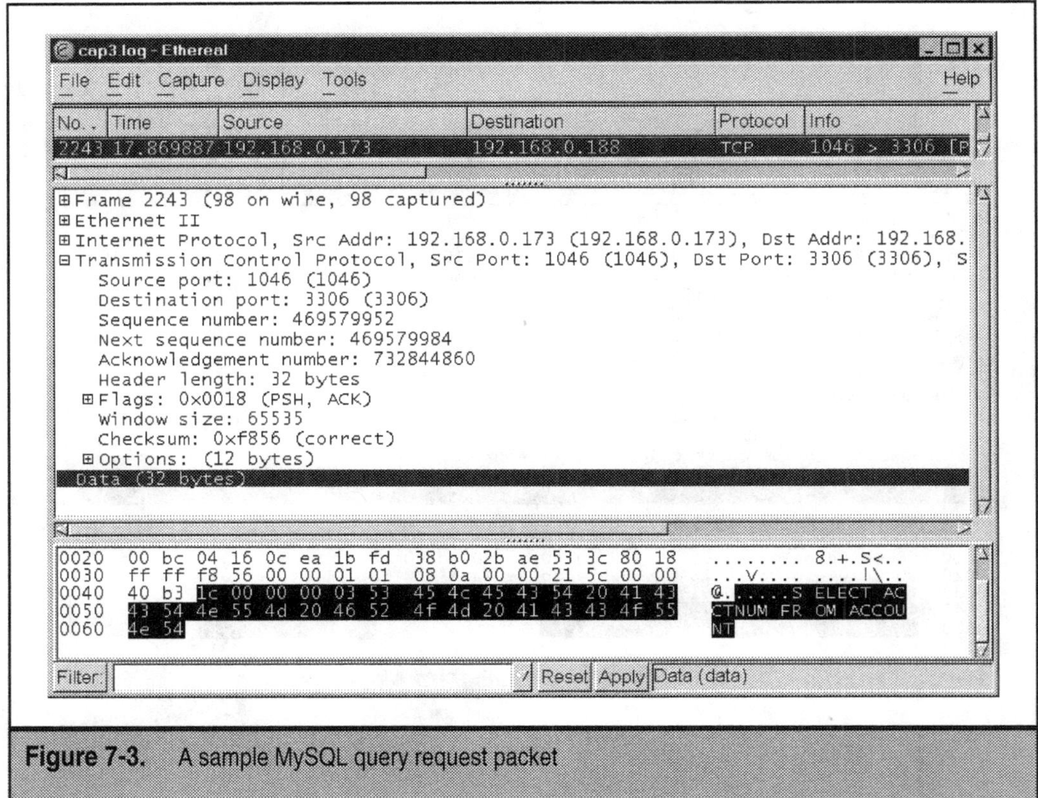

Figure 7-3. A sample MySQL query request packet

Countermeasure: Use a Secure Tunneling Package

If your JDBC driver will not connect to its server in a secure manner, the next best option is generally to implement a secure SSL tunnel between the database client and server. Typically, this involves running extra software on both the client and the server to set up and maintain the tunnel, but it will provide an acceptable level of security at a relatively low cost. A secure tunnel consists of two pieces: a client-side component, which runs on the same machine that hosts the client application, and a server-side component, which runs on the same physical machine as the database server. The tunnel works in the following manner:

1. The secure tunnel software is configured and running on both the client workstation and the server. For the purposes of this example, we will assume that the tunneling client is listening on port 5000 on the client workstation and the tunneling server is listening on port 5555 on the database server machine. The tunnel server needs to be configured to let it know which port on the server machine to forward its traffic to. In this case, we will assume that MySQL is running on the default port of 3306.

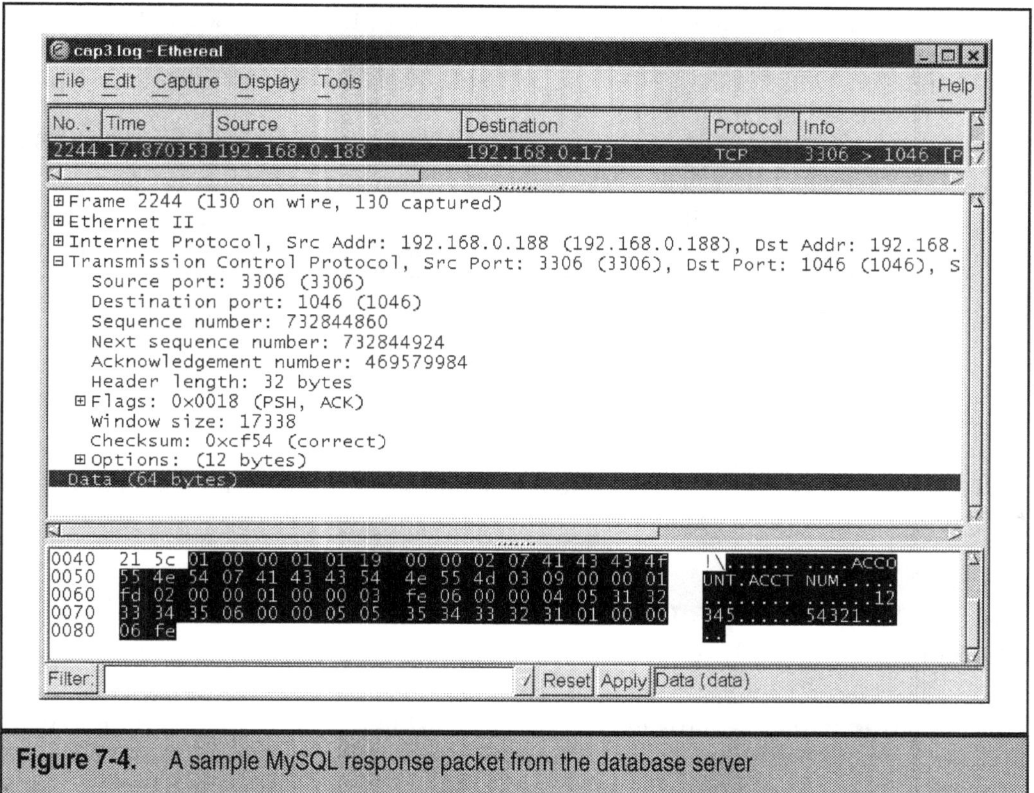

Figure 7-4. A sample MySQL response packet from the database server

2. A client wishing to use the tunnel connects to the tunneling client's port on the `localhost` (the client machine). This means that, in this example, we would set our connect URL for our JDBC driver in the client application code to `jdbc://mysql/localhost:5000/mysql`. This makes it look like we are connecting to a database located on the *client machine*, when in actuality, the MySQL JDBC driver will just be connecting to the client side of the tunnel. Because the tunnel client will seamlessly redirect the JDBC traffic, the JDBC driver will be tricked into thinking there is a database running on port 5000 of the local machine. The unencrypted JDBC traffic from the JDBC driver to the "phantom" database portrayed by the tunnel client will all be transmitted through the loopback interface of the client workstation and will not be sent across the network until the tunnel client has a chance to secure the transmission. This arrangement helps secure the client side of the JDBC connection.
3. The tunnel client (also running on the client workstation along with the user application) will accept the connection from the JDBC driver and connect across the network to the tunnel server listening on the server machine,

port 5555. This connection will use SSL to secure the remote socket-based connection to the tunnel server. The connection between the client and server machine will then be secure, and all traffic over this network will be encrypted. The tunnel client will merely forward all traffic it receives on port 5000 from the client JDBC driver to the tunnel server on the database server over the SSL connection.

4. The tunnel server will accept the SSL connection and transparently forward all incoming data to the database server (port 3306) on the server machine (it's `localhost`). Again, because the tunnel server is talking to the database server through the loopback interface, the unencrypted traffic between the tunnel server and the database server will never transit the network and hence, be secure.

Neither the client JDBC driver nor the database server needs to be aware that its traffic is being tunneled. Stunnel (www.stunnel.org) is an open-source example of secure tunneling software that is relatively easy to install and works quite well. Many other commercial and noncommercial packages that perform this valuable task are available.

Countermeasure: Implement an SSL Tunneling Client and Server Using JSSE

If you would like a Java-based solution, it is a relatively easy task to use the JSSE API to build your own tunneling software. Let's use JSSE to build a simple tunneling, or redirection, package that will allow us to create a secure network connection, using SSL/TLS, between two arbitrary hosts. Figure 7-5 illustrates how this tunneling works. Additionally, this package will log the traffic passing through it to a file. This will allow us to understand and evaluate exactly what traffic is being passed through the tunnel, for instructional purposes.

The Redirection Package Design

The redirection package has an abstract class, `AbstractRedirector`, which provides the majority of the functionality necessary to listen on a particular server socket and forward the traffic to another, arbitrary, host and port. There are three abstract methods in the `AbstractRedirector` class that must be implemented by a concrete subclass:

- The `getOutputSocket` method must return a socket connected to the specified host and port.
- The `getServerSocket` method must return a server socket listening on the specified local port.
- The `inboundSocketIsOK` method validates that a particular inbound socket, produced by the `ServerSocket.accept` method, is acceptable for an inbound connection. It can be used to deny connections from particular hosts, domains, subnets, and so on.

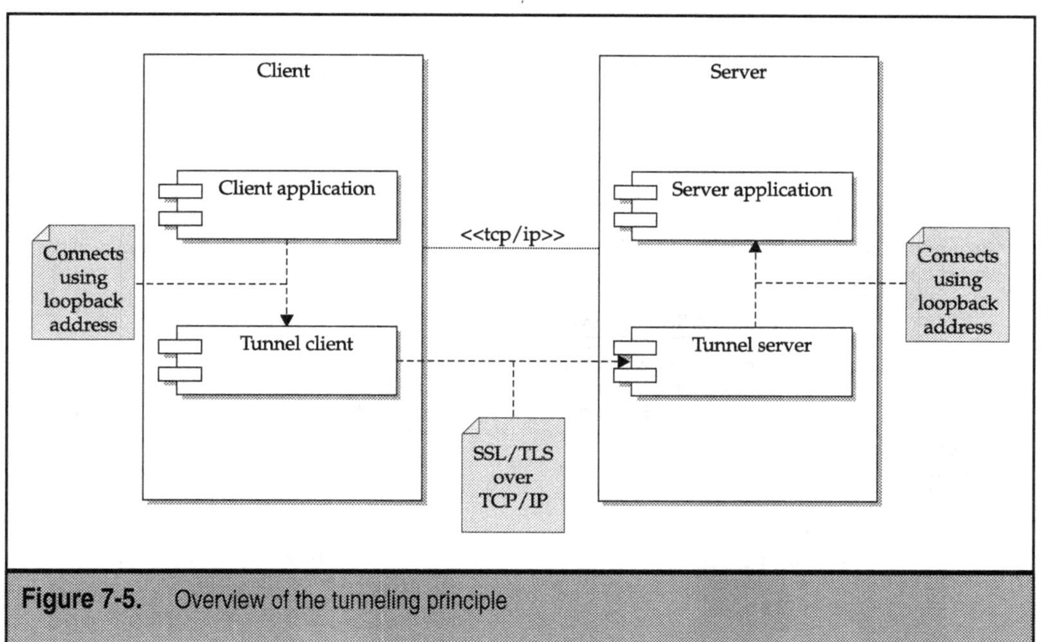

Figure 7-5. Overview of the tunneling principle

`AbstractRedirector` is then extended to create two separate classes: `SSLRedirectClient` and `SSLRedirectServer`. `SSLRedirectClient` is responsible for listening on an unsecured local socket and forwarding all traffic to a remote host and port via SSL/TLS. `SSLRedirectServer` receives the SSL connection from the `SSLRedirectClient` and forwards it to a different, unsecured port on the local machine. Essentially, this secures the connection between the client and the server. In practical use, a client would open a connection to `localhost` on the particular port on which the `SSLRedirectClient` was listening. All traffic bound for that port would be forwarded securely to the remote host, where it would be "retransmitted" using the loopback interface to the intended destination port. Figure 7-6 illustrates the redirection package design.

To the client, it looks like a connection is being made to an arbitrary port on the client's own machine. To the server, it looks like a connection is being made from another process running on the server machine. Of course, for all of this to work in a secure manner, the routing tables on both the client and server need to be configured to prevent broadcast of the loopback data over a live network interface.

A Brief Review of SSL/TLS Throughout this example, as well as examples in Chapter 8, the JSSE is used to provide SSL/TLS security at the socket level. Since the JSSE makes much of the SSL "handshake" process transparent to the application developer, we do not cover the SSL or TLS protocols in depth in this book. If you are interested in the details

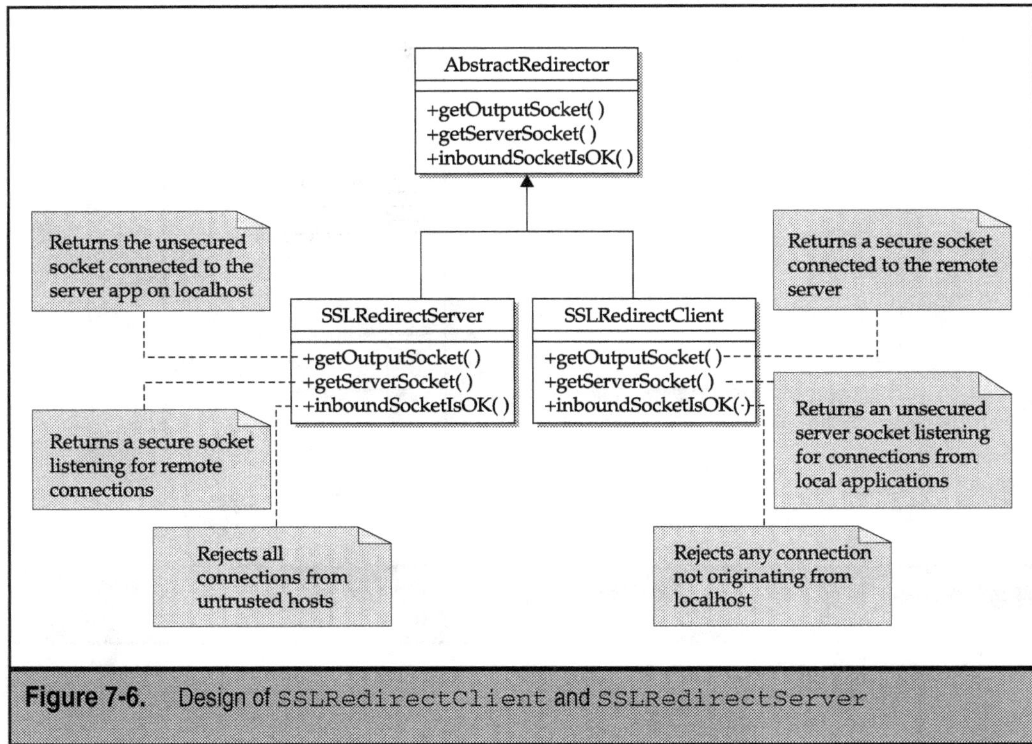

Figure 7-6. Design of `SSLRedirectClient` and `SSLRedirectServer`

of the TLS specification, they can be found at www.ietf.org/rfc/rfc2246.txt. For our purposes, we will distill the SSL/TLS connection process to the following general steps:

1. A SSL client requests a connection to a SSL server socket on a remote host.
2. The SSL server responds and, among other things, sends the client a copy of its signed digital certificate, signing it with the private key from the server's keystore.
3. The client checks the server's certificate to see if it was signed by someone the client trusts. The client's list of certificates and CAs that can be trusted is a Java keystore called a *truststore*. A default truststore which contains certificates from common CAs like Verisign and Thawte is distributed with the JDK and resides in the cacerts file in the lib/security directory of the JRE runtime.
4. If the server certificate, or a signer of the server certificate exists in the truststore, the connection is accepted and the two nodes agree on which ciphers and digest algorithms to use for communication. If the server certificate can not be verified by using the truststore, the connection is denied.

If SSL client authentication is not being used, the SSL connection process is complete after following the steps above. However, the server has the option of requesting that the client authenticate itself to the server too—this is called SSL (or TLS) with client authentication. If the server requests the client to authenticate, the following additional steps take place:

1. The client uses its private key from its keystore, which is a Java keystore that can be either the same as or different from the client truststore used in step 3 above, to create a signed certificate and sends it to the server.
2. The server verifies the client certificate using its own truststore. If the client certificate or a signer of the client certificate cannot be found in the truststore, the server refuses the connection. Otherwise the connection is accepted and secure communication begins using the previously agreed upon cipher and digest algorithms.

Notice that for normal, server authenticated SSL, the server requires a keystore to generate a signed certificate with its private key, and the client requires a truststore to verify either the server's signature or a CA's signature on the server certificate. When client authentication is used, both parties (client and server) must have both a keystore and a truststore. They need to present signed certificates to each other, which they both need to verify.

Understanding these techniques is integral to using the JSSE effectively, and also will help make the following example a little more clear.

If we look at our abstract base class, we see the three abstract methods that all subclasses of `AbstractRedirector` must implement.

```
protected abstract Socket getOutputSocket(String hostName, int port)
    throws IOException;

protected abstract ServerSocket getServerSocket(int port)
    throws IOException;

protected abstract boolean inboundSocketIsOK(Socket sock)
    throws IOException;
```

The SSLRedirectClient

The `SSLRedirectClient` class uses the JSSE to build the client side of a secure SSL connection. Because of this, when this code runs, the following system properties should be set:

- The `javax.net.ssl.keyStore` property contains the location of the keystore that stores the client's private key. This property can be eliminated if the SSL connection will not use client authentication.
- The `javax.net.ssl.keyStorePassword` property contains the password for the keystore specified above. Again, if client authentication is not being used, this property can be eliminated.
- The `javax.net.ssl.trustStore` property contains the keystore that stores the public certificates of all trusted hosts and CAs. This must be specified to initiate a valid SSL connection. If our server presents a certificate that is not in our truststore or signed by a CA that is not in our truststore, the connection will not be established.

Once these system properties are set, getting an SSL socket via JSSE is as easy as getting an instance of an `SSLSocketFactory` and using it to create a new secure socket.

The important code in this class looks like this:

```
package book.webserv.common;
import javax.net.ssl.SSLSocketFactory;
…
public class SSLRedirectClient extends AbstractRedirector {

  private SSLSocketFactory myFactory;

  public SSLRedirectClient(int listenPort, String redirectHost, int redirectPort)
      throws IOException {
    super("Client", listenPort, redirectHost, redirectPort);
    // Get the default JSSE secure socket factory.
    myFactory = (javax.net.ssl.SSLSocketFactory) SSLSocketFactory.getDefault();
}

  protected Socket getOutputSocket(String hostName, int port)
      throws IOException {
     // Create a secure socket to communicate with our server.
    Socket retVal = myFactory.createSocket(hostName,port);
    return retVal;
  }

  protected ServerSocket getServerSocket(int port)
      throws IOException {
    // We will be listening to a port on our local machine (loopback),
    // so we build a normal ServerSocket.
    return new ServerSocket(port);
  }
```

The following method ensures that our redirection client will accept connections only from a loopback network address. This will help defend against an attacker connecting to our tunnel from a remote machine and using our tunnel to connect to an otherwise secure server.

```
  protected boolean inboundSocketIsOK(Socket sock)
      throws IOException {

    // Only accept connections from the localhost.
    boolean retVal = false;
    if (sock.getInetAddress().isLoopbackAddress()) {
      // It's a loopback! Good.
      retVal = true;
    }
    return retVal;
  }
```

```
  public static void main(String[] args) {
. . .
    try {
      AbstractRedirector rc = new
SSLRedirectClient(listenPort,forwardHost,forwardPort);
      rc.acceptConnections();
    } catch (Exception e) {
      e.printStackTrace();
    }
  }
}
```

Notice that the `SSLRedirectClient` explicitly disallows any connections to its `ServerSocket` that do not originate from the loopback interface. This prevents a malicious outsider from hijacking the SSL connection from a remote machine and using the client certificate of the client machine (via SSL client authentication) to fool the server into thinking that requests were originating from the client machine, when they were actually being originated by the attacker.

The SSLRedirectServer

The `SSLRedirectServer` implements the server side of the SSL connection. It will receive remote SSL connect requests from our redirection clients and forward the traffic to a predetermined port on its local machine. The following system properties must be set when the redirection server is executed:

- The `javax.net.ssl.keyStore` property contains the location of the keystore that stores the server's private key. This should be included and should contain the private key corresponding to a certificate that is signed by a entity in the client's truststore.
- The `javax.net.ssl.keyStorePassword` property contains the password for the keystore specified in the `javax.net.ssl.keyStore` property.
- The `javax.net.ssl.trustStore` property contains the keystore that stores the public certificates of all trusted hosts and CAs. This must be specified if we want to use SSL client authentication. If a client presents a certificate that is not in our truststore or signed by a CA that is in our truststore, the connection will not be established.

Again, once the proper system properties are set, creating a SSL server socket is as simple as instantiating the factory and using it to create a new socket. The only additional nuance in the code is that we enable SSL client authentication by calling the `setNeedClientAuth` method on the server socket. This will force all SSL clients (our `SSLRedirectClient`) to present a certificate that is signed by an entity in our server truststore. If they don't, the connection will be refused.

Relevant code for this class looks like this:

```
package book.webserv.common;
import javax.net.ssl.SSLServerSocketFactory;
import javax.net.ssl.SSLServerSocket;
. . .
public class SSLRedirectServer extends AbstractRedirector {

  /**
   * A private member variable to hold our socket factory
   */
  private SSLServerSocketFactory myFactory;

  public SSLRedirectServer(int listenPort, int redirectPort)
      throws IOException {
    // We will only forward to ports on our server.
    super("Server", listenPort, "localhost", redirectPort);
    myFactory = (javax.net.ssl.SSLServerSocketFactory)
                               SSLServerSocketFactory.getDefault();
  }

  protected ServerSocket getServerSocket(int port) throws IOException {

    SSLServerSocket sock = (javax.net.ssl.SSLServerSocket)
                         myFactory.createServerSocket(port);

    // Force client authentication via SSL. This will guarantee that only
    // clients with certificates in our truststore can connect.
    sock.setNeedClientAuth(true);
    return sock;
  }

  protected Socket getOutputSocket(String hostName, int port)
      throws IOException {

    // For us, since we're a server, this will always be a non-SSL connection
    // to localhost.
    Socket retVal = null;
    retVal = new Socket(hostName,port);
    return retVal;
  }

  protected boolean inboundSocketIsOK(Socket sock)
      throws IOException {
    // Could check to see that remote machine is on a list of "approved"
    // hosts here. For now, we'll approve all inbound connections.
    return true;
  }
```

```
  public static void main(String[] args) {
...
    try {
      AbstractRedirector rs = new SSLRedirectServer(listenPort,forwardPort);
      rs.acceptConnections();
    } catch (Exception e) {
      e.printStackTrace();
    }
  }
}
```

Notice that for this particular server, the hostname of the remote host is not specified on the command line; it is hardcoded to be `localhost`. Because of this, the server will redirect traffic only to another port on the machine on which it is currently running. This prevents somebody from starting the server in a mode such that it will accept SSL connections and forward the data over an insecure connection to another remote host. This may or may not be desirable behavior, but we show it here to merely suggest the possibility of its use.

Generating the Keys

To do SSL client authentication, the client must have a copy of the server's public key (or a public key of a CA who signs the server's public key) in its truststore. Additionally, the server must have the client's key (or signing CA's key) in its truststore. To accomplish this, we need to configure the client and the server to generate the proper keys and keystores for a client-authenticated SSL connection.

To generate the keys, we'll run the following sequence of `keytool` commands. (See Chapter 2 for details on using the `keytool` utility.) In this example, we will be using the same physical keystore file as both a keystore and a truststore for an individual node. In a production environment, these would most likely be separated, with the keystore containing the server's private keys and the truststore containing trusted public certificates.

Here are the commands to generate the server key:

```
C:\sec\book\temp>keytool -genkey -keyalg RSA -keystore server.ks
Enter keystore password:  password
What is your first and last name?
  [Unknown]:  localhost
 -- Accept the defaults for everything else --
```

Remember that the CN piece of the certificate must contain the hostname of the server. Here are the commands for the client keystore (`client.ks`):

```
C:\sec\book\temp>keytool -genkey -keyalg RSA -keystore client.ks
Enter keystore password:  password
What is your first and last name?
  [Unknown]:  localhost
-- Accept the defaults for everything else --
```

Now, we export the public key information from each keystore and import it into the other keystore. After we complete this operation, the server keystore (`server.ks`) will contain the private server key and the public client key. The client keystore (`client.ks`) will contain the private client key and the public server key. When you import both certificates, answer "Yes" to the question "Do you want to trust this certificate?"

```
C:\sec\book\temp>keytool -export -keystore server.ks -file server.cer
Enter keystore password:  password
Certificate stored in file <server.cer>

C:\sec\book\temp>keytool -export -keystore client.ks -file client.cer
Enter keystore password:  password
Certificate stored in file <client.cer>

C:\sec\book\temp>keytool -import -keystore server.ks -file client.cer -alias
clientKey

C:\sec\book\temp>keytool -import -keystore client.ks -file server.cer -alias
serverKey
```

Running the Client and Server

To run the client and the server, we start up two command prompts, navigate to a directory where we want the log files to be written, and then execute the following command lines:

```
C:\sec\book\temp>java -Djavax.net.ssl.keyStore=server.ks
                      -Djavax.net.ssl.keyStorePassword=password
                      -Djavax.net.ssl.trustStore=server.ks
                       book.webserv.common.SSLRedirectServer 5555 3306
```

This command line starts the server component of the tunnel. This component will listen on port 5555 for remote SSL connections and forward them to port 3306 (the MySQL port) on the local machine, which, in our case, is the MySQL server.

To start the client component, we execute the following:

```
C:\sec\book\temp>java -Djavax.net.ssl.keyStore=client.ks
                      -Djavax.net.ssl.keyStorePassword=password
                      -Djavax.net.ssl.trustStore=client.ks
                       book.webserv.common.SSLRedirectClient 5000 localhost 5555
```

This starts the client side of the tunnel listening on port 5000 and forwarding all traffic over SSL to the server residing on `localhost`, port 5555. Note that any hostname could be used instead of `localhost`, and thus the tunnel could be established to any `SSLRedirectServer` running on an arbitrary machine.

As you can see, this is valuable technology for securing any network connection between two entities, not just a connection between a client and a database. However, to be truly production-ready, the code for the redirector should be upgraded to buffer the redirected data on both sides of the connection. Right now, in the `RedirectThread` class, we are logging and retransmitting data eight bits at a time. This is easy to write, but it's very inefficient. Ideally, the data would be buffered and then logged and transmitted in much larger chunks.

As usual, the complete, documented code for this package is available on our web site: www.hackingexposedjava.com.

Countermeasure: Encrypt the Data at the Application Level using the JCE

Another mechanism for securing data being passed between a client application and a database server is to use encryption. This solution is the same as the solution outlined for application database security earlier in the chapter (in the "Countermeasure: User-level Database Passwords and JCE for Encryption" section). Encrypting the application data directly using the JCE gives good security, but brings the liabilities of possible performance degradation and limitations on the ability to generate ad-hoc or complex SQL queries.

Now that we have covered some security issues surrounding the database server and the connection between the client and the server in a two-tier, client-server application with a fat client, it's time to address the client side. For the remainder of this chapter, we will concentrate on more techniques that we can use to improve the security stature of the client side of our sample application (the side that actually uses Java).

Protecting the Client-Tier

Now that we are networked, the possibility of an intruder placing unwanted or dangerous files on our client workstation is greatly increased. Attackers might succeed in somehow replacing segments of our good code with their nefarious code, especially with applets and Java WebStart applications, where remote class loading is almost a necessity.

Class File Spoofing

Popularity:	2
Simplicity:	5
Impact:	8
Risk rating:	5

How do we know that the code the client runs is actually the code that we, the developers, wrote? What can happen if it's not?

Suppose that attackers write their own version of our persistence service (called `book.cs.clientserv.MySQLPersistenceService`) that, instead of persisting data to our SQL database, returns a certain balance for every possible `get401Kbalance` query. Additionally, the attack code logs all `set401Kbalance` requests and also logs the username and password used to connect to the database. Now, assume that the attackers were able to trick the JVM into loading their `MySQLPersistenceService` instead of ours. For obvious reasons, this wouldn't be a good situation.

Here is what this attack might look like: The attacker writes a rogue version of the `MySQLPersistenceService`:

```
package book.cs.clientserv;

import javax.crypto.SecretKey;

...

public class MySQLPersistenceService
    implements book.cs.clientserv.RetirementAccountInfo {
  private SecretKey userKey;
  public MySQLPersistenceService(String uName, String pWord,
                                 String hostName, SecretKey key) {
    userKey = key;
  }
  public Number get401kBalance(String s)
    throws AccountNotFoundException, PersistenceException {
    System.out.println("This is the rogue code: getBalance");
    System.out.println("Here's your secret key: " + userKey);
    return new BigDecimal("99999.99");
  }

  public void set401kBalance(String s, BigDecimal bigDecimal)
    throws AccountNotFoundException, OperationNotAllowedException,
           PersistenceException {
    // Do nothing
    System.out.println("This is the rogue code: setBalance");
  }

  public void close() {
    // Do nothing
    System.out.println("This is the rogue code: close");
  }
}
```

As you can see, in this code we are merely printing some debugging messages and demonstrating that we have access to the secret key used to encrypt our database information. We easily could also display the username and password for the database, as well as spoof any possible get or set balance requests.

To trick the VM into loading our malicious class instead of the main application class, all we need to do is ensure that the attack code location (`./rclasses`) appears before the application code location (`./classes`) in the classpath. The following is a sample run of the malicious code where the user logs in and attempts to get the balance on a particular account:

```
C:\sec\book>java
  -Djava.security.auth.login.config=src/book/cs/clientserv/jaas.conf
  -Djava.security.policy=src/book/cs/clientserv/retirement.policy
  -cp ./rclasses;%CLASSPATH%  book.cs.clientserv.ClientFrame db

May 22, 2002 11:05:19 AM book.cs.clientserv.ClientFrame authenticateUser
...

This is the rogue code: getBalance
Here's your secret key: javax.crypto.spec.SecretKeySpec@4f9648e6
This is the rogue code: setBalance
This is the rogue code: close
```

Notice that all that needs to be done is to insert the `./rclasses` directory at the front of the classpath. Although, here, we forced this new classpath on the Java command line (using the `-cp` option), a much more likely scenario would be its addition to the `CLASSPATH` environment variable or actually replacing our distribution class with the rogue class in question. However it's done, once the spoofed class file is in place, the user still sees a normal login dialog box.

The application appears to function normally, and users are even presented with the reassuring "Java Applet Window" message to let them know that a security manager is running. But as we have seen, the code implementing the persistence portion of the code is not quite what the application developer intended.

Our sample attack would be even more dangerous if it covertly delegated all of our calls to the real `MySQLPersistence` service, silently watching for activity on a particular account, then stepping in and replacing the real results with something else. This type of attack is extremely hard to detect and can be quite damaging. Fortunately, Java provides several good options to counter this type of attack.

Countermeasure: Signed JAR Files and Package Sealing

JAR files are a great mechanism for distributing application code in an encapsulated, well-behaved manner. A fact about JAR files that many developers don't know is that they can also be used for security purposes, both by allowing code to be signed and by allowing the packages they contain to be sealed. Here, we will look at using package sealing to help us maintain the integrity of our application. We will cover signing JAR files later in the chapter, in the section about applet security.

Sealing packages within a JAR file is extremely easy and should generally always be done for production applications. Sealing is a technique that will tell the JVM that the packages contained in our JAR file are *atomic*. This means that any other class that claims to be a member of a package defined in our JAR file is invalid, even if that rogue class is loaded *before* the classes in our JAR file. This is a way of guaranteeing that our packages will run exactly as they are in the JAR file, or they will not run at all.

To seal a package within a JAR file, we need to generate a JAR manifest file, and then tell the JAR utility to add this manifest into our JAR file when we build the JAR file. The manifest file (called `Manifest.mf` in the source directory for the client server application) looks like this:

```
Sealed: true
```

This indicates that we want to seal the entire JAR file. The Java runtime will now detect any modifications and appropriately veto them.

NOTE As explained in Chapter 2, individual packages in a JAR file, rather than the whole JAR file, can be sealed. Developers of frameworks or other code that may be extended might want to seal individual packages. Usually, with a production application, most developers want to seal everything in the JAR file, not just a single package.

To build the sealed JAR file, we execute the following JAR command from the command line, specifying the JAR file to build, the manifest file, and the directory tree to compress:

```
C:\sec\book\classes>jar cfm ../jars/SealedRetirementApp.jar ../Manifest.mf *
```

Now, when we add the sealed JAR to our classpath, and try the same spoofing strategy, we encounter the following results:

```
C:\sec\book>java
  -Djava.security.auth.login.config=src/book/cs/clientserv/jaas.conf
  -Djava.security.policy=src/book/cs/clientserv/retirement.policy
  -cp ./rclasses;./jars/SealedRetirementApp.jar;%CLASSPATH%
   book.cs.clientserv.ClientFrame db

Exception in thread "main" java.lang.SecurityException: sealing violation
        at java.net.URLClassLoader.defineClass(URLClassLoader.java:232)
        at java.net.URLClassLoader.access$100(URLClassLoader.java:54)
. . .
        at java.lang.ClassLoader.loadClassInternal(ClassLoader.java:322)
```

As advertised, the class loader detects that we are attempting to impersonate a class in a sealed package and halts execution with a "sealing violation." This is just the type of behavior that we desire. You may notice that an attacker still could defeat our scheme by removing or altering the manifest in our JAR file, and we will cover a countermeasure for that tactic later in this chapter when we discuss signing JAR files.

Countermeasure: Specify the Classpath on the Command Line

It is generally considered good practice to always specify your application's classpath on the command line (via the `-cp` or `-classpath` options) in a read-only startup script. Do not rely on the `CLASSPATH` environment variable, because that opens a door for attackers to insert their own classes, as explained in the previous section. (This approach is a system policy countermeasure, and not one that the application programmer generally has much control over.)

The rationale behind specifying the classpath on the command line is the same as the reason for administrators typing fully qualified path names to any executable they wish to run when running a shell with superuser rights. It eliminates the option of a malicious individual placing a rogue executable in the current directory or somewhere else on the path before the application being executed. The same principle is true for Java classpaths.

Exploiting Unsynchronized User Credentials

Popularity:	1
Simplicity:	4
Impact:	5
Risk rating:	**3**

Currently, our sample application is performing authentication and authorization with two different mechanisms: We are using JAAS to verify the user's Windows NT identity, and then we are allowing our application to directly verify the user's identity through a JDBC connection with the database. This separation can possibly present an attacker with a certain window of opportunity in the following scenario.

Assume that an individual is transferred to another department, where they will no longer require access to the retirement application. As a matter of policy, their database account is revoked immediately upon the transfer. However, chances are that because they are only being transferred, not terminated, they will retain their Windows 2000 login. Also, because the user can't log into the database, the application developers figure that the application policy file doesn't need to be updated.

We now have the illusion of security with respect to this individual. They cannot log into the database, but if they run the application with anyone else's database password, they can still perform the work they used to be authorized to do, because the `grant` statements in the security policy file are based on their `NTUserPrincipal`, not any type of database access. Essentially, they are still authorized to use the *application*, even though their database password has been deactivated. If they can find some other way to access the database (someone else's credentials perhaps), they can still use the application to modify critical data.

This situation is incredibly common in large enterprises when users are transferred between departments. Centralized security staffs typically will revoke access for the user at the system level, but application-level access often remains unchanged for long periods of time.

In an ideal world, we want to have a *single* source of authentication and authorization for our entire application. With more complex architectures, this can be an extremely daunting task. However, with a two-tier application, JAAS provides an attractive solution.

Countermeasure: A Custom JAAS Login Module

Our approach will be to implement a custom login strategy that will authenticate all application users with the MySQL *database* and will additionally allow us to use that authentication for granting application permissions. Therefore, we can create accounts for each application user in our RDBMS and our application will accept authentication with the database server as authentication for the application also. This improves our situation because it enables us to have a single, platform independent, source of authentication and authorization for our application. This way, we won't need to authenticate with both the database and the operating system.

Another benefit of this approach is that it allows us to combine the database authentication, at a system level, with any other arbitrary JAAS login modules. Suppose that we later decide that we would like to perform JNDI authentication, and then get our database connection via a `DataSource` we find via a JNDI lookup. We can do this by making slight changes in our JAAS configuration file and in some code associated with our new `LoginModule`; we won't need to change any of the application code. Additionally, we can now distribute our `LoginModule` to other applications that can use it for authentication by adding a single line to their JAAS configuration files.

Also, we now will have the option of performing authentication (transparently to the user) with a *different* database than the one we use for our application, and generating a connection to the application database using potentially different credentials than the user originally supplied. Therefore, in the absence of LDAP, Kerberos, or some other enterprise authentication scheme, we could have a single database act as a shared "authentication server" for all of our client-server applications. By distributing our JAAS LoginModule to other client applications, we can work towards a low-tech solution to enterprise application access. All applications could then use the same `LoginModule`, which would conduct authentication using a single user repository.

To make this work, we will need to write three separate, but related, components:

- A custom JAAS `LoginModule` to authenticate the user with the database.
- A custom implementation of the `Principal` interface, which can be associated with a `Subject` and through which we can perform our application authorization. This `Principal` will be produced by the `LoginModule` we mentioned in step one and will contain all relevant information retrieved for the current user from the authentication data store.

- A custom implementation of a `Credential` object that will also be added to the `Subject` and will embody all information necessary to gain a connection to the database in question. This means that the `LoginModule`, in addition to attaching the user `Principal` to the prevailing JAAS `Subject`, will also attach a special "credential" which will allow that `Principal` (or user) to get a connection to the underlying application database, without reauthentication or providing another set of credentials.

As usual, the complete, working, documented version of the code can be found at www.hackingexposedjava.com.

Creating the Principal Interface Implementation

First, we will construct an implementation of the `Principal` interface specifically for our `LoginModule`. Our implementation of this `Principal` will be called `RetirementPrincipal` and will represent a user of our system authenticated against the MySQL database server.

Any information pertaining to a particular system user can be captured in a `Principal` object, but at a minimum, the interface requires a `getName` method. The name provided with this method will be used to match against names used in the `grant` clause of our application policy file.

The code for the `RetirementPrincipal` class follows.

```
package book.cs.customlm;

import java.security.Principal;

public final class RetirementPrincipal implements Principal {

  private String name;

  public RetirementPrincipal(String name) {
    this.name = name;
  }

  public String getName() {
    return name;
  }
```

Notice that we must override both the `equals` and `hashCode` methods we inherit from the `Object` class so that our object will be well behaved in collections.

```
  public boolean equals(Object o) {
    if (o instanceof RetirementPrincipal) {
      RetirementPrincipal that = (RetirementPrincipal) o;
      return this.name.equalsIgnoreCase(that.name);
    }
```

```
        return false;
    }
  public int hashCode() {
        return name.toUpperCase().hashCode(); }
    public String toString() {
        return "RetirementPrincipal: " + name;
    }
}
```

Creating the Credential Class

We also will develop a special `Credential` class that will wrap the database username and password. Because a `Credential` can be any object, we will also use this special object as a factory for our JDBC connections. This will give us a "poor person's" `DataSource`, which will be transparent to our application and enabled through the JAAS login module. Therefore, users will be able to get their `MySQLCredential` from the current JAAS `Subject` and ask the credential itself to produce a properly authenticated JDBC connection. This way, the application itself will never need to store, or even see, the user's database username and password. That information will have already been captured by the JAAS authentication subsystem. The implementation of the `MySQLCredential` class looks like this:

```
package book.cs.customlm;

import java.sql.Connection;
import java.sql.SQLException;
import java.sql.DriverManager;

public class MySQLCredential {

. . .

  private String userName = "";
  private char[] password = { };
  private String dbHostName= "";

  public MySQLCredential(String userName, char[] pWord, String dbHostName) {
    super();
    this.userName = userName;
    this.dbHostName = dbHostName;
    password = new char[pWord.length];
    System.arraycopy(pWord,0,password,0,pWord.length);
  }

  public String getUserName() {
    return userName;
  }
```

```
  public void clearSensitiveInformation() {
    Arrays.fill(password, ' ');
  }

  public Connection getDBConnection() throws SQLException {
    String dbURL = "jdbc:mysql://" + dbHostName + "/mysql";
    return DriverManager.getConnection(dbURL,userName,new String(password));
  }

}
```

As you can see, this is just a simple data object with the addition of some simple database connection logic. There is no reason why this class could not be "upgraded" to implement a full connection pool or serve as a facade for any other type of authenticated connection type. That said, generally you should strive to keep `Credential` objects relatively lightweight and free of business-specific functionality, so we will try not to go too overboard with this particular credential.

Building the Login Module

Last, we will build the custom JAAS `LoginModule` that will use both the `Principal` and `Credential` we developed. To do this, we implement the `LoginModule` interface and define five important methods:

- The `initialize` method will initialize the login module with the parameters specified in the JAAS configuration file. Typically, this method will run when the application constructs a `LoginContext` for a JAAS configuration entry that specifies that the custom `LoginModule` should be used at some point for authentication.
- The `login` method uses the `CallbackHandler` supplied in `initialize` to get the proper credential information, performs all necessary authentication, and returns true if the authentication has succeeded.
- The `commit` method adds the principal and credential information for this module to the `Subject` owned by the calling `LoginContext`.
- The `abort` method reinitializes the `LoginModule`. All credential information pertaining to the current login attempt should be released.
- The `logout` method removes the principal and credential information added to the `LoginContext`'s `Subject` in the `commit` method. It also reinitializes the `LoginModule` for future use.

Here is the implementation of the `MySQLLoginModule` class:

```
package book.cs.customlm;

import javax.security.auth.spi.LoginModule;
import javax.security.auth.Subject;
```

```
import javax.security.auth.login.LoginException;
import javax.security.auth.callback.*;
. . .
public class MySQLLoginModule implements LoginModule{

  private CallbackHandler ourCBH;
  private Subject ourSubject;

  private Principal tempPrincipal;
  private MySQLCredential tempCredential;

  private boolean ourLoginWasSuccessful = false;
  public void initialize(Subject subject, CallbackHandler callbackHandler,
                         Map sharedState, Map options) {
    ourCBH = callbackHandler;
    ourSubject = subject;
    String tempHostName = (String) options.get("DatabaseHostName");
    if (tempHostName != null) {
      dbHostName = tempHostName;
    }
  }
```

Notice that all that the `initialize` method does is extract information from the arguments and store it for later use. The real bulk of the work takes place in the `login` method, which appears next:

```
  public boolean login() throws LoginException {

  // Build the callbacks, which will allow us to get the DB username
  // and password from the user.
  NameCallback nameCallback = new NameCallback("Database Username: ");
  PasswordCallback pwCallback = new PasswordCallback("Database Password: "
                                                     ,false);
  Callback[] callbacks = { nameCallback, pwCallback };

  try {
    // Call the callback handler to get the DB username and password.
    // If the user has specified the DialogCallbackHandler, this will
    // display a dialog box asking the user for their userid and
    // password. Other callback handlers will behave differently
    ourCBH.handle(callbacks);
  } catch (IOException e) {
    throw new LoginException("Login Failure");
  } catch (UnsupportedCallbackException e) {
    throw new LoginException("Login Failure");
  }
```

```
    // Try to log in to the database with the provided information.
    tempPrincipal = new RetirementPrincipal(nameCallback.getName());
    tempCredential = new MySQLCredential(nameCallback.getName(),
                                         pwCallback.getPassword(),
                                         dbHostName);
    try {
      // Get the connection directly from the credential we just built.
      Connection c = tempCredential.getDBConnection();
      // We don't need the connection, we're just using it for authentication.
      c.close();
    } catch (SQLException e) {
      tempCredential.clearSensitiveInformation();
      throw new LoginException("Login Failure");
    }
    // Remember that we succeeded… We'll use this during the commit.
    ourLoginWasSuccessful = true;
    return ourLoginWasSuccessful;
  }
  public boolean commit() throws LoginException {
    if (ourLoginWasSuccessful) {
      // Add our principal and credential to the Subject.
      OurSubject.getPrincipals().add(tempPrincipal);
      ourSubject.getPrivateCredentials().add(tempCredential);
    }
    return true;
  }

  public boolean abort() throws LoginException {
    // Zero out our temporary principal and credential information.
    TempPrincipal = null;
    if (tempCredential != null) {
      tempCredential.clearSensitiveInformation();
    }
    tempCredential = null;
    return false;
  }
  public boolean logout() throws LoginException {
    // Remove our subject and principal from the Subject.
    if (ourSubject != null) {
      ourSubject.getPrincipals().remove(tempPrincipal);
      ourSubject.getPrincipals().remove(tempCredential);
    }
    tempPrincipal = null;
    tempCredential.clearSensitiveInformation();
    tempCredential = null;
    return true;
  } }
```

Integrating the Login Module into the Application

To integrate the new LoginModule into our application, we make modifications to our ClientFrame class. The authenticateUser method is unchanged, but the constructor of the MySQLPersistenceService class is modified to take an instance of MySQLCredential as an argument, instead of a RetirementCredential, which we used in the previous version. The new code in the main method of ClientFrame that extracts the credential from the Subject looks like this:

```
// Get the credential information for our user.
Set s = loginContext.getSubject().getPrivateCredentials(
                                    MySQLCredential.class);
Iterator I = s.iterator();
if (i.hasNext()) {
  MySQLCredential cred = (MySQLCredential) i.next();
  // Instantiate our model.
  model = new MySQLPersistenceService(cred,fileKey);
} else {
  secLogger.log(Level.WARNING,"No MySQLCredential for user");
  System.exit(ABNORMAL_COMPLETION);
}
```

Both the Subject doAsPrivileged call and the checkPermission call that we use in our application code to enforce authorization do not change. We can make all necessary authorization changes by modifying the JAAS configuration file and the appropriate policy file. To do this, we build our JAAS configuration file to look like this:

```
RetirementClient {
  book.cs.customlm.MySQLLoginModule required DatabaseHostName=localhost;
};
```

We also modify our security policy file to grant access based on our new custom Principal instead of our NTUserPrincipal:

```
grant principal book.cs.customlm.RetirementPrincipal "lester" {
  permission book.cs.common.RetirementAppPermission "setBalance";
};
```

We also need to add some more special permissions to our policy file to allow our application and LoginModule to add Principals and credentials to and read private credential information from the specified subject. This grant statement looks like this:

```
grant {
  permission javax.security.auth.AuthPermission "modifyPrincipals";
  permission javax.security.auth.AuthPermission "modifyPrivateCredentials";
  permission javax.security.auth.PrivateCredentialPermission
 "book.cs.customlm.MySQLCredential book.cs.customlm.RetirementPrincipal \"*\"",
 "read";
};
```

This is another permissive grant, and it should generally be used only in conjunction with a signed JAR file or some other secure codebase that refers specifically to our `LoginModule` code. We show it in a permissive manner here for demonstration purposes only.

When we run the application after our changes, we notice immediately that we are presented with a new dialog box. This dialog box is generated during the `LoginContext` `login` method when our custom `LoginModule` calls the `DialogCallbackHandler` we provided from our application to the `LoginContext`:

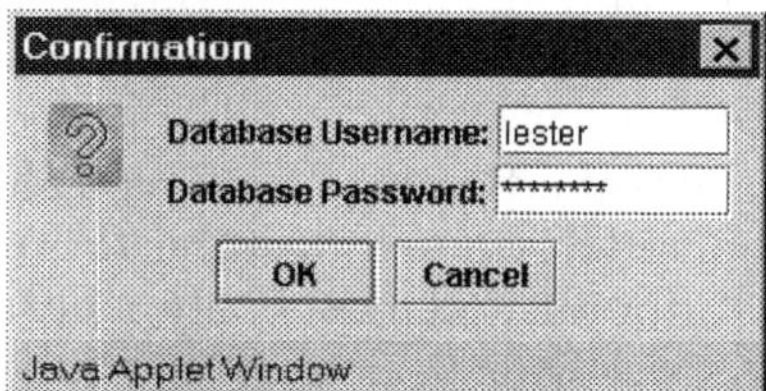

If we had supplied a `TextCallbackHandler` from our application instead of the `DialogCallbackHandler` when we built the `LoginContext`, all of the login-associated I/O would magically take place on the console instead of via dialog boxes. Since any client of our `LoginModule` can specify exactly how to query the user for login information through the assignment of an appropriate `CallbackHandler`, we now have the ability to reuse our `MySQLLoginModule`, `MySQLCredential`, and `RetirementPrincipal` across many domains and platforms, on both client and server-side implementations. Also notice that now the authorization is being done using our custom principal, not the NT principal, so our authentication and authorization are regulated from the same location.

Protecting Applet-based Clients

Applet technology was an early driving force behind the popularity of Java in the development community. In fact, one of the early suggested Java-based distributed architectures supported thin clients running securely in web browsers using CORBA to communicate across the Internet with various "object servers" to perform various business tasks for the client. The client would be responsible for only the presentation of information to the user, and the rest of the work would take place on the server side. The vision was that Java applet technology would enable this distributed object architecture.

Fortunately or unfortunately, depending on your perspective, applets never really caught on in the way that their original champions had thought they would. Traditionally, applets have suffered from several problems.

Each browser vendor implemented its own JVM. Some browsers had better specification compliance than others. Typically, browser VMs lagged behind normal VM technology by several revisions, so developers needed to write "lowest common denominator" code. In other words, they had to assume that they were running the most primitive VM in the most restrictive browser.

The early Java applet security models made it hard to build applets that performed nontrivial tasks without granting them full authority to roam the client system. Policy files were either nonstandard or nonexistent. Most applets were forced to live in an environment where they were constrained in such a way that converting a typical application presentation layer into an applet-based one was a long, arduous process.

Because of the youth of the Java specification and platform, along with the disparity in browser VM implementations, applets became well-known for various security-related weaknesses. Through numerous types of attacks, early browser VM implementations could be easily defeated to, in many cases, allow an applet to gain full access to a client system. Many users were afraid (and still are) to enable Java functionality in their browsers for fear that a malicious "attack applet" would seize control of their system. In earlier days, this fear was well-founded. However, with maturity in the Java platform has come maturity (and accompanying security) of the applet as a delivery mechanism for Java code to the client.

Applets do have one significant advantage over typical applications: We know that there will be a web server involved in our architecture. This will be an advantage from an application programmer's standpoint, and most likely, a headache for our system administrators and system security specialists. Because of the introduction of a web server, we have the ability to store certain files (such as our JAAS configuration file and the actual class files representing our code) remotely on a web server instead of on the client workstation. This is a huge advantage from a configuration management standpoint. We can easily push configuration changes and software updates down to the client at the earliest opportunity. However, the ability to use remote code and configuration information raises a number of important security concerns.

Applet-based Deployment Attacks

Popularity:	5
Simplicity:	5
Impact:	8
Risk rating:	**6**

In the early years of Java (1996 and 1997), it became somewhat notorious for its susceptibility to a number of attacks involving corrupted or modified bytecode. In their classic book on Java security, *Java Security: Hostile Applets, Holes and Antidotes*, Gary McGraw and Edward Felten outline several tactics that applets containing corrupted or craftily written bytecode could use to defeat the security in place in the common browsers of the day.

One of the more popular attacks was called a *type confusion* attack. In this type of attack, an attacker would develop bytecode that could confuse the VM into thinking that the same location in memory was home to two totally different objects. Essentially, the VM would be confused as to the type of the object at a particular memory location. Once this condition was established, information could be written to memory through one of the objects in question and read using another.

Obviously, if attackers could control one of the interfaces used to read and write, they could use that interface to penetrate and compromise various system-level objects, leading to a complete system compromise. This type of attack was extremely popular when many JVMs were on their early public releases.

Type confusion attacks were possible because of flaws in an underlying VM, not in the design of the Java security model itself. Therefore, some of the attacks would work only on a specific version, release, and patch level of a particular VM (for example, Netscape Navigator 3.0b5).

Other popular attacks took advantage of flaws in the bytecode verifiers embedded in particular VMs. There have been many attacks to date that have succeeded because of a particular verifier's failure to stop illegal class casting or accessing an object's private instance variables. Again, these attacks were usually confined to a particular verifier in a particular VM.

All of these attacks are realistic concerns that any application developer or Java applet user should have. However, in the current world of Java development, VMs have matured to the point that it is extremely rare to find *exploitable* flaws in bytecode verification or other VM-level security tasks. It still happens, but much less frequently.

Most applets now will run with the Java Plug-in instead of a browser's built-in VM (as discussed in the following countermeasure section). This gives the application developer the ability to require a certain type and version of VM on the client in order for an applet to run. Additionally, with the advent of JDK 1.2, and also with each successive JDK release, the security model has been updated to allow more flexibility, along with more compartmentalization, of remotely loaded code.

The salient point is that, if you have decided to use a Java applet, there is little as an application developer (or an application client for that matter) that you can do to prevent someone from exploiting a flaw in a particular version of a particular VM—just as there is little you can do to prevent someone from exploiting a flaw in your e-mail client or your native operating system.

Bytecode and VM-level attacks do pose risks to users, but in the opinion of the authors, these risks have been remedied to the point that they deserve to be classified with other system-level security bugs—discover them and install the appropriate patch. In this case, the best protection is information and diligence. Check the security bulletins from the manufacturer of your VM (Sun's bulletins are located at http://java.sun.com/sfaq/chronology.html). If possible, require your users to use something close to the most current version. Tools like the Java Plug-in allow you to use the latest version of the Sun VM to run an applet instead of the older VMs typically included with various web browsers.

Countermeasure: Use the Java Plug-in

For the reasons just mentioned, Sun Microsystems decided to attempt to standardize the VM on which applets run. The result of this standardization undertaking was the Java Plug-in, which is now delivered and bundled with the base installation of the JRE on a particular platform. This plug-in uses the extension facilities included with many popular web browsers to allow external, trusted applications to render web-based content for the browser. Macromedia Flash and the Real Network's RealPlayer are examples of plug-ins that are in common use.

The Java Plug-in works through a special tag embedded in an HTML page indicating that a Java applet is present. This can either be the standard `Applet` HTML tag or a special browser-specific tag that notifies the browser what type of content is included at the location of the tag and what handler should be used to render it. When the browser sees this tag, it ignores the browser's built-in VM and invokes the Java Plug-in, which uses Sun's JRE. This mechanism gives an application developer the following advantages:

- Application code will always run in a compliant VM, regardless of browser implementation.
- If users do not have the plug-in installed, they will be prompted by the browser to download it from Sun.
- The application code gains the optimization and performance enhancements contained in the Sun version of the VM.
- Although no VM will ever be totally impervious to illicit bytecode level attacks and type confusion attacks, it is generally acknowledged that the Sun VM implementation is more resistant to these forms of attack than the VMs built by many browser manufacturers.
- The application can now use many of the advanced security features (security management through policy files, JAAS, JSSE) that browser VMs do not support or support in a nonstandard manner.

Now we will convert the retirement application to an applet that will be used on a platform containing the Java Plug-in and a JDK 1.4-compatible JRE.

Applets and Security Policies

In some browser VMs, applets run using a separate security manager. However, with the Java Plug-in, applets will run, by default, with the default Java security manager—the same one we enabled in our stand-alone application. A difference with applets is that they *always* run with a security manager installed, for obvious reasons. The default security policy, as specified in the `java.policy` file in the `lib/security` subdirectory of the JRE installation, is extremely restrictive and does not give an applet much latitude in terms of its abilities or privileges. The following are some implications of the basic permissions in the default `java.policy` file on applets using the 1.4 JDK:

- It can listen on a port numbered 1024 or above on the local machine.
- It can read, but not modify, system properties that detail the current username; the version and vendor of the VM; the platform path and file separator; and the name, vendor, and version of the operating system.
- It can stop a thread by using the deprecated call to the `stop` method of the `Thread` class.

That's it. An applet running with a default policy file cannot do anything else requiring a particular permission. So, if you need to develop an applet that will be distributed via the Internet and must run on a default plug-in installation, your options are somewhat limited.

We could modify our application to meet these constraints, but instead, we will assume that we merely want to use applet technology as a vehicle to deliver our application to authorized users via a corporate intranet. Because of this assumption, and because of the fact that we will have many more security-related options to review, we will also assume that we have the ability to modify (usually through an install script) the security policy file in force when our applet runs.

Creating the Applet

To convert our application into applet form, we must undertake several tasks:

1. Modify or replace the application's main `JFrame` with a `JApplet`. The `JApplet` will have a fixed size that will be determined by its container.
2. Remove the `main` method from the application method and move the logic to the applet life cycle methods: `init`, `start`, `stop`, and `destroy`.
3. Build an HTML page to contain the applet.
4. Make a JAR file that contains all of the class files necessary for the applet to run and place it on a web server along with the HTML page.

Each of these tasks has security implications, which we will discuss as we perform each step.

Adding the ClientApplet Class Our first step will be to change our `ClientFrame` class into a class called `ClientApplet`, which will extend `JApplet` (instead of `JFrame`). The relevant code looks like this:

```
/**
 * Builds an instance of the ClientApplet
 */
public ClientApplet() {
  super();
}

public void init() {
  // These are both risky things to let a program do...
  // But we trust ourselves -- just make sure that the grants
  // for these permissions are done with the
  // signedBy attribute set in the policy file.
  System.setProperty("java.security.auth.login.config",
      "http://localhost:8080/RetirementApp/jaas.conf");
```

```
// Reset the policy file and refresh it.
System.setProperty("java.security.policy",
    "http://localhost:8080/RetirementApp/retirement.policy");

Policy.getPolicy().refresh();
```

Notice that we are setting the relevant system properties so that both our security policy and our JAAS configuration are loaded remotely from our web server (in this case, our local machine, as specified by `localhost`). We could also set the properties for and load our security logging configuration this way. In an ideal world, we would load these files using HTTPS with client authentication. This mechanism will be further discussed in later chapters. For now, we'll accept the possibility that someone could spoof our web server and download our policy file using HTTP.

Adding Applet Methods The main body of our `init` method is mostly extracted from our `main` method. Remember that the `init` method will run only once, when the plug-in loads the applet for the first time.

```
if (authenticateUser()) {

  try {

    // Build a SecretKey to instantiate our PersistenceService.
    sun.misc.BASE64Decoder decoder = new sun.misc.BASE64Decoder();
    SecretKeyFactory skf = SecretKeyFactory.getInstance("DESede", "BC");
    // Build a KeySpec from our stored key.
    SecretKeySpec secKeySpec =
        new
          SecretKeySpec(
                decoder.decodeBuffer(fileKeyBASE64),"DESede");
    // Generate the key itself.
    SecretKey fileKey = skf.generateSecret(secKeySpec);

    // Get the credential information for our user.
    Set s = loginContext.getSubject().getPrivateCredentials(
        MySQLCredential.class);
    Iterator i = s.iterator();
    if (i.hasNext()) {
      MySQLCredential cred = (MySQLCredential) i.next();
      // Instantiate our model.
      model = new MySQLPersistenceService(cred,fileKey);
      initComponents();

    } else {
      secLogger.log(Level.WARNING,"No MySQLCredential for user");
    }
  } catch (PersistenceException e) {
```

```
        appLogger.log(Level.SEVERE,"Persistence Exception", e);
      } catch (GeneralSecurityException e) {
        appLogger.log(Level.SEVERE,"Security Exception", e);
      } catch (IOException e) {
        appLogger.log(Level.SEVERE,"IOException", e);
      }
    } else {
      JOptionPane.showMessageDialog(null,
          "You have failed to enter the correct userid or password",
          "Login failure", JOptionPane.ERROR_MESSAGE);

    }
}
```

The `destroy` method (called when the applet reference is about to be released by the container) looks like this:

```
/
  public void destroy() {
    if (model != null) {
      model.close();
    }
    try {loginContext.logout();} catch (Exception e) {}
  }
```

Depending on our application design, we might want to write our code so that the JDBC connection to our database is dropped in the `stop` method instead of the `destroy` method and reestablished in the `start` method. For now, we will keep our applet simple, but extremely greedy from a resource standpoint, by keeping our database connection open until our applet is purged from the browser cache or the user closes the container.

Adding Applet Permissions We also need to add the following permissions to the `java.policy` file on the client machine, in addition to the permissions we already added for the custom `LoginModule` sample application:

```
grant { // New for applet
  permission java.util.PropertyPermission "java.security.auth.login.config", "write";
  permission java.util.PropertyPermission "java.security.policy", "write";
  permission java.lang.RuntimePermission
"accessClassInPackage.sun.security.provider";
  permission java.security.SecurityPermission "getPolicy"; };
```

These permissions allow any code running on our machine to modify the system properties associated with the security policy and the JAAS configuration. This is a condition that is not safe and we will fix shortly, but for now, we will merely add these statements to our `java.policy` file.

Creating the JAR File Next, we will add the classes needed for our applet to a JAR file. We will seal the JAR file using the same mechanism discussed earlier in this chapter. For our applet, our JAR file will be called `RetirementClient.jar`.

Building an HTML File Our final step before deployment will be to build an HTML file containing a reference to our applet. Traditionally, this reference has taken the form of an `APPLET` tag in a HTML file, in this case, called `ClientPage.html`, which looks something like this:

```
<HTML>
<HEAD><TITLE>Retirement Client Applet</TITLE></HEAD>
<BODY>
  <H1><CENTER>The Retirement Client</CENTER></H1><BR>
  <APPLET archive="RetirementClient.jar,mm.mysql-2.0.13-bin.jar"
      code="book.cs.applet.ClientApplet.class" width=400 height=200>
    <hr>
      Your browser does not appear to be Java-enabled.
    <hr>
  </APPLET>
</BODY>
</HTML>
```

The Java Plug-in is unable to override the `APPLET` tag of some implementations of older browsers, and if the user does not have the plug-in installed, the browser will attempt to run the applet with its own VM. This is not a desirable condition. For production use, instead of the `APPLET` tag, the HTML page containing the applet should be converted using the applet HTML Converter provided with JDK 1.4. It is a GUI-driven program that will add the necessary tags to the HTML page to allow your applet to run with an appropriate version of the Java Plug-in under most common browsers. The converter resides in the `lib` subdirectory of the JDK and can be run with the following command line:

```
java -jar %JAVA_HOME%/lib/htmlconverter.jar -gui
```

For simplicity, we will use the plain `APPLET` tag for our example.

Deploying the Web Application After we deploy this HTML file, along with the JAR files mentioned in the archive attribute of the APPLET tag, we need to place two more files on the web server: our JAAS configuration file and our policy file. Our code will load both of these remotely. This will help us, because our client will not need a local version of a JAAS configuration file with our custom `LoginModule` information embedded. In our case, we will deploy these files as part of a web application called `RetirementApp` with a context root of `RetirementApp`.

Running the Applet

When we type the URL `http://localhost:8080/RetirementApp/ClientPage.html` in our Netscape 6.2 browser, we see the following:

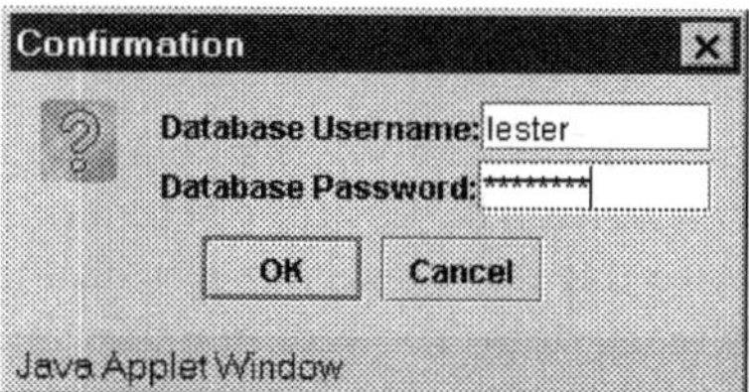

As you can see, the applet is using the custom JAAS login module we created earlier in the chapter and has full access to the database server. Once the user logs in, they are presented with the applet GUI shown in Figure 7-7.

Overall, with the proper policy file, applets are an extremely attractive way to deploy code. The user typically needs nothing but a web browser and a Java Plug-in to run the applet in question. However, by now, it should be obvious that we are granting permissions to our applet that we don't want other, potentially malicious, applets to be able to use. From a security standpoint, there is nothing wrong with wanting to write an applet

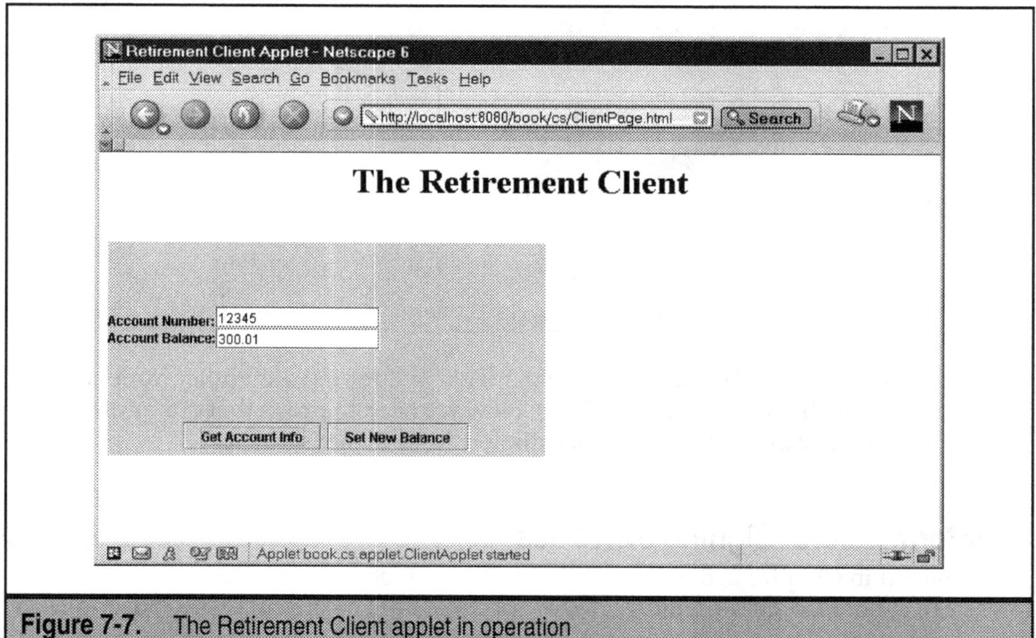

Figure 7-7. The Retirement Client applet in operation

that needs additional permissions. We merely need a way to prove that the applet that is attempting to run has been developed by us and has not been modified since. Once we can do that, users should feel confident giving our applet the same permissions that they would implicitly give a Java application by installing it on their workstation, while simultaneously forcing applets composed by unknown authors to run in a much more secure "sandbox."

The question then becomes, "How can we prove, beyond a shadow of a doubt, that the code on our web server was written by us and not just placed there by a malevolent attacker?" Earlier, you saw how to use digital signatures as a mechanism to validate the integrity and authorship of arbitrary data. We will use this same conceptual mechanism to demonstrate the authenticity of our applet code.

Now that we've got a working applet, let's remove the entries that we added to our system's `java.policy` file. After we do this, and then attempt to run the applet again, we see the following:

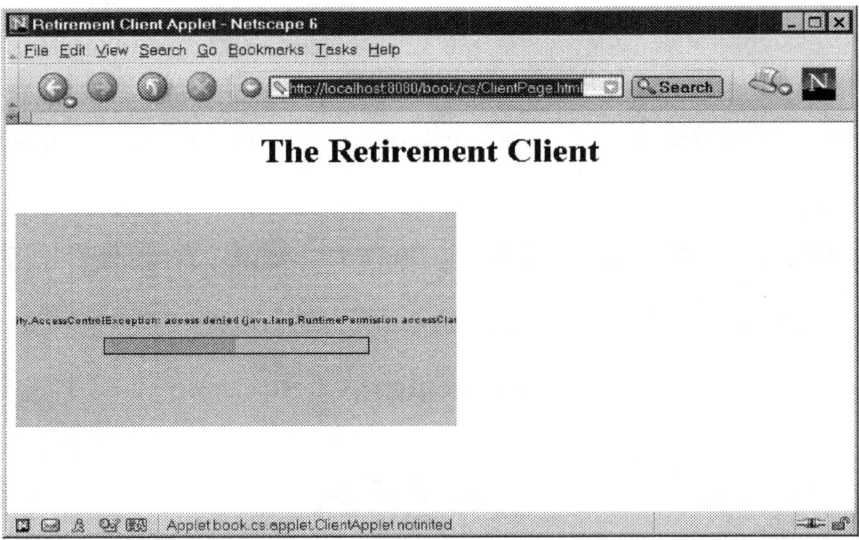

This is a good result. The Java security manager is stopping our applet from performing tasks that it isn't authorized to perform. Now we need to prove that our applet can be trusted, and then grant it the specific permissions that it needs.

Countermeasure: Signing JAR Files

As explained in Chapter 2, the `jarsigner` utility, which is distributed with the JDK, allows us to generate digital signatures for every class file in a particular JAR. So, implicitly, `jarsigner` generates a digest of each class file, then signs the digest with our private key. It also adds some extra files to the JAR and some extra entries to the JAR manifest to communicate the digital signature information.

To sign a JAR file with `jarsigner`, we need a private key, which we still have from our digital signature exercise earlier, and a JAR file to sign. To sign our `RetirementApp.jar` file, we perform the following command sequence:

```
C:\sec\book>jarsigner -keystore admin.ks -storetype JCEKS jars/RetirementClient.
jar adminkey
Enter Passphrase for keystore: password
```

A more subtle point is that we also need to sign the JAR file containing our JDBC driver (`mm.mysql-2.0.13-bin.jar`). We need to do this because we want the driver code to enjoy the same permissions as our application does.

After we sign the JAR files, if we attempt to run the applet again, we see the output shown in Figure 7-8.

By the simple act of signing the JAR file and proving to the user that we are responsible for its contents, the user now gets to choose whether to let our applet run once, run always, or not run at all. If the user elects to let our applet run, by clicking one of the Grant buttons, our applet will run with *full application permissions*. Essentially, the user can make the decision, and the applet will run as if it was an application installed locally on the user machine, with a security manager, but with `AllPermission` privileges.

This is extremely beneficial functionality, except for one problem: Implicitly, by turning the security manager off, the applet user defeats our application authorization scheme! All users will now be granted our custom `setBalance` permission, because the security manager has granted `AllPermission` to all principals using our code. This is not a good situation. There are three possible solutions for us at this point: Use negative

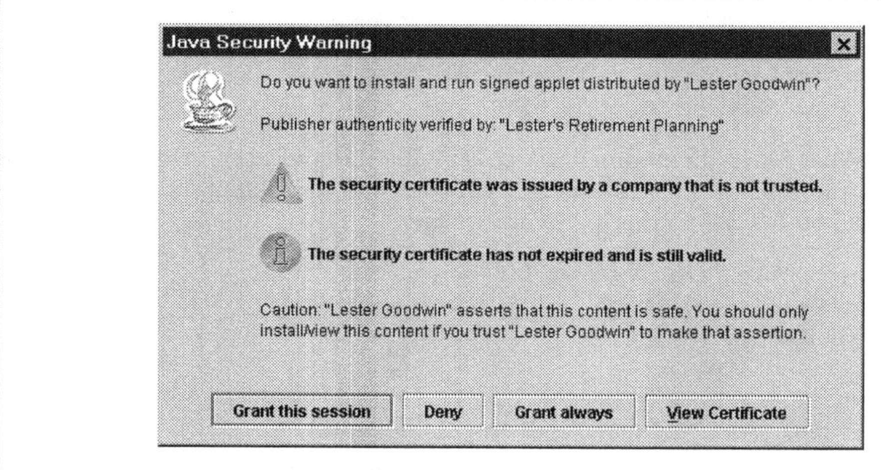

Figure 7-8. The applet security warning

security grants, change our authorization scheme, or disable the dialog that allows the user to grant full access to our code.

Using negative security grants means changing our authorization metaphor so that instead of having a `setBalance` permission, we would have a `cannotSetBalance` permission. Since permissions are always added to each other, granting `AllPermission` would prohibit the user from setting the balance. To give a user full access to our application, we would not grant them any application-specific permissions. To give a user no access, we would grant them all of our application permissions. This can be an effective mechanism, but it is generally confusing to administer and has some other subtle implications on the way we must write our application code.

Additionally, we may want to give the user the option to grant all permissions to our code or to make a conscious decision about using our applet. Even though we will discuss later in this chapter how to disable the "Grant Access" prompt box, it might not be the right option for all applet deployments.

It would be nice if we had an easier way to do our programmatic authorization which would enable our applet to blend in with the existing applet security model. Fortunately, we do.

Adding Programmatic Authorization Support

We have just built our own `MySQLCredential` object, which embodies a particular subject's rights with regard to our application running with a MySQL database as its persistence store. Let's extend our `Credential` object to support simple programmatic authorization. So now, instead of just being a token that allows us access to the database, it will also serve as a token that we can programmatically use to determine application-level authorization. To enable this scheme, we will add one simple method to `MySQLCredential` that returns true if the owner of the credential is authorized to perform application operations that write data (like setting an account balance) as follows:

```
public boolean canWriteData() {
  return userName.equalsIgnoreCase("lester");
}
```

Because we have already modified the `init` method of the `ClientApplet` to pass the credential into the `MySQLPersistenceService` through a slightly modified constructor, we will be able to use this to our advantage.

```
// Get the credential information for our user.
Set s = loginContext.getSubject().getPrivateCredentials(
    MySQLCredential.class);
Iterator i = s.iterator();
if (i.hasNext()) {
  MySQLCredential cred = (MySQLCredential) i.next();
  // Instantiate our model.
```

```
model = new MySQLPersistenceService(cred,fileKey);
initComponents();
```

When we actually need to check the permission, we insert the following code into our `set401KBalance` method in the `MySQLPersistenceService` class:

```
public void set401kBalance(String accountNumber, BigDecimal newBalance)
      throws AccountNotFoundException, OperationNotAllowedException,
             PersistenceException {

    // Do a programmatic check against our custom principal also.
    if (!userCredential.canWriteData()) {
      secLogger.log(Level.WARNING,"Unsuccessful setBalance attempt Subject: "
                  + userCredential.getUserName());
      throw new OperationNotAllowedException(
          "User not authorized to set the balance");
    }
    try {
      updateStmt.clearParameters();

 . . .
```

Currently, our `canWriteData` method is hardcoded in our `MySQLCredential` class, but we could easily extend this method to verify permissions based on calling a stored procedure or interrogating a read-only view of an application authorization table in the database.

Finally, in the environment of a typical corporate intranet, it would be nice to have a way to indicate that all applets constructed by the company should have one set of (potentially not comprehensive) privileges, while applets originating outside the intranet should be more restricted. We can do this by using the codebase attribute in our Java policy file.

Granting Special Permissions to Code

By using the `codebase` attribute, we can grant special permissions to code that originates from a certain URL or group of URLs. For example, we could include a `grant` statement like this in our policy file:

```
grant codebase "http://localhost:8080/-" {
  permission javax.security.auth.AuthPermission "createLoginContext.RetirementClient";
  permission java.lang.RuntimePermission "accessClassInPackage.sun.misc";
  permission javax.security.auth.AuthPermission "doAsPrivileged";
  permission javax.security.auth.AuthPermission "getSubject"; };
```

We are able to grant the listed permissions to all code originating on our local Tomcat web server. Initially, this may seem like a good idea, but when used with DNS names or groups of IP addresses, this scheme will break down under a spoofing attack. If attackers are able to spoof the IP address of our web server and insert their own, or trick our DNS server into misrepresenting a particular hostname, their attack code will have the same privileges as if it originated from the host in question.

Typically, it is a much better idea to use the `signedBy` clause in your `grant` statements. The `signedBy` clause will grant permissions based on the signer or signers of the JAR file where a particular class originates. This is a cryptographically strong way to assert the identity of code, as opposed to the weaker, codebase-centric technique.

TIP From a performance standpoint, it used to be much slower to load classes remotely out of JAR files, because potentially every JAR in the remote classpath would need to be downloaded and then unpacked to load a particular class file for the application. This caused many applet developers to shy away from using signed JAR files, preferring instead to load classes one at a time from the server and use codebase-centric policy files. However, with the advent of JAR file indexing, this class-loading behavior can be modified so that, with proper JAR file partitioning, remote classes are loaded in a much more efficient manner. See the documentation on JAR file indexing provided with JDK 1.4 for more information on this particular technology.

Once we have signed our JAR file, we can grant code originating in it permissions by adding a `signedBy` clause to the `grant` statements within our policy file.

To write a `signedBy` clause in our policy file, we need to specify two things: the public alias of a signed certificate that we would like to grant certain permissions to and the keystore we should use to load the certificate with the alias. If we don't specify a keystore, the default user keystore will be used. A password is generally not required, because public certificates can be read from the keystore without a password.

We will build a policy file that uses a remote keystore to read the certificate that we will use to verify the identity of the signer of our JAR file. We do this to demonstrate that a keystore can be loaded from any URL, not just the local file system. In a real application, to help protect against a spoofing attack, the keystore would be placed on a different web server than the applet code. To keep things simple and because, if you are following along with the code downloaded from www.hackingexposedjava.com, you are running only a single web server, we'll load our keystore from the same server as our applet code. The `keystore` entry and `grant` statement in the modified policy file look like this:

```
keystore "http://localhost:8080/RetirementApp/RetirementApp.ks", "JCEKS";
grant signedBy "admincert" {
. . .
};
```

If we add this entry to the default `java.policy` file for the system in question, and then invoke the applet, we see the same security warning box as earlier (Figure 7-8). However, this time, we will attempt to deny the applet's request for access. When we click the Deny button, the security warning goes away, but amazingly, the applet still runs. Why does this happen? The reason is that we have granted JAR files signed by `admincert` the necessary permissions in our prevailing policy file.

The security warning box controls only whether or not the applet will receive the `AllPermission` grant. If you deny the `AllPermission` grant through the dialog box, the applet will still run with the default security policy in force, which in our case is sufficient—we have granted the necessary permissions to any code signed by the owner of the certificate stored under the alias `admincert`. Fortunately, we can add an additional permission to the system policy file that will override the plug-in's display of the security warning dialog box. We can also add a permission to get rid of the "Java Applet Window" message from the status bar of our dialog boxes. Here are the necessary permissions:

```
// Turn off applet user interrogation.
permission java.lang.RuntimePermission "usePolicy";
```

This permission will force the plug-in to use the local policy files and prohibit the user from granting any signed applet unlimited access to the system. The next permission will remove the "warning" status bar from the bottom of all applet-generated dialog boxes:

```
// Disable Applet warning status bar.
permission java.awt.AWTPermission "showWindowWithoutWarningBanner";
```

This technique can also be used on normal applications running under a security manager to remove the warning message from the status bar.

Now, when we run the applet, we do not see the security warning dialog box, and our login dialog box looks this:

This is much more akin to the look and feel of a real application. There are many more issues surrounding the deployment of applets that are beyond the scope of this text, but we have outlined some simple steps that you can take to dramatically improve the security stature of your applet-based code. Now we will turn to security issues surrounding another Java technology: WebStart.

Protecting WebStart-based Clients

JDK 1.4 ships with built-in support for the Java Network Launching Protocol (JNLP) and API, more commonly known as Java WebStart. Java WebStart is a technology that attempts to combine the benefits of applet-based deployment (remote code and transparent version updates) with the benefits of stand-alone applications (ability to use GUIs based on `JFrames`, no need for a web browser or an applet container, and an application-like look and feel). In many ways, it succeeds in doing this. However, because code is being loaded remotely, you still need to take security precautions into consideration when using WebStart. Like applets, Java WebStart applications *require* that all archives containing application code be signed if the application would like any privileges beyond the default permissions. Unfortunately, at certain times, Java WebStart uses a different policy file than the typical `java.policy` file. The WebStart policy file is located in the Java WebStart directory and has the name `javaws.policy`. By default, this file gives the WebStart container (the Java WebStart Runtime and application launcher) the `AllPermission` permission, so that it can install a security manager but still run with full access to the client system.

Deployment information for the application is specified using XML in a JNLP file, which is placed on a web server, along with the application code and resources. To enable Java WebStart functionality, the user then traverses a link to the JNLP file in their browser, or runs Java WebStart from the command line, passing a URL to the JNLP file. This file is then processed, a local version of the Java Plug-in is started to accommodate the Java WebStart application, and the application is downloaded to the client machine, where optionally it can be cached to run offline at a later time. Every time the application runs, the web server is contacted to determine if an update has been made, and if so, the new version of the application is downloaded and replaces the older version residing in the workstation's Java WebStart cache.

Java WebStart also provides a group of "services" that implement the `javax.jnlp.BasicService` interface to extend the functionality of a WebStart application running with the default, highly restrictive security manager. These services allow an application to have limited access to local files, local printers, and the system clipboard, The application can also download code or data from an arbitrary URL, without violating the integrity of the restrictive security sandbox. For example, if an application attempts to open a file using the `javax.jnlp.FileOpenService`, the user will be prompted to locate the proper file using a Swing File Open dialog box. Therefore, the user has final authority over which files the application can access. These services are all available within the context of every Java WebStart application, and no additional security permissions or configuration is necessary.

Java WebStart-based Deployment Attacks

Popularity:	1
Simplicity:	5
Impact:	6
Risk rating:	**4**

Because WebStart code is loaded remotely, it is vulnerable to many of the same techniques that we saw in the Applets section earlier. Server spoofing, class replacement, and tricking unknowledgable users into granting wide-ranging system access are all very real possibilities with a WebStart deployment.

Countermeasure: Set Security in the JNLP File

Because most Java WebStart code is signed, it can be regulated via `signedBy` grants in the `javaws.policy` file or the system policy file, but Java WebStart gives the application developer two additional security settings, defined in the JNLP file for the application: the security AllPermissions attribute and the J2EE-Client attribute. These attributes can override any policy files in effect. The default settings give application developers a quick way to indicate that their application needs unfettered access to the system or the general security rights associated with a J2EE rich client application, respectively.

WebStart-enabling the Application

To demonstrate how to protect a WebStart deployment, we will WebStart-enable our retirement application. We will use the following strategy:

1. Compose a JNLP file for the retirement client application.
2. Deploy the JNLP file, along with the appropriate signed JAR files and other resources, to the web server.
3. Configure our client to use Java WebStart.

The JNLP file for our sample application looks like this and it relies on the full suite of code examples, which you can find at www.hackingexposedjava.com:

```
<?xml version="1.0" encoding="utf-8"?>
<!-- JNLP File for Retirement Client Application -->
<jnlp
  spec="1.0+"
  codebase="http://localhost:8080/book/cs/"
  href="WebStartClient.jnlp">
  <information>
    <title>Retirement Client Application</title>
    <vendor>finalize(), Inc.</vendor>
    <homepage href="index.html"/>
    <description>Allows the user to retrieve retirement account information</description>
    <description kind="short">Retirement Account Info Viewer</description>
    <icon href="money.jpg"/>
    <offline-allowed/>
```

The last line above allows our application to run in both connected and disconnected mode (using the local persistence service).

```
  </information>
  <security>
    <all-permissions/>
  </security>
```

This grants our application all permissions on the local system (based on user approval, of course).

```
  <resources>
    <j2se version="1.4"/>
    <jar href="RetirementClient.jar"/>
```

```
    <jar href="mm.mysql-2.0.13-bin.jar"/>
  </resources>
  <application-desc main-class="book.cs.webstart.ClientFrame">
    <argument>db</argument>
  </application-desc>
</jnlp>
```

No other special coding is involved. We don't even need to use the Java WebStart services for file access. The JNLP file allows users to give our application unlimited access to their machines. When we deploy the relevant files to our web server and configure our browser to direct `.jnlp` files to the proper content handler (according to the instructions contained in the Java WebStart documentation), we see the following interaction occur when we direct our browser to the URL `http://localhost:8080/RetirementApp/WebStartClient.jnlp`.

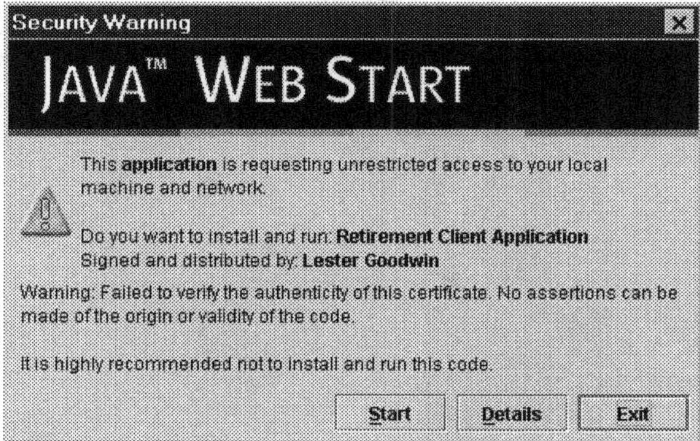

If we grant the permissions requested to our application, it will then run with the look, feel, and access of a normal, locally installed application with an `AllPermission` grant.

Now suppose we change our application's JNLP file to indicate that our application needs J2EE client permissions and not all permissions, by modifying the security entry to read as follows:

```
<security>
  <j2ee-application-client-permissions/>
</security>
```

The retirement client, in an ideal world, and according to the JNLP specification, will now run with the following permissions:

```
permission java.awt.AWTPermission "accessClipboard";
permission java.awt.AWTPermission "accessEventQueue";
permission java.awt.AWTPermission "showWindowWithoutWarningBanner";
permission java.lang.RuntimePermission "exitVM";
permission java.lang.RuntimePermission "loadLibrary";
permission java.lang.RuntimePermission "queuePrintJob"
permission java.net.SocketPermission "*" "connect";
permission java.net.SocketPermission "localhost:1024-" "accept, listen";
permission java.io.FilePermission "*" "read, write";
permission java.util.PropertyPermission "*" "read";
```

If we want to launch our application in the future, we can do so via the Java WebStart Application Manager, where our application now appears:

A very important point to remember is that with Java WebStart, granting permissions to the codebase where the application originates will not work. For example, a `grant` statement such as grant codebase "http://localhost:8080/RetirementApp/-" { permission java.security.AllPermission; }; will not give our Java WebStart application any additional permissions if it is started using the Web-Start Application Manager.

When our application is started via the WebStart Application Manager, it will run out of a local cache, and as such, its codebase will be from the local file system, not the remote server. This is somewhat deceptive. Consider a `grant` statement like this in the system `java.policy` file:

```
grant codebase "file:-" { permission java.security.AllPermission; };
```

This will implicitly give Java WebStart applications launched via the Application Manager full access to all of our system resources. A security warning dialog box will not even be displayed. This is not obvious, and is a potential vulnerability of many security policies currently in force. To avoid this vulnerability, if you are using Java Web-Start applications, exercise caution whenever granting permissions to codebases residing on the local file system.

Countermeasure: Signing JNLP Files

By this point, you may have noticed that an attacker could possibly modify our JNLP file to change the codebase or to request more permissive security settings than the original application developer desired.

Java WebStart provides a mechanism to prevent this by allowing a developer to sign a JNLP file. This is done by including the JNLP file in the signed JAR file used by the application to store its code and other resources. At runtime, the actual JNLP file from the web server will be compared with the signed version of the JNLP file in the JAR file. If there is a mismatch, the application will be terminated.

To sign our JNLP file, we first add the JNLP file to our archive in a file called `APPLICATION.JNLP` in the `JNLP-INF` subdirectory. Then we sign the JAR using normal JAR signing procedures. The embedded JNLP file will be signed along with the rest of the JAR. Now, if an attacker attempts to modify our JNLP file on the web server (perhaps by changing the name of the index page from `index.html` to `anotherindex.html`), we get the following error when we attempt to launch the JNLP file via a web link or the Application Manager:

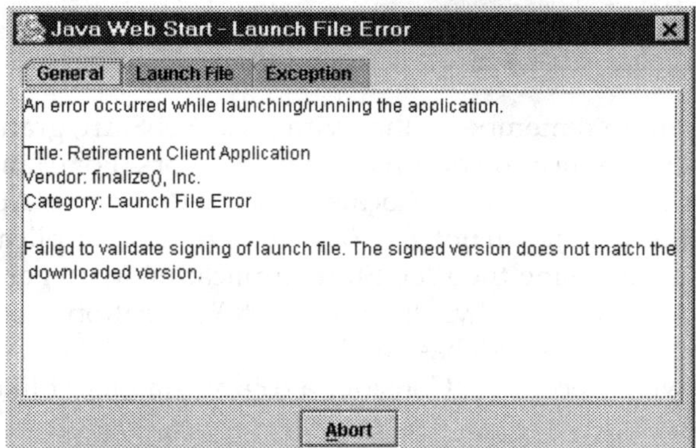

The WebStart runtime detects that the JNLP file has been changed outside our application and refuses to start, regardless of local security settings. This is an underutilized, but extremely important security-related feature bundled with Java WebStart.

SUMMARY

In a client-server application, as in a stand-alone application, application security cannot replace system-level security. However, smart application security design can work with system security techniques to make your application even more daunting to a potential attacker.

In this chapter, we have covered many issues revolving around client-server application security. We first looked at some high-level techniques for securing application data in a relational database and securing the connection between the client application and the database server. Then we focused on client security, describing how to implement the following techniques:

- Sealing packages to prevent class file spoofing
- Using remote JAAS configuration and policy files
- Building a custom JAAS `LoginModule` to perform authentication and authorization with an RDBMS via JDBC
- Building custom principals and credentials to track application-level access
- Implementing security with an applet-based client, including security with signed applets
- Implementing security with a Java WebStart client, including code distribution via JNLP and signing JNLP files

Here, we have covered the most commonly misunderstood and misused facets of client-side Java application security.

Next, we will discuss the implications of adding a new dimension to our architecture: Using Java RMI to communicate with business objects residing on a middle-tier object server.

CHAPTER 8

JAVA NETWORK
APPLICATIONS:
POTENTIAL
SECURITY FLAW
ATTACKS

In this chapter, we will look at securing an RMI application. With RMI, we can create a client that instantiates an object running on a computer somewhere on our network. RMI builds on many of the features of the Java language, such as serialization and platform-independent data types. It was designed to be a simple and flexible way to make method calls across the network. RMI does not include a high level of default security.

THE DANGERS OF RMI

Lester, our application developer, has discovered the benefits of distributed programming. He is thrilled the he can create a remote object and invoke methods on it from client applications on the network. Lester thinks that this is about as good as it gets.

But without knowing it, Lester has opened several security holes in his application. RMI doesn't include any provisions for security. It was designed with the expectation that the developer (preferably not a naive developer) would augment the RMI application with Java security features to provide the level of security needed. It appears that Lester has not done that.

RMI makes all method calls across the network in plain text without any authentication. This leaves applications open to a number of possible exploits, including allowing unauthorized users to access information they shouldn't have access to and to make method calls that they shouldn't be allowed to perform.

The Original RMI Application

We will look at five different versions of Lester's application, adding different levels of security as we continue to strengthen the application. Our first example will be the plain, straightforward version of the application created by Lester. All of the examples are launched by the same client and server classes and use whatever security method is indicated by a command-line parameter.

The Base Remote Object

The code in the following listing (as developed by Lester who has now started leaving his name out as the program author) is the object that exposes the server's functionality to the client applications.

```
package book.rmi;
import java.rmi.RemoteException;
import java.rmi.Remote;

/**
 * This interface defines the Remote Object for RetirementAccountInfo.
 * At this time it only allows for the checking of the account balance
 * for the 401K account.
 */
public interface RetirementAccountInfo extends Remote {
```

```
    /**
     * Get the balance of the account for the indicated account number.
     */
    public Number get401kBalance(String accountNumber)
        throws RemoteException, AccountNotFoundException;

    /**
     * Get the balance of the account for the indicated account number.
     * This method expects the account number to be encrypted and returns
     * the value encrypted.
     */
    public String get401KBalance2(String accountNumber)
      throws RemoteException, AccountNotFoundException;
    /**
     * Get the next challenge for the indicated account number. Requesting
     * a challenge voids all previous challenges.
     */
    public byte[] getChallenge(String accountNumber)
      throws RemoteException, AccountNotFoundException;
    /**
     * Get the account balance. If the response isn't the challenged encrypted
     * with the account's password, then a RemoteException is thrown.
     */
    public Number get401kBalance(byte[] response, String accountNumber)
      throws RemoteException, AccountNotFoundException;
}
```

As you can see in the code's comments, this is the base object that the system is built around. Several different method signatures are listed for `get401kBalance` because solving the security issues can require changes to be made at the business logic level. Those changes will be discussed later as we cover each solution.

The beginning of the file imports the necessary objects and declares the object as being an extension of the `Remote` interface. There are three different variants of the `get401Kbalance` method and a helper function, `getChallenge`, that is necessary for the fourth example.

The Server Program

The next listing is for the server code that offers the functionality to the client. This server program includes code that works with the later examples in this chapter.

```
package book.rmi;
import java.io.IOException;
import java.rmi.AccessException;
import java.rmi.RemoteException;

import java.rmi.registry.LocateRegistry;
import java.rmi.registry.Registry;
```

```
import java.security.Security;

/**
 * This class starts the RMI registry if necessary and then
 * makes one RetirementAccount available depending on the
 * command-line parameter. This class is intended to be run
 * from the command line using java.exe.
 */
public class ServerRMI  {

  /**
   * No one needs to create an instance of this class.
   */
  private ServerRMI() {
  }

  /**
   * Start the RMI Registry and make the RetirementAccount
   * available.
   * args[0] indicates which RetirementAccount to use.
   */
  public static void main(String[] args) {

    // Needed for the SSL Encryption of Communication Channel example
    try {
      Security.addProvider(new com.sun.net.ssl.internal.ssl.Provider());
    } catch (Throwable t) {
      t.printStackTrace();
    }

    // Needed for the Selective Encryption, Method Authentication,
    // and Socket Authentication examples
    try {
      Security.addProvider(new com.sun.crypto.provider.SunJCE());
    } catch (Throwable t) {
      t.printStackTrace();
    }

    // Set the RMI Socket factory for all objects that don't specify a socket
    // factory.
    if (args[0].equals("ex5")) {
      try {
        book.rmi.ex5.AuthenticatedSocketFactory.setSocketFactory(new
              book.rmi.ex5.AuthenticatedSocketFactory());
      } catch (IOException ex) {
        ex.printStackTrace();
      }
      // Set credentials. This is necessary for the server to communicate
      // among its various components (registry and registered objects).
```

```
      book.rmi.ex5.AuthenticatedSocket.setCredentials("server", "server");
    }
    // Create the object as necessary.
    try {
      Registry r = LocateRegistry.createRegistry(Registry.REGISTRY_PORT);
      if ("ex1".equalsargs[0])) {
        r.rebind("/RetirementAccount",
              new book.rmi.ex1.RetirementAccountImpl());
      } else if ("ex2".equals(args[0])) {
        r.rebind("/RetirementAccount",
              new book.rmi.ex2.RetirementAccountImpl());
      } else if ("ex3".equals(args[0])) {
        r.rebind("/RetirementAccount",
              new book.rmi.ex3.RetirementAccountImpl());
      } else if ("ex4".equals(args[0])) {
        r.rebind("/RetirementAccount",
              new book.rmi.ex4.RetirementAccountImpl());
      } else if ("ex5".equals(args[0])) {
        r.rebind("/RetirementAccount",
              new book.rmi.ex5.RetirementAccountImpl());
      } else {
    System.out.println("Invalid command line parameter " + args[0]);
      }
    } catch (RemoteException ex) {
      ex.printStackTrace();
    }

    // Print out all the objects bound to our registry. This should
    // be one object called /RetirementAccount. This helps to know
    // when server initialization is completed, since some of these
    // examples can take a few seconds to initialize (especially SSL).
    try {
      Registry r = LocateRegistry.getRegistry(Registry.REGISTRY_PORT);
      String[] remotes = r.list();
      System.out.println("Bound Names:  ");
      for (int i = 0; i < remotes.length; i++) {
        System.out.println("\t" + remotes[i]);
      }
    } catch (AccessException ex) {
      ex.printStackTrace();
    } catch (RemoteException ex) {
      ex.printStackTrace();
    }
  }
}
```

The `main` method is the entry point into the Java application when it's started in the VM. First, we add security providers to the runtime information. A security provider is a class that provides an implementation for a security algorithm. Providers can be added either in the source code, as is done here, or they can be added using the `java.security` properties file, found in the `jre/lib/security` directory. By doing this in the source code, we allow more flexibility in the user's system configuration. Also, editing the security file would affect all the applications run using the JVM, not just our application.

NOTE If we failed to add these security providers for JDK versions earlier than 1.4, exceptions would be thrown when we tried to use the security algorithms that they implemented.

After some processing specific to the fifth example (using an authenticated communications channel), we create the RMI registry on the default RMI port. It then adds an object to the registry, depending on the command-line parameter.

After the object has been added to the registry, we display all the objects that have been bound to our registry. This was found to be useful during the development of this sample application, because some of the encryption algorithms used by the examples (especially the third and fifth examples) can take some time to initialize themselves.

The Client Application

A simple client application accesses the server. This client was written so that it could access all the various servers shown in this chapter. There are a number of changes that this class goes through for the various examples, so only the part of the class needed for accessing the first example is explained here. The other code will be explained as necessary for the particular examples.

```
package book.rmi;

import java.io.IOException;
import java.rmi.NotBoundException;
import java.rmi.RemoteException;

import java.rmi.registry.LocateRegistry;
import java.rmi.registry.Registry;
import java.security.Provider;
import java.security.Security;
import book.rmi.ex5.AuthenticatedSocketHelper;
/**
 * This class looks up the Retirement Account Balance of an account.
 */
public class ClientRMI {
  /**
   * Look up the account balance and display it on System.out.
   * arg[0] is the security mechamism to use (i.e. ex1, ex2, etc)
   * arg[1] is the account number to look up
   * arg[2] is the account password, when used
   */
  public static void main(String[] args) {
    if (args.length < 3) {
```

```
  System.out.println("Missing parameters.");
  System.out.print("Correct usage:  java book.rmi.ClientRMI");
  System.out.println(" <example> <acct number> <account password>");

  System.exit(0);
}
// Needed for the SSL Encryption of Communication Channel example
try {
  Security.addProvider(new com.sun.net.ssl.internal.ssl.Provider());
} catch (Throwable t) {
  t.printStackTrace();
}

// Needed for the Selective Encryption, Method Authentication,
// and Socket Authentication examples
try {
  Security.addProvider(new com.sun.crypto.provider.SunJCE());
} catch (Throwable t) {
  t.printStackTrace();
}

if ("ex5"equals(args[0])) {
  try {
    book.rmi.ex5.AuthenticatedSocketFactory.setSocketFactory(
          new book.rmi.ex5.AuthenticatedSocketFactory());
  } catch (IOException ex) {
    ex.printStackTrace();
  }
  book.rmi.ex5.AuthenticatedSocket.setCredentials(args[1], args[2]);
}

try {
  Registry r = LocateRegistry.getRegistry(Registry.REGISTRY_PORT);
  RetirementAccountInfo acct =
         (RetirementAccountInfo)r.lookup("/RetirementAccount");
  Number num = null;
  if ("ex1".equals(args[0]) || "ex3".equals(args[0]) ||
      "ex5".equals(args[0])) {
    num = acct.get401kBalance(args[1]);
  } else if ("ex2".equals(args[0])) {
    byte[] bytes = args[1].getBytes();
    // Encrypt and encode bytes.
    String acctNum = EncryptionHelper.encode(
          EncryptionHelper.encrypt(args[1].getBytes(), "SecretKey"));
    String encrypted = acct.get401KBalance2(acctNum);
    String clearText = new String(EncryptionHelper.decrypt(
          EncryptionHelper.decode(encrypted), "SecretKey")).trim();
    num = new Double(clearText);
  } else if ("ex4".equals(args[0])) {
```

```
        byte[] challenge = acct.getChallenge(args[1]);
        byte[] response = EncryptionHelper.encrypt(challenge, args[2]);
        num = acct.get401kBalance(response, args[1]);
      }
      System.out.println("401K Account Balance " + num);
    } catch (RemoteException ex) {
      ex.printStackTrace();
    } catch (NotBoundException ex) {
      ex.printStackTrace();
    } catch (Exception ex) {
      ex.printStackTrace();
    }
  }
}
```

This class follows the same basic format as the server class: import the necessary RMI objects, declare the method, and install the security providers. The client then acquires a reference to the registry using our bound name and gets an instance of `RetirementAccountInfo`. Then it determines the account balance and prints it to the system console.

The Interface Implementation

The final class for the unsecured version of the application is the implementation of the `RetirementAccount` interface. Since each example is a separate package, this class goes in the `book/rmi/ex1` directory.

```
package book.rmi.ex1;

import java.rmi.RemoteException;
import java.rmi.server.UnicastRemoteObject;
import book.rmi.AccountNotFoundException;
import book.rmi.LocalPersistenceService;
import book.rmi.RetirementAccountInfo;
/**
 * A basic implementation of the RetirementAccountInfo interface as
 * a UnicastRemoteObject. This class only implements the basic
 * methods, not the alternates for the other examples.
 */
public class RetirementAccountImpl extends UnicastRemoteObject
      implements RetirementAccountInfo {

  /**
   * A reference to our persistence mechanism
   */
  private LocalPersistenceService persistence;
  private final String localFileName = "appdata.fil";
```

```
/**
 * Call our parent on creation to make sure initialization goes as it
 * should.
 */

public RetirementAccountImpl() throws RemoteException {
  super();
  try {
    persistence = new LocalPersistenceService(localFileName);
  } catch (Exception e) {
    throw new RemoteException("Unable to start persistence service");
  }
}

/**
 * Return the account balance.
 * It also prints to System.out every time someone gets their account
 * balance.
 */
public Number get401kBalance(String accountName)
    throws RemoteException, AccountNotFoundException {
  System.out.print(getClass().getName() + ": Received call to ");
  System.out.println("get401kBalance for " + accountName);
  return persistence.get401kBalance(accountName);
}

/**
 * Not implemented
 */
public String get401KBalance2(String accountNumber)
    throws RemoteException, AccountNotFoundException {
  throw new RemoteException(
          "This class only implements Example 1 methods");
}

/**
 * Not implemented
 */
public byte[] getChallenge(String accountNumber)
    throws RemoteException, AccountNotFoundException {
  throw new RemoteException(
    "This class only implements Example 1 methods");
}
```

```
  /**
   * Not implemented
   */
  public Number get401kBalance(byte[] response, String accountNumber)
      throws RemoteException, AccountNotFoundException {
    throw new RemoteException(
      "This class only implements Example 1 methods");
  }
}
```

This class provides an implementation for the basic version of get401kBalance, but throws exceptions for all other methods. This class, like all the classes in this chapter, uses the LocalPersistenceService used in the previous chapters. After printing the account number of the requester, this class returns the account's balance.

Running the RMI Application

To run this example, you will need to start the class book.rmi.ServerRMI in one JVM, and then run book.rmi.ClientRMI in the other, passing the parameters ex1 for the example and any string you want for the account number. This will then call the server, and both windows will print a line of text. The server will indicate which account called it, and the client will indicate the account balance.

Reading Transient Data

Popularity:	7
Simplicity:	5
Impact:	6
Risk rating:	**6**

In this application, the account number and account balance are transmitted between the server and the client. The RMI and serialization protocols don't indicate that any encryption must take place. Instead, these protocols describe how the data is to be written to the stream so that any other application compliant with the specification can read it. Since RMI sends information across the network, this information could be read in transit by a packet sniffer.

Countermeasure: Selective Encryption

One way to counter this type of attack is to encrypt all important information. In this approach, all sensitive information is encrypted before transmission. The information is then decrypted on receipt.

What Is a Packet Sniffer?

Network communication works by sending packets from one address to another. For Ethernet, one node makes a broadcast of its packet, and every other node receives the packet. If the packet is not addressed to the node, the packet is ignored. In a token-ring network, the packets are passed from node to node until the original node gets its packet back, and the passing is started again. Like Ethernet, token-ring adapters read the packet only if it is addressed to them. For wide area network (WAN) communication, a router attached to the local area network (LAN), usually using Ethernet or token-ring, reads the address and, because of its configuration, knows to read the packet. The packet is then transferred to another network connection, usually a link that directly connects the network to another, distant, network. The routers move the information over these direct links until it gets to the router at the other end, which puts the packet into that LAN.

Network adapters are built so that they read only the data addressed to them from the network. However, almost every Ethernet adapter and most recent token-ring adapters have a *promiscuous* mode. In this mode, the network adapter reads all packets on the network and sends them on to the operating system for processing. This mode was designed to help network administrators and network programmers view the traffic on the network to analyze and diagnose networking problems. Hackers, however, use this mode to view traffic on the network and attempt to intercept important information. The tool they use is a *packet sniffer*.

Hackers can also intercept data between the source and destination by compromising a router. They can then view the traffic as it goes across the router. They may even alter the routing information and send the information to a network that they control—either for capture and then forwarding or for pitching into a black hole, preventing the communication from taking place.

Encrypting the Account Number and Balance

To demonstrate this approach, we will modify our sample application so that the account number being passed to the server is encrypted and the account balance being returned to the client is decrypted. In this example, we will be using the 3DES encryption algorithm.

One downside for this particular example is that the key is hardcoded into the application. A better option would be to make a number of keys available to the client and server and have them select a key dependent on some determining factor, such as a calendar date, port number of the server, or mathematical operation on some numbers provided by the server. In this manner, the client and the server would select the appropriate key without explicitly transmitting the key on the network.

A Helper Class for Encryption

In the next listing, we will examine a helper class that will be used in most of the examples in this chapter. It provides a simple interface to the more complicated JCE API (discussed in Chapter 2).

```
package book.rmi;

import java.io.IOException;
import java.security.NoSuchAlgorithmException;
import java.security.InvalidKeyException;
import java.security.spec.InvalidKeySpecException;
import java.util.Arrays;
import javax.crypto.BadPaddingException;
import javax.crypto.Cipher;
import javax.crypto.IllegalBlockSizeException;
import javax.crypto.NoSuchPaddingException;
import javax.crypto.SecretKey;
import javax.crypto.SecretKeyFactory;
import javax.crypto.spec.DESedeKeySpec;
import sun.misc.BASE64Decoder;
import sun.misc.BASE64Encoder;

/**
 * This class holds all the methods necessary to perform encryption.
 * It performs triple DES encryption/decryption and Base 64
 * encoding/decoding.
 * This class requires Java's JSSE (Java Secure Sockets Extension)
 * and JCE (Java Cryptography Extension).
 * To use it, simply call its static methods.
 */
public class EncryptionHelper {

  /**
   * Since we will always use the same algorithm, we will create a
   * Cipher object for the course of execution. It's initialized on
   * first use.
   */
  private static Cipher cipher;
  /**
   * To make sure no one creates any instances of this object, we'll
   * declare this private.
   */
  private EncryptionHelper() {
  }
  /**
   * Encode the array of bytes using the Base64 algorithm.
   */
  public static String encode(byte[] cipherbytes) {
```

```
    BASE64Encoder encoder = new BASE64Encoder();
    return encoder.encode(cipherbytes);
  }
  /**
   * Encrypt the string of bytes so that it can be decrypted with the
   * key listed. It may return null if an error occurs (such as not
   * being able to load the necessary APIs).
   */
  public static byte[] encrypt(byte[] clearbytes, String key) {
    if (cipher == null) {
      // Create the cipher since it doesn't exist.
      try {
        cipher = Cipher.getInstance("DESede/ECB/NoPadding");
      } catch (NoSuchPaddingException ex) {
        ex.printStackTrace();
      } catch (NoSuchAlgorithmException ex) {
        ex.printStackTrace();
      }
    }
    // Keys need to be a certain number of bytes long. Provide a
    // base that is the correct length.
    String baseKey = "123456789012345678901234";
    StringBuffer sb = new StringBuffer();
    while (sb.length() < baseKey.length()) {
      sb.append(key);
    }
    key = sb.substring(0, baseKey.length());

    try {
      // Initialize the cipher for encryption.
      DESedeKeySpec keyspec = new DESedeKeySpec(key.getBytes());
      SecretKeyFactory keyfactory = SecretKeyFactory.getInstance("DESede");
      SecretKey skey = keyfactory.generateSecret(keyspec);

      cipher.init(Cipher.ENCRYPT_MODE, skey);

      // Data to be encrypted must be a multiple of 8 bytes long.
      // Pad with the NULL (0x00) value.
      if (clearbytes.length % 8 != 0) {
        byte[] fixedLength = new byte[clearbytes.length +
              ( 8 - (clearbytes.length%8) )];
        Arrays.fill(fixedLength, (byte)0);
        System.arraycopy(clearbytes, 0, fixedLength, 0, clearbytes.length);
        clearbytes = fixedLength;
      }
      // encrypt
      byte[] cipherbytes = cipher.doFinal(clearbytes);
      return cipherbytes;
    } catch (InvalidKeyException ik) {
```

```
      ik.printStackTrace();
    } catch (BadPaddingException bp) {
      bp.printStackTrace();
    } catch (IllegalBlockSizeException ibs) {
      ibs.printStackTrace();
    } catch (NoSuchAlgorithmException ex) {
      ex.printStackTrace();
    } catch (InvalidKeySpecException ex) {
      ex.printStackTrace();
    }
    return null;
  }

  /**
   * Decode the array of bytes using the Base64 algorithm.
   */
  public static byte[] decode(String s) throws IOException {
    BASE64Decoder decoder = new BASE64Decoder();
    return decoder.decodeBuffer(s);
  }

  /**
   * Decrypt the string of bytes with the indicated key.
   * It may return null if an error occurs (such as not
   * being able to load the necessary APIs).
   */
  public static byte[] decrypt(byte[] cipherbytes, String key) {
    if (cipher == null) {
      // Create the cipher.
      try {
        cipher = Cipher.getInstance("DESede/ECB/NoPadding");
      } catch (NoSuchPaddingException ex) {
        ex.printStackTrace();
      } catch (NoSuchAlgorithmException ex) {
        ex.printStackTrace();
      }
    }
    // Keys need to be a certain number of bytes long. Provide a
    // default that the password overwrites.
    String baseKey = "123456789012345678901234";
    StringBuffer sb = new StringBuffer();
    while (sb.length() < baseKey.length()) {
      sb.append(key);
    }
    key = sb.substring(0, baseKey.length());
    try {
      // Initialize the cipher for decryption.
```

```
      DESedeKeySpec keyspec = new DESedeKeySpec(key.getBytes());
      SecretKeyFactory keyfactory = SecretKeyFactory.getInstance("DESede");
      SecretKey skey = keyfactory.generateSecret(keyspec);

      cipher.init(Cipher.DECRYPT_MODE, skey);
      byte[] clearbytes  = cipher.doFinal(cipherbytes);
      return clearbytes;
    } catch (BadPaddingException bp) {
      bp.printStackTrace();
    } catch (InvalidKeyException ik) {
      ik.printStackTrace();
    } catch (IllegalBlockSizeException ibs) {
      ibs.printStackTrace();
    } catch (Exception ex) {
      ex.printStackTrace();
    }
    return null;
  }
}
```

This class has four methods: `encode`, `encrypt`, `decode`, and `decrypt`. The `encode` and `decode` methods perform the base 64 encoding and decoding, respectively. The `encrypt` and `decrypt` methods perform 3DES encryption and decryption.

The `encode` method wraps the `Base64Encoder` object. Similarly, the `decode` method wraps the `Base64Decoder` object.

The `encrypt` method creates a new `Cipher` object if one doesn't exist. The string used to create the cipher is where we specify the 3DES algorithm (DESede) in the ECB mode without any padding.

Next, we create the key that will be used to encrypt the data. In this example, we have a default value of the correct length. We will encrypt the password with itself; this way, a separate key is used for each user. To ensure that the encryption key is the correct length, we will repeat the password as many times a necessary to have the same number of characters, as is required. This provides a key of the correct length that doesn't use the same value for all of the missing characters and still provides a value that can be known to both the server and the client. The `SecretKey` object is created for the 3DES algorithm using the key that was just modified. The cipher is then initialized with the key and its mode.

The next lines pad the data with `null` (byte value of zero) to make the length of the array of bytes a multiple of 8. The encryption of the data takes only a single line of code, followed by a `return` statement. A series of `catch` statements catches all the exceptions that might be thrown during the encryption process.

The `decrypt` method works similarly to the `encrypt` method. We create the cipher, modify the key, and initialize the cipher. We then perform and return the decryption. Finally, we catch the exceptions.

A New Retirement Account Object and Get Balance Method

A new `RetirementAccountImpl` object has been created for this example, and the `get401KBalance2` method is listed next.

```
package book.rmi.ex2;

import java.io.IOException;
import java.rmi.RemoteException;
import java.rmi.server.UnicastRemoteObject;
import book.rmi.AccountNotFoundException;
import book.rmi.LocalPersistenceService;
import book.rmi.RetirementAccountInfo;
import book.rmi.EncryptionHelper;

/**
 * A basic implementation of the RetirementAccount interface as
 * a UnicastRemoteObject. This class only implements the encrypted
 * parameter and return call method get401kBalance2, not the other
 * methods.
 */
public class RetirementAccountImpl extends UnicastRemoteObject
    implements RetirementAccountInfo {

  /**
   * This method takes the account number as a parameter, encrypted
   * using the Triple-DES algorithm and a secret key. The return value
   * of the balance is then encrypted using the same algorithm and key.
   */
  public String get401KBalance2(String accountNumber)
      throws RemoteException, AccountNotFoundException {
    // Decode and decrypt account number.
    try {
      String acctName = new String(EncryptionHelper.decrypt(
            EncryptionHelper.decode(accountNumber), "SecretKey")).trim();
      System.out.print(getClass().getName() + ": Received call to ");
      System.out.println("get401kBalance for " + acctName);
      Number retVal = persistence.get401kBalance(acctName);
      // Encrypt and encode return value.
      String encrypted = EncryptionHelper.encode(
          EncryptionHelper.encrypt(retVal.toString().getBytes(),
          "SecretKey"));
      return encrypted;
    } catch (IOException ex) {
      throw new RemoteException("Error getting 401K Balance", ex);
    }
  }
```

This class defines an implementation of the RetirementAccount object. It implements only the method for this example and throws exceptions for all of the other methods.

We created the get401kBalance2 method specifically for this example, mainly for the simplicity of using strings to pass the values between the client and server. Alternatively, we could use a byte array and shift the values to reconstruct the values, but the additional complexity of the shifts reduces the clarity of the example.

The get401kBalance2 method determines the account number by first decoding the string containing the account number and then decrypting the value using our secret key SecretKey. We then trim the value to remove any excess spaces added by the padding of the data. Next, we log the request to System.out and determine the account balance. Following that is the encryption and encoding of the object.

First, we turn the object into a string, and then we get the bytes representing the object. We then encrypt this object using the same key as previously used and encode it using the base 64 algorithm. Finally, we return the encrypted value and catch the IOException that could be thrown, wrap the exception as a RemoteException, and throw the newly created exception.

The Client Encryption/Decryption Code

The following snippet is the code from ClientRMI that performs the encryption and decryption necessary to communicate with the modified server object.

```
} else if (args[0].equals("ex2")) {
  byte[] bytes = args[1].getBytes();
  // Encrypt and encode bytes.
  String acctNum = EncryptionHelper.encode(
        EncryptionHelper.encrypt(args[1].getBytes(), "SecretKey"));
  String encrypted = acct.get401KBalance2(acctNum);
  String clearText = new String(EncryptionHelper.decrypt(
        EncryptionHelper.decode(encrypted), "SecretKey")).trim();
  num = new Double(clearText);
```

This code performs the opposite actions of the get401kAccountBalance2 method. First, we encrypt and encode the account number using our secret key. Then we call the method on the server. Finally, we decrypt and decode the return value, and then convert it to the correct type for the method.

Advantages and Disadvantages of Selective Encryption

This example illustrates selectively encrypting sensitive information for its communication across the network. Using this approach, however, involves a number of tradeoffs and potential problems.

First, as previously mentioned, having both the client and server know the key to use for encryption without sharing that information with others is difficult with symmetric encryption. You could create a table of keys and use some other bit of information to choose which key in the table to use. Another alternative would be to use public key encryption. In this case, all of the clients use the same public key to encrypt the data. The server then uses its own private key to decrypt the communication. This solves the problem of key distribution, since the key was designed specifically for public distribution.

Another issue with this solution is that the encryption and decryption steps must be performed on both ends of the communication. If a different developer programs each side, then the communication won't work correctly—one side will be trying to use encrypted data as if it was never encrypted! If the same programmer develops both ends of the communication then the possibility exists that he might forget to perform the encryption. Normal testing wouldn't catch this since neither end of the communication would expect the data to be encrypted. Only code reviews or using packet sniffers could bring this vulnerability to light. Encrypting some of the fields in this manner reduces the clarity of the business logic because the encryption and decryption are intermixed. For some systems, this might not be an issue due to how the communication is structured. Some systems, especially those that are adding encryption after the system was already designed or even developed, might require extensive changes.

Lastly, encryption adds overhead processing. If a significant amount of the information needs to be encrypted, this processing can significantly slow down the system.

The benefit of using selective encryption over an encrypted communications channel, described next, is that you are spending resources on encrypting only the data that is sensitive. You are not encrypting public or other information that would not be useful to attackers.

Countermeasure: Encrypted Communication Channels

An alternative to selective encryption is to encrypt the entire communication channel between the client and the server. Using this approach, all the RMI calls are made through a socket that provides encryption. This method minimizes the security details present in the business logic and avoids problems with programmers making mistakes about what to encrypt.

Using an SSL Connection between the Client and Server

For this example, we will use an SSL connection between the client and server to protect all data in transient. The client and server software are essentially the same as in the original example. In both the client and server code, we added a security provider to guarantee that the SSL encryption package will be available. All we need to do is make RMI use the SSL sockets.

There are two ways to have RMI use SSL sockets. One approach is to extend `java.rmi.RMISocketFactory`, and then pass that class to `setSocketFactory`. This makes all RMI objects that are not associated with another socket factory use the socket factory specified. We'll use this method in the "Using an Authenticated Communications Channel" section later in this chapter. The other alternative is to set the socket factory through the `UnicastRemoteObject` constructor. This is the approach that we will use now.

The Socket Factories

To set the socket factories in the `UnicastRemoteObject`'s constructor, we first need to create two socket factories: one for the client and one for the server. The next listing shows the server socket factory.

```
package book.rmi.ex3;

import java.io.IOException;
import java.io.Serializable;
import java.net.ServerSocket;
import java.rmi.server.RMIServerSocketFactory;
import javax.net.ServerSocketFactory;
import javax.net.ssl.SSLServerSocket;
import javax.net.ssl.SSLServerSocketFactory;
public class SSLRMIServerSocketFactory
    implements RMIServerSocketFactory, Serializable {

  private static ServerSocketFactory sslFactory = null;

  public SSLRMIServerSocketFactory() {
  }

  public ServerSocket createServerSocket(int port) throws IOException {
    if (sslFactory == null) {
      sslFactory = SSLServerSocketFactory.getDefault();
    }
    SSLServerSocket sslSocket =
       (SSLServerSocket)sslFactory.createServerSocket(port);
    sslSocket.setEnabledCipherSuites
    (sslSocket.getSupportedCipherSuites());
    return sslSocket;
  }
  public boolean  equals(Object that) {
    return that != null && that.getClass() == this.getClass();
  }
}
```

The class we declare doesn't extend anything, but it does implement the `RMIServerSocketFactory` interface along with the `Serializable` interface.

We declare a `ServerSocketFactory` so that we will create this factory only once. There is only one method specified in the `RMIServerSocketFactory` interface: `createServerSocket`. This method takes an `int` value for the port to listen on and returns a `ServerSocket` that will accept connections on that port from any address.

First, we test the socket factory and create it if it doesn't exist. Next, we create the server socket and enable all of the supported cipher suites. If you don't enable any cipher suites, the client and server will never be able to communicate. This is because the server won't support any cipher suites, and the negotiation between the client and server will fail to find an acceptable match. Finally, the socket is returned.

The `equals` method aids in keeping the number of objects in memory down. The RMI library will discard duplicate socket factories and use just one instance when their `equals` method returns true. This implementation returns true whenever the instance of the object and the argument are the same class.

The client socket factory, shown below, is almost identical to the server socket factory. The only difference is that its method is called `createSocket` and it returns a connected socket.

```
package book.rmi.ex3;

import java.io.IOException;
import java.io.Serializable;
import java.net.Socket;
import java.rmi.server.RMIClientSocketFactory;
import javax.net.SocketFactory;
import javax.net.ssl.SSLSocket;
import javax.net.ssl.SSLSocketFactory;

public class SSLRMISocketFactory
    implements RMIClientSocketFactory, Serializable {
  private static SocketFactory sslFactory = null;

  public SSLRMISocketFactory() {
  }

  public Socket createSocket(String host, int port) throws IOException {
    if (sslFactory == null) {
      sslFactory = SSLSocketFactory.getDefault();
    }
    SSLSocket sslSocket = (SSLSocket)sslFactory.createSocket(host, port);
    sslSocket.setEnabledCipherSuites
    (sslSocket.getSupportedCipherSuites());
    return sslSocket;
  }
  public boolean  equals(Object that) {
    return that != null && that.getClass() == this.getClass();
  }
}
```

The RetirementAccount Interface

The code below provides the implementation of the `RetirementAccount` interface as a `UnicastRemoteObject`. Only the methods that are necessary for this example are shown. The other methods in the `RemoteAccountInfo` interface throw exceptions, since they aren't applicable to this example.

```
package book.rmi.ex3;

import java.rmi.RemoteException;
import java.rmi.server.UnicastRemoteObject;
import book.rmi.AccountNotFoundException;
import book.rmi.LocalPersistenceService;
import book.rmi.RetirementAccountInfo;
import book.rmi.EncryptionHelper;
/**
 * A basic implementation of the RetirementAccount interface as
 * a UnicastRemoteObject. This class only implements the basic
 * methods, not the alternates for the other examples.
 */
public class RetirementAccountImpl extends UnicastRemoteObject
    implements RetirementAccountInfo {

  /**
   * A reference to our persistence mechanism
   */
  private LocalPersistenceService persistence;
  private final String localFileName = "appdata.fil";

  /**
   * Create a RetirementAccountImpl that uses SSL as its communication
   * mechanism using any port available.
   */
  public RetirementAccountImpl() throws RemoteException {
    super(0, new SSLRMISocketFactory(), new SSLRMIServerSocketFactory());
    try {
      persistence = new LocalPersistenceService(localFileName);
    } catch (Exception e) {
      throw new RemoteException("Unable to start persistence service");
    }
  }

  /**
   * Return the account balance. This basic method always returns 12.
   * It also prints to System.out every time someone gets their account
   * balance.
   */
  public Number get401kBalance(String accountName)
      throws RemoteException, AccountNotFoundException {
    System.out.print(getClass().getName() + ": Received call to");
    System.out.println(" get401kBalance for " + accountName);
    return persistence.get401kBalance(accountName);
  }

}
```

This implementation of `RetirementAccountImpl` is almost identical to the implementation in the first example. The only difference is that the constructor has been modified. This modification calls the `UnicastRemoteObject` constructor, specifying the server and client socket factories to use with this object. It also specifies a port of 0, indicating that this object is allowed to bind to any port that is available on the server.

Advantages and Disadvantages of Using an Encrypted Communications Channel

Running this example illustrates the major drawback of this method. This version takes significantly longer to start up than the original version of the application. It also takes longer than the selective encryption example, because SSL is a complex protocol to set up on the socket and the encryption used taxes the CPU resources. Because of this slowdown, it is possible that normal usage of the system will slow the machine to a crawl. If you do use this approach, we advise you to load-test your application to verify that you will be able to support the necessary load.

The benefit of this method is that all information is encrypted, so the hacker will not know what information is being transmitted across the network. Additionally, you don't need to rely on the programmers to remember to encrypt all of the sensitive pieces of information. The only requirements are one line per `UnicastRemoteObject` must be modified and the security provider must be installed.

Invalid User Access

Popularity:	*8*
Simplicity:	*4*
Impact:	*10*
Risk Rating:	*7*

Sometimes, the data communicated between the client and the server doesn't need to be kept a secret, but you must be sure who the communication came from. An example of this would be when the company managing the retirement accounts changes the fees it charges. The amount of the fees themselves is public information. However, you don't want your clients to set the fees to zero, and you don't want your competition to set the fees prohibitively high. You only want to allow your employees to set the fees accordingly.

Countermeasure: Challenge/Response for Every Method

One way to prevent unauthorized users from accessing server-side functions is to alter the methods that are called across the network, so that the server can verify the user's identity. The most secure way to do this is to have the client request a challenge phrase. The client software then encrypts this random string of bytes with its password and returns it with the command the user wants to execute. This provides additional security, since every command is authenticated. If done properly, the challenge bytes are so infrequently used that hackers watching the communication channel wouldn't be able to send their own command using a previously viewed response before the client could send its own command.

Implementing Challenge/Response Authentication

To demonstrate the challenge/response approach, we will alter the methods that are used by the client and server for the RMI communication. Additionally, we will need to modify the manner in which these methods are called.

An Authenticated Implementation of the Interface

The next listing shows the new implementation of the `RetirementAccountImpl` for this example.

```
package book.rmi.ex4;

import java.rmi.RemoteException;
import java.rmi.server.UnicastRemoteObject;
import java.security.SecureRandom;
import java.util.Hashtable;
import java.util.Map;
import book.rmi.EncryptionHelper;
import book.rmi.AccountNotFoundException;
import book.rmi.LocalPersistenceService;
import book.rmi.RetirementAccountInfo;

 /**
 * An authenticated implementation of the RetirementAccount interface
 * as a UnicastRemoteObject. This class implements the methods that
 * provide user authentication on a per-method basis.
 *
 * To use this class, you need to call getChallenge, then encrypt the
 * resulting byte array using the Triple-DES algorithm and the user's
 * password as the key. This encrypted value is then the response and
 * is used to verify that users are who they say they are.
 */
public class RetirementAccountImpl extends UnicastRemoteObject
    implements RetirementAccountInfo {

  /**
   * Used to create the challenges. This class is static because it
   * takes a long time to initialize it.
   */
```

```
private static SecureRandom random = new SecureRandom();

/**
 * This class stores the challenges that have been issued.  This is
 * not static, so for each remote object that the user wants to use,
 * they will have to call the correct getChallenge method. It is a
 * Hashtable for thread-safe behavior.
 */
private Map challenges = new Hashtable();

/**
 * Get the challenge for the account number. Getting a challenge
 * will cancel all other challenges issued for the given account for
 * this object.
 */
public byte[] getChallenge(String accountNumber)
    throws RemoteException {
  byte[] challenge = new byte[256];
  random.nextBytes(challenge);
  challenges.put(accountNumber, challenge);
  return challenge;
}

/**
 * Get the 401K Balance for the indicated account. This method will
 * not return the correct value if the response is not the account's
 * encrypted password.
 */
public Number get401kBalance(byte[] response, String accountNumber)
    throws RemoteException, AccountNotFoundException {
  byte[] challenge = (byte[])challenges.get(accountNumber);
  byte[] expectedResponse =
    EncryptionHelper.encrypt(challenge, accountNumber);
  if (expectedResponse == null ||
      response == null ||
      expectedResponse.length != response.length) {
    throw new RemoteException("Error Occurred");
  }
  boolean authenticated = true;
  for (int i = 0; i < expectedResponse.length; i++) {
    authenticated &= expectedResponse[i] == response[i];
  }
  if (!authenticated) {
    throw new RemoteException("Error Occurred");
```

```
        }
        System.out.print(getClass().getName() + ": Received call to ");
        System.out.println("get401kBalance for " + accountNumber);
        return persistence.get401kBalance(accountNumber);
    }
}
```

Two methods are of interest in this example: `getChallenge` and `get401kBalance`. The `getChallenge` method creates an array of bytes and asks the `java.security.SecureRandom` class to randomly fill them. We use `SecureRandom` instead of `Random` because the numbers returned are less predictable. This lower level of predictability makes it more difficult for hackers to launch a *replay attack*, which is when the hackers record a conversation and then perform the same actions as in the recorded conversion. If hackers can successfully predict which challenge they will receive, then they can know that they have a valid response. If hackers can't predict the next challenge generated by the server, then their only option is to begin a conversation with the server and hope that the server's challenge is one for which they have recorded a response.

The signature of the `get401kBalance` has been modified from the original method signature so that the response can be returned to the server. The method first encrypts the challenge for the user using the account's password. Then it checks that the expected response and the actual response match; if they don't match, the code throws an exception. We next log the request to `System.out` and return the value.

The Client Challenge Code

The snippet below shows the portion of `ClientRMI` relevant to call the modified `RetirementAccountInfo` object.

```
} else if (args[0].equals("ex4")) {
        byte[] challenge = acct.getChallenge(args[1]);
        byte[] response = EncryptionHelper.encrypt(challenge, args[2]);
        num = acct.get401kBalance(response, args[1]);
```

In this snippet, the client first asks the server for a challenge phrase. The client encrypts the challenge using the user's password, and then makes the method call to the server with the encrypted challenge and the account number.

Advantages and Disadvantages of Using Challenge/Response Authentication

The major benefit of this approach is that the server knows that the user on the other end at least knows the password of an authorized user. With password-based security, this is the best security a system can provide.

The drawbacks of this approach are similar to those of the selective encryption approach. This method relies on the programmers handling the authentication. This leaves the possibility of certain methods not having the required authentication. It also requires that the security information be part of the business objects. For new systems, this might not be much work to incorporate, but this does present a considerable reengineering effort for existing systems.

This system works at about the same speed as the selective encryption system. The number of method calls has doubled, due to the necessity of obtaining the challenge bytes. The client performs some encryption, and this might be more or less than the encryption that the selective encryption method needs to perform; therefore, the performance of these two methods will vary depending on the specific application.

The challenge/response version performs a little slower than the original version of the application because of the additional network communication and processing for the encryption. This version is faster than the secure communication channel using SSL version because of the limited encryption used in this example and SSL overhead in the other version.

This countermeasure is most suitable when certain methods need to be performed by authenticated users, and the other methods in the system can be executed by any user.

Countermeasure: Authenticated Sockets

One way to authenticate the users that are accessing the system is to use an authenticated communication channel. In this approach, the socket connection between the client and the server performs the authentication before the connection is given to the RMI framework.

Using an Authenticated Communications Channel

In order to use an authenticated communication channel, we must create an authenticated socket class to perform the authentication. Then we must create a socket factory so that RMI can use our new sockets. We must also create a `RetirementAccount` object that knows how to access the user information. Finally, we need to modify the client and server applications to use the new object.

The AuthenticatedSocket Class

The `AuthenticatedSocket` class for the server implements our authentication protocol on top of a normal socket.

```
package book.rmi.ex5;

import java.io.DataInputStream;
import java.io.DataOutputStream;
import java.io.IOException;
import java.net.InetAddress;
import java.net.Socket;
```

```
import book.rmi.EncryptionHelper;

/**
 * This class implements an authentication protocol on top of a normal
 * socket. This is the server side and corresponds to the
 * AuthenticatedSocket client side class.
 *
 * In order to authenticate after the socket is opened, the
 * server reads a Java UTF string. It then sends 256 bytes of random
 * data. The client encrypts those bytes using the Triple-DES
 * encryption algorithm and the user's password as the key. The client
 * then returns the 256 encrypted bytes. If the user is allowed to
 * connect and the encrypted bytes were encrypted with the password,
 * then the server sends the UTF string "OK".  Otherwise, the server
 * sends the string "No" and closes
 * the connection.
 */
public class AuthenticatedSocket extends Socket {

  /**
   * The username to connect to the server with. Only one user/password
   * combination is allowed in the JVM at a time because the RMI
   * architecture makes it difficult to set the client's credentials
   * before contacting the server.
   */
  private static String username = null;

  /**
   * The password to connect to the server with
   */
  private static String password = null;

  /**
   * Set the username and password to use with the server. Setting
   * this once will set it for all instances in the JVM. Resetting
   * this will not invalidate old connections but will be used for all
   * new connections.
   */
  public static void setCredentials(String u, String p) {
    username = u;
    password = p;
  }

  /**
   * Boolean to indicate if this socket was created unconnected, a sign
   * that the socket is a server socket and should log the user out on
   * close.
   */
  private boolean serverSocket = false;
```

```
  /**
   * Create an unconnected socket. Need to allow package access to
   * this method so that AuthenticatedServerSocket can create these.
   */
  AuthenticatedSocket() throws IOException {
    super();
  }

  /**
   * Connect to the server and log in.
   */
  public AuthenticatedSocket(InetAddress address, int port)
      throws IOException {

    super(address, port);
    authenticate();
  }

  /**
   * Connect to the server and log in.
   */
  public AuthenticatedSocket(InetAddress address, int port,
                             InetAddress localAddr, int localPort)
      throws IOException {
    super(address, port, localAddr, localPort);
    authenticate();
  }

  /**
   * Connect to the server and log in.
   */
  public AuthenticatedSocket(String host, int port)
      throws IOException {
    super(host, port);
    authenticate();
  }

  /**
   * Connect to the server and log in.
   */
  public AuthenticatedSocket(String host, int port,
                             InetAddress localAddr, int localPort)
      throws IOException {
    super(host, port, localAddr, localPort);
    authenticate();
  }

  /**
```

```
   * Cause the socket to perform the authentication protocol. This
   * method will throw an exception if the username hasn't been set
   * or if the credentials are incorrect.
   */
  protected void authenticate() throws IOException {
    if (username == null || username.length() == 0) {
      close();
      throw new IOException("Can not send an empty username");
    }
    DataInputStream in = new DataInputStream(getInputStream());
    DataOutputStream out = new DataOutputStream(getOutputStream());

    out.writeUTF(username);
    byte[] challenge = AuthenticatedSocketHelper.readChallengeResponse(in);
    byte[] response = EncryptionHelper.encrypt(challenge, password);
    out.write(response);

    String authenticated = in.readUTF();
    if (!authenticated.equals("OK")) {
      in.close();
      out.close();
      throw new
        IOException("Unable to authenticate credentials with the server");
    }
  }

  /**
   * Calling this method sets the flag that indicates the socket should
   * log out on closing. Needed on the server sockets.
   */
  public void setLoggedIn() {
    serverSocket = true;
  }

  /**
   * Log the user out of the authenticated socket and then close the
   * socket.
   */
  public void close() throws IOException {
    if (serverSocket) {
      AuthenticatedSocketHelper.logout(
        this.getInetAddress().getHostAddress());
    }
    super.close();
  }
}
```

This class keeps one username and password for all instances of the class in the JVM and has a `setCredentials` method to set this information. Several alternatives to this implementation strategy could be used, but this method keeps the security information away from most of the application. One alternative that would still keep the security information isolated would be to define a callback mechanism that would either prompt the user for the credentials or use cached information.

In order to make the extension of `ServerSocket` possible, we declare a no-argument constructor. This constructor does not perform authentication because the socket is not connected at the end of the initialization process. Next, we implement the various constructors declared in the `Socket` superclass. Each of the constructors calls its parent implementation to connect the socket, and then calls the `authenticate` method of this class in order to authenticate the socket to the server. The RMI framework doesn't use all of these methods; they are supplied in case the socket needs to be used for non-RMI communication.

The `authenticate` method performs the important work of this class. First, it verifies that the username is valid and generates an exception if it isn't. Then it opens the streams to perform the communication. We then implement our custom authentication protocol. First, we send our username to the server. Then we read the challenge and encrypt it to create the response. We send the response to the server and read the server's response. If the server's response is "OK," the method silently returns. If the server's response isn't "OK," the communication channels are closed and an exception is thrown.

The `setLoggedIn` method sets the flag that indicates that the socket needs to log out when the socket is closed. This is important for the server side because it allows a client's IP address to be used by another user. The `close` method is overridden to perform the logout action if the flag is set.

Calling this on the client side does not cause any problems, but performs several operations that are unnecessary.

The AuthenticatedServerSocket Class

The `AuthenticatedServerSocket` class extends the `java.net.ServerSocket` class to add the authentication protocol to the socket-connection procedures.

```
package book.rmi.ex5;

import java.io.IOException;
import java.io.DataInputStream;
import java.io.DataOutputStream;
import java.net.InetAddress;
import java.net.ServerSocket;
import java.net.Socket;
import java.security.SecureRandom;
import book.rmi.EncryptionHelper;

/**
 * This class implements an authentication protocol over a normal
 * socket. This is the server side and corresponds to the
 * AuthenticatedSocket client side class.
```

```
 *
 * In order to authenticate after the socket is opened, the
 * server reads a Java UTF string. It then sends 256 bytes of random
 * data. The client encrypts those bytes using the Triple-DES
 * encryption algorithm and the user's password as the key. The client
 * then returns the 256 encrypted bytes. If the user is allowed to
 * connect and the encrypted bytes were encrypted with the password,
 * then the server sends the UTF string "OK". Otherwise, the server
 * sends the string "No" and closes the connection.
 */
public class AuthenticatedServerSocket extends ServerSocket {

  /**
   * The random number generator used for generating the challenges
  */
  private static SecureRandom random = new SecureRandom();

  /**
   * Constructor defined by the ServerSocket class
   */
  public AuthenticatedServerSocket(int port) throws IOException {
    super(port);
  }

  /**
   * Constructor defined by the ServerSocket class
   */
  public AuthenticatedServerSocket(int port, int backlog)
      throws IOException {
    super(port, backlog);
  }

  /**
   * Constructor defined by the ServerSocket class
   */
  public AuthenticatedServerSocket(int port, int backlog,
                                   InetAddress bindAddr)
      throws IOException {
    super(port, backlog, bindAddr);
  }

  /**
   * The accept method calls implAccept and then performs the
   * authentication. If the user correctly authenticates, then the
   * socket is returned; otherwise, an exception is thrown.
   */
  public Socket accept() throws IOException {
    AuthenticatedSocket s = new AuthenticatedSocket();
    // If you call super.accept instead of implAccept, then it seems
```

```
// that only one socket at a time can be authenticating.
this.implAccept(s);

// Check that the other end is authenticated.
DataInputStream in = new DataInputStream(s.getInputStream());
DataOutputStream out = new DataOutputStream(s.getOutputStream());

String username = in.readUTF();
String password = getPasswordForUser(username);

byte[] challenge = getChallenge();
out.write(challenge);
byte[] response = AuthenticatedSocketHelper.readChallengeResponse(in);
byte[] expectedResponse = EncryptionHelper.encrypt(challenge, password);

// Check that the response and expected response match.
boolean authenticated = true;
if (expectedResponse == null) {
  authenticated = false;
} else {
  for (int i = 0; i < challenge.length; i++) {
    authenticated &= (response[i] == expectedResponse[i]);
  }
}

if (authenticated) {
  try {
    AuthenticatedSocketHelper.setUser(
      s.getInetAddress().getHostAddress(), username);
  } catch (Exception ex) {
    // Most likely because someone else is connected from
    // that machine
    authenticated = false;
  }
}
if (authenticated) {
  out.writeUTF("OK");
  s.setLoggedIn();
  // Don't close the streams here; this closes the underlying
  // socket in the corresponding direction (half closed sockets).
  return s;
} else {
  out.writeUTF("NO");
  in.close();
  out.close();
  s.close();
  // This IOException never gets reported anywhere, but we throw
  // it so that RMI knows the socket is bad.
  throw new IOException(
```

```
        "Unable to authenticate credentials with the server");
    }
  }

  /**
   * Get the random challenge.
   */
  private byte[] getChallenge() {
    byte[] challenge = new
      byte[AuthenticatedSocketHelper.CHALLENGE_LENGTH];
    random.nextBytes(challenge);
    return challenge;
  }

  // Could use any source for the password here: database, JAAS, etc.
  protected String getPasswordForUser(String username) {
    return username;
  }
}
```

First comes the declaration and initialization of the random-number generator used to generate the challenge bytes. Then we implement all the constructors declared in the `ServerSocket` class. These have been implemented to allow the class to be used for non-RMI communication.

The `accept` method overrides the `ServerSocket.accept` method. First, we get a socket and connect it with a client. Then we obtain the streams for communicating with the client. Next, we get the username from the client and look up the user's password. We then generate the challenge bytes, send them to the client, read the response, and create the expected response.

The next fragment of code determines if the expected response and the actual response are the same. If the responses are the same, we attempt to store the host from which the user is connected. This might fail because another user is already logged in from that computer, which is not allowed. If the username is set correctly, the client is informed of the status and the socket is returned for usage by the application. If the responses don't match or another user is connected from that computer, the socket is closed and an exception is reported.

The `getChallenge` method uses the random-number generator to create an array of bytes for the challenge. The `getPasswordForUser` method returns the password for the user in question. In this simplistic implementation, the password is the same as the username.

The Helper Methods

This `AuthenticatedSocketHelper` class implements methods that help the authenticated socket classes.

```
package book.rmi.ex5;

import java.io.DataInputStream;
```

```
import java.io.IOException;
import java.util.Hashtable;
import java.util.Map;

/**
 * This class provides methods that are necessary to both the
 * AuthenticatedSocket and the AuthenticatedServerSocket.
 */
public class AuthenticatedSocketHelper {

  /**
   * The challenge length. Setting this high decreases the chances
   * that the hacker can randomly create a string to match what the
   * password would generate, but it also increases compute and
   * transmission time. This should be a multiple of 8.
   */
  public static final int CHALLENGE_LENGTH = 256;

  /**
   * Read the challenge or response from the input stream. This will
   * loop until CHALLENGE_LENGTH bytes are read or an exception is
   * thrown. Note that it may take several reads to get all the data,
   * especially the larger CHALLENGE_LENGTH becomes.
   */
  static byte[] readChallengeResponse(DataInputStream in)
      throws IOException {
    byte[] challenge = new byte[CHALLENGE_LENGTH];
    int start = 0;
    while (start < challenge.length) {
      int len = in.read(challenge, start, challenge.length - start);
      start += len;
    }
    return challenge;
  }

  /**
   * Map to store the current users and where they are connected from.
   * Implemented as a Hashtable to provide thread-safety.
   */
  private static Map activeUsers = new Hashtable();

  /**
   * Store the fact that a particular user is connected from a
   * particular host.
```

```
 */
static void setUser(String hostname, String username) {
  LoginInfo info = (LoginInfo)activeUsers.get(hostname);
  if (info != null) {
    if (username == null || !username.equals(info.username)) {
      throw new RemoteException(
        "Another user is logged in from that address");
    } else {
      info.loginCount++;
    }
  } else {
    info = new LoginInfo();
    info.username = username;
    info.loginCount = 1;
    activeUsers.put(hostname, info);
  }
}

/**
 * Get the current user for the thread we are run in. This depends
 * on how RMI names the threads that it creates. For Sun JVMs 1.2,
 * 1.3, and 1.4 on Windows, this method works, but only when each
 * user has their own unique hostname (i.e. firewalls will probably
 * mess this up).
 */
static String getCurrentUser() {
  Thread.currentThread().getName();
  String hostname = threadName.substring(threadName.indexOf('-')+1);
  int index = hostname.indexOf('/');
  if (index > 0) {
    hostname = hostname.substring(index+1);
  }
  LoginInfo info = (LoginInfo)activeUsers.get(hostname);
  if (info != null) {
    return info.username;
  } else {
    return null;
  }
}
/**
 * Remove one socket from the current user on the host from the list
 * of current connections. If the count is zero, then allow all users
 * to log in from that host.
 */
```

```
  static void logout(String hostname) {
    LoginInfo info = (LoginInfo)activeUsers.get(hostname);
    if (info != null) {
        info.loginCount--;
        if (info.loginCount <= 0) {
          activeUsers.remove(hostname);
        }
    }
  }
  /**
   * Private class to track how many times a user has logged in from
   * a particular host.
   */
  private static class LoginInfo {
    public String username;
    public int loginCount = 0;
  }
}
```

We define the length of the challenge array to be 256 bytes. This needs to be long enough to prevent a hacker from easily guessing what the encrypted bytes will be without knowing the password. This also needs to be short enough to avoid having its processing cause too much overhead, since each challenge will be encrypted by the client and the server.

The `readChallengeResponse` method is a package-accessible method that reads the challenge or response from the input stream. We declare an array of the proper length, and then continually read the stream until the correct number of bytes are read or an exception is thrown, which is passed on to the calling method of this function.

The remainder of the file deals with knowing which user is making each method call. The solution presented here has a number of flaws, but in certain situations, it is adequate. RMI does not provide any context for a method call and doesn't allow the server object access to the socket that is being used for the communication. Consequently, we must find a way to get around this limitation.

Sun's implementation of the JVM on the Windows platform, and possibly other platforms, names the thread on which the server object is running. This name, while varying between the different versions, is basically the same for JVMs 1.2 through 1.4: They all end with the IP address of the client computer. The `setUser` method, which is called when a socket is accepted, keeps track of how many times a user is connected from a computer and allows only one username to be used by the client computer. The `getCurrentUser` method parses the thread's name and determines the user associated with that host, which it returns. The `logout` method removes one connection for the particular user at the client address. If the count is zero or less, the login information is removed from the internal table, which allows another user to log in.

Tracking which user is logged in from which host in this manner is not perfect. Any proxy server between the client and the server will create problems, because the request will appear to come from the same host computer. In order to prevent users from gaining permissions they shouldn't normally have because another user logs in from the same proxy server, only one user per IP address is allowed. For applications that are available to the general public, this restricts the users to one per company. For internal applications where all the users are on the same network and no proxy or firewall servers are present, this approach will work.

The RMI Socket Factory Implementation

The next code listing implements the `RMISocketFactory` using `AuthenticatedSockets`, so that all RMI method calls use `AuthenticatedSockets`.

```
package book.rmi.ex5;

import java.io.IOException;
import java.io.Serializable;
import java.net.ServerSocket;
import java.net.Socket;
import java.rmi.server.RMISocketFactory;

/**
 * The RMISocketFactory for Authenticated Sockets
 */
public class AuthenticatedSocketFactory extends RMISocketFactory
    implements Serializable {

  /**
   * Create the server socket. This returns an
   * AuthenticatedServerSocket.
   */
  public ServerSocket createServerSocket(int port) throws IOException {
    return new AuthenticatedServerSocket(port);
  }

  /**
   * Create the client socket. This returns an AuthenticatedSocket.
   */
  public Socket createSocket(String host, int port) throws IOException {
    return new AuthenticatedSocket(host, port);
  }

  /**
   * This returns true for any two instances of this class. This
   * allows for more aggressive caching of the object.
   */
  public boolean  equals(Object that) {
```

```
    return that != null && that.getClass() == this.getClass();
  }
}
```

The `AuthenticatedSocketFactory` class extends the `RMISocketFactory`. This class is the basis for creating sockets used by RMI. It implements both client and server socket factories and provides several static methods to set and retrieve the current socket factory. By extending this class, we are able to set the default socket factory, making modifications of the remote objects unnecessary.

The implementation of this class, similar to the `SSLSocketFactory` class in the SSL connection version (in the "Using an SSL Connection between the Client and Server" section earlier in the chapter), is very straightforward. The `createServerSocket` creates a new `AuthenticatedServerSocket` for the indicated port. The client version of `createSocket` returns a connected, authenticated socket.

The Interface Implementation for Authenticated Sockets

The next code listing shows this example's implementation of the `RetirementAccountInfo` interface.

```
package book.rmi.ex5;

import java.rmi.RemoteException;
import java.rmi.server.UnicastRemoteObject;
import book.rmi.AccountNotFoundException;
import book.rmi.LocalPersistenceService;
import book.rmi.RetirementAccountInfo;

/**
 * A basic implementation of the RetirementAccount interface as
 * a UnicastRemoteObject. This class only implements the basic
 * methods, not the alternates for the other examples. This object
 * is only secured if the underlying RMI Object Factory is
 * secured. It is assumed that the communication channel is an
 * AuthenticatedSocket.
 */
public class RetirementAccountImpl extends UnicastRemoteObject
    implements RetirementAccountInfo {
  /**
   * Return the account balance. It also prints to System.out every
   * time someone gets their account balance. It checks with the
   * AuthenticatedSocketHelper to find out the user's true identity.
   */
  public Number get401kBalance(String accountNumber)
      throws RemoteException, AccountNotFoundException {
```

```
    String currentUser = AuthenticatedSocketHelper.getCurrentUser();
    if (accountNumber == null || !accountNumber.equals(currentUser)) {
      throw new RemoteException("Invalid Account Number");
    }
    System.out.print(getClass().getName() + ": Received call to ");
    System.out.println("get401kBalance for " + currentUser);
    return persistence.get401kBalance(currentUser);
  }
```

This example of the `RetirementAccountImpl` is similar to the implementation in the unsecured example and in the SSL example. The constructor simply calls `super` and does not set the socket factory to be used because this class is implemented to use the default socket factory. It does initialize the `LocalPersistenceService` that is used for retrieving the account balances. In the client and the server, we will modify the default socket factory so that the authenticated sockets are used.

The `get401kBalance` method gets the current user using the `AuthenticatedSocketHelper` class. It then checks that the current user and the requested account are the same. If they aren't, an exception is thrown. If the username and the account number match, the request is logged to `System.out` and the balance is returned.

The Client and Server Code

This listing provides the relevant code for the `ClientRMI` class for this example.

```
if (args[0].equals("ex5")) {
   try {
     book.rmi.ex5.AuthenticatedSocketFactory.setSocketFactory(
       new book.rmi.ex5.AuthenticatedSocketFactory());
   } catch (IOException ex) {
     ex.printStackTrace();
   }
   book.rmi.ex5.AuthenticatedSocket.setCredentials(args[1], args[2]);
 }
```

First, we install our `AuthenticatedSocketFactory` as the default socket factory. This will make all classes that don't specify a socket factory use authenticated sockets for communication. The other line for this example sets the username and password for the user. The `RetirementAccountImpl` is then accessed the same way as it was in the original example—simply by calling the method as shown below.

```
// Set the RMI Socket factory for all objects that don't specify a
// socket factory
if (args[0].equals("ex5")) {
  try {
    book.rmi.ex5.AuthenticatedSocketFactory.setSocketFactory(
      new book.rmi.ex5.AuthenticatedSocketFactory());
  } catch (IOException ex) {
    ex.printStackTrace();
```

```
    }
    // Set credentials. This is necessary for the server to communicate
    // among its various components (registry and registered objects)
    book.rmi.ex5.AuthenticatedSocket.setCredentials("server", "server");
}
```

The snippet above is the code from `ServerRMI` that was presented at the beginning of the chapter. This code is specific to this example and not needed for the other examples. First, the default socket factory is set, just as in `ClientRMI`. Also, the credentials are set at the end of the snippet. The credentials need to be set because when the default socket factory is set, all communication occurs over `AuthenticatedSockets`, including communicating with the registry to register new objects. Since our `AuthenticatedSocket` doesn't have a mode for unauthenticated communication, the registration communications need to be authenticated as well. For this purpose, we have created a dummy account named `server` that is only allowed to connect, not actually run any of the methods in the application.

Advantages and Disadvantages of Using Authenticated Sockets

Since RMI does not provide any context for the server method calls, the authenticated socket countermeasure is limited in its usefulness. However, if your application can operate within the restrictions provided, this approach can be effective.

This countermeasure allows the authentication mechanism to be localized. Client programmers just need to remember to set the socket factory and user credentials just once during the application. Server programmers only need to set the socket factory and then call the `AuthenticatedSocketHelper`'s `getCurrentUser` method to determine who the user is. This way, programmers don't need to deal with keeping track of who the user is.

THE DANGERS OF LOADING CLASS AND JAR FILES REMOTELY

RMI allows you to alleviate some application distribution headaches by allowing the class and JAR files to be loaded from a remote location. This is especially useful for RMI applications because of their sensitivity to varying versions of class files that might exist for applications that are frequently updated. To do this, you set the `java.rmi.server.codebase` property when you start the JVM, as demonstrated by:

```
java -Djava.rmi.server.codebase=http://appserver/jars/app.jar MyClass
```

This listing will cause RMI to load classes from the JAR file `app.jar`.

While this method does provide a convenient distribution mechanism, it also gives hackers a mechanism to attack your system and your user's computer. If hackers could modify the code and convince the users to run it, they could control the system.

Hacker Replaces Class Files in Transit

Popularity:	*5*
Simplicity:	*3*
Impact:	*10*
Risk Rating:	***6***

The first step for hackers to attack a system using this attack would be to find an application that is distributed in this manner. The most likely avenue for hackers to discover this would be from listening in on your network traffic. When the hackers observe the repeated HTTP requests for JAR or class files, they will identify their target—not only the application, but also the server providing the application and the particular JAR file that they will attack.

Another method for an attacker to discover an application is to be an insider, such as a developer of the system or a user. The insider has access to the application and can determine how the application is distributed, giving the attacker the knowledge of which server and JAR file to target.

Once hackers have figured out what to attack, they will download the application for themselves. Most hackers will try to execute the application and compromise the application using its interface. Hackers who want to compromise the computer systems of the users, rather than the application, will decompile the application, converting the class files into source code. The hackers are looking for a method that they are sure will be executed. Good candidates would be classes with `main` methods or classes named in a manner that indicates they are the primary class, such as `MyApplication`, `Application`, or `ApplicationStart`.

Hackers using this attack are trying to execute code on the user's computer of their choice. They will insert one or two commands into the application where they believe the commands will be executed. These commands will call the hackers' own class. The hackers will then repackage the JAR file, including the modified class of the original application and their own new class. Hackers could then get the users to run the application in one of two ways:

- Attack the application server and replace the JAR file on that machine. Because the machine is an application server, this attack might be detected by an intrusion detection system (IDS) before all the users executed the application.
- Use a "man-in-the-middle attack." In this case, the hackers convince the users that the application server they need to consult is one that the hackers control. This could be accomplished by Address Resolution Protocol (ARP) or Domain Naming Service (DNS) attacks against the network, which would also possibly be detected by an IDS system.

Hackers could then configure the system that they control to relay all requests on to the real application server and act as a relay between the user and the server. For certain requests, the hackers could indicate that their file should be returned instead of a relayed response. (The server would continue to relay the request, so that the traffic patterns on the server still appear the same.) In this attack, the hackers would modify only the relayed JAR file to be their own.

This class will spawn a new thread, allowing the hackers' code to run simultaneously with the application. The hackers' class will probably try and download an application from a website that the hackers control, and then execute that application. Depending on the `java.policy` file that the application is executed with, a successful exploitation of this attack would be the first step into taking complete control of the user's computer system.

Countermeasure: A Secure java.policy File

Implementing a strong `java.policy` file for your application will make this attack almost useless in compromising the users' computers. If you prevent the application from opening any sockets, the hackers cannot download any external applications.

By preventing the external applications, you require the hackers to embed all of their attack code in the JAR file, either as Java class objects or as JNI libraries. Because most exploits are specific to the particular operating system, the hackers would need to include a variety of exploits in the JAR file, making its file size balloon and increasing the chances that someone would notice the attack. Also, restricting access to the `Runtime.exec` methods would also prevent the hackers from executing external tools, which might install servers that act as a backdoor to the system.

If you need to allow your application to access sockets or external applications, you should explicitly grant permissions to only those sockets and applications that are necessary and deny all other permissions.

It is possible to digitally sign a JAR file so that users can be confident that code being executed is the code that the application creator produced. This would seem to be the perfect answer to countering this attack—use a method to detect if any code has been modified or added to a JAR file. The problem is that signed JAR Files were developed for applets and the Java runtime does not check the signature of JAR files it downloads for the RMI codebase system property.

SUMMARY

In this chapter, we have examined the major security issues associated with RMI and presented some solutions. We began with Lester's unsecure implementation, and then proceeded to add security measures. We added encryption selectively, encrypted all information going across the network, used challenge/response authentication, and finally, implemented an authenticated communications channel. We also looked at problems involving remote code loading.

These are not the only steps that need to be taken, however. RMI applications can also fall victim to the more generalized Java networking attacks that were discussed in the previous chapters and those countermeasures should also be used.

PART III

CHAPTER 9

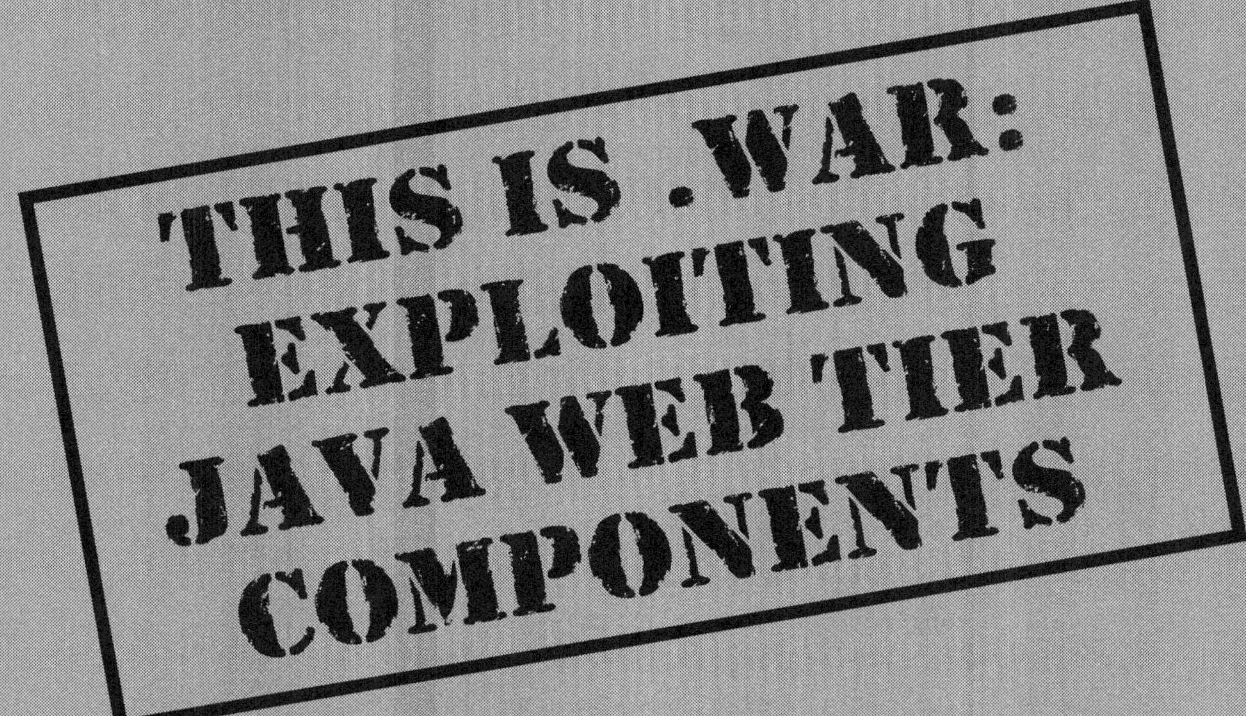
THIS IS .WAR:
EXPLOITING
JAVA WEB TIER
COMPONENTS

A web application, especially one deployed on the Internet, is a much more appealing target to potential attackers than a typical stand-alone or client-server application. There are several reasons for this:

- **Availability and accessibility** Many web applications are available to public users at any time, day or night. Because web servers must be accessible to public users, they typically reside in a DMZ and don't enjoy the luxury of the full-perimeter security of a typical enterprise's firewalls.
- **Familiarity** Most attackers, even unsophisticated ones, are familiar with a web-based interface. A web browser is easy to obtain and is one of the most common pieces of application software. The HTTP protocol is well defined, and many hacking tools and exploits exist that are specifically geared toward helping an attacker penetrate and compromise a web-based application.
- **Ease** Configuring a web server, web container, and web application for public use is extremely complex, especially if you add servlets and JSP. Attackers often can take advantage of this complexity by exploiting deficiencies in the system or application configuration.
- **Publicity** Some skilled attackers are driven by publicity, fame, ego, or a simple desire to prove that they can do something that few others can do. Defacing or compromising a popular website has far more "PR" value than compromising an internal application used by several dozen corporate employees.

Because of these factors, the demographics of the people who choose to attack public web applications are slightly different than those of the people who choose to attack internal business applications. We will take this into account as we review our sample application.

System-level security is extremely important for any web application. Many fine references are available that detail exactly how to configure web container security for just about any platform—that is not the focus of this text. In this chapter, our goal is to review the steps that you, as a J2EE *application developer*, can take to protect both your application and your data. As with the previous chapters, you should implement your application security measures in conjunction with, not instead of, proper system security measures.

In the course of the following chapters, we will see how the following techniques can be applied to our sample web application to improve its security stature:

- Hiding application structure and enabling more granular declarative authorization by passing *some* servlet parameters in the URL instead of in the HTTP header
- Configuring certain servlets to deny HTTP GET requests
- Implementing a solid web application exception-handling scheme
- Overriding container defaults for directory listing and servlet invocation
- Implementing a form-based authentication scheme
- Building a web application that can resist "session stealing" attacks

- Implementing and requiring HTTPS via SSL to be used for all browser to container connections (with and without SSL client authentication)
- Implementing a J2EE CLIENT-CERT authentication scheme
- Using servlet filters to implement a client cache control strategy
- Mapping container roles to application-specific roles

THE SAMPLE APPLICATION: WEB-ENABLED

Since business has been going well for Lester, he has decided to put a web interface on his retirement planning application. His design goal is to enable authorized users to view and set balances from a common web browser (without using applet or WebStart technology). To enable this, he built a web application utilizing several technologies:

- JSP and servlets
- Static HTML content
- The Tomcat web container / web server

Even though the sample application that we will examine is small, it has been constructed in such a way that it will allow us to cover most of the relevant, common, security-related attacks to which a web application might be exposed. We will also review viable countermeasures for those attacks.

The architecture of the sample retirement application, shown in Figure 9-1, is relatively common. As you can see, a web client, typically a browser, connects to the web container using HTTP. The application code, deployed in the web container, responds to the request and, when necessary, accesses the application data in the MySQL database using `MySQLPersistenceService`, developed in Chapter 7. For the purposes of this chapter, we assume that the database server is behind a corporate firewall and relatively safe

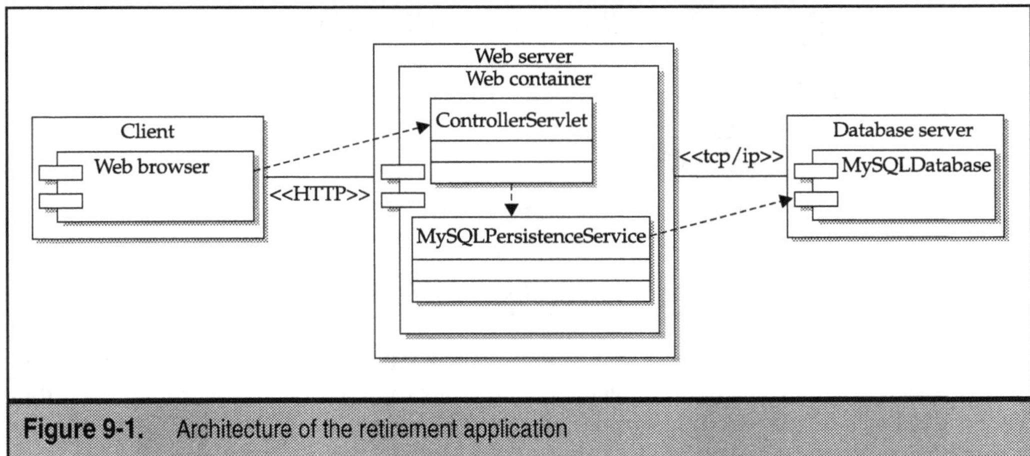

Figure 9-1. Architecture of the retirement application

from attack. Our focus will be on analyzing the security requirements of the web client (browser), the web container, and the application running within that container.

Let's take a quick tour of our sample application. To initiate a session, the user navigates to the entry page (`entry.html`) under the application root context.

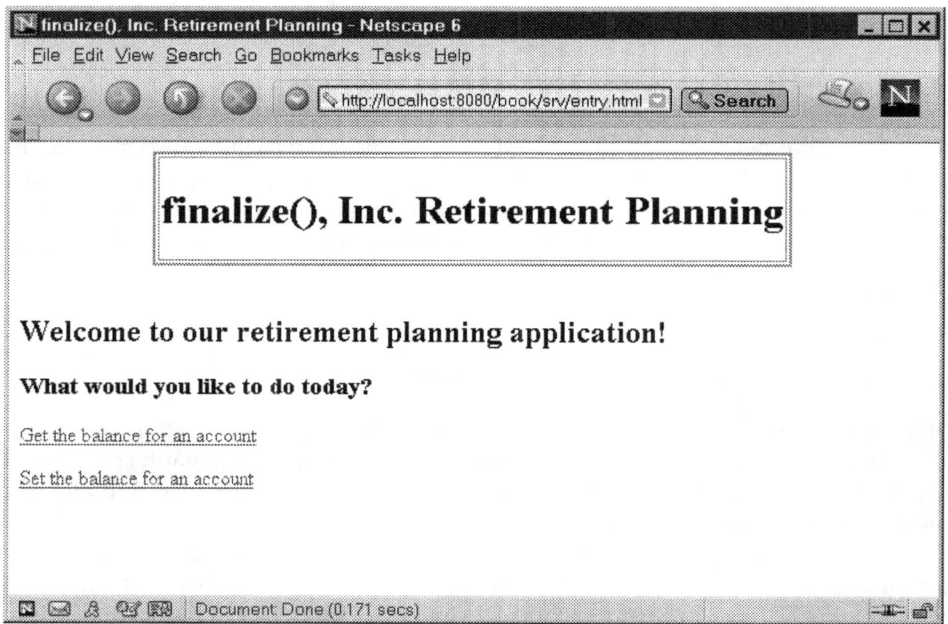

The user then has the option to either get or set the balance for a particular account. If they click the `Get The Balance For An Account` link, they are asked to authenticate using the HTTP BASIC authentication method.

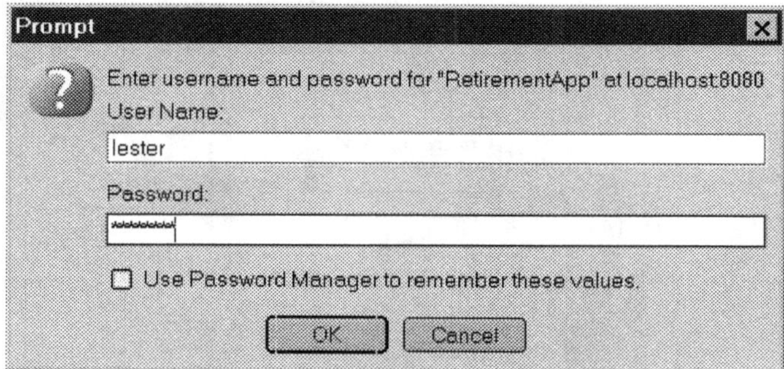

After authentication, if the user is authorized to view the `getbalance.html` page, they are presented with a form that enables them to enter the account number for which they want the balance displayed. The form is submitted to an instance of `ControllerServlet` (a servlet that serves as the controller for our J2EE Model 2 architecture).

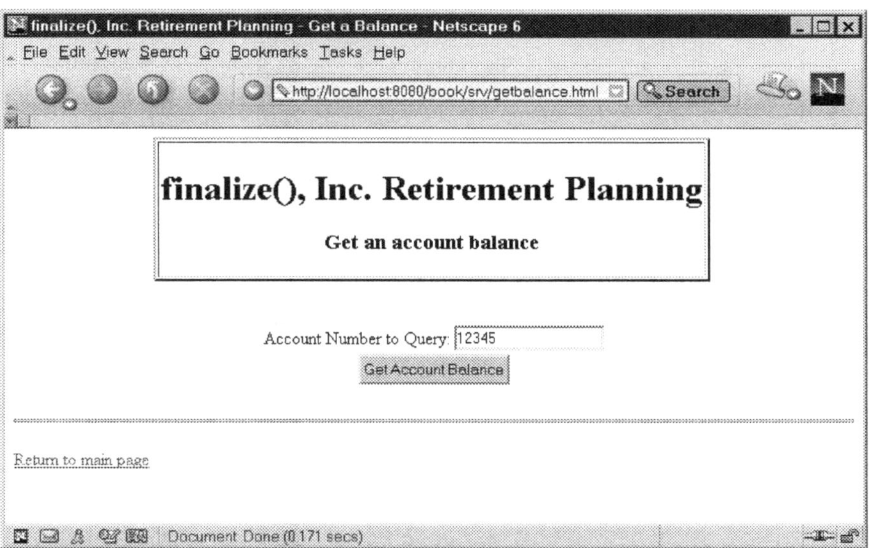

When the servlet receives the request, it processes the form action, creates an instance of `MySQLPersistenceService` to read from the MySQL database, calls the `get401KBalance` method to read the balance in question, and then closes the instance of `MySQLPersistenceService` along with its corresponding database connection. An instance of the `AccountDataTrans` class is created to hold the results of the query and is attached to the current user's session. The current request is then forwarded to the `displaybalance.jsp` page, which retrieves the `AccountDataTrans` object from the current session, and then uses it to display the balance to the user.

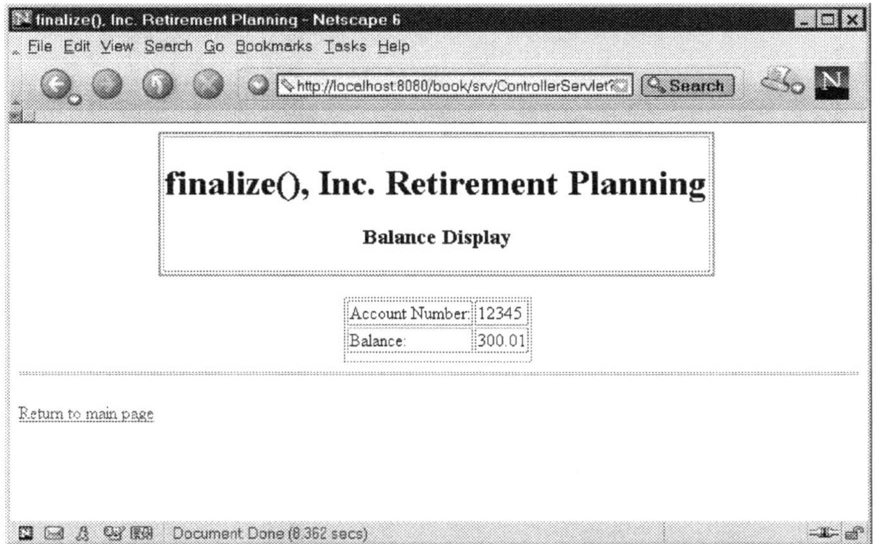

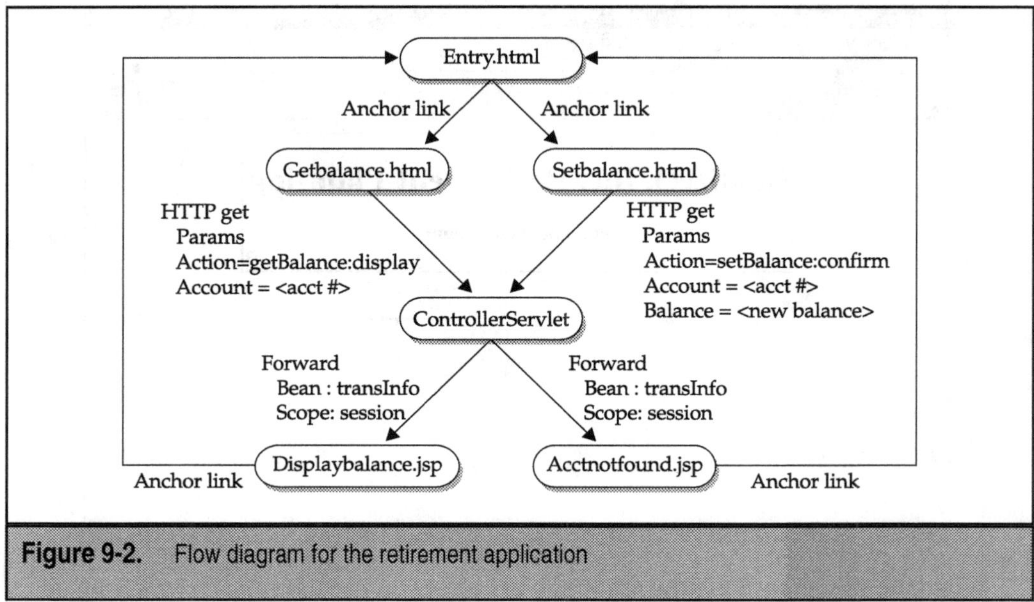

Figure 9-2. Flow diagram for the retirement application

The set balance functionality works in a similar manner. When the user navigates to `entry.html`, they click the `Set The Balance For An Account` link.

A flow diagram for this web application, shown in Figure 9-2, demonstrates that a common entry page (`entry.html`) feeds two static HTML pages (`getbalance.html` and `setbalance.html`) with the input forms necessary to feed the `ControllerServlet`. The `ControllerServlet` then directs the traffic to the `displaybalance.jsp` page (the view), but with different values in the instance of `AccountDataTrans` depending on what operation has just been performed.

Lester's application is currently configured to use HTTP BASIC authentication, and the two pages that are protected are the `getbalance.html` and `setbalance.html` pages (the pages with the HTML forms to request relevant data from the user). Only users in the `admin` role are allowed access to the `setbalance.html` page, while any authenticated user is allowed to use the `getbalance.html` page. The corresponding entries in the `web.xml` file to enable this level of access are formatted in bold:

```
<security-constraint>
    <web-resource-collection>
      <web-resource-name>GetBalance</web-resource-name>
      <description>Get Balance Functionality</description>
      <url-pattern>/getbalance.html</url-pattern>
    </web-resource-collection>
    <auth-constraint>
      <role-name>*</role-name>
    </auth-constraint>
```

```
  </security-constraint>

  <security-constraint>
    <web-resource-collection>
      <web-resource-name>SetBalance</web-resource-name>
      <description>Set Balance Functionality</description>
      <url-pattern>/setbalance.html</url-pattern>
    </web-resource-collection>
    <auth-constraint>
      <role-name>admin</role-name>
    </auth-constraint>
  </security-constraint>

  <!-- The type of authentication to do -->
  <login-config>
    <auth-method>BASIC</auth-method>
    <realm-name>RetirementApp</realm-name>
  </login-config>
```

The entries in the `web.xml` file depend on the following entries in the `tomcat-users.xml` file, which give `brian` the role `employee` and `lester` the role `admin`. The `tomcat-users.xml` file resides in the `conf` subdirectory of the Tomcat installation and is the default mechanism for defining users, groups, and passwords in the Tomcat environment. Users defined in the `tomcat-users.xml` file are defined for *all* web applications running in the container, so when we specify above that any role can access `/getbalance.html`, we're saying that any user who provides the container with a username and password stored in the tomcat-users file is OK to use that page. Similarly, in order for a user to access Lester's `/setbalance.html` page (as shown earlier) that user must have the role `admin` as defined in the `tomcat-users.xml` file:

```
<tomcat-users>
  <user name="lester" password="password"
roles="javaguru,admin,employee,manager"/>
  <user name="brian"  password="password" roles="employee"/>
</tomcat-users>
```

As we examine the flow of the application and look at the general architecture, an attacker could potentially focus on the following areas:

- The network client (in this case, the browser)
- The connection between the client and the server (HTTP)
- The servlets and JSP residing in the web container
- The connection between the web container and the database server
- The database server itself

In Chapter 7, we have already reviewed security issues for both the database server and the connection between an arbitrary Java client and a database server, so we will not cover those in this section. Instead, we will focus on the following key topics:

- Protecting the application at the client browser
- Securing the connection between the browser and the web container
- Securing the application logic residing in the web container itself

Exploiting URL Information

Popularity:	3
Simplicity:	6
Impact:	8
Risk rating:	**6**

Upon only casual inspection, we can see some problems with the security of this application. One of the most obvious weaknesses is that the application transmits all of its form data by appending the information to the URL using an HTTP GET request. Here's a sample excerpt of the `form` tag:

```
<form action="ControllerServlet" method="get">

<table summary="Set Balance Info" align="center">
<tr>
  <td>Account Number to Query:</td>
  <td><input type="text" name="account"></td>
</tr>
<tr>
  <td colspan="2" align="center">
    <button type="submit">Get Account Balance</button>
  </td>
</tr>
</table>
<input type="hidden" name="action" value="getBalance:display">
</form>
```

Additionally, notice that the form has a hidden input field called `action` that passes the value `getBalance:display` to the `ControllerServlet`. When the user submits the form, the `action` field, along with all relevant form data, is displayed in the URL field of the browser:

```
http://localhost:8080/book/srv/ControllerServlet?account=12345&action=getBalance%3Adisplay
```

This gives an attacker two very important pieces of information: the direct URL mapping of the ControllerServlet, and the action that the servlet should take (passed in the form of a parameter). In fact, by directly typing the preceding URL into a browser, a potential attacker, even one with little knowledge of programming or HTML, could enumerate through possible common "actions" by trying to guess common strings and then examining error messages.

More importantly, if we look at the following excerpt of the web.xml file for this application, we can see that the getbalance.html page (the one that requests the servlet) is secured, but *the servlet itself is not*. This is a very common security mistake in web applications: protecting the resources that invoke a critical component, but not protecting the component itself.

```
<!-- Security Information -->
 <security-constraint>
  <web-resource-collection>
   <web-resource-name>GetBalance</web-resource-name>
   <description>Get Balance Functionality</description>
   <url-pattern>/getbalance.html</url-pattern>
  </web-resource-collection>
  <auth-constraint>
   <role-name>*</role-name>
  </auth-constraint>
 </security-constraint>
```

As you can see above, because we have specified a role-name of *, any *authenticated* user can access the getbalance.html page. However, because it is not specified in the security-constraint tag section of the web.xml file, *any* user—*even an unauthenticated user*—can access the ControllerServlet itself. This may not matter too much for the get balance functionality, but it would if an unauthorized user could set balances. In fact, let's try to set a balance by directly submitting data to the controller servlet. To do this, we simply need to match the URL format for the set balance functionality. Perhaps we could capture this information by looking over an authorized user's shoulder, looking at the user's history entries in the browser's history, sniffing network traffic, or just guessing parameters:

```
http://localhost:8080/book/srv/ControllerServlet?account=12345&balance=
6000&action=setBalance%3Aconfirm
```

If we open a new browser window, type the preceding URL into the URL field of the browser, and change the balance to something better (like $3,000,000), we see the following results.

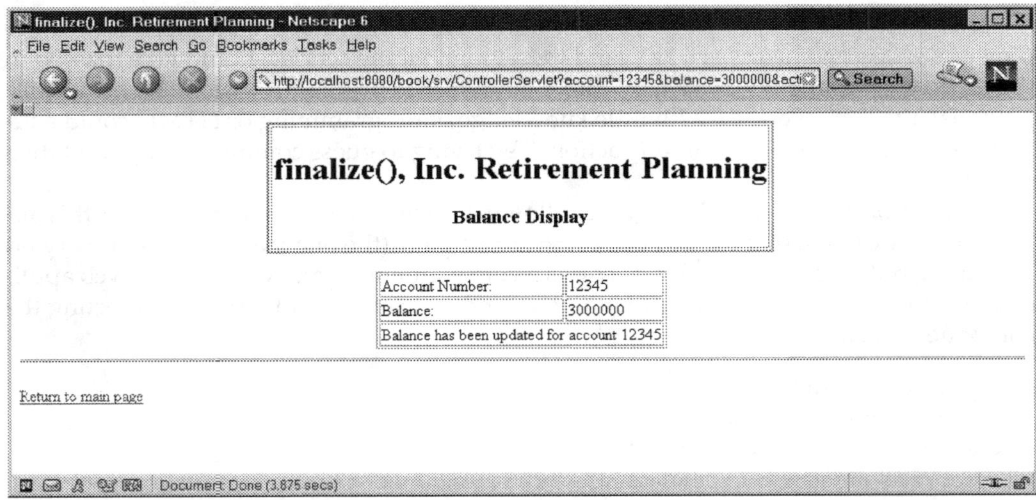

Obviously, allowing anybody who can figure out our servlet's URL and parameter syntax to arbitrarily set balances is not good. Once an attacker discovers our URL and parameters, they essentially have full access to our application.

A common first attempt to fix this problem is to change our `security-constraint` to deny access to our `ControllerServlet` to everybody but users in the `admin` role. Unfortunately, if we do this, normal users who need to use the `ControllerServlet` for get balance or other functionality will not be authorized to access it, because they will not be in the `admin` role. All is not lost, though; several countermeasures are available that enable us to restrict access to our application while also providing the added benefit of shielding our application structure from prying eyes.

Countermeasure: Map Multiple URLs to the Same Servlet

One huge advantage that we have with servlets is the `servlet-mapping` tag in the `web.xml` file. This allows us to map an arbitrary URL to a particular servlet. The benefit of this approach is that we can map several URLs to the *same* servlet…*and* we can secure each of those URLs separately. Additionally, instead of using a parameter to request some behavior from the servlet, we can have the servlet examine the incoming URL to determine what behavior to take. This approach has several advantages:

- It hides the true name of our servlet. This helps prevent any direct enumeration of the servlet itself (although an attacker could still attempt to enumerate URLs).
- It allows us to secure various servlet actions declaratively.
- It masks the structure of our web application from the user. If we really want to confuse potential attackers, we could change the URL extension for our mappings to `.asp`, `.php`, or something along those lines.

A sophisticated attacker would see through these measures relatively easily, but it would just be one more step they would need to take to understand our application structure.

To make this change, we need to take the following actions:

1. Modify the calling pages (`getbalance.html` and `setbalance.html`) to submit the forms to the new URLs.
2. Modify the `ControllerServlet` so that it determines its action by reading the URL instead of the `action` parameter.
3. Modify the `web.xml` file to map the new URLs to the servlet.
4. Add the appropriate declarative security for the new URLs in the `web.xml` file.

We modify the `setbalance.html` page in the following manner. Notice that we are removing the hidden input field and replacing it with a new relative URL, `/actions/setbalance`.

```
<form action="actions/setbalance"
      method="get" name="AccountSelect"
      title="AccountSelect">
. . .
</form>
```

Then, we apply the same modifications to the `getbalance.html` page, directing the form to submit to `actions/getbalance` instead.

Now, we must modify the `ControllerServlet` to examine the request URI instead of the request parameters. To do this, we change our code and replace our call to `request.getParameter` with a call to `request.getURI`. This method will give us the entire URI of the request, but will not include the scheme (HTTP, HTTPS, and so forth) or the host information. So, when a user types

```
http://localhost:8080/a/b/c
```

into the URL line of their browser, the `getURI` method will return the string "/a/b/c" as a result. Once we modify our servlet code to accommodate the change, it looks like this:

```
private void processRequest(HttpServletRequest request,
                            HttpServletResponse response)
    throws ServletException, IOException {

      String reqURI = request.getRequestURI();

   if (reqURI.indexOf("actions/") !=
      reqURI.lastIndexOf("actions/"))
   { // Handle the possibility of us being deployed under
     // a root context that contains 'actions/' }
```

```
    reqURI = reqURI.substring(reqURI.indexOf("actions/"));

    if (reqURI.equals("actions/getbalance")) {
      // Handle the display of the balance
      processGetBalanceDisplay(request,response);
    } else if (reqURI.equals("actions/setbalance")) {
      // Handle the display of the balance
      processSetBalanceDisplay(request,response);
    } else {
      // Handle other actions that require other processing
    }
  }
```

Then, we make the appropriate modifications to the `servlet-mapping` segment of the `web.xml` file for our application to map the URLs to our `ControllerServlet`. The mapping looks like this:

```
<servlet-mapping>
  <servlet-name>ControllerServlet</servlet-name>
  <url-pattern>/actions/getbalance</url-pattern>
</servlet-mapping>
<servlet-mapping>
  <servlet-name>ControllerServlet</servlet-name>
  <url-pattern>/actions/setbalance</url-pattern>
</servlet-mapping>
```

Again, both URLs are mapped to the same servlet. The servlet itself will determine how to direct the particular requests by examining the URI of the request.

Finally, we will change the security constraint for the web application to actually protect the critical resource instead of protecting the page that calls the resource. From the simplest security standpoint, we really don't care if a user can see the `getbalance.html` or `setbalance.html` pages. What we *do* care about is whether or not that user can then *actually* get or set a balance. So, instead of securing the pages that request the information, we will secure the URLs that refer to our `ControllerServlet`, which actually reads or modifies the information. Note that in an ideal world, we would require authentication and authorization for all of our web resources, and we will focus on that topic later in the chapter. But, for now, we can gain a significant measure of protection by making relatively small changes in one servlet and the deployment descriptor for the application. After we make the changes, the `security-constraint` section of the `web.xml` file looks like this:

```
<!-- Security Information -->
<security-constraint>
  <web-resource-collection>
    <web-resource-name>GetBalance</web-resource-name>
```

```
    <description>Get Balance Functionality</description>
    <url-pattern>/actions/getbalance</url-pattern>
  </web-resource-collection>
  <auth-constraint>
    <role-name>*</role-name>
  </auth-constraint>
</security-constraint>

<security-constraint>
  <web-resource-collection>
    <web-resource-name>SetBalance</web-resource-name>
    <description>Set Balance Functionality</description>
    <url-pattern>/actions/setbalance</url-pattern>
  </web-resource-collection>
  <auth-constraint>
    <role-name>admin</role-name>
  </auth-constraint>
</security-constraint>
```

Now, when we try to run the application and get a balance, we are asked to authenticate when the servlet is invoked instead of when the `getbalance.html` page is served to us. Once we get the balance, we can see in the browser's URL field that the new URL is being used. For our purposes, we will authenticate as `brian`–someone who doesn't have authority to set balances, but can get them.

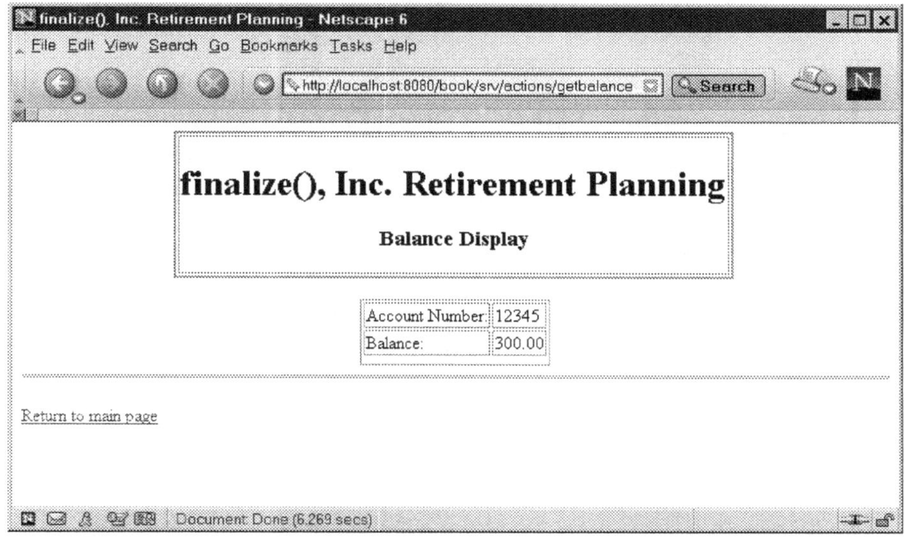

When Brian attempts to set a balance, however, he gets the expected response from the server:

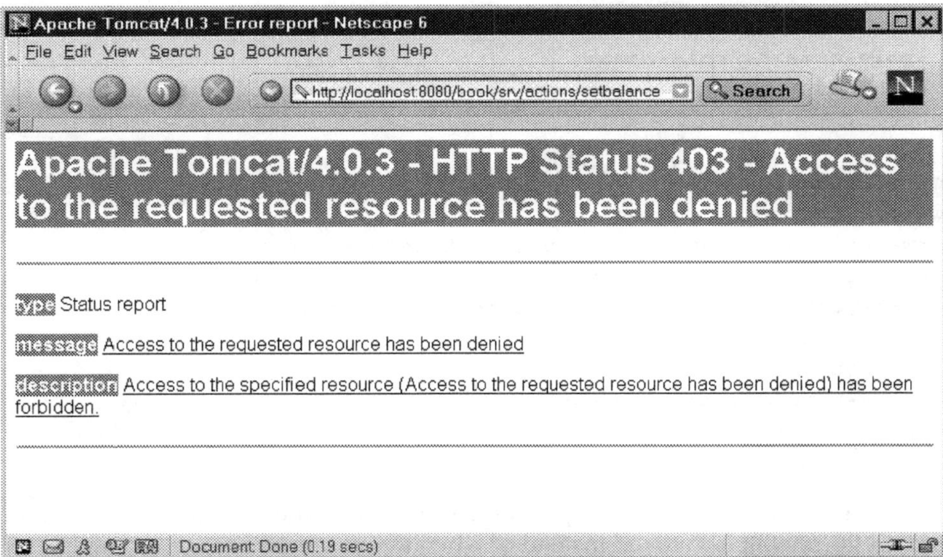

This is exactly the behavior we want. Now we are able to control access declaratively based not just on a resource, but also, in a limited way, on requested functionality. Furthermore, it is somewhat more difficult for an attacker to enumerate parameter options because it is not clear exactly what resource is providing the set balance functionality.

Countermeasure: Prefer HTTP POST to HTTP GET

As you can see in the previous illustration, the servlet parameters are still clearly visible in the URL field of the browser. This can have several negative consequences for our application:

- It is easy for a casual observer to see what parameters are being passed to the server-side code.
- Browsers often cache information based on URL—and the information contained within a HTTP GET request is usually part of the cached URL. This can cause the browser to improperly retrieve a response from cache instead of re-executing the servlet. Also, a person viewing the browser history can see exactly which parameters were submitted at which times.
- Because all the information is in the URL, the servlet (along with the proper parameters) can be added to the browser bookmarks or forwarded to somebody in an email. This may be desired functionality, but may also be a vulnerability in some cases.

▲ Although the HTTP 1.1 specification does not specify a maximum length for a URL, certain browsers limit the length of them anyway. For example, with all versions of Internet Explorer before version 6 (5.5 and below), the URL length was limited to 2,048 bytes (see http://support.microsoft.com/default.aspx?scid=kb;EN-US;q208427). So, if our application needs to pass a lot of data to the server as parameters, using HTTP GET can cause truncation or loss of data with some browsers.

We can easily correct this issue by building our forms to use the POST method instead of the GET method. This will cause the forms to embed all parameter information in the HTTP request header instead of appending it to the URL. Consequently, the parameter information will not be displayed in the URL field in the browser and a person viewing the browser history will not be able to retrieve the data submitted either.

Using the POST method does not protect the parameter values during transport; it merely makes them harder to see. Even if we change our forms to POST data to our servlet (as opposed to using HTTP GET), a user with a little knowledge can still uncover the parameter names by merely looking at the HTML source in their browser and examining the `form` tags. But since we get some tangible gains without any major drawbacks, we'll convert our sample application's forms to use HTTP POST instead of HTTP GET. To do this, we convert the HTML code in question (`getbalance.html` and `setbalance.html`) to use the POST method of submission:

```
<form action="actions/setbalance" method="post"
      name="AccountSelect" title="AccountSelect">
```

Now, when we set the balance, we see the following in our browser:

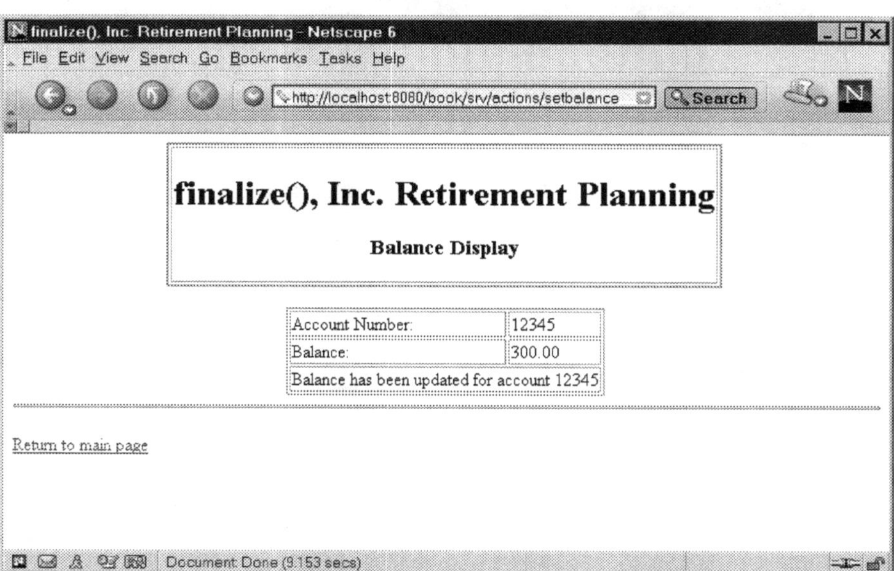

Our forms no longer use the GET method to submit data to our servlet. However, a user still could manually type in the URL of the servlet into their browser's URL field, and then use the HTTP GET syntax to pass the relevant parameters . With our current mode of operation, a user could do this and the servlet would still work. To remove this possibility, we modify our servlet so that it does not respond to HTTP GET requests. This absolutely guarantees that all information is coming to us via the proper method. To do this, we change the behavior of the `doGet` method in our servlet as follows:

```
protected void doGet(HttpServletRequest request,
                      HttpServletResponse response)
      throws ServletException, IOException {

response.sendError(HttpServletResponse.SC_METHOD_NOT_ALLOWED,
        "The GET method is not supported by this application");

}
```

We leave the `doPost` method unchanged. A client who attempts to send a GET request to our servlet will receive an HTTP status code of 405, which means that the requested method is not supported by the resource.

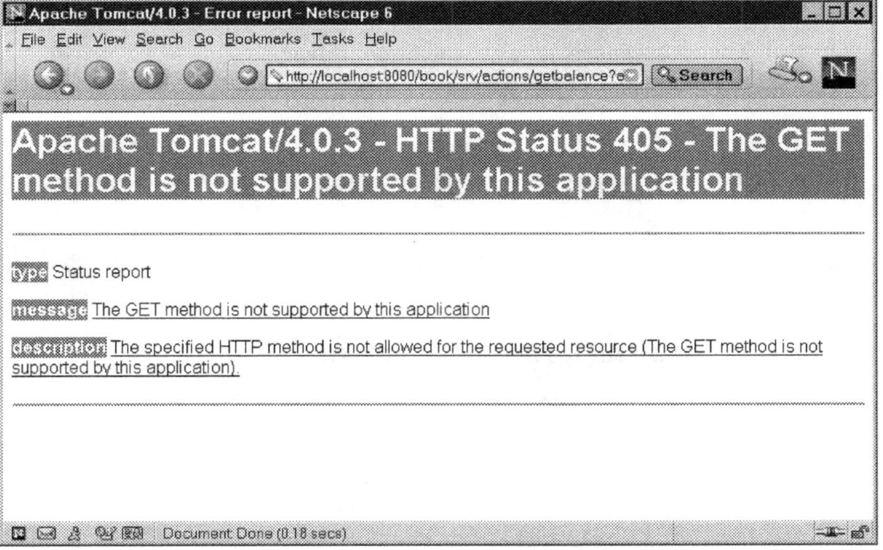

An alternate approach is to completely remove the `doGet` method from our `ControllerServlet`. If we do this, our parent class will send a similar code on its own. However, because it is common for most servlets to have both the `doGet` and `doPost` methods implemented, we will leave the `doGet` implemented so that future maintainers of our code know that our refusal to handle GET requests was a conscious decision, not an omission.

Exploiting Poor Error Handling

Popularity:	4
Simplicity:	7
Impact:	6
Risk rating:	**6**

Now that we have our application configured in such a way that it partially hides its structure from a casual observer and is enforcing simple declarative authorization, the next issue that we'll focus on is how it behaves when given improper input or parameters. For most web-based systems, attacks that use improper or malformed input are some of the most common *application*-level attacks used. Developers often are forced to compromise robustness of error handling to deliver a particular application on-time. What we will investigate is how sloppy error or exception handling can give a potential attacker quite a bit of information about our system.

If we look at the HTTP 405 error depicted above, we see that we can determine some information about our system just by looking at an application error page. Most notably, we can easily see the name and version number of the server software. The version number especially is valuable information for any attacker, because it can provide them with information about current patch levels and, consequently, vulnerabilities to particular exploits. Typically, this information can be found anyway by manually examining the HTTP header, but sometimes system administrators will remove the version information from the HTTP header yet forget to remove it from the server error pages. This is a system-level security issue and not our primary focus as application developers, but we should do our part to make sure that our application doesn't give away any more information than necessary about the system it's running on.

Continuing on the topic of exception handling exploits, let's look at what happens if we try to confuse the application with some bad input. On the `setbalance.html` page, let's try to enter a string of letters for the balance instead of numbers, shown next.

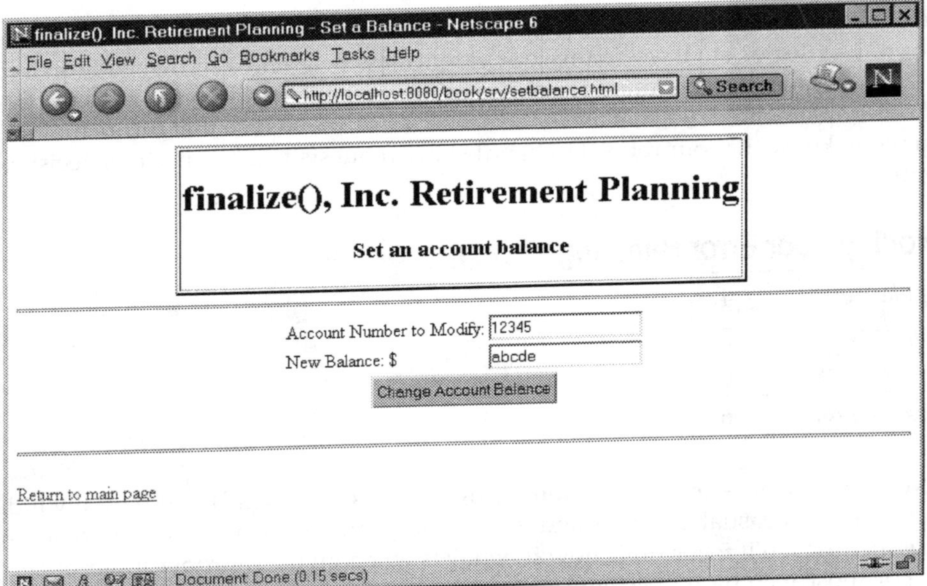

When we do this, we get the following result:

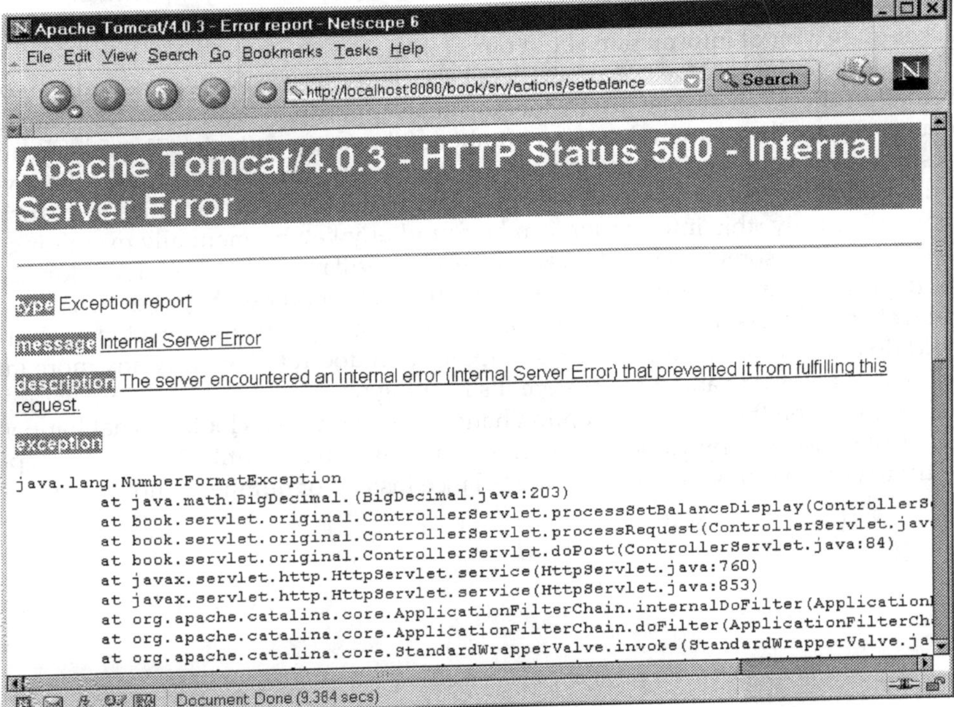

This situation has two problems:

- Our application does not properly handle invalid input—it throws an uncaught `NumberFormatException`.
- The container displays a complete stack trace of the exception, along with line numbers, class names, and the entire contents of the stack.

Obviously, as application developers, we need to fix the first problem. However, it is unrealistic to expect that an application, no matter how thoroughly tested, will make it to production without any possibility of throwing an uncaught `RuntimeException`, `ServletException`, or `IOException` that the container must catch. Therefore, in addition to writing solid code, we should also strive to configure our application in such a way that it doesn't give an attacker an exorbitant amount of information *if* there happens to be an exception we don't catch.

So, instead of immediately fixing our code to catch the `NumberFormatException`, let's examine the mechanism that the servlet API gives us to tell the container exactly what to display when confronted with an uncaught exception or the need to return a server-generated HTTP error or warning.

Countermeasure: Build Comprehensive Application-Level Error Handling

In the deployment descriptor for our web application, we can specify a URL to which the request will be forwarded if a particular HTTP error or Java exception is processed by the web container. To do this, we specify the following `error-page` information in our `web.xml` file:

```
<web-app>
 … Erroneous information removed …
</servlet-mapping>
<!-- Error handling information -->
  <error-page>
    <exception-type>javax.servlet.ServletException</exception-
type>
    <location>/gen_errorpage.jsp</location>
  </error-page>
  <error-page>
    <exception-type>java.lang.Exception</exception-type>
    <location>/gen_errorpage.jsp</location>
  </error-page>
  <error-page>
    <error-code>404</error-code>
    <location>/gen_errorpage.jsp</location>
```

```
  </error-page>
  <error-page>
    <error-code>405</error-code>
    <location>/gen_errorpage.jsp</location>
  </error-page>
  <security-constraint>
  . . .
  </security-constraint>
</web-app>
```

These tags request the container to redirect all uncaught Java exceptions, along with the 404 and 405 HTTP errors, to the URL `/gen_errorpage.jsp`. The URL specified is relative to the application context root URL. We can display quite a bit of information to the user (if we want to) on our error display page. A sample, but much too informative, error page might look like this:

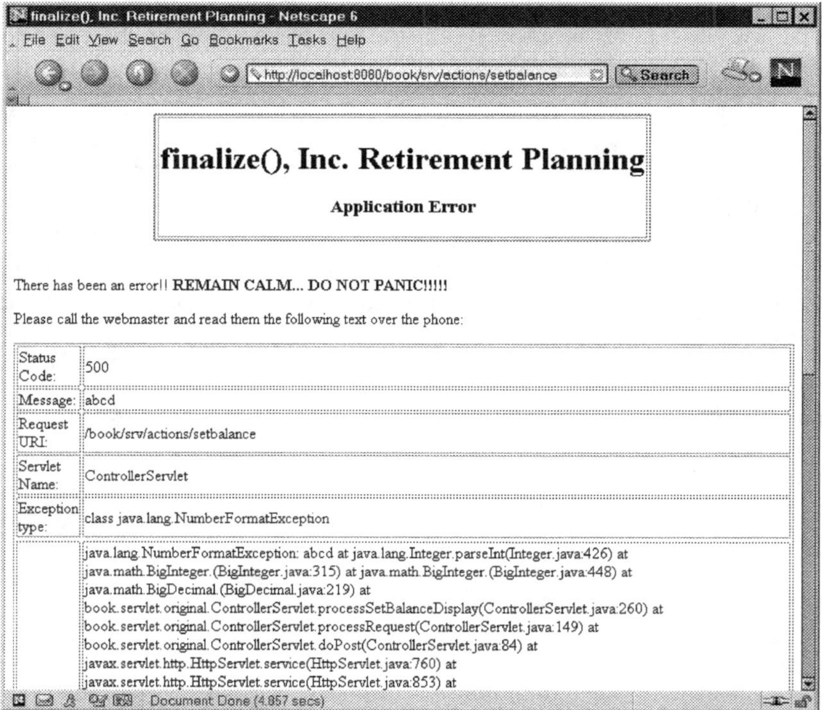

This page succeeds in removing the server information from the error description, and is probably appropriate for use in a development environment. However, it is still unsuitable for a production environment, because it displays a lot of internal information to the user. This would most likely be confusing for the user at best, and dangerous for us (if the user is an attacker) at worst.

Instead, let's build an error page that displays only the error code and message, and then logs the rest of the relevant information in a file on the server. Using this scheme, if an exception is generated, the page gives the user a reference number that they can use when talking to an appropriate support staff member. That way, the help desk personnel can look up the exact error the user received in the application log, and the user will not have any relevant internal system information.

To do this, we will modify our JSP to log the appropriate information along with a key value based on the current server time, in milliseconds. For demonstration purposes, we will write the information to the Tomcat server log, but we could also use the Java Logging API that we presented in Chapter 4. When writing multiple entries to a shared server log, it is important to either write our error message to the log in a single operation or write the timestamp for our particular error with every piece of data so that a server race condition will not interleave our error messages with the messages of another application or another thread within our application.

Here is an extract of what `gen_errorpage.jsp` looks like with the addition of the relevant logging code:

```
<p>There has been an error!! <strong>REMAIN CALM... DO NOT
 PANIC!!!!!</strong></p>
<p>Please call the webmaster and read them the following text
over the phone:</p>
<% java.util.Date timeStamp = new java.util.Date(); %>
<% application.log(timeStamp.getTime() + " : URI : " +
request.getAttribute("javax.servlet.error.request_uri")); %>
<% application.log(timeStamp.getTime() + " : Name : " +
request.getAttribute("javax.servlet.error.servlet_name")); %>
<% application.log(timeStamp.getTime() + " : Exception : " +
request.getAttribute("javax.servlet.error.exception_type")); %>
<% Throwable exception = ((Throwable)
request.getAttribute("javax.servlet.error.exception"));
   if (exception != null) {
     StringWriter sw = new StringWriter(2000);
     PrintWriter pw = new PrintWriter(sw);
     exception.printStackTrace(pw);
     application.log(timeStamp.getTime() + " : Stack : " +
sw.toString());
   }
%>

<table summary="Error Info" align="center" border="1">
<tr>
```

```
  <td>Status Code: </td>
  <td><%= request.getAttribute("javax.servlet.error.status_code")
%></td>
</tr>
  <td>Message: </td>
  <td><%=
request.getAttribute("javax.servlet.error.message") %></td>
</tr>
  <td>Error Reference Number: </td>
  <td><%= timeStamp.getTime() %></td>
</tr>
</table>
```

When we re-create the same error now, we see the following page displayed:

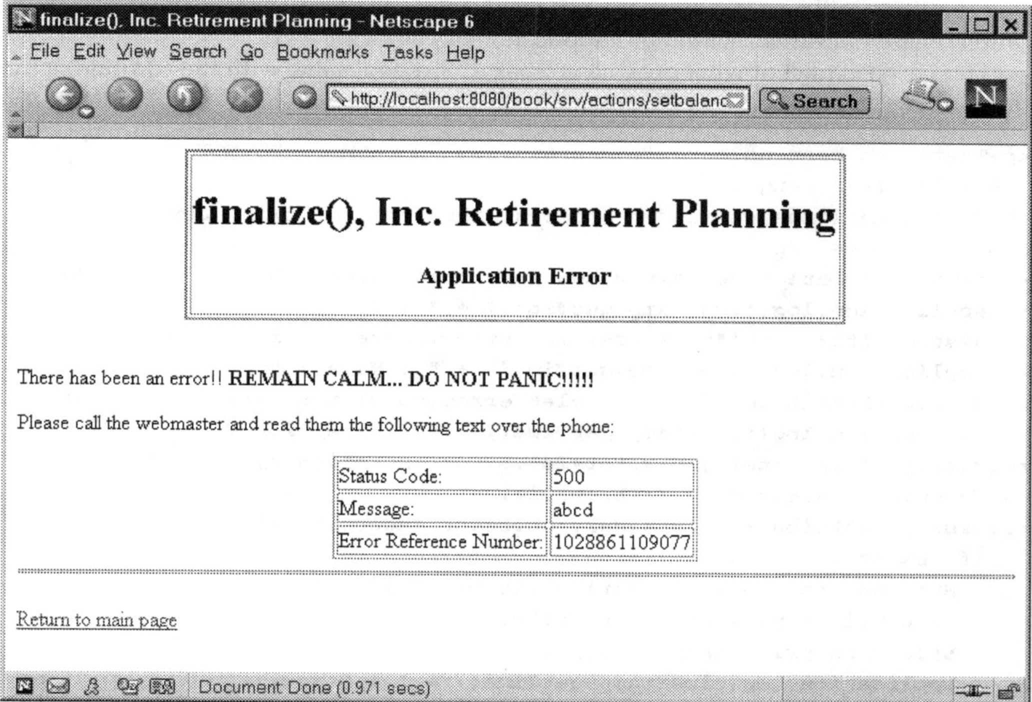

This improves our situation quite a bit. Now the user knows that an unexpected error has occurred, and has the capability to resolve it (with help from a person who has access to the application logs). Speaking of logs, if we look in the appropriate Tomcat log file, we see the following information:

```
2002-06-04 15:42:45 1028861109077: URI : /book/srv/actions/setbalance
2002-06-04 15:42:45 1028861109077: Name : ControllerServlet
```

```
2002-06-04 15:42:45 1028861109077: Exception : class
java.lang.NumberFormatException
2002-06-04 15:42:45 1028861109077: Stack :
java.lang.NumberFormatException: a
      at java.lang.Integer.parseInt(Integer.java:426)
      at java.math.BigInteger.<init>(BigInteger.java:315)
      at java.math.BigInteger.<init>(BigInteger.java:448)
<< rest of stack trace deleted >>
```

This is just about everything we need to fix the problem. Notice that JSP can also use this mechanism without having to specify the JSP `errorPage` page directive.

In this particular application, it would be much more user friendly, and generally a better design practice, to catch the `NumberFormatException` in code and tell the user that they need to reenter a valid number. The system error-handling mechanism (along with logging) does not need to be invoked for that purpose. However, our example demonstrates how that exception would look if our code made it into production without the appropriate exception handling (a bug) and a user entered a bad number. We would have all necessary information to quickly find, isolate, and repair the defect, and the user would have no knowledge of the internal structure of our application.

Exploiting Direct Translation of User Input to SQL

Popularity:	*8*
Simplicity:	*7*
Impact:	*7*
Risk rating:	*7*

Sometimes, user input that doesn't cause an exception can be damaging also. Let's look at an example to see why.

Imagine that Lester wanted to expand his application to provide a "customer search." To do this, Lester adds a field to his `account` table in the database called `name`, which contains the customer name for the corresponding account. A user would then enter a customer's name, and the application would respond with a listing of account numbers that match that name (some customers might have more than one account). A code snippet for this piece of the application functionality might look something like this:

```
String name = request.getParameter("name");
String sql = "SELECT number FROM Account "
             + "WHERE name like '" + name +"'";
. . . < Code to run the query and display the result set > . . .
```

So, if we pass in `lester` as the parameter name on our HTML form, we would get back a list of all account numbers that contain the value `lester` in the `name` field. This is exactly the functionality we desire.

However, we have a small problem. What if a user types in `%` in the name field on the HTML form? Recall that in SQL `%` is a wildcard character that will, if used in the LIKE clause of a SELECT statement, match any entry for the field in question. With our code, if the user passes `%` in for the parameter name, the application will return *all* account numbers in our database. This is not a good result. Furthermore, the user could type in `b%` and get all account numbers for individuals whose names start with the letter *b*. This isn't good either.

All of the preceding issues are disconcerting, but they aren't the major problem. Here is the major problem with the preceding code fragment: If the user types in this text as their name parameter:

```
%' AND balance > 100000 AND number LIKE '%
```

it will effectively run the following query for the user:

```
SELECT number FROM account WHERE name LIKE '%' AND balance >
100000 AND number LIKE '%';
```

which will unwittingly give the user *carte blanche* access to query our account table for just about any information they'd like. It is simply amazing to see the number of production applications that make this very mistake.

Countermeasure: Validate All User Input

The countermeasure for this attack is simple: Never pass user input directly through your web component to the database or any other method, CGI program, or resource for that matter.

Whenever using the LIKE operator, always parse the user input for `%` and the other SQL pattern-matching characters. Also, in any input, parse the expression for the semicolon character (;), which denotes the end of a SQL statement, and for the single or double quote characters. Some databases will allow you to execute multiple queries in a single string by chaining them with semicolons. For example:

```
SELECT number FROM account WHERE name LIKE 'lester'; DELETE FROM
account;
```

Using a JDBC `PreparedStatement` instead of

```
statement.executeQuery("<SQL Query Here>");
```

is also a good defense against this type of attack. With most JDBC drivers, a prepared statement is bound to the database *before* you fill in the user input, and as such will only compare the text passed in for its argument with the field specified in the original query used to prepare the statement.

Taking Advantage of Weaknesses in BASIC Authentication

Popularity:	*3*
Simplicity:	*5*
Impact:	*10*
Risk rating:	***6***

Currently, our application is using HTTP BASIC authentication to authenticate the client browser with the web container. To enable this type of authentication, we must let the container know what *realm* the web application belongs to. The realm name we specify will be stored on the client browser along with the hostname of our system, the client username, and the client password. The username and password will be automatically included in the HTTP header each time a request is made to the host and realm for which the authentication was initially requested.

As we saw in Lester's original application, configuring BASIC authentication is quite easy. We just have to add the following clause toward the end of the `web.xml` file for our application:

```
<web-app>
  . . .
  <login-config>
    <auth-method>BASIC</auth-method>
    <realm-name>RetirementApp</realm-name>
  </login-config>
  . . .
</web-app>
```

The following table, which contains excerpts of HTTP headers sent between the client and the web server, summarizes the communication that occurs when a resource is requested that requires BASIC authentication:

Client Sends	Server Responds
GET /protected/index.html.	HTTP/1.1 401 Unauthorized WWW-Authenticate: Basic realm="RetirementApp"
GET /protected/index.html Authorization: Basic QWxhZGRpbjpvcGVuIHNlc2FtZQ==	Contents of the /protected/index.html

Notice that the client sends two GET requests. When responding to the first request, the server sees that the resource is protected and, because there is no authentication information attached, denies the request but sends back the authentication type (BASIC) and realm name. When the browser sees that authentication is required, it attaches the authorization block for the realm in question to the HTTP request header and resubmits the request. In this example, the username and password are sent to the server encoded in the Authorization header field. This field is simply encoded using the base 64 encoding algorithm and can easily be decoded. Its format is *<username>*:*<password>*.

With BASIC authentication, the *client browser,* not the web server, remembers the client's username and password. For every request to a resource in the specified realm, the browser will resend the base 64 encoded user ID and password information in the authorization header of the HTTP request (without prompting the user again). So, when you, as a user, are accessing a site using BASIC authentication, your base 64 encoded user ID and password are being sent over the network with *every* request for a protected resource, not just the first request.

Alternative Mechanisms for Container Authentication

It should be apparent that for large installations, maintaining all user credential information in flat files on an application server or, in the worst case, on a web server in the corporate DMZ is not a good idea. Therefore, most web container vendors provide several other choices for user authentication:

- **JNDI realms** These authenticate a subject against a JNDI-compliant naming service, usually LDAP.
- **JDBC realms** These authenticate subjects against some custom tables located in a JDBC-compliant database.
- **JAAS realms** Support for these is somewhat new in most web containers (Tomcat 4.1 and beyond, WebLogic 7, and WebSphere 5), but extremely promising. JAAS realms allow authentication to be performed using any combination of JAAS-compliant login modules. This approach offers incredible flexibility along with the possibility for true enterprise single (or global) sign-on. Refer to Chapters 4, 5, and 7 for more in-depth coverage of JAAS. With this approach, we could even instruct our container to use the custom JAAS `LoginModule` we built in Chapter 7 to authenticate users for our web application!

Using each one of these options not only is container dependent, but also is site dependent. As such, we will not cover them more deeply in this text. However, to the web application developer, the realm used to authenticate is relatively transparent. The container handles all authentication details, and the application developer merely specifies the type of authentication desired with the client browser, not how the container should go about validating that authentication.

An application can have only one method of authentication in force at a particular time. Therefore, the body of the `web-app` portion of a `web.xml` deployment descriptor can have only one `login-config` entry.

Once the authentication method is set, the container will automatically request the appropriate type of authentication whenever the client requests a protected resource (as specified in the `security-constraint` section of the `web.xml` file). The supplied credentials will be checked against the appropriate server-side realm to verify their validity. For Tomcat, the default security realm is called the `MemoryRealm`, and can be configured with the contents of the `tomcat-users.xml` file in the `/conf` subdirectory of the Tomcat install directory.

BASIC authentication is better than no authentication, but has some significant drawbacks:

- The information is sent over the network in the clear. However, as we will see in Chapter 10, the information can easily be sent over an SSL connection to shield it from prying eyes. So, even though this is a security issue for our sample application in its current form, it is not a reason to exclude BASIC authentication as an option.
- The browser remembers the client credentials for a host/realm combination as long as it is running. In most cases, to log out of a particular application, the client browser must be completely closed (all windows) and the browser process must terminate. It is possible to circumvent this to force a logout programmatically (by manually setting a response header to tell the browser that the credentials are no longer valid), but doing so is not straightforward. Furthermore, it is very difficult from the server side to time out a user logged in using BASIC authentication.
- Many browsers offer to "help" the user by permanently remembering their credentials (username and password) for them. This is a dangerous feature that exposes our application to the possibility that an attacker gaining access to a client machine could gain free access to our application just by starting up the browser.
- Finally, the dialog box that most browsers display does not usually match the presentation scheme of most web applications. This is a minor issue from a security standpoint, but a major one for many content developers.

Countermeasure: Use an Alternate Method of Authentication

The J2EE specification provides developers with three other authentication schemes (in addition to BASIC):

- **FORM** Uses an HTML-based form, developed by the application developer, to elicit credential information from the user. This information is then submitted to the container, which verifies it and associates the results of the authentication with the user's session. This mechanism is often used instead of BASIC authentication because it is almost as easy to use, but gives a much more visually appealing login screen to the end user. Additionally, in many containers, a user can be easily logged out using FORM authentication merely by invalidating the session. This is a huge advantage compared to BASIC authentication. Unfortunately, credential information is still sent via a simple HTTP POST operation and thus can be easily intercepted.

- **DIGEST** Similar to BASIC authentication, except instead of sending the user password with base 64 encoding, the password, along with a nonce (similar to a salt value, as discussed in Chapter 4), is hashed using a secure digest algorithm and sent to the server. The server then computes a digest of the stored password and nonce and compares it to the digest sent by the client. This eliminates the propagation of the plaintext user credentials over the network. Within short time periods, DIGEST authentication is still vulnerable to replay attacks, but overall it is much more secure than BASIC authentication. However, DIGEST authentication is rarely used, because more secure alternatives are available. We will discuss these alternatives later in this chapter when we cover SSL in its various forms.
- **CLIENT-CERT** From a security standpoint, probably one of the best mechanisms available for client authentication. However, it has some drawbacks that make it impractical in many environments. With CLIENT-CERT, the client authenticates by digitally signing a piece of data and sending it to the server. The server then verifies the signature on the data and authenticates the client in that manner. CLIENT-CERT authentication is extremely secure, and we will see how to configure Tomcat to use the CLIENT-CERT authentication mechanism later in this chapter.

At this point, though, we will replace our BASIC authentication method with form-based authentication. This gives us several nice capabilities, enabling us to do the following:

- Provide users with a more pleasing authentication experience. We can provide numbers to call for lost passwords, online help, and a common look and feel with the rest of our web site.
- Invalidate or time out a user's login based on inactivity.
- Provide users with a mechanism to manually log out if needed.

To modify our application to use form-based authentication, we need to do several things:

1. Modify our application to support session tracking.

2. Build a login page to accept the user's login.
3. Build a login error page to display failed login attempts.
4. Add logout functionality.
5. Modify the `web.xml` file to enable form-based authentication.

First, because the FORM login method in Tomcat uses sessions to track login information, we need to make sure that our application is built in such a way that it will support sessions. If the client browser is set to accept cookies, this is no problem: The container will install a cookie on the client browser that represents the session. Or, if the client is using SSL to connect to the server, the server has the option of using the SSL session ID to track the client session.

However, if we also want to support browsers that are configured to deny cookies and aren't using SSL, we need to make some changes to our application, the most notable of which is to insert calls to `response.encodeURL` at every point that our application generates a URL to be returned to the client browser. When the `encodeURL` method is called, if the client browser is not accepting cookies, an element called `JSESSIONID`, along with a unique session identifier, is appended to the URL. Then, we return that modified URL back to the client browser. This needs to be done throughout the entire application. One implication of this is that most static HTML pages need to be converted to JSP so that we can insert the call to `encodeURL`. For some applications, this may be cost-prohibitive, but we will configure our application in this manner to demonstrate the technique. For example, when we convert the link section of our entry page using this technique, it looks like this:

```
<p>
  <a href="<%= response.encodeURL(request.getContextPath() +
              "/getbalance.jsp") %>">
    Get the balance for an account
  </a>
</p>
```

Next, we will build a login JSP with an embedded form that will POST its results with the action *j_security_check*—note the use of `encodeURL` here also. This will notify the container that the form contains login information. Our application will never see the request associated with the form; it will be intercepted by the container and authenticated using the realm currently in effect. The username input field on the form must be named `j_username`, and the user password must be named `j_password`. Our new application login page will look like this (we'll call it `login/login.jsp`):

```
<html>
. . .
<hr>
<form action="<%= response.encodeURL("j_security_check") %>"
      method="post" name="LoginForm"
```

```
      title="LoginForm">
<table summary="Login Info" align="center">
<tr>
  <td>User Name:</td>
  <td><input type="text" name="j_username"></td>
</tr>
<tr>
  <td>Password: </td>
      <td><input type="password" name="j_password"></td>
</tr>
<tr>
  <td colspan="2" align="center"><button
type="submit">Login</button></td>
</tr>
. . .
</html>
```

As you can see, it's just an HTML form with some embedded JSP expressions to encode the URLs. But, from the user's perspective, it matches the scheme of the rest of our application much better than a browser-initiated login dialog box.

Now, we need to develop the login error page. This is the page that the container will display if the user-supplied credentials cannot be authenticated. Our login error page is an extremely straightforward HTML-based page that informs the user that their login request was denied and directs them back to the main application page.

To add logout functionality, we will modify our entry page to detect whether a session is present. If a session exists, we additionally give the user the option to log out. If the user chooses to log out, we will forward them to our `ControllerServlet`, which will invalidate the user session and direct them back to our entry page. We will not provide a login mechanism; the container will do that for us automatically when the user attempts to access a protected resource.

The following are the changes that we need to make to enable logout functionality for our application:

1. Add a line to our entry JSP (`entry.jsp`) to make sure that it does not unilaterally create a new session for the user. We let the container authentication mechanism handle that piece.

   ```
   <%-- Set this to false so that a session is not automatically
        created for us --%>
   <%@ page session="false"  %>
   ```

2. Add a block to display a custom message to the user, if needed. This will be used by the `ControllerServlet` to display a Logout Successful message to the user when the logout is complete.

```
. . .
<h2>
<% if (request.getAttribute("banner_message") != null) { %>
  <%= request.getAttribute("banner_message") %>
<% } else { %>
    Welcome to our retirement planning application!
<% } // end else %>
</h2>

 . . .
```

3. Add code which adds a new link to logout only if there is a currently authenticated user. We can discover who generated the request by using the `getUserPrincipal` method, which will return an instance of `java.security.Principal` that corresponds to the currently authenticated user. This feature is more commonly used for programmatic authorization, but in this case, we use it to determine whether or not authentication has occurred yet.

```
<% if (request.getUserPrincipal() != null) { %>
<p><a href="<%= response.encodeURL(request.getContextPath() +
                 "/actions/logout") %>">Logout</a></p>
<% } // end if %>
</body>
</html>
```

4. Modify our `ControllerServlet` to receive the `/actions/logout` action and act appropriately. We log the user out by invalidating their entire session, along with all of their session-based data. Note that if your application is storing important or sensitive information in an `HttpSession` object, you might want to present the user with a confirmation before the logout, or plan to persist the session information in some other way.

Here is what the `processRequest` method in the `ControllerServlet` looks like with the appropriate changes (in bold):

```
private void processRequest(HttpServletRequest request,
                            HttpServletResponse response)
    throws ServletException, IOException {

  String reqURI = request.getRequestURI();
  if (reqURI.indexOf("actions/") !=
      reqURI.lastIndexOf("actions/"))
  { // Handle the possibility of us being deployed under
    // a root context that contains 'actions/' }
```

```
    reqURI = reqURI.substring(reqURI.indexOf("actions/"));

    if (reqURI.equals("actions/getbalance")) {
      // Handle the display of the balance
      processGetBalanceDisplay(request,response);
    } else if (reqURI.equals("actions/setbalance")) {
      // Handle the display of the balance
      processSetBalanceDisplay(request,response);
    } else if (reqURI.equals("actions/logout")) {
      request.getSession().invalidate();
      request.setAttribute("banner_message","You have been
logged out!");
      RequestDispatcher dispatcher =
getServletContext().getRequestDispatcher("/entry.jsp");
      dispatcher.forward(request,response);
. . .
```

The last action that we need to take is to configure the `web.xml` file to support form-based authentication, add special security for our login-related JSPs, and map incoming traffic to our new entry page:

```
<web-app>
. . .
  <servlet>
    <servlet-name>EntryPage</servlet-name>
    <jsp-file>/entry.jsp</jsp-file>
  </servlet>
. . .
  <servlet-mapping>
    <servlet-name>ControllerServlet</servlet-name>
    <url-pattern>/actions/logout</url-pattern>
  </servlet-mapping>
  <servlet-mapping>
    <servlet-name>EntryPage</servlet-name>
    <url-pattern>/entry.html</url-pattern>
  </servlet-mapping>
. . .
```

The preceding entries map the `entry.html` pattern to our new `entry.jsp` page. This allows us to insert a JSP without breaking existing bookmarks in client browsers and without having to recode all of the references to `entry.html` in our code.

Next, we add a special `security-constraint` for our login-related pages. Notice that the `role-name` attribute is empty. This will deny *all* users direct access to all resources located beneath the `/login` subcontext.

```
  <!-- Security Information -->
. . .
  <security-constraint>
    <web-resource-collection>
      <web-resource-name>LoginPages</web-resource-name>
      <description>Login Functionality</description>
      <url-pattern>/login/*</url-pattern>
    </web-resource-collection>
    <auth-constraint>
      <role-name></role-name>
    </auth-constraint>
  </security-constraint>
. . .
```

You might be thinking, "Why would we include a empty `role-name` tag and prohibit *all* users from accessing our `LoginPages` resource?" The reason is that even though no user can access the pages *directly*, the container has no such restriction and can access them with impunity. This means that we can use `RequestDispatcher.forward` or `include` methods to process them, or the container can do it automatically.

CAUTION An often overlooked aspect of the `security-constraint` tag is that it protects the specified resource only from *client* access, not from server-side components belonging to the same web application, or applications that are able to get another application's `ServletContext`, because cross-context mapping is allowed in the server configuration.

Finally, we specify that we would like form-based authentication, along with the login and error pages that should be used by the container to conduct the login:

```
  <!-- The type of authentication to do -->
  <login-config>
    <auth-method>FORM</auth-method>
    <form-login-config>
      <form-login-page>/login/loginpage.jsp</form-login-page>
      <form-error-page>/login/loginerror.jsp</form-error-page>
    </form-login-config>
  </login-config>
</web-app>
```

And that's it! Because our `ControllerServlet` is still protected by the security constraints we covered earlier in this chapter, whenever access to that resource is requested, FORM login will be used by the container to authenticate the user.

Now, when we deploy and run our application, we see the following results after we try to set or get a balance:

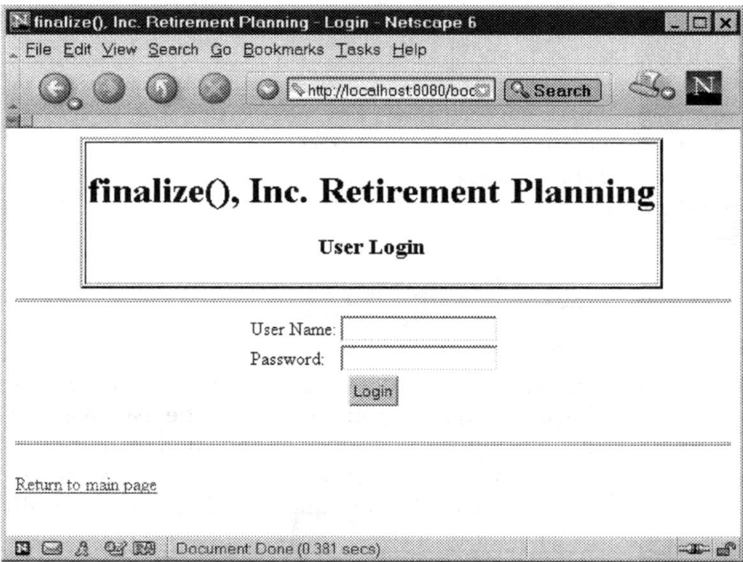

Once the user authenticates, the proper operation is performed, and then they are directed back to the main page, where they see a new item (logout) appear at the bottom of their list of choices.

If the user elects to end their session by clicking the Logout link, the `entry.jsp` page is displayed again, but this time the Logout anchor is missing and a special message is displayed for the user informing them that they have been logged out.

Client Cache Analysis

Popularity:	5
Simplicity:	10
Impact:	7
Risk rating:	7

With most common web browser configurations, viewed pages are cached on disk so that they can be later retrieved without the overhead of another HTTP request. While this is a good idea for image files, static, unsecure HTML content, and other web resources, it is definitely *not* a good idea for a secure web application. Let's take a look at what happens when we navigate to our web client cache directory and search for the string "Balance Display," which is the title of our balance display page. We see the following results, most with quite cryptic filenames:

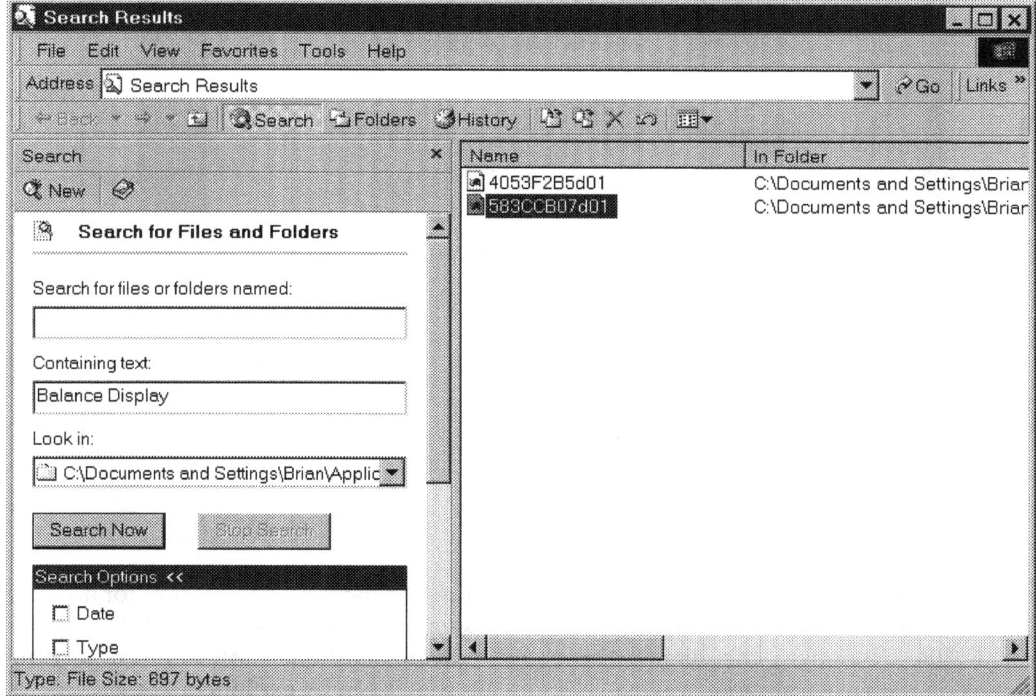

Even though the filenames don't make sense to us, we do know that these files contain the string "Balance Display." If we open one of the files in a text editor, we see the following disturbing results.

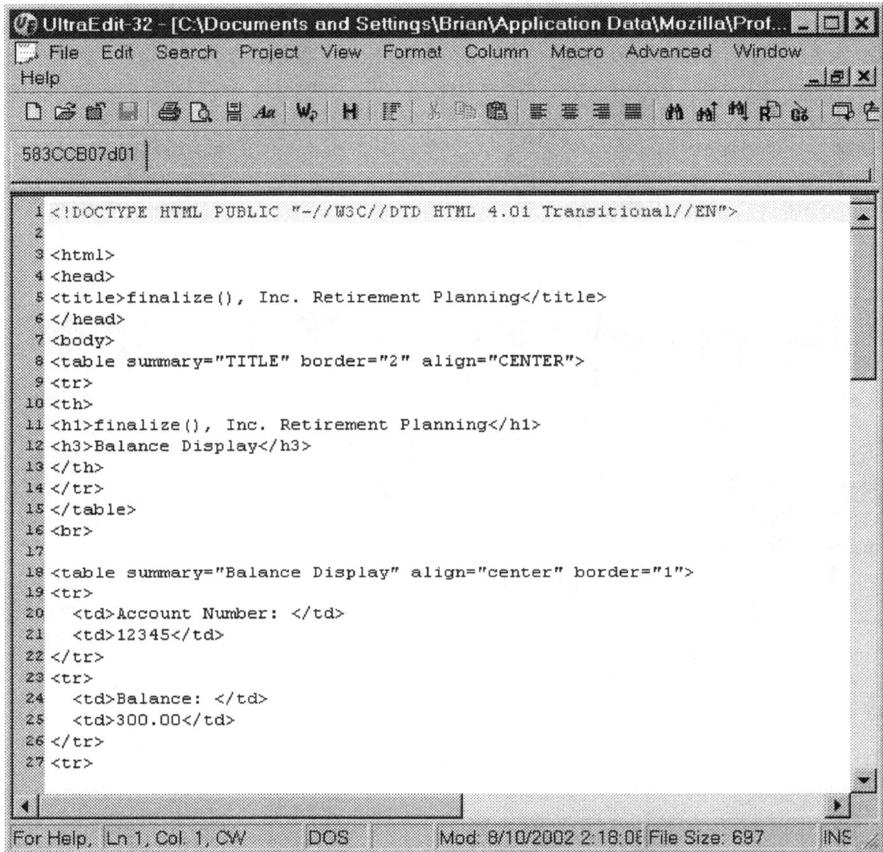

As you can see, this is the raw HTML containing the balance information for account 12345. These files are stored on the client's workstation and are never deleted until the cache fills. Obviously, the client is probably unaware that such information is being stored on their workstation, and even less aware that it can be exploited as easily as we have shown.

Countermeasure: Cache Control via Servlet Filters

One possible countermeasure is to require the client to disable caching entirely in their browser. This is not practical for most clients. It can dramatically increase the time and resources necessary to visit an arbitrary website.

Instead, we will use a built-in mechanism in the HTTP 1.1 protocol that allows our application to inform the browser that the information contained on a page should never be cached, or even written to a temporary file on disk.

To do this, we will set a field called `Cache-Control` in the HTTP response header to a value of `no-store`. This tells the browser that it should never write the contents of the response to disk in any circumstances. There is also an option called `no-cache`, which tells the browser not to use the response to serve a future request, but *does not* prohibit it from writing the response to a temporary file for its own internal use. Additionally, the option `private` will tell the browser that it can cache the response, but it must do so in a location that is only accessible to the user currently running the browser. Because most Windows-based installations are effectively single-user (even if there are multiple users defined, most users will have local administrative access on the local NT workstation and can look at other people's files), specifying `Cache-Control` as `private` really will not have much of a constructive effect on a typical Windows platform. The `Cache-Control` setting has several other options that are not as relevant for security purposes, but may be interesting nonetheless. You can look them up at www.w3.org/Protocols/rfc2616/rfc2616-sec14.html.

If we want to set the `Cache-Control` response header for a particular page, we can include the following code in our servlet or JSP:

```
response.addHeader("Cache-Control", "no-store");
```

Remember that response header information must be set *before* the first chunk of data is sent from the container to the client—this should be obvious, because the header data needs to get sent at the *beginning* of the response. Therefore, to be safe, all code that sets header values should appear before any code that writes to the payload of the HTTP response.

Implementing our Cache-Control Strategy

However, we still have a slight logistical problem: What if we don't want *any* of our pages for the application to be cached by the client (or at least any pages that fall within a certain subcontext of our application)? This is a realistic requirement, especially for a secure web-based application. Hand-coding the `addHeader` method call in all of our code can be tedious at best. We have two real solutions that we can use to address this issue:

- Server-side includes
- Servlet filtering

If we use server-side includes, we would place a `response.addHeader` call in a servlet or JSP, which would be included in every relevant web page on our system. This would still require hand-coding the "include" in both servlets and JSPs, but in many enterprise development environments, there is a standard "corporate" include that (by internal standard) must be placed at the beginning of each file anyway. This is much more of an issue with servlets, though, as the servlet developer must remember to include a call to `RequestDispatcher.include` in their `doGet` and `doPost` methods. Additionally, if servlets are chained and requests are being forwarded (as is the case in our application), sometimes the same header will get set twice. This is no problem *as long as data hasn't already been sent to the client*. With a large web application, keeping track of all the possibilities and guaranteeing that the `Cache-Control` header is always getting set properly can turn into a bit of an administrative headache.

Writing a Servlet Filter to Control the Client Browser Cache

As you may have expected, there *is* a better way to handle this situation: servlet filtering. Servlet filters, new in the 2.3 version of the servlet specification, give us the ability to let the container apply a filter to an incoming request/response pair *before* the web application involved even gets to see it. In the filter, we can set some fields in the response header, and then pass the request on to the web application, which will continue to respond appropriately.

To write a servlet filter to perform this task for us, we need to take two steps:

1. Write the filter.
2. Modify the `web.xml` file to let the container know when it should be invoked.

To write a servlet filter, we merely have to implement the `javax.servlet.Filter` interface, which contains three methods: `init`, `destroy`, and `doFilter`. Here is what our implementation looks like (for a fully documented version of this code, download the complete working code examples for this text at www.hackingexposedjava.com):

```
package book.servlet.original;

import javax.servlet.*;
import javax.servlet.http.HttpServletResponse;
import java.io.IOException;

/**
 * This filter will add a Cache-Control header of the
 * proper type to the supplied HttpResponse.  The
 * value of the Cache-Control header <B>*MUST*</B>
 * be set in the init parameter called
 * <code>CacheControlType</code>
 */
public class CacheControlFilter implements Filter {
  protected FilterConfig config;
  private String cacheControlType;
  public void doFilter(ServletRequest servletRequest,
                       ServletResponse servletResponse,
```

```
                        FilterChain filterChain)
        throws IOException, ServletException {

      // We know this is an HTTP response, so cast it:
      if (servletResponse instanceof HttpServletResponse) {
        HttpServletResponse resp =
            (HttpServletResponse) servletResponse;
        // Add the cache-control header to the response
        resp.addHeader("Cache-Control", cacheControlType);

      } else {
        throw new ServletException("Invalid response in filter");
      }
      // Continue Processing
      filterChain.doFilter(servletRequest, servletResponse);
    }

    public void init(FilterConfig filterConfig)
      throws ServletException {
      // Store the FilterConfig object for future use
      this.config = filterConfig;
      cacheControlType =
config.getInitParameter("CacheControlType");
      if (cacheControlType == null) {
        throw new ServletException("No cache control specified");
      }
    }

}
```

Most of the processing occurs in the `doFilter` method. We add the proper header to the response and then call the next filter in our filter chain. In the `init` method, we will read one initialization parameter: `CacheControlType`. This will allow the user of our filter to set the `cache-control` type to anything that they'd like: `no-store`, `no-cache`, `private`, and so forth.

To notify the web container about how to use and apply this filter, we add the following entries to our deployment descriptor (`web.xml`):

```
<!-- Application filter information -->
<filter>
  <filter-name>CacheControlFilter</filter-name>
  <filter-class>
      book.servlet.original.CacheControlFilter
  </filter-class>
```

```
  <init-param>
    <param-name>CacheControlType</param-name>
    <param-value>no-store</param-value>
  </init-param>
</filter>

<!-- Map the filter to all resources under
     our root context -->
<filter-mapping>
  <filter-name>CacheControlFilter</filter-name>
  <url-pattern>/*</url-pattern>
</filter-mapping>
```

This material must appear in the `web.xml` file *before* the first servlet is defined. These entries tell the container to map requests for all servlet and JSP resources to our filter first, and then to the resource. Now, once we deploy our application and restart the server, the `Cache-Control` header will silently be added to every request for every resource in our application. This is a security administrator's dream!

If we clear our browser cache manually, and then visit our application again and request a balance, we will see that the balance is successfully displayed. But, when we search our browser's cache for the string "Balance Display," we will also see the following pleasing results:

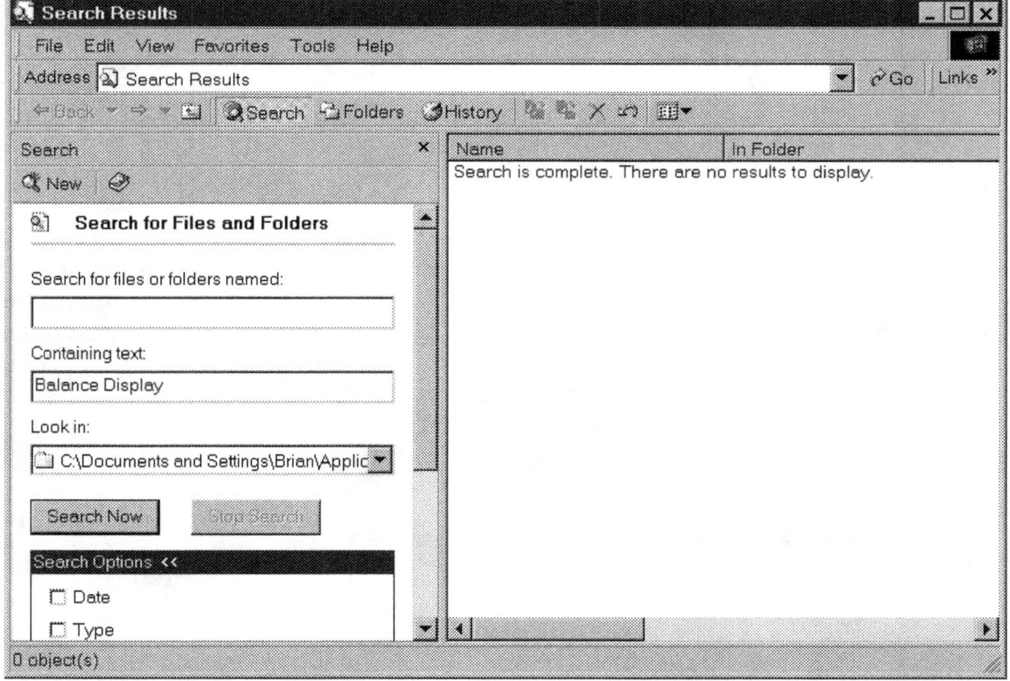

Our servlet filter is working and the client browser is not retaining any information that we don't want it to retain.

From a security standpoint, servlet filters are extremely powerful technology. They can be used to implement logging, single sign-on (SSO)-style authentication via nonstandard authentication methods—perhaps using a CICS connector to authenticate a client on a mainframe—or just standard enterprise policies for request or response composition. In fact, a servlet filter can even look at the contents of a request and deny it outright, before the servlet or JSP to which it is directed is even invoked. Filters are an extremely pleasing development in the servlet API, and one that has incredible potential for creative and labor-saving application in industry.

SUMMARY

In this chapter, you learned how to apply the following techniques to a sample web application to improve its security stature:

- Hide application structure and enable more granular declarative authorization by passing select servlet parameters in the URL instead of in the HTTP header
- Configure certain servlets to deny HTTP GET requests
- Implement a web application exception-handling framework with nonrevealing error handling
- Implement a form-based authentication scheme
- Use servlet filters to implement a client cache control strategy

In the next chapter, we will continue to explore how you can fully utilize the services of your host web container to develop more comprehensive web application security.

CHAPTER 10

SHAKING THE FOUNDATION: WEB CONTAINER STRENGTHS AND WEAKNESSES

Often, improper server configuration—something that an application developer may have little control over—can pose security problems too. That is the focus of this section: things that you, as an application developer, can do to help your web application fully utilize (or fully avoid) common features provided by your web container. Most of the examples in this chapter will focus on the Tomcat web container, but we have specifically chosen examples that apply to many other web containers, too.

Exploiting Improperly Configured Applications and Containers

Popularity:	*8*
Simplicity:	*5*
Impact:	*8*
Risk rating:	*7*

As if installing and configuring a J2EE-compliant web container wasn't difficult enough, many organizations compound the difficulty by not employing application server administrators. Rather, they assign the duty to one of the following two categories of employee:

- Overworked, underappreciated system administrators who know little about J2EE, application servers, or web development, but are gurus at dealing with OS-level administration and configuration
- Overworked, underappreciated application developers who understand J2EE, but have little experience installing and configuring server software

Usually, neither of these groups is properly equipped or trained to know the nuances of application server installation, configuration, and maintenance. In many cases, web containers get installed with the default options and receive just enough configuration to get an application up and running. Sometimes, the application developer does not have the authority to reconfigure the container to alleviate any perceived security problems. However, some simple actions can be taken at the application level, without requiring server reconfiguration, to overcome shortcomings in a faulty container setup.

The following are two common configuration errors that (in many web containers) an application developer has the ability to correct without modifying the server configuration itself:

- Directory listings are enabled in the container
- The invoker servlet is active

The Effects of Directory Listing

Let's address these in order. First, a common configuration mistake, especially on lightly used web containers, is to leave the directory listing capability turned on. With this feature enabled, the container, when asked for a resource that maps directly to a directory on the server, will, in the absence of an appropriate welcome file (like `index.html`) in the directory, return an HTML-formatted directory listing instead of a 404 (resource not found) error. Since the main page for our application is called `entry.html`, and that doesn't appear in our list of welcome files for our web application, we get the result shown in Figure 10-1 when we type in the base URL for our application.

For obvious reasons, this result is not good. Even if the directory listing capability were originally disabled, sometimes it can be reenabled during a careless patch installation or system upgrade. With Tomcat, the directory listing feature is enabled by default, and can be configured by setting the `listings` parameter to the default servlet in the `web.xml` file located in the `conf` subdirectory of the Tomcat installation.

Figure 10-1. A listing of our application root directory

However, if you are an application developer, you may not have access to that directory, or the server administrator may refuse to turn off the directory listing capability—there may be other users of the container who depend on it. We will see a simple solution that allows you, as an application assembler or deployer, to regain control over how your pages are displayed underneath your application context.

The Invoker Servlet

An additional security-related configuration issue is that most web containers come with something called an "invoker" or "invoker servlet" installed by default. This allows developers to easily access a servlet without including a `servlet-mapping` tag in the `web.xml` file for a particular application. With Tomcat, if we append `/servlet/` followed by the fully qualified class name of the servlet that we wish to run to the application context root URL, Tomcat will magically run our servlet, *even if* we have a separate mapping for the servlet that is secure. This hole, combined with poor error handling that displays a stack trace (containing the class name of the servlet) when confronted with an exception, makes it possible for an attacker to quickly access the servlets installed under a particular context. They can then call those servlets directly without regard to security settings that may be in force for the particular web application.

In Tomcat, to use the invoker to call our `ControllerServlet` directly, without authentication, we type the following URL:

```
http://localhost:8080/book/srv/servlet/book.servlet.original.ControllerServlet
```

As our application stands now, our `ControllerServlet` would return a 405 code (method not supported), because we disabled support for HTTP GET earlier. If we had not disabled HTTP GET support, an attacker would be able to freely use our servlet at this time. Furthermore, even with GET support disabled, an attacker could easily manually submit POST requests to this servlet by changing the action on an arbitrary HTML form to the preceding URL.

Countermeasure: Override the Invoker Servlet and the Default Servlet

To address both of these security issues, we have a powerful tool at our disposal: the application-level deployment descriptor (`web.xml`). We will modify this file to instantiate a new version of Tomcat's default servlet, with the directory listing capability turned off. Additionally, we will configure the servlet mappings so that this servlet, not the one configured by the system administrator, will handle all requests for our application's resources.

The servlet we are using is the *same* servlet that Tomcat uses by default to handle web requests. We are just creating a new instance of it, with the parameters set the way we want them set—most notably, with the directory listing capability turned off.

Additionally, we will override the mapping for the invoker servlet and direct all requests for the /servlet subcontext of our application to the new default servlet also. This will fix both issues, and will not require server reconfiguration.

To enable these features, we will make the following changes to our web.xml file:

```
<web-app>
. . .
```

The following is the configuration for Tomcat's default servlet. Notice that we are setting the listings parameter to false, which turns off the feature that generates directory listings.

```
<servlet>
  <servlet-name>AppDefault</servlet-name>
  <servlet-class>
     org.apache.catalina.servlets.DefaultServlet
  </servlet-class>
  <init-param>
    <param-name>debug</param-name>
    <param-value>0</param-value>
  </init-param>
  <init-param>
    <param-name>listings</param-name>
    <param-value>false</param-value>
  </init-param>
  <load-on-startup>1</load-on-startup>
</servlet>
```

Next, we map the newly created servlet to our root application context as well as the /servlet subcontext:

```
  <servlet-mapping>
    <servlet-name>AppDefault</servlet-name>
    <url-pattern>/</url-pattern>
  </servlet-mapping>
  <servlet-mapping>
    <servlet-name>AppDefault</servlet-name>
    <url-pattern>/servlet/*</url-pattern>
  </servlet-mapping>
  . . .
</web-app>
```

After we perform this mapping, when we try to get a listing for the root context of our application, we see the following error:

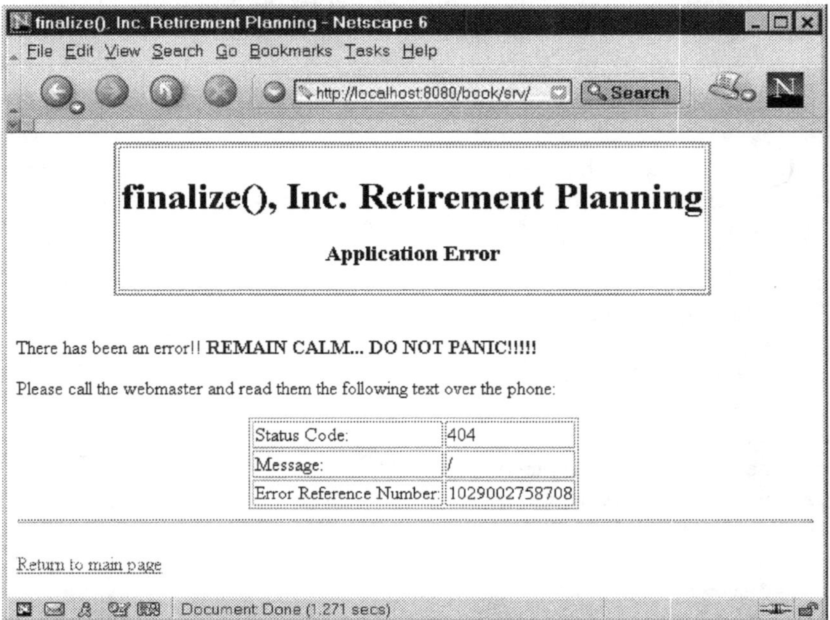

We also get the same error if we try to access a servlet directly by using the invoker servlet.

Different containers have different versions of both the invoker and the default request handler, and with some implementations, the invoker is mapped to a subcontext other than `/servlet` by default. Therefore, the dynamics of this solution differ slightly based on which web container is in use. Additionally, some containers do not have Java-based request handlers or invokers, but instead implement the necessary functionality in some other language, like C. However, even if your container does not include a servlet-based request handler, you can still write your own error servlet and map the `/servlet` subcontext to it. This will at least override the built-in invoker and prevent external users from having direct, unauthorized access to your servlets. Additionally, you can prevent unwanted directory listings by guaranteeing that every directory contains a file that matches the definition of a "welcome file" for the container, for example, a file with a name like index.html. Of course, you could also talk to your system administrator and get them to configure the container the way you would like it to be configured, but in some environments, this just isn't practical.

Session Hijacking

Popularity:	4
Simplicity:	6
Impact:	10
Risk rating:	**8**

As we saw in the last chapter, when not using HTTPS, the web container maintains session awareness with its web clients in one of two ways:

- Cookies
- URL rewriting

To make it easier to demonstrate the session hijacking attack, we will use URL rewriting to manage our sessions throughout this section. The technique we illustrate will also work, with slight modifications, against a cookie-based session tracking scheme.

Let's modify our entry page slightly to display the actual principal name of the current user (if there is one) so that we can get more information regarding exactly who the container thinks we are. To do this, we'll modify `entry.jsp` in the following manner (shown in bold):

```
<% if (request.getUserPrincipal() != null) { %>
<p>
   <a href="<%= response.encodeURL(request.getContextPath()
                + "/actions/logout") %>">
      Logout user <%= request.getUserPrincipal().getName() %>
   </a>
</p>
<% } // end if %>
```

If we disable cookies in our browser, after we either get or set a balance, log on using form-based authentication, and return to the entry page, we see some interesting information appended to our URL:

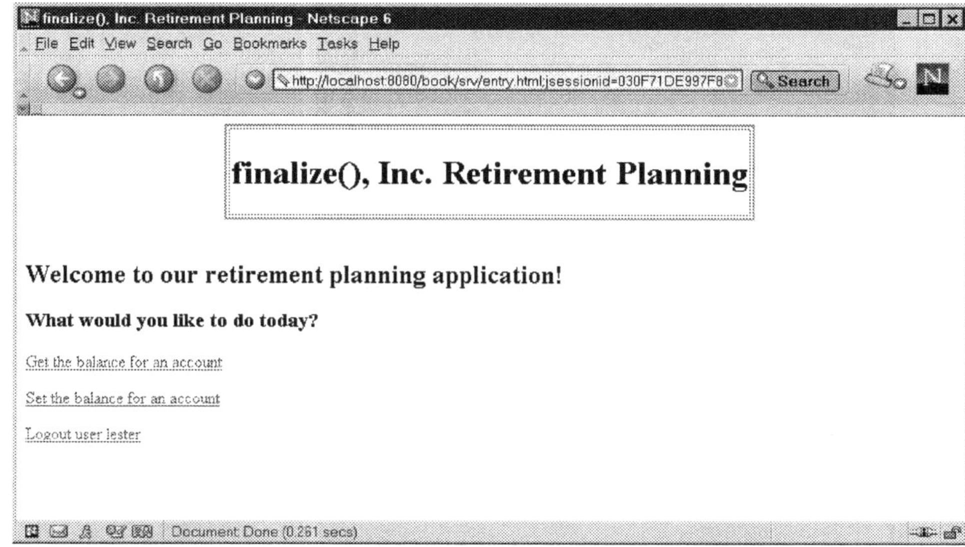

Particularly, pay attention to the URL line, the full text of which is:

```
http://localhost:8080/book/srv/entry.html;jsessionid=030F71DE997F85F8A406DBEC1A7EA87B
```

The `jsessionid` portion of the URL has been added by the container and represents the ID that it uses to distinguish us from all other users. In Tomcat, the session ID is computed by generating a secure random number (using the `SecureRandom` class) and computing its digest using a message digest algorithm.

Stealing a Session

Here is the dangerous part: Let's take the URL from our first browser session, including the session ID, paste it into a different browser, and bring up the entry page.

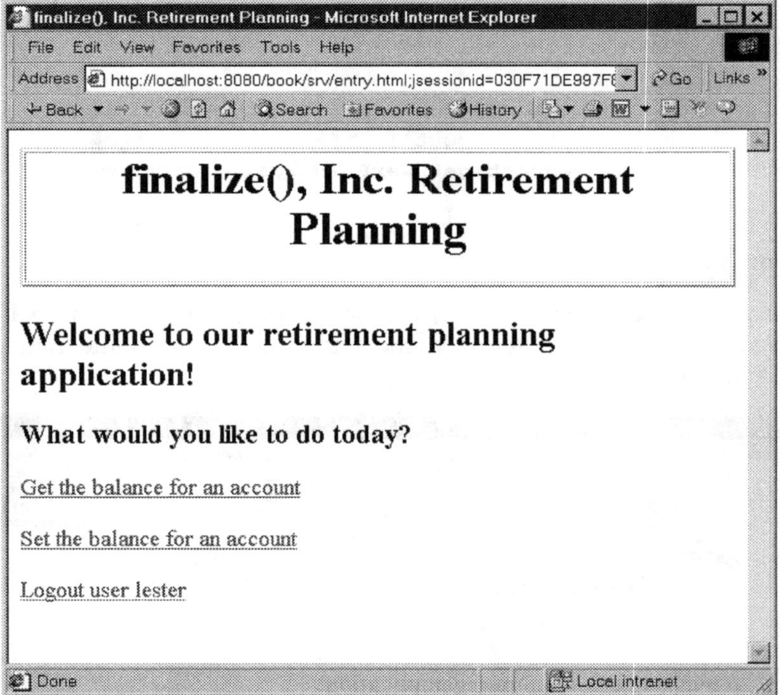

Notice the last link on the page: The container thinks we are Lester! Because we were able to reproduce the session ID, the container does not ask us to authenticate, but merely assigns the principal associated with the current session to the new client. If we were using cookies instead of URL rewriting, the session would be stored in a cookie on the client browser called JSESSIONID and would contain the same information. So, if we can duplicate (or guess) the session ID and install it on our browser, we can masquerade as the other user for as long as the server will let us.

Countermeasure: Proper Session Configuration

It should be clear by now that this is an extremely dangerous attack. There are several techniques that we can use to defend ourselves, but none of them (except one) is even close to being totally secure. As long as our connection between the client and the server is unprotected, the session ID will be sent with every HTTP request made. An attacker anywhere on the route between the client and server can intercept a packet containing the header, inspect the session information, and then use it to impersonate us. Additionally, an attacker that is able to impersonate the web container can request the cookie or read the `jsessionid` parameter themselves.

Here are some techniques we can use to reduce our risk of being victimized by an attack such as this:

- Secure the connection between our client and server. We will cover this in the upcoming section "Countermeasure: Require a HTTPS Connection for All Browser-Server Communication." Note that if you choose to use this method, the *entire* communication needs to be secure, not just the authentication piece. Because the session ID is sent with every request, it only takes one unsecured request to broadcast our session to the world. Adding client authentication to the HTTPS connection makes this method even more secure.
- Modify the `web.xml` file to add a `session-timeout` element. This instructs the container to timeout a session after a certain period of inactivity. Many times, old sessions are left on the server for hours or sometimes days—although this is not the default setting for most containers. This not only poses a security risk, but also is a waste of server resources, so getting rid of unused or inactive sessions is in everyone's best interest.
- Add logout functionality to the application. Allowing users to end their own sessions is another nice way to avoid server resource overload and defend against session theft.
- Configure the server so that the session IDs are generated in a truly random manner. Tomcat is configured in this manner by default, but some older application servers (along with older versions of Tomcat) generated their session IDs by using either a predictable random-number-generation algorithm with a seed based on the server startup time or, even worse, sequential numbers. Both of these mechanisms are extremely weak because they allow an attacker to guess possible session identifiers without actually having to intercept traffic.
- Modify your controller servlet or servlets to inspect the client IP address or hostname. This technique is usually not appropriate for public web applications because IP addresses or hostnames often can change based on proxy server configuration or loss of a DHCP lease. However, if you know that you have a situation where client IP addresses will not change (perhaps an intranet with static IP assignment), feel free to use the `getRemoteHost` or `getRemoteAddr` method to get the remote hostname or IP address, respectively. You can then

associate that IP address with the session and recheck it each time you receive a request. Servlet filters, new in the 2.3 version of the servlet API, are extremely useful for this purpose.

To address the session timeout issue, let's update the `web.xml` file for our application to set a default session timeout. In most containers, the default session timeout is 30 minutes. The timeout refers to the time the session is inactive, not the elapsed time since the session was created. To configure our application for a 15-minute session timeout, the `web.xml` entry would look as follows:

```
<session-config>
    <session-timeout>15</session-timeout>
</session-config>
```

Intercepting Information from an Insecure Browser-Server Connection

Popularity:	3
Simplicity:	2
Impact:	9
Risk rating:	5

As we saw previously, as long as our transport is unsecured, we really have no surefire way to address a session-stealing attack or any other exploit based on the ability to view the data passed between the client browser and the web container. So, let's see how we can add another countermeasure to this attack by falling back upon the web application developer's best friend: HTTPS via SSL/TLS.

Countermeasure: Require an HTTPS Connection for All Browser-Server Communication

In Chapter 7, you saw a redirection package that uses SSL to create secure connections between two arbitrary computers. Then, in Chapter 8, you learned about using SSL to secure connections between RMI clients and RMI object servers. In this section, we will focus on how SSL can be used by the web application developer to not only provide secure communication between a browser and the web container, but also to authenticate the identity of both the client and the server.

Properly configuring a web container to enable HTTPS using SSL/TLS is no easy task, and this certainly is not a book on server administration. However, by reviewing the steps necessary to configure Tomcat to use SSL, we will gain more insight about how exactly SSL applies to a web application, what options the web developer has, and what decisions need to be made during an SSL installation. This can help you determine whether using HTTPS is a viable option for your particular application.

To enable SSL in Tomcat, you need to take the following steps, the details of which are described in this section:

1. Create a digital certificate and have it signed by a trusted certification authority. This will be the server's mechanism for demonstrating its identity to potential clients.
2. Import the certificate and secret key into a Java keystore and place it in a location that is accessible to the Tomcat server process.
3. Modify the Tomcat `server.xml` file to enable the SSL connector and redirect HTTPS requests to the appropriate HTTPS port.

Generating a Server Key

First, we will use `keytool` to create a new keystore with our own secret key stored within:

```
C:\sec\book>keytool -genkey -alias serverkey -keyalg RSA
                    -validity 1095 -keystore tomcatserver.ks
                    -storetype JCEKS
Enter keystore password:  password
What is your first and last name?
  [Unknown]:  localhost
What is the name of your organizational unit?
  [Unknown]:  servers
What is the name of your organization?
  [Unknown]:  Lester's Retirement Planning, Inc.
What is the name of your City or Locality?
  [Unknown]:  Anywhere
What is the name of your State or Province?
  [Unknown]:  AK
What is the two-letter country code for this unit?
  [Unknown]:  US
Is CN=localhost, OU=servers,
   O="Lester's Retirement Planning, Inc.",
   L=Anywhere,
   ST=AK, C=US correct?
  [no]:  yes

Enter key password for <serverkey>
        (RETURN if same as keystore password):
```

We *must* enter the DNS hostname of the server in the "first and last name" section of the key generation prompts. The client browser will match this hostname against the hostname in the URL provided by the user to connect. If the names don't match, the user of the web browser will receive a message stating that the server certificate does not match the server address. This prevents potential attackers from stealing the server certificate and using it to spoof the application website from a different location.

Once the key has been generated, we need to send it to a certificate authority (CA) for certification. This is the step where the CA will digitally sign our certificate to assert its identity. Because we will use this server for test purposes only, we will self-sign our certificate instead of spending money to have it professionally signed by a CA. By self-signing our certificate, the client browser will display a warning message to the user informing them that the authenticity of the certificate cannot be assured. But, since we are in development mode, and we trust ourselves, we'll accept the inconvenience of the message in the interest of saving some money.

The step to self-sign our certificate looks like this:

```
C:\sec\book>keytool -selfcert -alias serverkey
                    -keystore tomcatserver.ks
                    -storetype JCEKS
Enter keystore password:  password
```

Now, we have a keystore that contains two things:

- A signed certificate
- The private key corresponding to that certificate

Next, we move the keystore into a location where the Tomcat server can see it; the CATALINA_HOME directory (the base Tomcat installation directory) will suffice.

Enabling HTTPS in Tomcat

Now, we will modify the `server.xml` file in the `conf` subdirectory under the Tomcat base directory to enable SSL support. First, we need to uncomment the definition for the SSL connector. It looks something like the following (entries which are different than the Tomcat default appear in bold):

```
<!-- Define an SSL HTTP/1.1 Connector on port 8443 -->

<Connector
className="org.apache.catalina.connector.http.HttpConnector"
           port="8443" minProcessors="5" maxProcessors="75"
           enableLookups="true"
           acceptCount="10" debug="0"
           scheme="https" secure="true"
 >
 <Factory
 className="org.apache.catalina.net.SSLServerSocketFactory"
           clientAuth="false" protocol="TLS"
           keystoreFile="tomcatserver.ks"
```

```
        keystorePass="password"
        keystoreType="JCEKS"
  />
</Connector>
```

Notice that our HTTPS port is defined to be 8443. If this were a production server, we would configure the port to be the standard HTTPS port of 443. Also, notice that we've added entries to reflect the name of our keystore file, the password, and the fact that it is a JCEKS and not a standard JKS keystore.

We next tell Tomcat's normal HTTP connector to forward all HTTPS requests to our secure HTTPS port (in our case 8443), by modifying the connector definition (again in `server.xml`):

```
<!-- Define a non-SSL HTTP/1.1 Connector on port 8080 -->
<Connector
className="org.apache.catalina.connector.http.HttpConnector"
           port="8080" minProcessors="5" maxProcessors="75"
           enableLookups="true" redirectPort="8443"
           acceptCount="10" debug="0" connectionTimeout="60000"
 />
```

Testing the Installation

Now that our server is configured, all that remains is a test. When we open our browser and type the following URL, we see this display:

```
https://localhost:8443/book/srv/entry.jsp
```

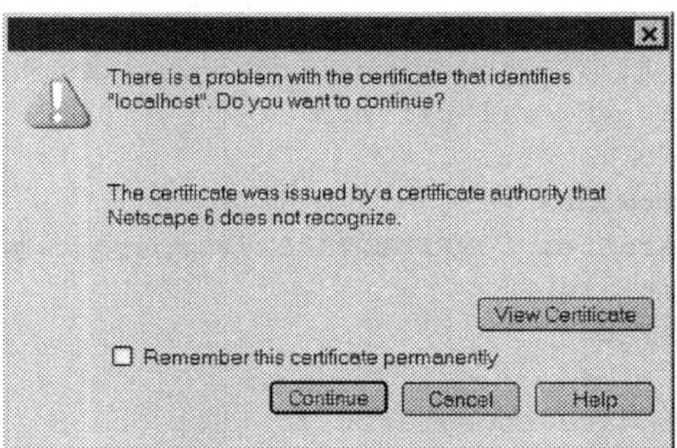

This is Netscape's way of warning the user that our site is supplying a certificate that has not been signed by a trusted CA. Both Netscape and Internet Explorer are distributed with a set of certificates from "trusted CAs" preloaded. If the browser cannot match the signature on a certificate with one of these CAs, the preceding warning box appears. If we wanted to get rid of the warning box, we could add our self-signed certificate to the browser's "trusted" list—on Netscape, this can be done by selecting the Remember This

Certificate Permanently check box in the dialog box shown. This will alleviate the warning, but then the browser in question will automatically be predisposed to trust content signed with that certificate in the future. This is probably not the behavior we want for a development certificate stored on our local workstation. Once we click the Continue button in the dialog box, we have a secure connection between the client browser and the container. All login credentials, along with sensitive application data, will be passed over the secure connection.

There is still a slight problem with our configuration, though: The user has to know enough to type "https" in the browser URL window instead of "http." The server will still respond to HTTP requests, as it should, and potentially the user could be fooled into thinking their connection is secure when, in fact, it isn't.

Adding a Transport Guarantee

J2EE gives us a way to specify that all communication with our application must either take place using SSL/TLS or not take place at all: the `transport-guarantee` tag in the `web.xml` file. For a particular resource collection, we can, in addition to specifying the authorization level, specify the sensitivity level of the data. For example, if we want to protect the data from unauthorized changes in transit, we can specify that the transport needs to be INTEGRAL. If we also want to ensure that the data can neither be changed nor read or viewed in transit, we can specify that the information is CONFIDENTIAL. We specify these values using the `transport-guarantee` tag.

By adding the `transport-guarantee` tag (shown in bold) to all of our security constraints, we tell the web container that we require secure delivery of those resources:

```
    <security-constraint>
    <web-resource-collection>
      <web-resource-name>AllJSPResources</web-resource-name>
      <description>All JSP-based resources</description>
      <url-pattern>*.jsp</url-pattern>
    </web-resource-collection>
    <user-data-constraint>
      <transport-guarantee>CONFIDENTIAL</transport-guarantee>
    </user-data-constraint>
  </security-constraint>
  . . .
<!-- Repeat the user-data-constraint for all other
     security-constraints -->
```

These entries specify that all relevant resources in our web application should be sent using a secure mechanism. For Tomcat, this means using HTTPS/SSL. Now, even if the user types in a URL like this:

```
http://localhost:8080/book/srv/entry.jsp
```

they will be seamlessly redirected to:

```
https://localhost:8443/book/srv/entry.jsp
```

It is important to remember that enforcing SSL for only one or two resources in an application is almost like not enforcing it at all. The application will still be vulnerable to most session stealing/impersonation attacks because the session-tracking cookie is sent with every session-related request. If some of those requests happen to use plain HTTP, the cookie is sent in the clear. Additionally, if you decide to only use SSL on one or two pages that deal with sensitive data, make sure that you use the `transport-guarantee` tag to secure not only the servlet handling the sensitive data, but also the *forms that post the secure data* so that those forms are *loaded* using SSL also. Otherwise, the form will post the data to an insecure URL in the clear using HTTP, and then the client browser will be redirected by the container to repost the data to a secure URL using HTTPS. The data will be submitted twice: once in the clear, and once in a secure manner.

Client Certificate Authentication

There are some disadvantages to using SSL for all transactions between the browser and the container. The biggest disadvantage is performance/resource use. It takes more resources (server memory, client and server CPU, and network bandwidth) to establish and maintain an SSL connection. Thus, many people shy away from using SSL frequently, especially on corporate intranets. However, if configured and used correctly, SSL has one major, usually overlooked, feature that makes it attractive for reasons other than connection integrity and confidentiality: SSL is capable of authenticating both the server *and the client* before establishing a secure connection. This authentication is performed using digital certificates—a much stronger mechanism than username/password authentication or client and server IP address verification.

If we enable SSL client authentication in our container, the option of using the CLIENT-CERT *application* authentication method in the `login-config` tag in the `web.xml` file also becomes available. To perform CLIENT-CERT-based authentication, we need to perform several steps:

1. Configure the server to perform SSL with client authentication instead of server-only authentication. This is usually not the default option, as the server typically requires more configuration to get this piece to work correctly.
2. Establish an internal Public Key Infrastructure (PKI) to sign client certificates. For certificate-based client authentication to work, each user must have their own digital certificate signed by a trusted CA. If you are considering using the CLIENT-CERT authentication method, it might be well worth your while to set up your own CA and add its root certificate to your server's "trusted CA" list. A more expensive, but usually more reliable, option is to purchase individual client certificates for all of your users from a commercial CA. Some CAs even give you the option of running your own "intermediate" CA under their

auspices. This can be the best of both worlds, costing less than individually purchasing certificates for all users, but also giving you the flexibility and self-administration of your own CA.

3. Have your clients install their personal signed certificates in all browsers that they will use to access your application.
4. Enable the CLIENT-CERT authentication method by modifying the application's `web.xml` file.
5. Make sure that the server authentication realm is properly configured to handle certificate-based authentication. Instead of providing usernames and passwords, users will be providing digital certificates, so the values to be looked up in the default realm (whether it is a file on disk, or a LDAP directory) for authentication must be modified slightly.

In this section, we will see a short example detailing exactly how to configure Tomcat and a Netscape browser to perform client authentication. For the purposes of this example, we're going to assume that the user of the client browser already has their own personal certificate signed by a trusted CA. You can obtain a free signed certificate for personal use from Thawte (www.thawte.com), and you can also obtain signed test certificates for server use with SSL. This is the mechanism that we will use. If you'd like more control, you can always establish a CA for your enterprise and sign client certificates yourself.

Configuring Tomcat to use SSL with Client Authentication

Our first step will be to configure our web container to support client authentication on its SSL sessions. In Tomcat, this can be done with a simple modification (shown in bold) to the SSL connector entry in the `server.xml` file:

```
<!-- Define an SSL HTTP/1.1 Connector on port 8443 -->

<Connector
 className="org.apache.catalina.connector.http.HttpConnector"
           port="8443" minProcessors="5" maxProcessors="75"
           enableLookups="true"
           acceptCount="10" debug="0"
           scheme="https" secure="true">
  <Factory
   className="org.apache.catalina.net.SSLServerSocketFactory"
           clientAuth="true" protocol="TLS"
           keystoreFile="tomcatserver.ks"
           keystorePass="password"
           keystoreType="JCEKS"/>
</Connector>
```

Notice that all we have done is set the `clientAuth` attribute to `true`. This informs the container that for every SSL session, it should try to authenticate the client before establishing the connection. The server will ask the client for a signed certificate. If the signature on the client certificate does not come from a CA the server trusts, the connection will be denied. Once we make this setting (and restart the server, of course), if we attempt to access our application using a web browser with no certificate installed, we see the following confusing message:

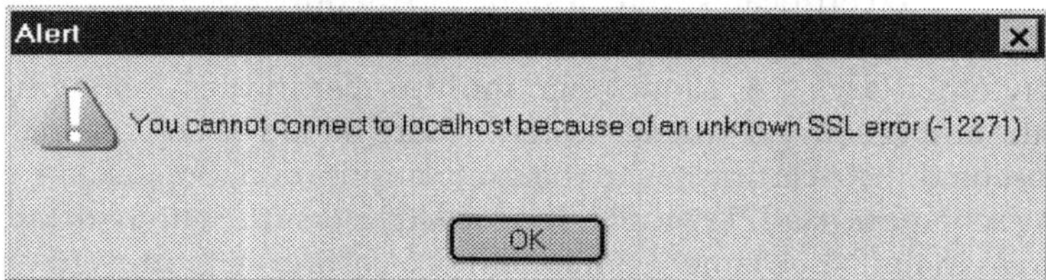

This is the web container's way of telling our browser that it will not establish a HTTPS connection without trusted client credentials. Obviously, it would be better if our browser gave us a more user-friendly error message, but the result is correct: The server is denying connections from users it does not trust.

This authentication will now happen for all SSL connections on the server regardless of how we have our web application configured. So, right now, even though the web container is enforcing the policy that our clients must have a valid, trusted certificate to connect via SSL, our application is still using form-based authentication. This is fine, and still very secure, because we have configured our application in such a way that our form-based authentication is being performed over an SSL connection.

Container Authentication Using a Client Certificate

However, it would be nice if we could take advantage of the fact that the container already has a signed, certified certificate from the client and perhaps use that to authenticate the client for our application too. In fact, we can do this quite easily, by enabling the CLIENT-CERT authentication option in our `web.xml` file:

```
<login-config>
  <auth-method>CLIENT-CERT</auth-method>
</login-config>
```

In practice, for CLIENT-CERT authentication to work, we must be using SSL or have some other secure connection with the client. So, CLIENT-CERT cannot be used unless you are willing to establish an HTTPS connection at some point in your application life cycle. This is not a totally unrealistic requirement, though. If you need an authentication mechanism as secure as digital certificates to protect your application, you probably should be conducting all communication over SSL/TLS anyway.

Once our deployment descriptor specifies that we require CLIENT-CERT authentication, we need a way of mapping the certificate provided by the client to roles in our web container's authentication realm. We will see how to do this using Tomcat's memory realm, but the concept can easily be extended to JNDI realms, JDBC realms, or even JAAS-based realms.

The modification we make will be in the `tomcat-users.xml` file, located in the Tomcat `config` directory. This may seem unintuitive at first, but makes sense if you look at the big picture. X509 certificates were designed to identify potentially everybody in the world. Because of this, some standardization needed to be done. Obviously, VeriSign or Thawte, or any other large CA, cannot sign multiple certificates, belonging to different people, with the ambiguous username "lester." There would be confusion if all Lesters in the world presented their certificates to the same application. So, instead, a much more robust naming scheme is used. Typically, it is considered sufficient to include a name *and* an email address in the "username" component of a certificate to prevent naming confusion. Organizational and location-based information can also (and should) be added to protect against namespace confusion and overlap.

The point of this discussion is that we cannot keep using `lester` and `brian` as usernames if we plan to use CLIENT-CERT authentication. We need to be much more specific about which Lester or Brian we are authorizing to use our application. To do this, we need to configure Tomcat in such a way that it will match the full subject information stored in the certificate. This is the information that we must add as a key to our authentication realm. Here is what the corresponding entry in our `tomcat-users.xml` file would look like for Lester's client certificate:

```
<user
name="EMAILADDRESS=lester@javajockey.com, CN=Thawte Freemail Member"
password="" roles="admin,employee"
/>
```

Notice that we are leaving the password field blank. It's not needed, because the client has already authenticated themselves (in a much more secure way than password-based authentication) by demonstrating that they are in possession of a private key for a signed, trusted certificate endorsed by a CA.

At this point, we are assuming that our client has generated a key pair, had their public key signed by a CA, and installed the signed certificate back into their browser. Once we redeploy our application and restart the server to enable the SSL client authentication, we see the following results when we try to access the entry page for our application:

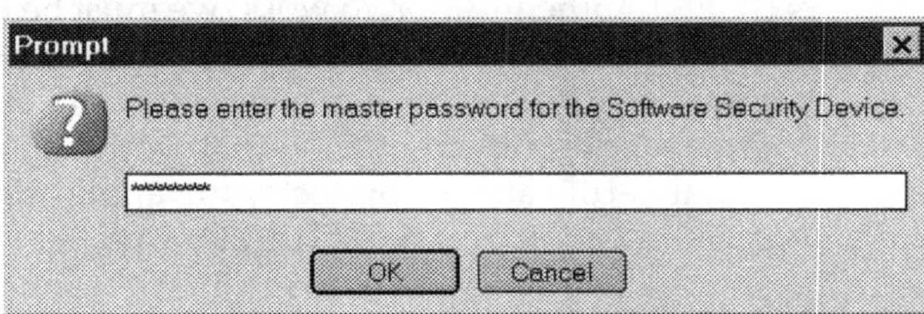

This is Netscape prompting the user to "unlock" their keystore, which contains their private key. Netscape needs the user's private key to sign the certificate that our server is requesting. This "private keystore" feature protects us from someone starting our browser and using it (and the embedded certificates) without our authorization. Internet Explorer, in its default mode, does not operate this way. It will send our client certificate automatically (or prompt us to select one without authentication). It assumes that we are already authenticated with the OS, so we don't need to authenticate again. Both methods are acceptable, but just make different assumptions about who could be using the browser.

Once the user types in their Netscape keystore password, the application behaves as normal. When the user, whom we have configured to only have employee access, tries to access the get balance functionality, *no further authentication is done*. The connection is already authenticated, so the container knows with certainty that all requests sent over that connection are being sent by the authenticated user. Using client certificates to authenticate users is incredibly attractive for a number of reasons:

- It can provide single sign-on functionality across web applications and servers with a minimum of configuration and relative transparency to the user.
- It is the most secure means of remote client authentication available. But remember, the method is only as secure as the client's keystore. If someone can steal the client's key, they can still impersonate the client. However, stealing a digital private key usually is much more difficult than stealing a plaintext password.
- The client owns their own credentials. The server (or application) has no need to administer or reset passwords, or store secret client information. The server needs to store only the subject's identifying information and a list of trusted CAs. This distributes the valuable information. Now, instead of being able to get the administrator's credentials by hacking the server, an attacker would need to find the administrator's keystore and somehow hack that. This "many eggs, many baskets" approach can make an attacker's job much more difficult.

The major disadvantages related to using client certificates to authenticate users are:

- A PKI must be in place to grant, revoke, deliver, and sign certificates for clients.
- Clients must be educated regarding the concept of digital certificates, their storage, and their use.

Because key storage is decentralized, detecting an attack on our application is more difficult also. If an attacker was attempting to use a password guessing attack on our server, we could detect the attack and take countermeasures. However, to defeat the CLIENT-CERT authentication, an attack would be directed at our client's keystore (to steal their private key). Our client, not us, would have the responsibility of detecting and preventing such an attack. From a philosophical standpoint, this makes sense: every person should protect their own identity. However, from a pragmatic perspective, typically we, as owners of the web container, are much better equipped to defend the client's credentials than the end user of our application.

These are not simple disadvantages to overcome, and many times are the driving forces behind organizations not adopting an effective authentication approach based on public keys. However, the benefits of having a PKI in place are quite large and extend past secure web applications. Secure email, file transfer, telnet sessions, VPNs, RMI, CORBA IIOP connections, and many more applications are based on the concept of public key cryptography and can benefit from an integrated PKI approach.

Gaining Valuable Information by Exploiting Container Configuration Files

Popularity:	5
Simplicity:	5
Impact:	9
Risk rating:	**6**

A breach in security often can have a domino effect. If one component is breached, the attacker can develop information to attack other components. This is also true with our sample application. If you have downloaded the full code examples from www.hackingexposedjava.com, you may have noticed already that the definition for the `ControllerServlet` in our `web.xml` file has the following interesting information:

```
<servlet>
  <servlet-name>ControllerServlet</servlet-name>
  <servlet-class>book.servlet.original.ControllerServlet</servlet-class>
  <init-param>
    <param-name>DB_URL</param-name>
    <param-value>jdbc:mysql://localhost/mysql</param-value>
  </init-param>
  <init-param>
    <param-name>DB_USER_NAME</param-name>
    <param-value>lester</param-value>
  </init-param>
  <init-param>
    <param-name>DB_PASSWORD</param-name>
    <param-value>password</param-value>
  </init-param>
 . . .
</servlet>
```

The database login information that the application uses to establish its JDBC connection with the MySQL database is stored in the `web.xml` file. Typically, this is not a problem, because the Tomcat server will refuse any requests for data that resides in an application's WEB-INF subcontext. However, if an attacker is able to breach the server security at the system level, the web.xml file for our application would be freely available to them. Once they have access to that file, they could easily read our application's database credentials and use those to establish a connection to the database server.

Countermeasure: Encrypt Credential Information Whenever Possible

Fortunately, initialization parameters are just strings. A simple countermeasure for this form of attack would be to encipher the credentials, using the techniques we learned in Chapter 4, and decipher them in the init method of the appropriate servlet. Even though this countermeasure is so simple, it is rarely implemented, and server configuration files in a J2EE environment continue to be a bonanza of information for nefarious attackers.

Another option to counter this attack would be to use a JDBC DataSource to connect to the database, as discussed in Chapter 7. This is also a good option and is much more secure than storing the information in cleartext in the web.xml file.

Exploiting Coarse-Grained Authorization

Popularity:	5
Simplicity:	10
Impact:	4
Risk rating:	**6**

As our application stands right now, we have the option to grant or deny a particular role the ability to set the balance for an account. What if we want to enforce a business rule that says that normal employees can set a balance as long as it does not exceed $5,000, and administrators have unlimited balance-setting potential? Given our current scheme, we can't do this without creating an entirely new action for our servlet, called actions/setbalanceunder5k or something to that effect.

Because this requires extra time, some application developers have been known to not enforce the rule—and instead merely give employees the same access to the set balance action that administrators have. Obviously, this is not a good solution and needlessly puts our application at risk of attack by internal authorized users who for some reason (deliberate or, more commonly, accidental) attempt to overstep their authorized bounds.

Countermeasure: Use Programmatic Authorization

The web container gives us an easy way to determine whether or not the user invoking our page belongs to a particular role: by using the isUserInRole method in the HttpServletRequest class. By invoking this method, our servlet or JSP can inquire, at any time, as to which role the calling principal belongs. We will use this method to determine whether or not a caller is authorized to perform the set balance operation appropriately.

To do this, we just have to add an `if` statement to our code to test the role and send a 403 (not authorized) response back to the client if the operation is not allowed. Here is what the code looks like in the `processSetBalance` method of the `ControllerServlet` class to accomplish this task:

```
if (newBalance.compareTo(new BigDecimal(5000)) == 1) {
  // The request to change the balance is greater than $5000
  if (!request.isUserInRole("admin")) {

    // The user is not authorized to perform this operation.
    response.sendError(HttpServletResponse.SC_UNAUTHORIZED,
                       "User not authorized to set balance of $"
                       + newBalance);
  }
}
```

Next, we will modify our `web.xml` file to allow users in the role "employee" to post data to the `actions/setbalance` URL. Previously, we turned off this access as part of our declarative security scheme.

```
<security-constraint>
  <web-resource-collection>
    <web-resource-name>SetBalance</web-resource-name>
    <description>Set Balance Functionality</description>
    <url-pattern>/actions/setbalance</url-pattern>
  </web-resource-collection>
  <auth-constraint>
    <role-name>admin</role-name>
    <role-name>employee</role-name>
  </auth-constraint>
</security-constraint>
```

Now, any employee can freely set balances of under $5,000, but when a non-administrator attempts to set a balance above $5,000, they receive a 403 (unauthorized) error.

Dealing with Overlapping Application Roles

There's just one problem with this approach: Our roles are enforced and coded at the servlet level, but they are assigned at the container (or possibly the enterprise) level. Because we're using Tomcat's memory realm, we have to associate roles and users there, for the whole container. This becomes an issue if we want to start using prepackaged web components like taglibs or third-party web components.

Imagine this situation: We give our application to another company, XYZ Corp. The container administrators at XYZ Corp. have *already* defined the roles `admin` and `employee` in their container. And, unfortunately, their definitions do not agree with ours. If the administrator at XYZ Corp. were to install our web-application right out of the box, all users who previously had the admin role would automatically have administrative access to our application. The container administrator (acting in the role of deployer) at XYZ Corp. would then have to make the tough decision of one of the following approaches to mitigate the problem:

1. Allowing the previous admin users administrative access to our application too, and granting new users who need administrative access to our application administrative access to everything in the container.
2. Revoking admin access from all existing users who have it and only granting it to administrative users of our application.
3. Rewriting or reconfiguring one or more applications so that the global role names can be changed, perhaps to RetirementAppAdmin and XXXXApplicationAdmin, and so forth.

These are not attractive options. Again, J2EE comes to the rescue with a relevant solution to this problem: a technique called *role-mapping*. Role mapping allows us as the application deployer or assembler to map roles that exist in the container to roles that exist in our application.

Let's imagine that we are the administrator at XYZ Corp. confronted with the situation just outlined. What we would like is the ability to create a role in our container called RetirementAppAdmin and then have the container answer true for users possessing this role when the retirement application makes the call isUserInRole("admin"). This would require no code changes in the application (good), and allows several applications with programmatic references to admin to exist simultaneously without overlap; for each application, different people could be in the admin role.

Implementing Role Mapping

This is an extremely simple technique to implement. We need to make two changes. First, we will modify the web.xml file for our application to include the security-role-ref tag in the appropriate servlets. The only place where we are doing the programmatic checking is in the ControllerServlet, so we will perform the mapping there only:

```
<servlet>
    <servlet-name>ControllerServlet</servlet-name>
    <servlet-class>book.servlet.original.ControllerServlet</servlet-class>
  . . .
    <security-role-ref>
      <role-name>admin</role-name>
      <role-link>RetirementAppAdmin</role-link>
    </security-role-ref>
. . .
  </servlet>
```

This will map the admin role in our servlet to the RetirementAppAdmin role in the prevailing authentication realm for the container (Tomcat). Also, we need to map every appearance of the admin role in our deployment descriptor itself to the RetirementAppAdmin role. The mapping that we just defined only takes place for the servlet in question. It is assumed that an application assembler or deployer has access to the deployment descriptor, but not the code, so changing the web.xml file is well within their J2EE job description. Here's an example change (in bold):

```
<security-constraint>
    <web-resource-collection>
      <web-resource-name>SetBalance</web-resource-name>
      <description>Set Balance Functionality</description>
      <url-pattern>/actions/setbalance</url-pattern>
    </web-resource-collection>
    <auth-constraint>
            <role-name>RetirementAppAdmin</role-name>
      <role-name>employee</role-name>
    </auth-constraint>
    <user-data-constraint>
      <transport-guarantee>CONFIDENTIAL</transport-guarantee>
    </user-data-constraint>
  </security-constraint>
```

We'll now make a slight change to our tomcat-users.xml file to configure the user represented by our certificate to belong to the RetirementAppAdmin role:

```
<tomcat-users>
<user
name="EMAILADDRESS=lester@javajockey.com, CN=Thawte Freemail Member"
password="" roles="RetirementAppAdmin"
/>
</tomcat-users>
```

Role-mapping is an incredibly important concept in J2EE application security and will also be covered in Chapter 12, which focuses on developing secure Enterprise JavaBeans.

SUMMARY

In the course of Chapter 9 and this chapter, you've seen how you can apply the following techniques to a sample web application to improve its security stature:

- Hide application structure and enable more granular declarative authorization by passing select servlet parameters in the URL instead of in the HTTP header
- Configure certain servlets to deny HTTP GET requests
- Implement a solid web application exception-handling scheme with nonrevealing error handling
- Override container defaults for directory listing and servlet invocation
- Implement a form-based authentication scheme
- Employ techniques for resisting attempts to "steal" user sessions
- Implement and require HTTPS via SSL to be used for all browser to container connections with and without SSL client authentication
- Implement a client certificate–based authentication scheme
- Use servlet filters to implement a client cache control strategy
- Map container roles to application-specific roles

To gain a better appreciation of what the entire sample web application looks like, and how it behaves while using each of these techniques, download the sample code and installation scripts from our website: www.hackingexposedjava.com.

Securing web applications is an incredibly difficult task. The velocity of development that typically accompanies any web-enabled technology means that it is very difficult to insert security "after the fact" as we have done in Lester's application. In most web development environments that the authors have seen, if something doesn't get done the first time, it doesn't get done at all—there just isn't enough time. Hopefully, in the previous two chapters, you've learned some simple, easy-to-use techniques that can help you implement a relatively secure web application from the beginning…the first time through!

In the next chapter, you will see how to apply many of these same techniques to the middle tier—more specifically, to web services–based applications.

CHAPTER 11

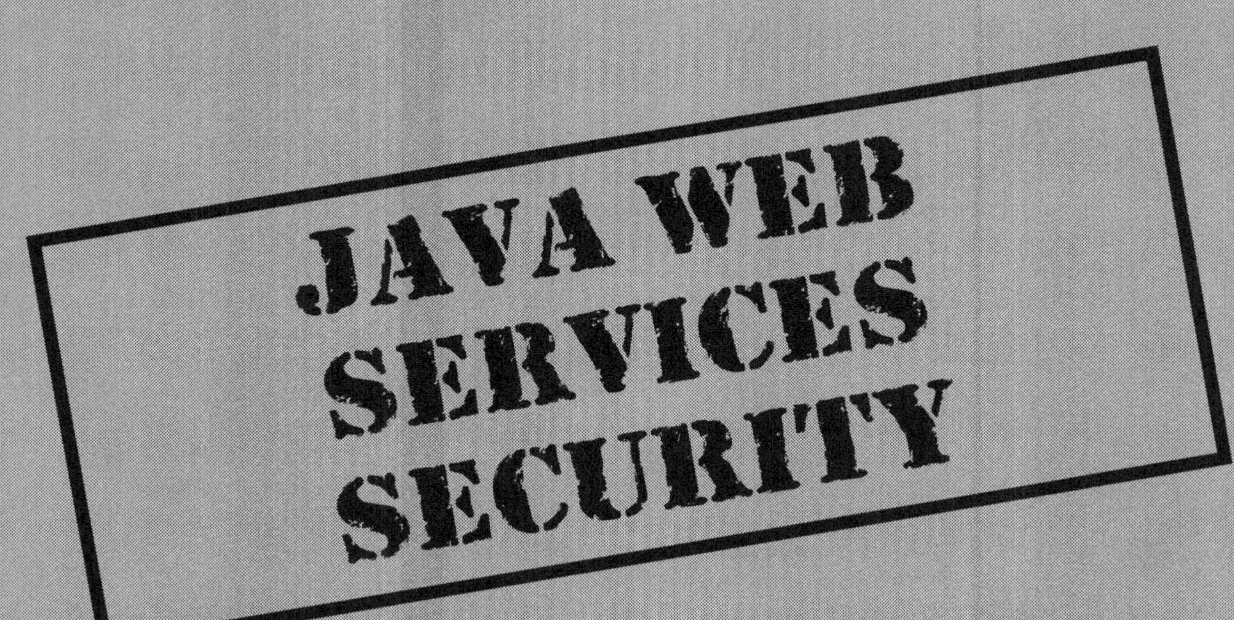
JAVA WEB
SERVICES
SECURITY

Recently, there has been much industry uproar regarding the dawning of the age of web services. As the current leading contender for the "Silver Bullet of the Moment" award, web services, regardless of their promise, will have a hard time living up to the hype about them. This hype, as usual, has not been generated by those who developed the technology, but instead by marketing and sales personnel worldwide. However, regardless of how overrated or underrated web services may currently be in the eyes of the technical media, the concept is here to stay. Web services will most likely be the future of inter-enterprise electronic commerce and cooperation.

The foundation of web services is XML. All notable web services technologies use XML as a mechanism to exchange data. Because XML messages are self-descriptive and can be easily transported using any protocol that can handle a string of text, they are ideal to use as the basis for all other relevant technologies, so they are ideal for use in web services. In this chapter, we will cover the most prevalent web services technologies: Simple Object Access Protocol (SOAP), Web Services Description Language (WSDL), and Universal Description Discovery and Integration (UDDI).

WEB SERVICES IN JAVA

At a high level, the term *web services* refers to the ability to publish, discover, or invoke a set of services in a platform-independent manner, using XML and standard, web-based protocols (like HTTP) for transport. This independence is the one missing factor in inter-enterprise computing today. Businesses find it hard to electronically interoperate in a controlled, secure manner. Much of this difficulty is caused by differences in platforms and transports, which necessitate tedious conversion of data and functionality in order for two businesses with different architectures to interoperate.

For example, suppose that Lester has a friend who runs a service that provides online stock quotes. Lester wants to provide these stock quotes to his clients from within the context of his own application. Without web services, he has few options for getting the stock quote programmatically from a third-party and displaying it to his end user.

In the early days of the Internet, it was thought that CORBA would be the enabling technology for secure, dynamic invocation of services and exchange of information between business entities. With CORBA, Lester would make a remote call to an ORB at the quote provider to request the service and receive the response. However, for many reasons, CORBA never reached the critical mass of acceptance that would make it the *de-facto* standard for Internet business messaging.

Much of CORBA's unpopularity stems from its thoroughness, its perceived lack of flexibility (although this isn't the case, it is perceived by many to be true), and its inability to handle asynchronous messaging in a straightforward manner. CORBA is a truly massive standard. There are few developers who understand it well enough to use it effectively. For a "web of commerce" to become a reality, it must be possible for a relatively small enterprise to make services available to others with minimum cost. Part of cost reduction is complexity reduction, so something less complex than CORBA is necessary.

CORBA remains popular for intra-enterprise services. CORBA is the basis for RMI-IIOP, which is a required transport for EJB invocation, and unbeknown to many of its users, CORBA has facilities for dynamic discovery and invocation of remote methods. However, it is less popular for use between different computing entities.

Another possible solution to Lester's quandary would be to invoke a custom servlet published by the quote provider, passing it the necessary data as part of a HTTP POST request. This would be a more lightweight solution, and in fact was the way much business-to-business electronic commerce was conducted pre-web services. Its disadvantage is that it is completely proprietary. If Lester wanted to programmatically use the services of many external parties, he would need to learn many different proprietary communication protocols, or ways to format the HTTP POST data he was sending. Similarly, he would need to write custom code to contact each service provider. Again, this is not an ideal solution.

What if there was a standard way of transporting data or invoking a service on a remote system? What if this standard was relatively lightweight (sacrificing robustness and expressiveness to reduce complexity), platform-neutral, and could be used over just about any transport, including the most prolific of all transports, HTTP? This would be ideal, and it would be a first step toward a world of "hands-off" electronic commerce. This is what web services seek to achieve.

Web Services Technologies

There is nothing mystical about web services. They are merely another mechanism for building distributed systems (albeit somewhat more flexible than previous mechanisms). Typically, for any general-purpose distributed system to work, it must contain at least three components: a naming service or registry, a mechanism to describe the interfaces for the services provided, and a methodology for actually transporting the request, along with the interface description to the service provider. Web services are no exception. Here is a list of the three foundational technologies in the web services world:

- **UDDI** This is the naming service, where service providers can advertise their services to prospective clients. UDDI technologies are used as a clearinghouse for interface information, along with other relevant business information regarding providers of web services. A service provider publishes its service in a UDDI registry. A client then looks up the service provider in the registry, enumerates the services, chooses the one it wants, and asks the registry for the location of the interface description (WSDL) that describes the service in question.
- **WSDL** This is the interface description. WSDL's XML-based grammar is the mechanism for the service description. It describes the capabilities of a particular web service. If the service supports a synchronous request-response model, WSDL contains the description of the arguments or parameters for each request, instructions for how to marshal the arguments for transport, and the structure and marshalling information for any response.

- **SOAP** This technology is used for the actual invocation of web services. It provides a platform-neutral, XML-based mechanism to request services or send messages from one application to another. SOAP supports either synchronous or asynchronous messaging.

NOTE An interesting feature of SOAP is that it supports workflow-based messaging, which is discussed in the "Web Services Workflow Security" section later in this chapter.

To lend a little more perspective to the function of the three cornerstone web services technologies, here is a quick comparison of how they relate to CORBA and Java RMI:

	CORBA	Java RMI	Web Services
Naming service	COSNaming	rmiregistry	UDDI
Interface description	IDL	Remote interface that extends `java.rmi.Remote`	WSDL
Wire Protocol	IIOP	JRMP or RMI-IIOP	SOAP

This is not meant to be an exact comparison, but if you are already familiar with CORBA or Java RMI, the analogies provided above may be of some use to you.

The Web Services Developer Pack

In CORBA or Java RMI, very rarely do programmers write native IIOP or JRMP code. More commonly, they use helper classes and utilities that generate the proper stubs and skeletons for them. Those helper classes, stubs, and skeletons then use the proper communication protocols in a way that is transparent to the application programmer. Again, web services are no exception.

In June of 2002, Sun released the first version of the Web Services Developer Pack (WSDP). This release contains several "helper" technologies, which are intended to make the development of web services simpler and more developer friendly:

- **JAXM** This is a Java interface that can be used to generate SOAP messages (or other kinds of messages). Instead of needing to manually compose a SOAP XML request for some remote service, a developer can use JAXM to automate part of the message creation.
- **JAX-RPC** This technology sits on top of JAXM and essentially gives an application developer an RMI-like interface to web services. It is geared directly toward a synchronous remote procedure call (RPC)-based model, and as such doesn't support asynchronous messaging. However, it makes WSDL parsing and SOAP request generation a snap. It will likely be one of the more commonly used technologies for building synchronous web services clients in Java.

- **JAXR** This technology allows convenient Java access to UDDI-based registries. It is much like JNDI, except geared toward web services registries.
- **A Host for Web Services Endpoints** A reference implementation of a web services container implemented using servlets running on Jakarta Tomcat.

We will use the WSDP as our mechanism for exploring web services security in this chapter. Note that other vendors have proprietary Java implementations of web services containers, as well as proprietary Java APIs for web services access. The majority of the information that we present in this chapter can be applied to web services in Java, regardless of the container. However, it is generally thought that the Sun community-based standards for Java access to web services will prevail, so those are the ones we will specifically examine. Also note that even though the Java mechanisms for accessing web services functionality may differ, the fundamental request protocol (SOAP) remains the same.

As a model, we will use JAX-RPC and a synchronous, request-response-based web services architecture. Our focus will be on how to secure your web services-based application. As usual, the complete code for this chapter, along with installation, deployment, and configuration instructions, can be downloaded from www.hackingexposedjava.com.

For more information about how to program for or deploy applications to the WSDP, consult the Sun Web Services Tutorial, which can be found at http://java.sun.com/webservices.

THE WEB SERVICES-ENABLED APPLICATION IMPLEMENTATION

Lester has been reading many industry publications, and he is convinced that web services will allow him to expand his customer base by allowing remote clients, running on disparate architectures, to access his retirement application. Because the business model for his application is mostly synchronous (the `get401KBalance` and `set401KBalance` methods), he decided that these would be good features to make available via SOAP/HTTP. Because JAX-RPC is a developer-friendly way to implement an RPC-like interface over SOAP, Lester implemented the original version of his code using that standard.

The architecture of the web services-enabled retirement application is similar to the RMI-based architecture described in Chapter 8. It includes a Java client, connecting to a remote business tier using RPC-like functionality. However, there are significant differences, as you can see in the application overview shown in Figure 11-1.

The most notable difference in our application is that, instead of connecting to an RMI server application using JRMP or RMI-IIOP, this client will use HTTP to POST a SOAP request to a special servlet (`com.sun.xml.rpc.server.http.JAXRPCServlet`, distributed as part of the WSDP). The servlet will then parse the SOAP request, unmarshal the arguments, and call the implementation of the remote interface (`RetirementAccountInfoImpl`).

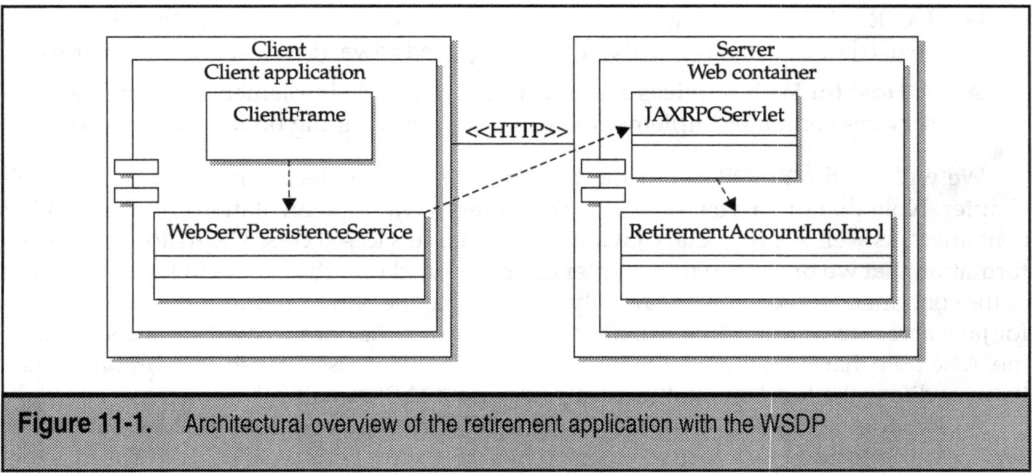

Figure 11-1. Architectural overview of the retirement application with the WSDP

This implementation of the remote interface is very similar to an implementation class that extends `UnicastRemoteObject` or `PortableRemoteObject` for an RMI application. Once the implementation object returns the result, the servlet marshals the return value and returns it via SOAP encoding in the HTTP response to the client. Essentially, the `JAXRPCServlet` is playing the role of a RMI skeleton.

The Retirement Web Services Suite: Server Side

On the server side, to facilitate the JAX-RPC presentation of services, Lester needed to write an implementation class that would run within the web services container and actually perform the `get401KBalance` and `set401KBalance` methods. To do this, he developed the `RetirementAccountInfoImpl` class. This class is similar to a typical RMI implementation class. The class merely implements the necessary service methods using the `MySQLPersistenceService` to perform the I/O with the database.

Then Lester generated the necessary encoder, decoder, stub, and skeleton code to enable the SOAP transport by using the `xrpcc` utility, which is distributed with the WSDP. This utility can generate all necessary support files and WSDL from a Java `Remote` interface, or it can generate the support files from an arbitrary WSDL document. To make an RMI analogy, `xrpcc` is similar to the `rmic` program distributed with the JDK. The client and the server applications will use these support files to communicate via SOAP. This is the strength of JAX-RPC: It allows both the client and server to be developed without an in-depth knowledge of SOAP.

The Configuration File

To use `xrpcc`, Lester developed a `config.xml` file, which contained all of the necessary configuration information for his web service:

```
<?xml version="1.0" encoding="UTF-8"?>
<configuration xmlns="http://java.sun.com/xml/ns/jax-rpc/ri/config">
  <service name="RetirementServerOriginal"
      targetNamespace="http://javajockey.com/wsdl"
      typeNamespace="http://javajockey.com/types"
      packageName="book.webserv.original">
      <interface
        name="book.webserv.original.shared.RetirementAccountInfo"
        servantName=
          "book.webserv.original.server.RetirementAccountInfoImpl"
      />
   </service>
</configuration>
```

In the config.xml file, the service name, public interface name, and the server class name need to be specified. xrpcc uses this information to generate the appropriate client-side and server-side code.

Running xrpcc

To run xrpcc, use the following command line:

```
C:\sec\book>xrpcc -classpath classes -both
                  -s src -d classes -keep
                  src/book/webserv/config.xml
```

This generates the class RetirementServerOriginal_Impl, which the client will use to generate the proper stub to communicate with the web service.

The web.xml File

Once all of the files were generated, Lester built a web.xml file to configure the JAXRPCServlet to service incoming SOAP requests and redirect them to his implementation class. The web.xml file, with relevant entries shown in bold, looks like this:

```
<?xml version="1.0" encoding="UTF-8"?>

 <!DOCTYPE web-app PUBLIC
     "-//Sun Microsystems, Inc.//DTD Web Application 2.3//EN"
     "http://java.sun.com/j2ee/dtds/web-app_2_3.dtd">

<web-app>
   <display-name>RetirementWSApplication</display-name>
   <description>Retirement App (Web Services)</description>
   <servlet>
      <servlet-name>JAXRPCEndpoint</servlet-name>
```

```
        <display-name>JAXRPCEndpoint</display-name>
        <description>
           Endpoint for Retirement Application
        </description>
        <servlet-class>
          com.sun.xml.rpc.server.http.JAXRPCServlet
        </servlet-class>
        <init-param>
           <param-name>configuration.file</param-name>
           <param-value>
            /WEB-INF/RetirementServerOriginal_Config.properties
          </param-value>
        </init-param>
    </servlet>
    <servlet-mapping>
        <servlet-name>JAXRPCEndpoint</servlet-name>
        <url-pattern>/jaxrpc/*</url-pattern>
    </servlet-mapping>
    <session-config>
        <session-timeout>60</session-timeout>
    </session-config>
</web-app>
```

Notice that one servlet, `JAXRPCServlet`, will be a part of this web application and will be mapped to the `/jaxrpc/*` URL pattern. This servlet is distributed with the WSDP and is the servlet that receives incoming SOAP requests and forwards them to the implementation class specified in the `config.xml` file.

How does this servlet know to do this? It uses the data contained in the `RetirementServerOriginal_Config.properties` file.

The Properties File

A properties file is also generated by the `xrpcc` utility and passed as an `init` parameter to the servlet. The contents of the `.properties` file look like this:

```
# This file is generated by xrpcc.

port0.tie=book.webserv.original.shared.RetirementAccountInfo_Tie
port0.servant=book.webserv.original.server.RetirementAccountInfoImpl
port0.name=RetirementAccountInfo
port0.wsdl.targetNamespace=http://javajockey.com/wsdl
port0.wsdl.serviceName=RetirementServerOriginal
port0.wsdl.portName=RetirementAccountInfoPort
portcount=1
wsdl.location=/WEB-INF/RetirementServerOriginal.wsdl
```

Lester has added the last line, shown in bold, to make the WSDL for his application publicly available via the web service. That way, any clients who want to connect can contact the server and look up the proper interfaces without needing to contact Lester directly. Also notice that the properties file contains the name of the server class along with the `xrpcc`-generated tie object, which will be used to map client requests to the server implementation object.

The Retirement Web Services Suite: Client Side

On the client side, to enable the web services connection, Lester has developed a custom persistence manager that uses web services, called `WebServPersistenceService` in the `book.webserv.original` package. The `ClientFrame` application (from Chapters 4, 5, and 7) uses this persistence service in place of the `LocalPersistenceService` or the `MySQLPersistenceService`. The relevant code that builds and uses the client-side stub to communicate with the web service is depicted in bold. Remember that when the client calls the stub, the JAX-RPC runtime will generate a well-formed SOAP message requesting the service and transmit it to the server over an HTTP connection.

```
package book.webserv.original.client;
...
import javax.xml.rpc.Stub;

import java.math.BigDecimal;
import java.rmi.RemoteException;

/**
 * This is a basic implementation of a web
 * services-enabled persistence service that
 * uses the JAX-RPC API to communicate with the server.
 * Additionally, it uses statically generated stub classes.
 */
public class WebServPersistenceService
  implements RetirementAccountInfo {
. . .
  private Stub myStub;

  public WebServPersistenceService(String servURL) {
    serviceURL = servURL;

    // Build an instance of our stub and set the
    // endpoint to the server URL.
    Stub tmpStub = (Stub)
      (new
      RetirementServerOriginal_Impl().getRetirementAccountInfoPort()
      );
```

```
    tmpStub._setProperty(
             javax.xml.rpc.Stub.ENDPOINT_ADDRESS_PROPERTY,
             serviceURL);

    // Cast the stub to something that implements
    // our remote business interface.
    myStub = (RetirementAccountInfo) tmpStub;

  }

  public BigDecimal get401kBalance(String accountNumber)
      throws AccountNotFoundException, PersistenceException {
    BigDecimal retVal = null;
    try {
      // Delegate the call to our stub.
      retVal = myStub.get401kBalance(accountNumber);
    } catch (RemoteException e) {
      // Handle the exception
    }
    return retVal;
  }

  public void set401kBalance(String accountNumber,
                             BigDecimal newBalance)
      throws AccountNotFoundException,
             OperationNotAllowedException,
             PersistenceException {
    try {
      // Delegate the call to our stub.
      myStub.set401kBalance(accountNumber,newBalance);
    } catch (RemoteException e) {
      // Handle the exception
    }
    return;
  }

  public void close() {
    try {
      myStub.close();
    } catch (Exception e) {
      // Handle all exceptions.
    }
  }
}
```

In the `main` method of the `ClientFrame` class, Lester added the following block of code to build the proper instance of the `WebServPersistenceService` and attach it to the client frame. The only argument passed on the command line is the URL to the web service provider, in this case, `http://localhost:8080/book/webserv/original/jaxrpc/RetirementAccountInfo`.

```
if (args.length == 1) {
  model = new WebServPersistenceService(args[0]);
} else {
  System.out.println("Usage: java ClientFrame <web service URL>");
  System.exit(ABNORMAL_COMPLETION);
}
cf = new ClientFrame(model);
```

Figure 11-2 shows how the client-side and server-side of this implementation work together.

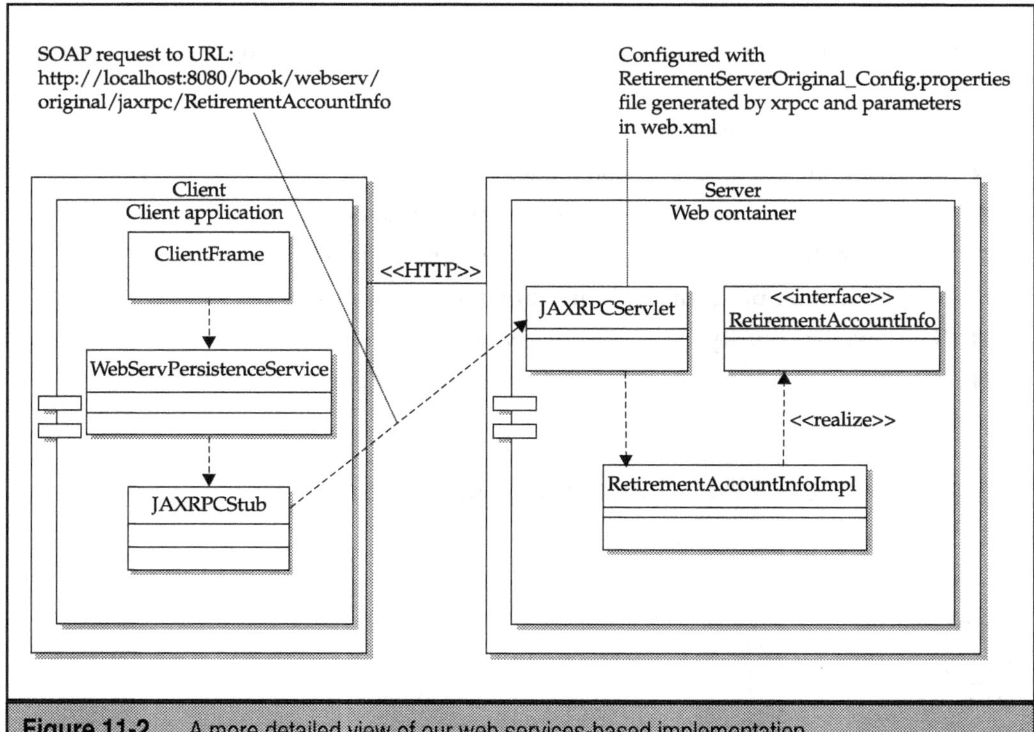

Figure 11-2. A more detailed view of our web services-based implementation

WEB SERVICES APPLICATION VULNERABILITIES

As you may have noticed, compared to a stand-alone architecture, the web services architecture has many more "moving parts." These extra layers give SOAP/HTTP-based applications much more flexibility. They also present more possible access points to the determined attacker. Here are a few of the possible vulnerabilities that we'll want to address when attempting to secure a web services application:

- The transport between client and server is done via HTTP, and requests and responses are encoded using SOAP/XML, which is easily viewable or changeable with a common text editor.
- The WSDL metadata necessary to invoke the service is usually available to the general public, either as an adjunct to the web services container or as part of a reference from a UDDI directory entry.
- Propagation of security identity or credentials between the client and service is not standard and can be quite problematic, especially in a workflow-based architecture. There are emerging standards for credential propagation, message integrity, and confidentiality, but these are still disparate and somewhat vendor-specific.

Throughout the course of this chapter, we will cover the following aspects of web services security:

- Authentication with web services
- Securing the client/server connection
- Connecting web services via secure tunneling over SSL
- Implementing declarative authorization for web services
- Implementing programmatic authorization for web services
- Options for security in a workflow-based environment
- Confidentiality and integrity of payload information
- Propagation of credential information

Manual Invocation of Web Services with Modified or Contrived SOAP Requests

Popularity:	5
Simplicity:	5
Impact:	8
Risk rating:	**6**

Let's take a look at the traffic that passes between the Java client and the web services server during a typical operation. To eavesdrop on the traffic, we could use a packet sniffer, but instead, we'll use the tunneling redirection utility that we built in Chapter 7. This package allows us to place some code between the client and the server to monitor, and log the data being passed back and forth so that we can see exactly what the JAX-RPC classes are sending over the wire.

First, we run the `ClientFrame` code and, instead of directing the JAX-RPC API to connect to `localhost` port 8080 (the port to which the WSDP Tomcat instance is listening), we change the URL we pass on the command line to connect to our redirector on port 5000. This will allow us to log all HTTP traffic between the client and the server.

```
C:/sec/book> java book.webserv.original.client.ClientFrame
             "http://localhost:5000/book/webserv/
                     original/jaxrpc/RetirementAccountInfo"
```

The first request we see from our client to the server is an HTTP POST request to the JAX-RPC servlet that looks like this:

```
POST /book/webserv/original/jaxrpc/RetirementAccountInfo HTTP/1.1
Content-Type: text/xml; charset="utf-8"
Content-Length: 532
SOAPAction: ""
User-Agent: Java1.4.0
Host: localhost:5000
Accept: text/html, image/gif, image/jpeg, *; q=.2, */*; q=.2
Connection: keep-alive

<?xml version="1.0" encoding="UTF-8"?>
<env:Envelope
     xmlns:env="http://schemas.xmlsoap.org/soap/envelope/"
     xmlns:xsd="http://www.w3.org/2001/XMLSchema"
     xmlns:xsi="http://www.w3.org/2001/XMLSchema-instance"
     xmlns:enc="http://schemas.xmlsoap.org/soap/encoding/"
     xmlns:ns0="http://javajockey.com/types"
     env:encodingStyle="http://schemas.xmlsoap.org/soap/encoding/">
     <env:Body>
        <ans1:get401kBalance
           xmlns:ans1="http://javajockey.com/wsdl">
             <String_1 xsi:type="xsd:string">
                 12345
             </String_1>
        </ans1:get401kBalance>
     </env:Body>
</env:Envelope>
```

By looking at the body of the SOAP envelope, more specifically the bolded text, we can see that this request is a `get401kBalance` request, and that the one argument is a string, with the value 12345. Having used this application, we know that this is the account number. The reply looks similar:

```
HTTP/1.1 200 OK
Content-Type: text/xml; charset="utf-8"
SOAPAction: ""
Transfer-Encoding: chunked
Date: Thu, 04 Jul 2002 16:59:12 GMT
Server: Apache Coyote HTTP/1.1 Connector [1.0]

223
<?xml version="1.0" encoding="UTF-8"?>
<env:Envelope
   xmlns:env="http://schemas.xmlsoap.org/soap/envelope/"
   xmlns:xsd="http://www.w3.org/2001/XMLSchema"
   xmlns:xsi="http://www.w3.org/2001/XMLSchema-instance"
   xmlns:enc="http://schemas.xmlsoap.org/soap/encoding/"
   xmlns:ns0="http://javajockey.com/types"
   env:encodingStyle="http://schemas.xmlsoap.org/soap/encoding/">
   <env:Body>
     <ans1:get401kBalanceResponse
        xmlns:ans1="http://javajockey.com/wsdl">
       <result xsi:type="xsd:decimal">
         6001.00
       </result>
     </ans1:get401kBalanceResponse>
   </env:Body>
</env:Envelope>
```

The `setBalance` invocation looks similar. In fact, if we merely open a socket to the web service server and send the same SOAP request that we see above, but change the account numbers, we can interrogate the web service to get the balances of any account in the system. Similarly, we can set an arbitrary account's balance by using the same technique.

We used a redirection server to gain this information, but it should be clear that an arbitrary attacker could use a packet sniffer or any other type of network-monitoring device to get the same results.

Countermeasure: Use SSL/TLS for All Non-public Web Service Ports

Web services effectively expose the business tier of our application to the world. If we don't want everybody with a text editor and a beginner's knowledge of network programming to be able to intercept, modify, and exploit messages directed toward our web services, we need to develop a scheme for protecting them. We will start at the foundation by requiring SSL connections for all clients of our web service.

Requiring SSL Connections

In Chapter 10, we described how to configure the Tomcat SSL connector. All we need to do is configure the connector on our web services host and add an entry to the JAX-RPC web application to require a secure transport for all connections. This entry would look something like this:

```
<security-constraint>
    <web-resource-collection>
       <web-resource-name>RPCEndpoint</web-resource-name>
       <url-pattern>/jaxrpc/*</url-pattern>
       <http-method>GET</http-method>
       <http-method>POST</http-method>
    </web-resource-collection>
    <auth-constraint>
      <role-name>*</role-name>
    </auth-constraint>
    <user-data-constraint>
      <transport-guarantee>CONFIDENTIAL</transport-guarantee>
    </user-data-constraint>
  </security-constraint>
```

This will require that SSL be used whenever a client attempts to access our JAX-RPC processing servlet.

Sometimes, we may need to keep a particular web service open for non-SSL traffic as well as SSL traffic. To keep our application secure in an environment such as this, we can remove the transport guarantee from the `web.xml` file, but still use the SSL port (in this case, 8443) to connect to the service. Alternatively, if SSL is not enabled on the server, we can use our tunneling redirection package from Chapter 7 to build an SSL tunnel to the server in question. However, publishing web services on a public server without the benefit of SSL exposes us to the possibility that somebody could monitor or modify the business information being passed between our clients and our services. Also, although SSL/TLS will help us secure the transport layer of our application, there is still much that it doesn't do for us. We will discuss these issues in the following sections.

Invocation of Service by Unauthorized Client

Popularity:	*8*
Simplicity:	*7*
Impact:	*8*
Risk rating:	*8*

Even though the connection between a client and our server is now secured using SSL, it is still possible for an unknown client (unless we are using SSL client authentication) to connect to our web service and invoke various methods. To do this, the attacker must first know what format the SOAP messages should be in. Fortunately, because we have SSL-enabled our connection, an attacker can no longer gain information through passive eavesdropping. However, there is still a major weakness in our scheme. To discover it, we will disable SSL between our client and server to make monitoring the connection somewhat easier, but be aware that this technique will work even if SSL is enabled on the server.

If we invoke the JAX-RPC servlet on the server from a common web browser, we see the following response:

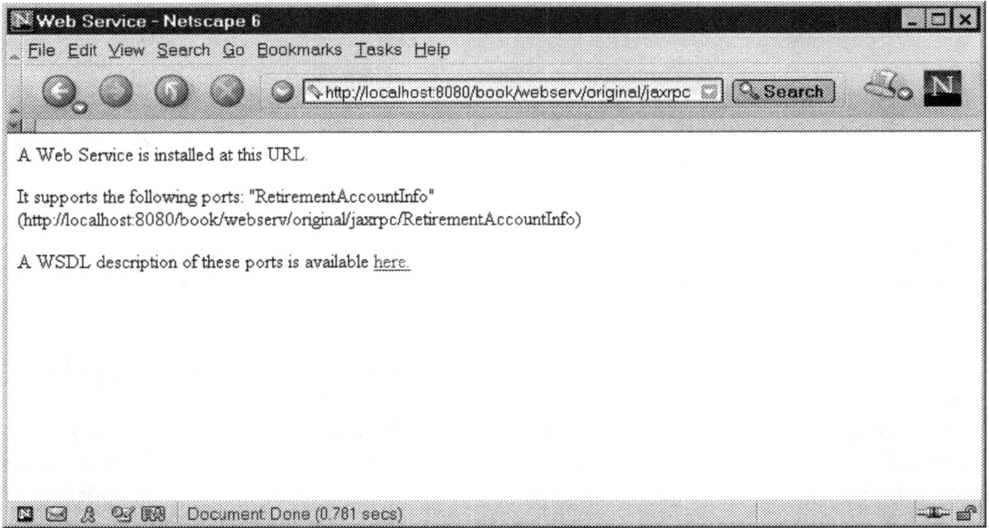

It's good to be user friendly, but this is taking friendliness a little too far! As you can see, the servlet kindly identifies which ports are active *and* gives us a link to the WSDL that defines the necessary format for our SOAP messages. This easy availability of metadata is a key component of SOAP—it gives automated agents the ability to discover how to invoke our service automatically. However, it's less than ideal from a security standpoint.

If we follow the link for the WSDL document, we get the following information (we need to use the View Source option in our browser, since it won't automatically render WSDL, but the data is there nonetheless):

```
<?xml version="1.0" encoding="UTF-8"?>
<definitions name="RetirementServerOriginal"
             targetNamespace="http://javajockey.com/wsdl"
             xmlns:tns="http://javajockey.com/wsdl"
             xmlns="http://schemas.xmlsoap.org/wsdl/"
             xmlns:soap="http://schemas.xmlsoap.org/wsdl/soap/"
```

```
            xmlns:xsd="http://www.w3.org/2001/XMLSchema"
            xmlns:ns2="http://javajockey.com/types">
  <types>
    <schema targetNamespace="http://javajockey.com/types"
        xmlns:xsi="http://www.w3.org/2001/XMLSchema-instance"
        xmlns:tns="http://javajockey.com/types"
        xmlns:soap-enc="http://schemas.xmlsoap.org/soap/encoding/"
        xmlns:wsdl="http://schemas.xmlsoap.org/wsdl/"
        xmlns="http://www.w3.org/2001/XMLSchema">
      <import
         namespace="http://schemas.xmlsoap.org/soap/encoding/"/>
      <complexType name="PersistenceException">
        <sequence>
          <element name="message" type="string"/>
          <element name="localizedMessage"
                   type="string"/>
        </sequence>
      </complexType>
      <complexType name="AccountNotFoundException">
        <sequence>
          <element name="message" type="string"/>
          <element name="localizedMessage"
                   type="string"/>
        </sequence>
      </complexType>
. . .
    <soap:binding
       transport="http://schemas.xmlsoap.org/soap/http"
       style="rpc"/>
  </binding>
  <service name="RetirementServerOriginal">
    <port name="RetirementAccountInfoPort"
          binding="tns:RetirementAccountInfoBinding">
      <soap:address
          location="REPLACE_WITH_ACTUAL_URL"/>
    </port>
   </service>
</definitions>
```

What is even more troubling is that once we have the WSDL for our web service, we can use the `xrpcc` tool to reverse-engineer the stubs necessary to call the service from Java. To a designer of a public web service, this ability is merely good advertising and desirable. To the security-conscious web service developer who wants limited public access, this is extremely dangerous.

To use the xrpcc tool to generate the necessary files, we save the WSDL in a temporary file (let's call it temp.wsdl). Then we must build a config.xml file for the xrpcc tool that tells it where our WSDL is located and which package to put our generated Java code into. This does not need to match the package structure of the code on the server, because package information is lost during SOAP encoding. Here is what a simple config.xml file might look like:

```
<?xml version="1.0" encoding="UTF-8"?>
    <configuration
     xmlns="http://java.sun.com/xml/ns/jax-rpc/ri/config">
        <wsdl location="temp.wsdl"
              packageName="mypackage">
        </wsdl>
    </configuration>
```

This configuration file requests that the xrpcc tool use the WSDL in the file temp.wsdl and place the results in a package called mypackage. We then run the xrpcc tool using the following command line:

```
C:\sec\book\temp\reveng>xrpcc -client -d . -s . -keep config.xml
```

We see that after it runs, a directory called mypackage is created under our current directory. Inside that directory are all of the stub and helper files necessary to invoke our web service from Java. In fact, even the *Java remote interface* for the web service has been faithfully re-created from the WSDL document. We can see it if we look at the RetirementAccountInfo.java file in the mypackage subdirectory:

```
// Helper class generated by xrpcc, do not edit.
// Contents subject to change without notice.

package mypackage;

public interface RetirementAccountInfo extends java.rmi.Remote {
    public void close() throws java.rmi.RemoteException;
    public java.math.BigDecimal
           get401KBalance(java.lang.String string_1)
           throws mypackage.AccountNotFoundException,
                  mypackage.PersistenceException,
                  java.rmi.RemoteException;

   public void set401KBalance(java.lang.String string_1,
                              java.math.BigDecimal bigDecimal_2)
           throws mypackage.PersistenceException,
                  mypackage.AccountNotFoundException,
                  mypackage.OperationNotAllowedException,
                  java.rmi.RemoteException;
}
```

Even though the variable and package names are different, it should be apparent that this interface is functionally equivalent to our actual remote interface.

Now that we have the proper helper classes, we can write a simple client to interrogate our web service and get and set balances. We'll call our unauthorized client `UnauthClient` and place it in a file called `UnauthClient.java`:

```
import mypackage.RetirementServerOriginal_Impl;
import mypackage.RetirementAccountInfo;

import javax.xml.rpc.Stub;
import java.math.BigDecimal;

public class UnauthClient {
  public static void main(String[] args) {
    try {
      RetirementAccountInfo myStub;
         // Build an instance of our stub and set
         // the endpoint to the server URL.
      Stub tmpStub = (Stub)
      (new
      RetirementServerOriginal_Impl().getRetirementAccountInfoPort()
      );
      tmpStub._setProperty(
                 javax.xml.rpc.Stub.ENDPOINT_ADDRESS_PROPERTY,
                 args[0]);

      // Cast the stub to something that implements
      // our remote business interface.
      myStub = (RetirementAccountInfo) tmpStub;
      System.out.println("Balance for acct 12345 is "
                        + myStub.get401KBalance("12345"));
      myStub.set401KBalance("12345",new BigDecimal(30000.00));
      System.out.println("Balance for acct 12345 is "
                        + myStub.get401KBalance("12345"));
    } catch (Exception e) {
      // Handle the exceptions
    }
  }
}
```

When we run our client, we see the following results:

```
C:\sec\book\temp\reveng\java UnauthClient
              "http://localhost:8080/book/webserv/
                      original/jaxrpc/RetirementAccountInfo"
```

```
Balance for acct 12345 is 6000.00
Balance for acct 12345 is 30000
```

As you can see, given nothing but the URL of the JAX-RPC servlet, we were able to access all of its services with a simple Java program. Here is a review of the steps we performed:

1. Use the default behavior of the JAX-RPC servlet to enumerate the active ports and to get the location of the WSDL document that describes the active services.
2. Download the WSDL document.
3. Use the `xrpcc` tool to read the WSDL document and generate Java stub, encoding, and interface files to use.
4. Write a simple Java client that uses the generated helper classes to call the web service.

Obviously, this behavior is not desirable for a typical web service. Ideally, we want to control access to both our metadata and the service itself. Fortunately, there are some techniques that we can use to enable this functionality.

Countermeasure: Use HTTP Authentication for Web Services Clients

The first approach that we can take to address this weakness in our application is to use HTTP authentication to allow only authorized users access to the web service. Because the JAX-RPC SOAP processor is a servlet, we can configure the container so that it requires all of the servlet's clients to be authenticated using HTTP authentication. This could take the form of BASIC, DIGEST, or CLIENT-CERT authentication.

Implementing HTTP Authentication

We can implement HTTP authentication by making the following modifications, shown in bold, to the `web.xml` file:

```
    <web-resource-collection>
     <web-resource-name>RPCEndpoint</web-resource-name>
     <url-pattern>/jaxrpc/*</url-pattern>
     <http-method>GET</http-method>
     <http-method>POST</http-method>
  </web-resource-collection>
  <auth-constraint>
     <role-name>manager</role-name>
  </auth-constraint>
</security-constraint>
<login-config>
  <auth-method>BASIC</auth-method>
</login-config>
```

With this `web.xml` file, the container will require HTTP BASIC authentication from all clients of the JAX-RPC servlet and will allow only those clients who hold the role of `manager` to execute the servlet. Note that we could have also constrained this authorization to a particular SOAP port on the servlet by using a more specific `url-pattern` property than just `/jaxrpc/*`.

We still are presented with a small problem though. When we were using BASIC authentication with our servlets, the client browser took care of collecting the username and password from the user and adding it to the HTTP header on the next request to the designated realm. But now we are invoking the web service programmatically, not through a browser. How can we pass this credential information?

JAX-RPC has a facility for the client code to pass the username and password to the JAX-RPC runtime, which will then transmit it as part of the HTTP request header. To access this functionality, we will modify the constructor in the `WebServPersistenceService` as follows:

```
public WebServPersistenceService(String servURL, String uName,
                                 char[] password)
{
  serviceURL = servURL;
  Stub tmpStub = (Stub)
  (new
   RetirementServerBasicAuth_Impl().getRetirementAccountInfoPort()
  );
  tmpStub._setProperty(
          javax.xml.rpc.Stub.ENDPOINT_ADDRESS_PROPERTY,
          serviceURL);
  tmpStub._setProperty(javax.xml.rpc.Stub.USERNAME_PROPERTY,
                       uName);
  tmpStub._setProperty(javax.xml.rpc.Stub.PASSWORD_PROPERTY,
                       String.valueOf(password));

  myStub = (RetirementAccountInfo) tmpStub;

}
```

When we construct the `WebServPersistenceService` in the `ClientFrame`, we merely pass the username and password from the active `RetirementCredential` object to the constructor listed in the code fragment above. Then, if we look at the HTTP traffic between the client and the server, we see the following welcome field, in bold, added to the request header:

```
POST /book/webserv/basic/jaxrpc/RetirementAccountInfo HTTP/1.1
Content-Type: text/xml; charset="utf-8"
Content-Length: 532
SOAPAction: ""
Authorization: Basic bGVzdGVyOnBhc3N3b3Jk
```

```
User-Agent: Java1.4.0
Host: localhost:5000
Accept: text/html, image/gif, image/jpeg, *; q=.2, */*; q=.2
Connection: keep-alive

<?xml version="1.0" encoding="UTF-8"?>
. . .
```

Now, if we provide an invalid username or password, we will be denied access to the web service by the container. This is much better than allowing any public user to access our web services.

Remember that BASIC authentication encodes only the username and password using base 64 encoding. However, we would be connecting over SSL if we were not using this application for an example, so there is little danger in using the BASIC authentication mechanism.

Countermeasure: Disable Public Distribution of WSDL Documents

Public availability of the WSDL that describes our services may be good from an ease-of-use perspective, but as most security professionals know, things that contribute to ease of use usually also contribute to relaxation of security. As you saw previously, it's possible to reverse-engineer a client for our web services by merely gaining access to the WSDL document describing our services.

For all but totally public applications, it is good practice to guard the WSDL description of the service and distribute it in only a controlled manner. This will help prevent an arbitrary attacker from collecting valuable information about the structure of our application.

Disabling WSDL Distribution

To disable distribution of the WSDL for an application, we just need to remove the following line from the `RetirementServerOriginal_Configuration.properties` file:

```
wsdl.location=/WEB-INF/RetirementServerOriginal.wsdl
```

When we redeploy the application and restart the server, the link to the WSDL document describing our services will be removed.

This same principle applies to publishing references to WSDL in a public UDDI registry. By making information about our services publicly available, we are giving potential attackers quite a bit of information about how to use our application maliciously.

Does this mean that we shouldn't participate in the budding world of web services? Absolutely not! The fact is that most real users of web services right now don't use information from a public UDDI registry. Instead, they contact the administrator of the service in question and obtain the necessary information (WSDL, usage information, documentation, and so on) directly from the administrator. Sure, it will be much harder for arbitrary Internet users to hook up their favorite spreadsheet or word processor to dynamically extract information from our web service, but then again, most applications don't require this type of arbitrary anonymous access.

So, as is the case with most other security decisions, it's up to you to decide what you allow and disallow. If the gain from public access to your WSDL outweighs the potential loss due to a system compromise, then it's good to distribute your WSDL. Otherwise, keep it confidential and distribute it to only those with a need to know.

Access of Particular Application Functionality by Unauthorized Users

Popularity:	5
Simplicity:	5
Impact:	5
Risk rating:	**5**

As we've discussed in previous chapters, attackers could gain access to our application's `set401KBalance` function. With our current security configuration for the web services application, we cannot restrict access to this function to only administrators.

Currently, we have enabled only a Boolean access policy to our service: Users are either authorized to access the web services port or they are not authorized. This is the best that we can do, because we can apply servlet authentication only to a URL pattern. But what if we want to get the user's identity information and use it at runtime to make security decisions? In servlets, we could call the `isUserInRole` or `getUserPrincipal` methods in the servlet context to get information about our caller. However, as things stand right now, we don't have access to any contextual information from our web services container.

Countermeasure: Use JAX-RPC Support for Programmatic Authorization

Fortunately, the developers of the JAX-RPC standard knew that our server-side components would need to retrieve some sort of contextual information from their host container, so they included the `ServiceLifecycle` interface as part of the `javax.xml.rpc.server` package.

The `ServiceLifecycle` interface contains two methods: `init` and `destroy`. If we implement this interface in our server implementation class, the container will call the `init` method whenever it activates our server object, and then it will call the `destroy` method before it releases the server object instance. This is beneficial because the argument to the `init` method is an instance of `javax.xml.rpc.server.ServletEndpointContext`, which, in turn, contains a method called `getServletContext`, which allows us to get a reference to the `ServletContext` for the servlet that is hosting (or calling) our server implementation object. Better yet, the `ServletEndpointContext` class has a method called `getUserPrincipal`, which allows us to extract the principal information for the current client of our service. We'll use this method to enforce our programmatic authorization scheme in our server object.

Enabling Programmatic Authorization

We will make the following modifications to our implementation (`Impl`) class to enable programmatic authorization.

- Implement the `ServiceLifecycle` interface.
- Code the `init` method to retain the `ServletEndpointContext`.
- Check the context in the `set401KBalance` method to make sure that the principal is `lester`.

Principal-based Authorization

Here are the relevant contents of our new server implementation class:

```
public class RetirementAccountInfoImpl
    implements RetirementAccountInfo, ServiceLifecycle {
```

Our class must implement the `ServiceLifecycle` interface to provide hooks for the container to invoke our life cycle methods.

```
. . .

  private ServletEndpointContext epContext;
```

We will keep a reference to our endpoint context. This will allow us to get the user `Principal` information as necessary. In the following `set401KBalance` method, we will check the prevailing `Principal` object and compare it with our "list" of authorized users. Right now, Lester is the only authorized user of this method.

```
  public void set401kBalance(String accountNumber, BigDecimal newBalance)
      throws AccountNotFoundException, OperationNotAllowedException,
      PersistenceException {
    if (epContext.getUserPrincipal().getName().equals("lester")) {
      Connection c = getConnection();
      MySQLPersistenceService model =
         new MySQLPersistenceService(c,secretKey);
      model.set401kBalance(accountNumber,newBalance);
      model.close();
    } else {
      throw new OperationNotAllowedException(
               "Invalid user attempting to set balance");
    }
  }

...
```

In the init life cycle method, we grab the ServletEndpointContext and store it in our private member variable:

```
public void init(Object o) throws ServiceException {
  epContext = (ServletEndpointContext) o;

  System.out.println("Context name: "
        + epContext.getServletContext().getServletContextName());
}
```

We don't need to do anything for now in the destroy method, but this is where we would release any resources we specifically allocated in the init method above.

```
    public void destroy() {
      System.out.println("BasicAuth destroy.");
    }
}
```

With these changes in place, Lester is able to get and set balances, but when user brian attempts to set a balance, he is confronted with an OperationNotAllowedException. So, by using this mechanism, we have implemented a limited ability to implement authorization within our code.

The JAX-RPC server programming model does not include equivalents for the isCallerInRole or isUserInRole methods that other J2EE components can use. For this reason, we must use a much more rigid authorization model than we use with typical J2EE components. However, at least the principal identity is propagated to us, and if we needed to, we could write our own application-level "role-mapper," which would map user Principal objects to their appropriate roles.

Role-based Programmatic Authorization

The JAX-RPC specification requires only the getUserPrincipal method in the ServletEndpointContext method, but there is no reason why the container could not allow the server implementation class to see the actual HttpServletRequest that was received by the JAX-RPC servlet. In fact, the WSDP Reference Implementation from Sun gives us that capability. However, by using this capability, we will be writing nonstandard code that will depend on a servlet (instead of an EJB or other component) being used to receive messages for our service. Furthermore, we will have to assume that the servlet will be the JAX-RPC servlet from the Sun WSDP reference implementation. Most other vendors that provide servlet-based web service endpoints provide this same functionality, but they all do it in a somewhat different manner.

Let's say we've decided to sacrifice container independence to gain flexibility in security administration through the use of roles. We'll live on the edge for a moment and write container-specific code to use role-based programmatic authorization instead of the principal-based approach that we used previously. To do this, we modify the `set401KBalance` method as follows:

```
public void set401kBalance(String accountNumber, BigDecimal newBalance)
    throws AccountNotFoundException, OperationNotAllowedException,
    PersistenceException {
  // Cast our endpoint context to a vendor-specific one.
  com.sun.xml.rpc.server.http.ServletEndpointContextImpl ctx =
    (com.sun.xml.rpc.server.http.ServletEndpointContextImpl)
      epContext;

  HttpServletRequest req = ctx.getHttpServletRequest();
  if (req.isUserInRole("RetirementAdmin")) {
    Connection c = getConnection();
    MySQLPersistenceService model =
      new MySQLPersistenceService(c,secretKey);
    model.set401kBalance(accountNumber,newBalance);
    model.close();
  } else {
    throw new OperationNotAllowedException(
              "Invalid user attempting to set balance");
  }
}
```

Then we give Lester the role `RetirementAdmin` in the `tomcat-users.xml` file:

```
<user username="lester" password="password"
      roles="admin,manager,provider,RetirementAdmin"/>
```

NOTE We could also do role-mapping in the `web.xml` file for the JAX-RPC servlet to map the `admin` role to a role specific to our particular web service. That process would be identical to what we already have covered in previous chapters, so we won't cover it here.

Now, when we run the client, we find that Lester can still set balances and Brian still gets an `OperationNotAllowedException`. However, we can feel much better as developers because we have a scalable way to administer our security policies for this web service. We can't pat ourselves on the back too much though, because we relied on nonstandard functionality to accomplish this task.

So far, we have dealt with only servlet-based endpoints for web service requests. According to the draft specification for the EJB 2.1 standard, EJBs will be able to provide web service endpoints in the future (as a matter of fact, some vendors are doing this already in a proprietary manner). Thus, the direct invocation of EJB methods via SOAP will be enabled, and the EJB implementation class will have full access to the typical security-related methods available from its session, entity, or message-driven context object. The

EJB 2.1 draft specification mandates the use of JAX-RPC if web service endpoints are supported, so the techniques we apply here should apply to EJB web service endpoints in the future.

Passing Database Passwords As Context Parameters

In the original version of the sample application, the MySQL database username and password are hardcoded into the server implementation object. We need a better solution.

In the servlets that we developed in previous chapters, we passed the database credential information into the servlet via initialization parameters. However, because the initialization parameters are available only via the `ServletConfig` object, which, in turn, is available to only the servlet class itself, we can't use the same technique to get initialization parameters from our web services container. However, we do have access to the `ServletContext`, and because we do, we *can* access context parameters.

To populate our server implementation object with the relevant database credential information, we will modify the `web.xml` file to contain the proper context parameters, and then get them from the `ServletContext` object.

Be aware that context parameters are available to *every* servlet in the web application, not just the JAX-RPC servlet. This is an important point to keep in mind when considering servlets for addition to the web application.

To pass the database credential information by using context parameters, we'll make the following additions to the `web.xml` file for our service:

```
<web-app>
   <display-name>RetirementWSApplication</display-name>
   <description>Retirement App (Web Services)</description>
   <context-param>
     <param-name>DB_URL</param-name>
     <param-value>jdbc:mysql://localhost/mysql</param-value>
   </context-param>
  <context-param>
    <param-name>DB_USER_NAME</param-name>
    <param-value>lester</param-value>
  </context-param>
  <context-param>
    <param-name>DB_PASSWORD</param-name>
    <param-value>password</param-value>
  </context-param>
   <servlet>
      <servlet-name>JAXRPCEndpoint</servlet-name>
      . . .
   </servlet>
      . . .
</web-app>
```

Similarly, we add the following code to the `init` method of our server object to extract the parameters and store them internally:

```
public void init(Object o) throws ServiceException {
  epContext = (ServletEndpointContext) o;
  System.out.println("Class: " + epContext.getClass().getName());
  System.out.println("Context name: "
        + epContext.getServletContext().getServletContextName());

  // Load the database configuration info from our init parms.
  dbUserName =
   epContext.getServletContext().getInitParameter("DB_USER_NAME");
  dbPassword =
   epContext.getServletContext().getInitParameter("DB_PASSWORD");
  dbURL = epContext.getServletContext().getInitParameter("DB_URL");
}
```

To reinforce an already belabored, but very important, point, realize that we are depicting the credentials—in particular, the database password—in cleartext for instructional purposes only. In a production application, you would encipher the password, base 64 encode it, put it in the `web.xml` file, and then decode and decipher it as you extract it. You would store your key information for the decryption in a separate location. Even if you do something as simple as embed the key as a final variable in your class file, this still provides a much higher degree of security than having password information stored in plaintext in an `.xml` file on the server.

If your server does not enforce these types of security practices (for example, Tomcat forces users to store plaintext passwords for `DataSources` in the `server.xml` file), try to take things into your own hands. A possible solution for the Tomcat example would be to build the `DataSource` without an embedded password, then use `theDataSource.connect` method that accepts a username and password instead of the one with no arguments. This way, you could encrypt the password and store it with the application configuration instead of with the server configuration.

Leaving plaintext credentials, especially those for other systems (like databases) on a server enables a "domino effect" if a compromise should occur.

WEB SERVICES WORKFLOW SECURITY

Another aspect of web services involves asynchronous, workflow-style processing. In a typical workflow model, a sender generates a message and then sends the message to a receiver. The first receiver may not be the ultimate destination for the message, but may instead be required to perform only partial processing on the message. Then the message is forwarded from the initial receiver to the next receiver in line, and so on until it reaches its final destination. In SOAP parlance, these receivers are called *actors*.

For example, the workflow could go something like this:

1. A client generates a SOAP message requesting that a current sales brochure be sent to a customer with a particular ID.
2. The message is routed to the first actor, who is responsible for translating the customer ID into a mailing address and adding it to the message body.
3. The newly modified message is forwarded to an actor (or service) that converts the brochure name to a printable block of data (perhaps PostScript or some other format).
4. The message is forwarded to a printing and mailing component, which prints the printable content and ensures that it is mailed to the provided mailing address.

Figure 11-3 illustrates this workflow process. The lure of web services is that potentially each of these services could be provided by a different enterprise, or even an entirely different organization or company.

SOAP currently provides much of the basic functionality necessary to enable this type of workflow, but unfortunately, it is totally lacking in security to support it. Let's take a look at the types of security that are necessary in a workflow-based environment such as this.

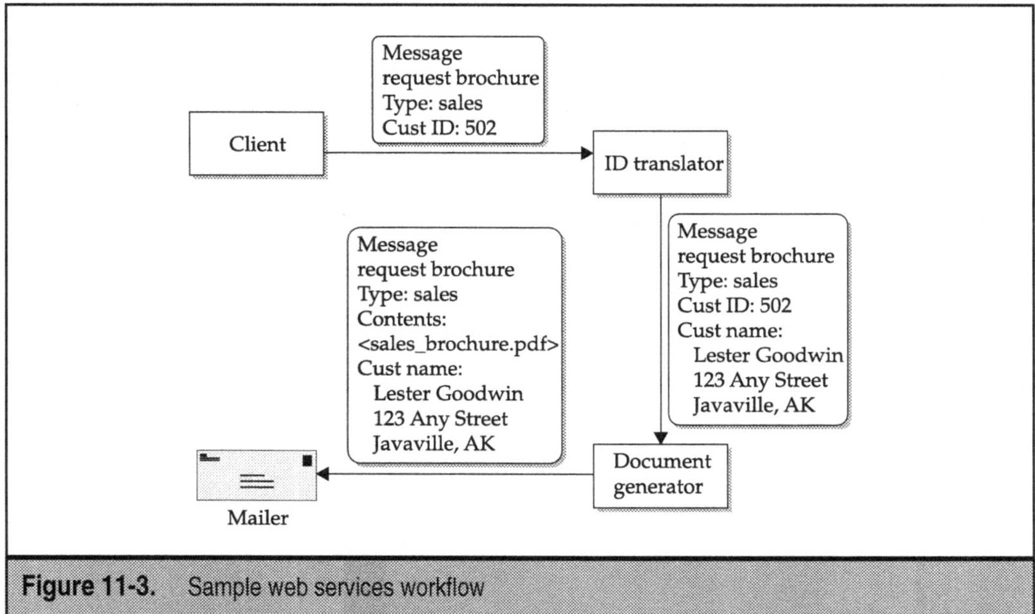

Figure 11-3. Sample web services workflow

Unauthorized Modification of a Web Services Request by an Intermediate Actor

Popularity:	2
Simplicity:	8
Impact:	8
Risk rating:	**6**

We need a way to guarantee that the mailing service (the last actor in line) knows who generated the *original* request and that the providers of the intermediate services (document generation and mailing address generation) were all trusted by the originator of the message. So, there needs to be a secure way to propagate an authentication token throughout the workflow. Considering that some complex workflows could take days to complete, this becomes a daunting problem. Right now, there is no real standard solution to deal with this issue.

We will look at future standards that address this problem in the next section. But what if you need to build a web services application that has this functionality today, and your vendor does not provide proprietary support for propagation of security credentials?

Use the JCE to Add Sender Identification and Message Integrity

The best short-term solution to this problem would be to include a digital signature of both the original message content and a timestamp or serial number in the user data section of the message to verify its origin. The final receiver can then verify the signature and know that the entity that generated the original data was in possession of the private key of the originator.

Additionally, to verify the identities of the intermediate processors, each processor or actor could include a digital signature of the information that they added to the message using certificates that had been signed by the message originator. This would prove two things:

- That the intermediate processors were trusted by the originator (because they have their certificates signed by the client)
- That the information included in the message was generated by them and nobody else

Unauthorized Retransmission of a Web Services Request

Popularity:	4
Simplicity:	9
Impact:	5
Risk rating:	**6**

You may also want to incorporate a signed timestamp or serial number into the authentication token to help protect against "replay" attacks. For example, suppose that you order a new sports car from the manufacturer using its web services interface. Your request is digitally signed, so attackers cannot modify it. However, they can capture the request and send the same one over and over again. You might not even know about it until you get a message from the dealer telling you it's time to pick up 54 new cars.

Include a Timestamp or Serial Number with Each Message

If a timestamp is included in the signed message, the receiver can see that 53 of the messages are identical and discard them. Additionally, if for some reason, it takes your message an excessive length of time to arrive at its destination, it can also be rejected as invalid.

Unauthorized Retrieval of Information from a Web Services Request by an Intermediate Actor

Popularity:	*4*
Simplicity:	*8*
Impact:	*3*
Risk rating:	***5***

What if we need to keep our information private in a workflow process? Using SSL, as we did in Lester's system (see Figure 11-3), will only guarantee the confidentiality of data as it passes between nodes. Once our information is on a particular node, SSL does nothing to protect it.

Using Lester's workflow system, let's assume that we want to keep the customer mailing address secret from the company that is doing our document generation. The document generation company doesn't need the mailing address to do its job, and if this service were provided by an external vendor, we wouldn't want them to build a list of our customers merely by lifting the information out of all SOAP messages passing through their service.

Use the JCE to Provide Message Confidentiality

Again, SOAP does not provide a standard way to handle data confidentiality, although this feature will be addressed in future specifications. If you absolutely must implement a system that has this need right now, you can fall back on the JCE and encrypt the relevant information with the public key of its recipient. However, there's a small problem with that approach: What if multiple, but not all, nodes along the workflow need to look at the information. A better solution is to encipher the sensitive data with a symmetric key, then encipher, or wrap, the symmetric key with the public key of the intended recipient.

So, if there were three possible recipients of the data in the workflow, you would encipher the same symmetric key three times: once with each possible recipient's public key. Then you would include all three asymmetrically enciphered keys in the message body along with the symmetrically enciphered data. That way, each of the three intended receivers could decipher the symmetric key using their private key and then use that symmetric key to decipher the data. Any unauthorized receivers would not be able to decipher the sensitive information, because they wouldn't have the private key necessary to decipher one of the enciphered symmetric keys.

Obviously, implementing an infrastructure like this is difficult. In fact, it is so difficult, yet the need is so common, that there are many people working on building standards to satisfy this need right now. In the next section, we'll present a quick summary of the current state of web services security standardization.

THE FUTURE OF WEB SERVICES SECURITY

It is probably apparent to you by now that web services are an extremely nascent technology. Indeed, just as is the case with many business applications, security is being added to web services somewhat as an afterthought. Because of this, we can be assured that the world of Java web services security will continue to change. Fortunately, web services use XML as their basis, and XML is very amenable to dynamic modification of structural schema information.

Security may very well be the primary show-stopper that stands in the way of the business acceptance of web services technology. It will merely be a race to determine if security standardization will occur before the next new idea for business-to-business messaging and collaboration emerges. However, with the enormous amount of industry backing that web services are receiving, it seems almost certain that web services will win the race. What they will look like when they cross the finish line is another matter entirely.

Many web services-related security technologies are currently under development, including SOAP Security Extensions: Digital Signature, the proposed Web Services Security standard (WS-Security), and the Security Assertion Markup Language (SAML). These technologies are not mutually exclusive, but in the future, there may be some implementations of containers or SOAP parsers that support the first, but not the second and vice versa. In fact, the proposed WS-Security standard supercedes many aspects of the SOAP Security Extensions: Digital Signature standard.

There is also a bevy of emerging XML-level standards for key management, message digests and signatures, message confidentiality, and more. We had to draw the line somewhere, so we chose to focus on only those technologies that are directly relevant to web services.

SOAP Security Extensions: Digital Signature

The proposed SOAP Security Extensions: Digital Signature standard addresses adding digital signature information to SOAP messages in a standard way. It has the status of an official W3C note (not a standard) and as such, has received some industry acceptance to date.

Essentially, the SOAP Security Extensions: Digital Signature proposal allows a sender to add a message digest and signature to the header of a SOAP envelope in a standard way. This allows the receiver to look at the header, verify the integrity of the digest by using the digital signature, and then verify the integrity of the message body by comparing it with the attached digest.

For more information about SOAP, refer to http://www.w3.org/TR/2000/NOTE-SOAP-20000508/ and for more information about the SOAP Digital Signature Proposal, refer to http://www.w3.org/TR/SOAP-dsig/.

This feature provides for message integrity only. There are no provisions in this specification for confidentiality. However, especially in workflow-style SOAP-processing networks, where messages can pass through many processing nodes, message integrity is an extremely important technology. This technology, originally developed by Microsoft, will most likely be superceded by WS-Security.

WS-Security

The proposed WS-Security specification (http://www-106.ibm.com/developerworks/library/ws-secure/) is much more comprehensive, and as such, may encounter some industry-wide resistance, especially since portions of the standard appear to directly compete with the OASIS SAML specification (specifically, the authentication and authorization portion). However, recently the developers of WS-Security have submitted it to OASIS as a proposed standard, so the chances are good that any overlap will eventually be worked out.

The WS-Security recommendation has been developed by Microsoft, IBM, and Verisign. It proposes a much more elaborate security model for web services. In fact, it threatens to take the "simple" out of SOAP (Simple Object Access Protocol), if it hasn't been removed already. The developers of this specification rightly decided that for true enterprise interoperability to exist, especially when goods and services are being exchanged as a result of computation, a robust interoperable security framework is necessary. Thus, the WS-Security standard provides one of the best hopes for a framework that organizations can rely on for electronic commerce and the automated pursuit of business.

The WS-Security proposal contains support for secure propagation of security credentials. Credentials can be username/password-based, username/digest-based, or digital credentials, such as Kerberos tokens or X509 certificates. Additionally, WS-Security uses the XML signature and encryption standards to facilitate end-to-end message-level security (integrity and confidentiality). One interesting aspect of WS-Security is that it supports the concept of *trust domains*. This means that an arbitrary node in the middle of a SOAP workflow could add its credentials to a message and "vouch" for its authenticity, validity, or level of authorization, even if the ultimate receiver of the message has no knowledge of the original sender. This technology is critical for enabling cross-enterprise business workflows.

IBM and Microsoft are already supporting WS-Security in portions of their product line, and with its submission to OASIS, many other vendors will probably follow suit.

SAML

SAML was developed by OASIS, and it focuses almost exclusively on authentication and authorization, not message integrity or confidentiality, as WS-Security does. SAML's primary goal is to address authenticating a user and then propagating that user's identity in a secure manner. This allows a user to authenticate with one organization, perhaps a trustworthy entity like Microsoft (remember, this is just a hypothetical example), which then would generate a series of SAML assertions that could be used to vouch for the user at remote sites. Then the user could attach the SAML token to his or her requests to other web services, perhaps a hardware ordering and configuration service at Sun Microsystems. Then, if Sun Microsystems trusts Microsoft, there would be no need to reauthenticate the user, because Microsoft had already authenticated the user. All of this information can be gleaned from a SAML token attached to a SOAP message.

The end result of this initiative would be single sign-on functionality across organizations, and perhaps across the Internet itself. Will this ever happen? I don't know... Will Sun ever trust Microsoft? We'll have to wait and see.

SUMMARY

In this chapter, we focused on web services and how they relate to Java and J2EE security. You have seen that web services in Java do have some security-related features, which can be used to secure simple, point-to-point applications quite well.

For more complex applications, there are many possible ways to construct secure web services applications. But today, those security mechanisms are extremely labor-intensive and nonstandard. This makes dynamic interoperability, which is one of the key design goals of web services, almost impossible. Therefore, unless there are compelling reasons to do so, most organizations would most likely be better off waiting for the technology to mature before exposing corporate business logic to the general public, or even external clients, via web services. Of course, exposing web services to internal clients via an intranet or some other trusted communication medium is somewhat more appropriate at this time, but you still must realize that any security solution built today will most likely be superceded by an industry-standard framework in the near future.

An organization that exposes its services electronically needs to be assured that the users of those services are authorized and that the services themselves cannot be exploited. Failure to do that would be similar to a car dealer allowing people to order a new car from the factory over the phone, without even asking for their names. The dealer would have nothing to worry about if everyone in the world was honest. But all it takes is a few dishonest or irresponsible people to put the entire dealership out of business. The same is true with web services. Before we can realize their full promise, web services must be secure, reliable, and trustworthy. You wouldn't want to trust *your* hard-earned money to anything else, would you?

CHAPTER 12

ENTERPRISE JAVA BEANS: SECURITY FOR THE BUSINESS TIER

Lester was almost comfortable with his application, but then he realized that it was missing something. Lester's retirement application was not using EJBs, one of the best features that J2EE has to offer.

As you learned in Chapter 3, EJBs operate in a container that provides a useful set of services, such as life cycle management, transactions, and security. EJBs allow business logic to be encapsulated in components and then run within a container. Using a multitiered model for application development, the presentation tier can focus on how to display information to the user and respond to user interaction, and the business tier can focus on implementing business logic and exposing this business logic as services.

Lester would very much like to avail himself of the benefits of EJBs. For Lester's application, the process of retrieving and setting 401K account balances represents business logic, and these are the components we will model as EJBs.

Recall that there are several different types of EJBs we can use to implement our components: an *entity* bean represents persistent data, a *session* bean represents a conversation with a client and is used to manage the business processing for a client session, and a *message-driven* bean allows asynchronous messages to be processed by an EJB component. Lester believes that an entity bean would be appropriate for representing his 401K account balance information, a session bean could be used to interact with his retirement account client application, and a message-driven bean would be useful to allow changes to accounts from asynchronous clients (whoever they may be).

THE EJB APPLICATION IMPLEMENTATION

Lester, confident and motivated, has created a version of his retirement account application that uses EJBs. As usual, strong security is lacking, but we will help him fix that. Luckily, if we merely use the standard J2EE security services provided for us by our container, Enterprise Java Beans are one of the easiest types of J2EE component to secure. In fact, most of our efforts in this chapter will focus on that very task: letting the container do the hard work of security for us. For now though, let's take a look at what Lester hath wrought with his application.

The retirement client application we've looked at previously used a GUI for user interaction. The process of persisting the data that the user has entered was abstracted to a persistence service. Throughout the course of the book, this service has taken the form of a `LocalPersistenceService` (using the local file system), a `MySQLPersistenceService` (using a MySQL database via JDBC), and a `WebServPersistenceService` (using SOAP via JAX-RPC).

For EJBs, we modify our tried-and-true persistence service to use EJBs to manage the application data. This is accomplished with a new class, the `EJBPersistenceService`. This class will perform a JNDI lookup to find a home interface for and create an instance of a stateless session bean (the `RetirementAccountInfoBean`).

Once the persistence service has the remote reference to the session bean, it uses the reference to interact with the EJB and perform two operations: get the 401K account balance and set the 401K balance. The interaction between these components is shown in

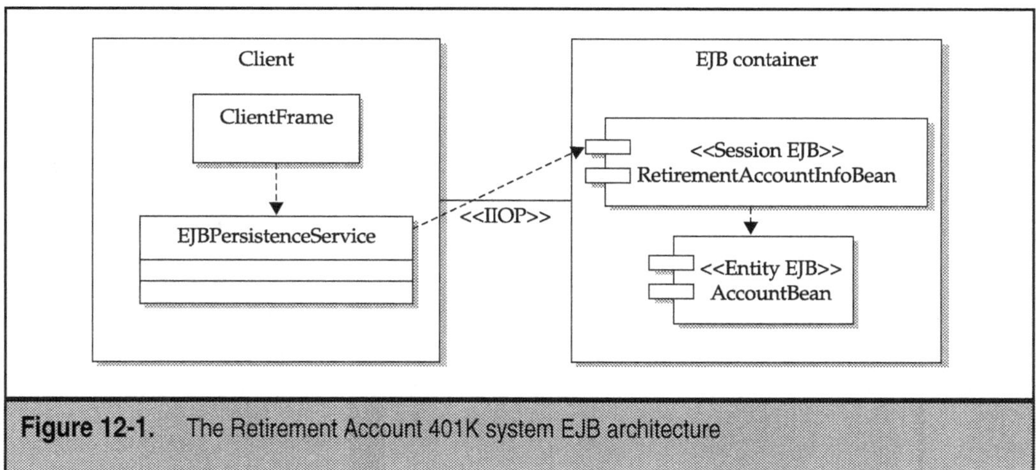

Figure 12-1. The Retirement Account 401K system EJB architecture

Figure 12-1, and as usual, the complete working code for this example is available from www.hackingexposedjava.com.

Although we use a GUI client for our EJBs in this chapter, the techniques we demonstrate are quite relevant for web clients of EJBs also.

The EJB Persistence Service

The code for the `EJBPersistenceService` is shown next.

```
/**
* Constructs an instance of this service, which will use the home interface
* residing at the provided JNDI Name for its persistence services.
* @param servJNDIName The JNDI name of the home interface for
* the bean.
*/
  public EJBPersistenceService(String servJNDIName) {
    serviceJNDI = servJNDIName;

    try {
      Context c = new InitialContext();
      Object o = c.lookup(serviceJNDI);
      RetirementAccountInfoHome raih = (RetirementAccountInfoHome)
                              PortableRemoteObject.narrow(o,
                              RetirementAccountInfoHome.class);
      myStub = raih.create();
```

```
    } catch (Exception e) {
      e.printStackTrace();
    }
  }
```

We know that to use an EJB, we must obtain a reference to the home object for the bean. To get this reference to the home object, we use the naming service provided by our application server. The `EJBPersistenceService` constructor obtains access to the naming service using the initial context, and then uses the `lookup` method to obtain a reference to the home for the EJB. This home reference is obtained through a name (a string) passed into the constructor for the `EJBPersistenceService` class. The call to the `Context lookup` method will return an object reference, which must be narrowed to obtain the reference to the `RetirementAccountInfoHome` object. We then use this home object to get the remote reference to the `RetirmentAccountInfo` session bean. This is the session bean that the client will use to obtain and change retirement account information.

The Get and Set Balance Methods

The `EJBPersistenceService` class exposes two methods to provide for the manipulation of the 401K account data: the `get401kBalance` and the `set401kBalance` methods, which are part of the `RetirementAccountInfo` interface we have been using throughout this book. These methods use the remote reference (which Lester refers to as a *stub*) to use the session bean to manipulate the accounts. The code for these methods is shown next.

```
public BigDecimal get401kBalance(String accountNumber)
      throws AccountNotFoundException, PersistenceException {
    BigDecimal retVal = null;
    try {
      // Delegate the call to our stub.
      retVal = myStub.get401kBalance(accountNumber);
    } catch (RemoteException e) {
      e.printStackTrace();
      throw new PersistenceException("RemoteException");
    }
    return retVal;
  }

  public void set401kBalance(String accountNumber,
         BigDecimal newBalance,
         RetirementCredential cred)
      throws AccountNotFoundException, OperationNotAllowedException,
      PersistenceException {
    try {
```

```
      // Delegate the call to our stub.
      myStub.set401kBalance(accountNumber,newBalance,cred);
    } catch (RemoteException e) {
      e.printStackTrace();
      throw new PersistenceException("RemoteException");
    }
    return;
  }

  public void close() {
    try {
      myStub.close();
    } catch (Exception e) {
      // Handle all exceptions.
    }
```

The `set401KBalance` method takes parameters for the account number, new balance, and security credentials of the user who has logged in to the system. This method merely takes that information and makes a call to a method of the same name using the remote reference (the stub).

The `get401kBalance` method takes a parameter for the account number and returns the current balance in the account. It does not require security credentials for the user who has logged in to the system, instead giving any user that capability.

The Beans

Lester has created several beans to provide the business services for his application. In Lester's first attempt at using EJBs, he created an entity bean and a session bean. The `AccountBean` is an entity bean used to provide access to the retirement account resource. The `RetirementAccountInfoBean` is a session bean which, as you just saw, will be used by the client's `EJBPersistenceService` class to provide access to EJB resources.

The AccountBean

The code for the `AccountBean` entity bean is shown below. Since this bean uses container-managed persistence, the code that provides the database access will be supplied by the container. For this reason, many of the methods provided are empty body implementations and have been eliminated from this listing. A remote interface is also declared for this class, but is not shown here for brevity. This interface provides the signature for the `setAccountBalance` and `getAccountBalance` methods, thus allowing components or applications that obtain a reference to the remote interface for the entity bean to make calls on these methods.

```
package book.ejb.original.ejb;

import javax.ejb.*;
```

```
import java.rmi.RemoteException;
import java.math.BigDecimal;
public abstract class AccountBean implements EntityBean {

  private EntityContext ctx;

  // Required abstract getters and setters for CMP 2.0
  public abstract String getNumber();
  public abstract void setNumber(String newNum);
  public abstract BigDecimal getBalance();
  public abstract void setBalance(BigDecimal newBal);

  public BigDecimal getAccountBalance() {
    return getBalance();
  }

  public void setAccountBalance(BigDecimal newBal) {
    setBalance(newBal);
  }
  public void setEntityContext(EntityContext entityContext) {
    ctx = entityContext;
  }

  public void unsetEntityContext() {
    ctx = null;
  }
…
  public String ejbCreate(String aNum, BigDecimal balance) throws CreateException {
    setNumber(aNum);
    setBalance(balance);

    // We're CMP, so return null
    return null;
  }
  public void ejbPostCreate(String aNum, BigDecimal balance) {

  }
}
```

This bean contains a method to set the account balance (`setAccountBalance`) for the retirement account, and a method to retrieve the account balance (`getAccountBalance`). These methods, in turn, map to the respective `get` and `set` methods of the bean.

The `ejbCreate` method for the entity bean, which is also shown above, takes an account number and a balance. This is used to set the initial balance for the bean instance.

The RetirementAccountInfoBean

The `RetirementAccountInfoBean` bean is the session bean responsible for interacting with the client application to get user responses. It also interacts with the entity bean, which will provide access to the data resource. This is effectively a controller object, which on a small scale, controls access to other important resources. The code for this class is shown next.

```
public class RetirementAccountInfoBean implements SessionBean {
  private SessionContext ctx;
  private AccountHome acctHome;

  public void ejbCreate() throws CreateException {
     acctHome = getAccountHome();
  }
  public void setSessionContext(SessionContext sessionContext) {
    ctx = sessionContext;
  }

  public void ejbRemove() {
    ctx = null;
    acctHome = null;
  }

  public void ejbActivate() {
  }

  public void ejbPassivate() {
  }

  public BigDecimal get401kBalance(String accountNumber)
      throws AccountNotFoundException {
    System.out.println("Getting balance");
    BigDecimal retVal = null;
    try {
      Account a = acctHome.findByPrimaryKey(accountNumber);
      retVal = a.getAccountBalance();
    } catch (FinderException fe) {
      throw new AccountNotFoundException(
              "Account not found");
    } catch (RemoteException e) {
      throw new EJBException("Bad call to Account Bean", e);
    }
    return retVal;
  }

  public void set401kBalance(String accountNumber,
                             BigDecimal newBalance,
```

```
                                  RetirementCredential cred)
      throws AccountNotFoundException,
             OperationNotAllowedException,
             PersistenceException {

    if (cred.getUserName().equalsIgnoreCase("lester") &&
        new String(cred.getPassword()).equals("password")) {
      BigDecimal retVal = null;
      try {
        Account a = acctHome.findByPrimaryKey(accountNumber);
        a.setAccountBalance(newBalance);
      } catch (FinderException fe) {
        // If we can't find the account, add it.
        // This is for example purposes only. Would want to have
        // a separate "add account" method for a real system.
        try {
          acctHome.create(accountNumber,newBalance);
        } catch (Exception e) {
          throw new EJBException("Can't create new account",e);
        }
      } catch (RemoteException e) {
        throw new EJBException("Bad call to Account Bean", e);
      }
    } else {
      throw new OperationNotAllowedException(
               "User not authorized to set balance");
    }

  }
. . .

  private AccountHome getAccountHome() {
    AccountHome retVal;
    try {
      Context c = new InitialContext();
      Object o = c.lookup("java:comp/env/ejb/AccountHome");
      retVal = (AccountHome)
                 PortableRemoteObject.narrow(o,
                     AccountHome.class);
    } catch (Exception e) {
```

```
        throw new EJBException("Trouble finding AccountHome",e);
      }

      return retVal;

   }
}
```

As you can see, this class contains the `set401KBalance` method and the `get401kBalance` methods. Again, this session bean will not talk directly to the database; it delegates that work to the `AccountBean` entity bean.

The `get401kBalance` method needs to obtain a reference to the entity bean to contact. This requires the home object for the entity bean, which is obtained using the `InitialContext lookup` method provided with the name associated with the entity bean.

Once the `get401kBalance` method has received the home reference for the bean, it calls a finder operation on the home interface to retrieve the remote reference for the entity bean instance that corresponds to the account that will be modified. The remote reference is then used to retrieve the information required.

The `set401kBalance` method performs the same operation to obtain a reference to the entity bean home interface. This method has the added responsibility to check the identity of the user who sent the request. This information is passed in the form of a `Credential` object. For our purposes, the `Credential` object contains a username and password, which are checked to determine if the user has permission to set the 401K account balance.

NOTE It may seem as if the session bean is not adding much value—it is merely passing data through to the entity bean and providing a customized authorization scheme. However, we have intentionally added it as an example of the common *session façade* J2EE design pattern. It will give us a great mechanism to explore security concepts in the context of this most common EJB configuration.

The home interface for the `RetirementAccountInfoBean` session bean contains method signatures for both the `set401kBalance` and the `get401kBalance` methods, thus exposing both of those methods to client applications. There is currently no EJB security associated with these beans, which as we will see, has left Lester's application somewhat vulnerable.

EJB APPLICATION VULNERABILITIES

As you have learned in earlier chapters, two important aspects of application security to manage are *authentication* and *authorization*. Authentication involves verifying that the user is who he or she says they are. Authorization involves determining whether the authenticated user is authorized to perform the action he or she is requesting.

The EJB specification does not concern itself with many authentication issues; that is left to the container implementation. The majority of the security portion of the EJB specification is concerned with authorization. Actions are interpreted to be method invocations, and the EJB specification details that an authenticated user (a principal) is mapped to a security role, and that security role is granted permission to execute specific methods in specific components, as shown in Figure 12-2.

At runtime, when an EJB is invoked, the principal who invoked the method is assigned to the context of the method call. Just as in web applications, that principal can be a member of one or more J2EE roles. When a client session attempts to invoke a method on an EJB, the container checks to determine whether the security role currently assigned to the principal invoking the method has been granted permission to execute the method.

If the authentication is being done using a web-tier client, various security realm mechanisms are available to authenticate the user and map the authentication to a security principal. These authentication mechanisms can be combined with very strong confidentiality and integrity mechanisms such as SSL to make it very difficult for an attacker to access this information.

Mapping the authenticated user to a J2EE role is the responsibility of the realm mechanism. Application server vendors then provide a mechanism to map the security principal to a security role. Unfortunately, this mapping mechanism falls outside the EJB specification and is proprietary, with each vendor offering its own set of tools.

If the client is not a web-tier client (a thin client), as is the case with Lester's application, some other mechanism is required to authenticate the user and relay this authentication information to the application server. This must be done in a secure fashion, since the information may be moving over an unsecured network. The J2EE specification, in combination with the EJB specification, provides something of a mandate for security with these applications, which are referred to generically as J2EE application clients. More specifically, for our purposes, these are non-web J2EE clients, also referred to as *rich clients*.

A J2EE client application can perform authentication, which is then mapped to an EJB security role. Then, using IIOP security transport semantics, the authentication credentials

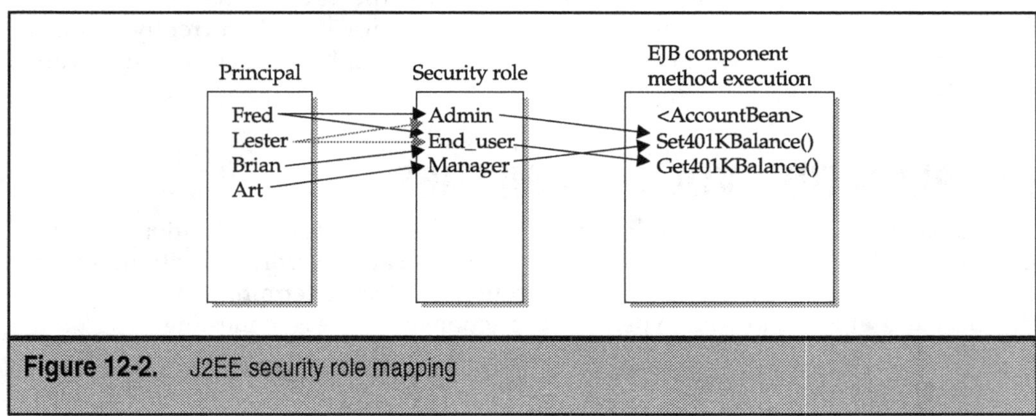

Figure 12-2. J2EE security role mapping

can be transported securely from the client ORB to the container. It is possible for the IIOP connection between the client's ORB and the application server ORB to be tunneled through an SSL connection to provide an additional level of confidentiality and integrity. Most production application servers provide methods to secure the connection between EJB clients and the application server itself, whether this connection is from a RMI-IIOP client or via a connector or plug-in from a web server.

Using SSL to secure connections between application servers adds a slight performance cost, but can be invaluable for the protection of sensitive enterprise data. Additionally, SSL with server authentication will protect clients from a spoofing attack, but more important, if SSL client authentication is used to allow connections only from authorized clients, it can defend your application server from many denial-of-service (DoS) attacks.

To run J2EE Application Clients, Sun's J2EE reference implementation uses the `runclient` utility, which wraps the Java application with a small program that prompts the user for a username and password, as shown here.

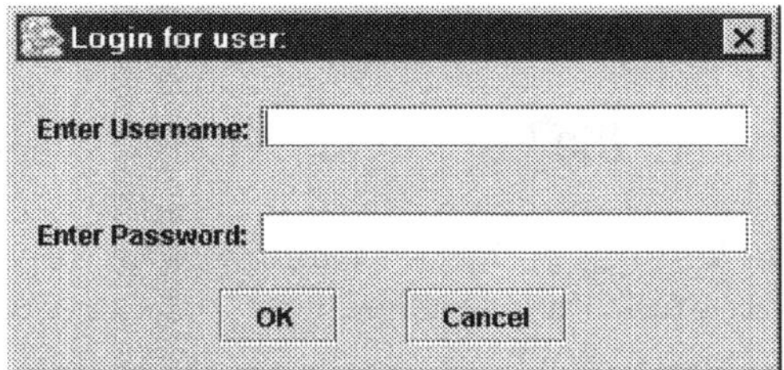

The reference implementation also provides various screens that allow the authenticated user to be mapped to a group, which is, in turn, mapped to a security role. What is important to note is not the specifics of how security will be mapped, but that the EJB implementation will allow the container to enforce security and using that security is the best practice for EJBs. Without this security mechanism, any remote user (including potential attackers) with access to the EJB server and knowledge of the interfaces of remotely deployed beans (those not declared as local beans) could access the server and execute remote methods. Declarative security should be the norm for deployed EJBs that present remote interfaces to enterprise clients.

Unauthorized Access to the Naming Service

Popularity:	3
Simplicity:	7
Impact:	4
Risk rating:	5

A potential attacker can gain much information without even calling our EJBs merely by looking at the contents of the JNDI-compliant naming service presented by our application server. Every home object, for every bean with a remote interface that resides on the server, is stored in the naming service. A skillful attacker could write some code, or use a utility to traverse the namespace via JNDI. Once they were able to assess the structure of the namespace, they could get the home objects for particular beans and then examine the metadata for the beans by using the `getEJBMetaData` method in the `EJBHome` interface. If the application server is configured to dynamically generate and remotely serve the .class files for its stubs, an attacker could discover all relevant information about our bean and invoke methods upon it without even having a copy of its remote interface. This technique is similar to the one we applied in Chapter 11 when we were able to invoke a web service without the proper stub files, instead using the WSDL to build the stubs ourselves.

Additionally, an attacker could potentially remove references to our beans from the naming service and replace them with their own. Then, when clients looked up the home interface for our bean, they would instead get the attacker's home interface, built to spoof our bean.

Countermeasure: Secure the Naming Service

Most common application servers give administrators the ability to restrict access to bind, rebind, and even look up objects in the naming service. However, for unknown reasons, in many production application servers, these features are never enabled. It could be that the administrators don't know that they can be enabled, or maybe they are disabled in the name of performance. Regardless, your application server's naming service is its front door. Allowing unrestricted access to it is analogous to allowing anonymous users to freely browse the file systems on your servers: it's not a good idea.

The specifics of how to secure a particular application server's naming services are obviously server specific and beyond the scope of this book, but for most common application servers, the procedure is relatively straightforward.

Securing the namespace is the first step to securing the server itself. Controlling who can add, remove, and view entries in your namespace is critical to controlling who can access your application. Don't forget this important step.

Packet Sniffing to Get User Credentials and Calling the Session Bean Directly

Popularity:	*8*
Simplicity:	*3*
Impact:	*7*
Risk rating:	***6***

As we return to our example, we see that although Lester has made good use of a middle-tier technology (EJBs), he has once again left a security hole in his application. Lester is sending the username and password unencrypted to the server in his own custom Java object. Any determined hacker with a packet sniffer could capture the username and password.

Assuming our attackers are knowledgeable insiders, they could easily combine the user security credentials with the interface for the session bean to create their own malicious application to set 401K account balances as they see fit.

If you remember, the `set401kBalance` method on the session bean is exposed to client applications in the remote interface. Clever attackers could easily construct their own application to connect to the server and pass valid credentials to the `set401kBalance` method, thus increasing the balance on their target account.

Unauthorized Access to the Entity Bean

Popularity:	5
Simplicity:	3
Impact:	8
Risk rating:	**5**

An even larger security hole is created by the design of the entity bean. While the session bean requires valid security credentials, in the form of a custom Java object, to be able to call the `set401kBalance` method, the entity bean `setAccountBalance` method has no such requirement. Any application that can obtain a reference to the remote object for an instance of the `AccountBean` could make a call to the `setAccountBalance` method.

The path of least resistance for our technical attacker would be to create a simple application that takes the account number and balance as arguments, calls the finder method to obtain the corresponding entity bean for the account number, and then makes calls on the `setAccountBalance` method. Even though Lester's application accessed the entity bean from another EJB—a session bean—since the entity bean presents a *remote* interface, there is nothing precluding a client application created by a malicious programmer from accessing the entity bean in an application using code similar to the following.

```
...
        //
        // Obtain the home interface for our entity bean.
       //
       Context c = new InitialContext();
       Object o = c.lookup("java:comp/env/ejb/AccountHome");
       AccountHome ah = (AccountHome)
            PortableRemoteObject.narrow(o,AccountHome.class);
       try {
         //
         // Find our account.
         //
```

```
        Account a = ah.findByPrimaryKey(accountNumber);
        //
        // Set the balance.
        //
        a.setAccountBalance(newBalance);
...
```

Countermeasure: Use Local Interfaces with Entity Beans

Fortunately, we have several tools in our bag of tricks that can counter malicious hackers. First and foremost, we should secure our most valuable resource, our data. We can do this by creating the entity bean using an EJB *local interface* (which is a new feature in the EJB 2.0 specification), thus limiting its access to only local components. A *local bean*—a bean that extends the local EJB interfaces—cannot be accessed from outside the container in which it is running. Since entity beans should not be directly accessed by client applications, virtually every entity bean should be declared as a local bean. Local beans also provide a performance improvement, since the container can avoid the local loopback network communication channel and use more efficient interprocess or intraprocess communication mechanisms.

Both the home and remote interfaces for the `AccountBean` must extend the appropriate interfaces. For the `AccountHome` interface, it must extend the `EJBLocalHome` interface, as shown next.

```
...
public interface AccountHome extends EJBLocalHome {
  public Account create(String accountNumber,
                        BigDecimal initBal)
     throws RemoteException, CreateException;

  public Account findByPrimaryKey(String accountNumber)
     throws FinderException, RemoteException;
}
```

For the `AccountBean` remote interface, the `EJBLocalObject` interface can be extended as follows.

```
...
public interface Account extends EJBLocalObject {
  public BigDecimal getAccountBalance() throws RemoteException;

  public void setAccountBalance(BigDecimal newBal)
     throws RemoteException;
```

The deployment process also must be aware that local interfaces are being used. The deployment descriptor entry to define the `AccountBean` entity bean as a local bean is shown next.

```
...
<enterprise-beans>
    <entity>
      <display-name>AccountBean</display-name>
      <ejb-name>AccountBean</ejb-name>
      <local-home>book.ejb.moresecure.ejb.AccountHome</local-home>
      <local>book.ejb.moresecure.ejb.Account</local>
      <ejb-class>book.ejb.moresecure.ejb.AccountBean</ejb-class>
      <persistence-type>Container</persistence-type>
      <prim-key-class>java.lang.String</prim-key-class>
      <reentrant>False</reentrant>
      <cmp-version>2.x</cmp-version>
      <abstract-schema-name>Account</abstract-schema-name>
      <cmp-field>
        <description>no description</description>
        <field-name>balance</field-name>
      </cmp-field>
      <cmp-field>
        <description>no description</description>
        <field-name>number</field-name>
      </cmp-field>
      <primkey-field>number</primkey-field>
      <security-identity>
        <description></description>
        <use-caller-identity></use-caller-identity>
      </security-identity>
    </entity>
...
```

Countermeasure: Let the Container Perform Authentication and Transport User Credentials

Instead of prompting for and subsequently transporting user credentials by using a custom Java object, we should let the container take care of that function for us. After all, part of the allure of EJB technology is that the container can manage many aspects of distributed computing that we as application developers would like to avoid, like transactions, persistence, and *security*. By removing the custom credential from our application, and letting the container authenticate the client, either through the `runclient` utility (for rich clients) or by using the techniques we explored in Chapters 9 and 10 for web-based clients, we are guaranteed that we will always be able to get the associated principal from our methods, regardless of platform or container. Also, we can be assured that the credentials will be transported in a much more secure, standardized manner than any custom solution that we might build.

To enable this functionality in our application, we just need to remove the credential parameter from our `set401KBalance` method in our `RetirementAccountInfo` bean, as shown in Figure 12-3. Once we enable declarative authorization for our EJB, the container will *automatically* require credentials from any client, in a standard format the container can understand.

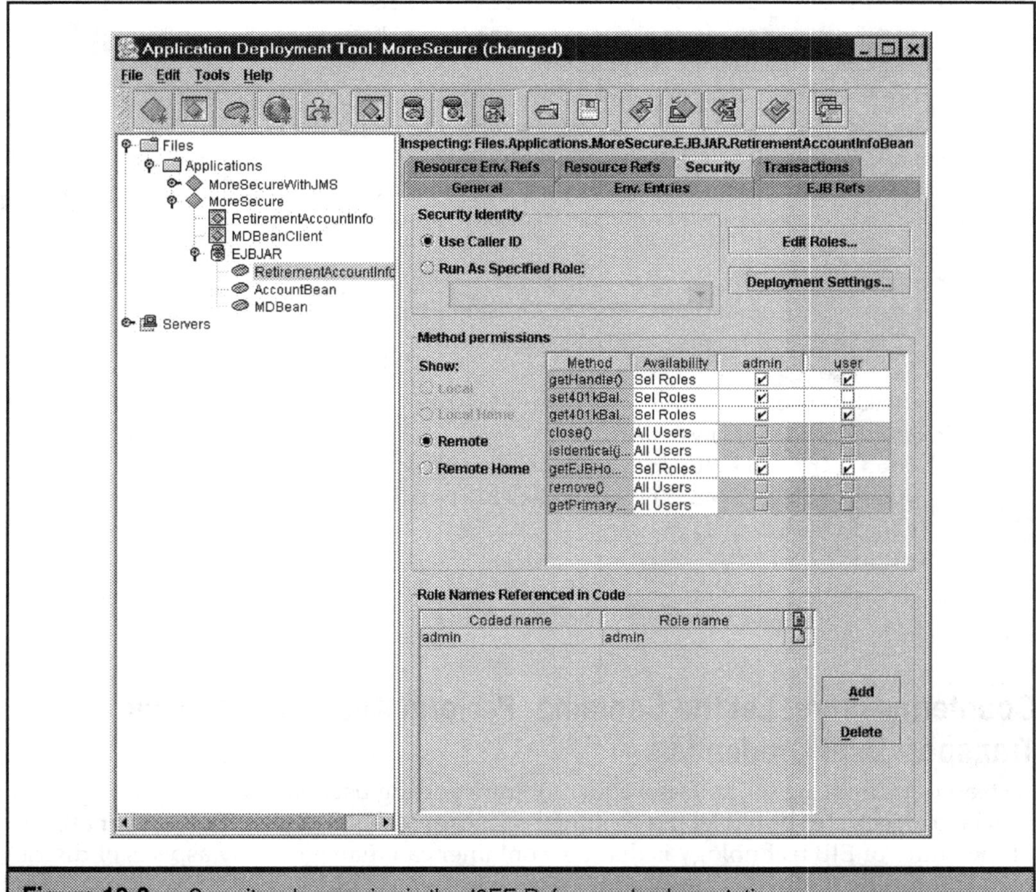

Figure 12-3. Security role mapping in the J2EE Reference Implementation

This approach is beneficial from another perspective also: Application code no longer has to handle a user's username and password information. Now, any application can gain the benefits of authentication and authorization without having access to, or needing to explicitly check client credentials.

Countermeasure: Use Declarative and Programmatic Security to Validate Roles

For our purposes, we need to secure both the EJB session bean (`RetirementAccountInfoBean`) and the entity bean (`AccountBean`), since they are both potentially accessible (the local interface for the entity bean is accessible through the session bean or from any other bean deployed in its container). Both the home and remote references should use declarative security. The security mapping performed in the J2EE Reference Implementation maps users and groups of users to security roles, as shown in Figure 12-3.

To avoid having virtually any unauthorized user with knowledge of EJBs accessing an EJB, we need to institute security within the EJB container. As discussed in Chapter 3, J2EE declarative security allows entries in the EJB deployment descriptor to describe the security for the application.

One major advantage of the declarative security approach is the flexibility it provides, allowing security decisions to be made at deployment time instead of at development time. This allows components to be developed generically and then integrated into various applications with different security requirements. This integration is easier than the alternative programmatic approach, where addressing different security requirements would mean costly changes to application code. It is also less error prone, since the developer does not need to constantly insert programmatic security checks into the code; the code is instead secured by nature of the fact that declarative security is being used.

EJBs also support programmatic authorization and provide the ability to map those programmatic checks to other security roles if needed. In the EJB code, the security state for the bean is available through the associated context: `SessionContext` for session beans, `EntityContext` for entity beans, and `MessageDrivenContext` for message-driven beans.

In the session bean code shown previously, the `RetirementAccountInfoBean` contained a `set401KBalance` method that performs the secure operation of changing the 401K account balance. We can secure this code programmatically using the code shown next.

```
...
public void set401kBalance(String accountNumber, BigDecimal newBalance)
      throws AccountNotFoundException, OperationNotAllowedException,
      PersistenceException {
    System.out.println("Setting Balance");
```

```
    if (ctx.isCallerInRole("admin")) {
      BigDecimal retVal = null;
      AccountHome ah = getAccountHome();
      try {
        Account a = ah.findByPrimaryKey(accountNumber);
...
```

As this code shows, we can use a simple call to the `isCallerInRole` method to determine whether the caller is in the required security role. This use of programmatic security requires an entry in the deployment descriptor indicating that a particular role is being used and linking the role used in the code to a security role. This entry is required, even if the security role names are the same, as shown in the following deployment descriptor fragment.

```
<session>
      <display-name>RetirementAccountInfoBean</display-name>
      <ejb-name>RetirementAccountInfoBean</ejb-name>
      <home>
        book.ejb.moresecure.shared.RetirementAccountInfoHome
      </home>
      <remote>
        book.ejb.moresecure.shared.RetirementAccountInfoRemote
      </remote>
      <ejb-class>
        book.ejb.moresecure.ejb.RetirementAccountInfoBean
      </ejb-class>
      <session-type>Stateless</session-type>
      <transaction-type>Container</transaction-type>
      <ejb-local-ref>
        <ejb-ref-name>ejb/AccountHome</ejb-ref-name>
        <ejb-ref-type>Entity</ejb-ref-type>
        <local-home>book.ejb.moresecure.ejb.AccountHome</local-home>
        <local>book.ejb.moresecure.ejb.Account</local>
        <ejb-link>ejb-jar-ic.jar#AccountBean</ejb-link>
      </ejb-local-ref>
      <security-role-ref>
        <role-name>admin</role-name>
        <role-link>admin</role-link>
      </security-role-ref>
      <security-identity>
        <description></description>
        <use-caller-identity></use-caller-identity>
      </security-identity>
    </session>
```

If a method contains code that can be used by users in a variety of security roles, and only certain blocks of code within the method need to be restricted, then programmatic security is appropriate. But more commonly, work is divided into methods that perform very specific operations, which sometimes require security (as with our `set401KBalance` method). In this case, J2EE declarative security offers a cleaner solution.

With declarative security, entries are made in the deployment descriptor to identify security roles and to then associate those security roles with EJB methods. In our retirement account application, we have identified a security role named `admin` and associated that role with a number of different methods, as shown next.

```
...
  <assembly-descriptor>
    <security-role>
      <description>Administrative User</description>
      <role-name>admin</role-name>
    </security-role>
    <security-role>
      <description>Authorized user</description>
      <role-name>user</role-name>
    </security-role>
    <method-permission>
      <role-name>admin</role-name>
      <method>
        <ejb-name>AccountBean</ejb-name>
        <method-intf>LocalHome</method-intf>
        <method-name>findByPrimaryKey</method-name>
        <method-params>
          <method-param>java.lang.String</method-param>
        </method-params>
      </method>
     <method>
        <ejb-name>RetirementAccountInfoBean</ejb-name>
        <method-intf>Remote</method-intf>
        <method-name>set401kBalance</method-name>
        <method-params>
          <method-param>java.lang.String</method-param>
          <method-param>java.math.BigDecimal</method-param>
        </method-params>
      </method>
      <method>
        <ejb-name>RetirementAccountInfoBean</ejb-name>
        <method-intf>Remote</method-intf>
        <method-name>get401kBalance</method-name>
        <method-params>
```

```
        <method-param>java.lang.String</method-param>
      </method-params>
    </method>
...
```

This example shows the assignment of several security roles, including the `admin` security role (shown in bold). In the `method-permission` section, the `admin` security role is associated with a number of methods, including the all-important `set401KBalance` method and the `get401KBalance` method. Now, only authenticated users who have been assigned to these security roles will be allowed to execute these methods. (A number of other `method-permission` assignments are made but are not shown here.)

Securing session and entity beans is generally much more straightforward than securing standalone applications or web-based applications. The reason is that if you let the container do its job, it does most of the hard work for you: authentication, authorization, transport, and propagation of credentials and identity. Where most people go wrong is trying to circumvent the standard J2EE approach and working against the container by implementing a custom security mechanism that works *in place of* the container's mechanism. Not only can this lead to security weaknesses, but at the very least it can lead to extra work, lack of interoperability, and an increased maintenance burden. Get your money's worth! Use your container; that's what it's there for!

COMMON PITFALLS WHEN USING MESSAGE-DRIVEN BEANS

So far, our application only uses entity and session beans. The other type of bean in the current EJB specification is a message-driven bean (MDB). MDBs listen to a message queue or topic served by a message broker. These beans are invoked asynchronously, meaning the client that sent the message usually does not wait for the requested action to complete; it merely posts the message. The message may, in fact, be placed on a message queue, where it is processed at some later point in time. The details of message queues and topics are beyond the scope of this text. We care about security, and as it happens, MDBs represent a very serious potential security hole.

When a message is received by the messaging system within the application server, there is no client. Unlike session beans or entity beans, with MDBs, there is no persistent connection to the application server. Although the message header does contain information about the message, such as a reply-to destination and a provider-specific message ID, it does not provide any built-in authentication of the sender.

Many message brokers require authentication before an individual can add a message to a queue or publish a message to a topic. However, in many enterprise messaging applications, messages are reformatted, retransmitted, altered, forwarded by automated workflow managers, and more. In this process, header information is often somewhat unreliable, because it is usually overwritten by the most recent transmitter. When credentials are propagated, they are usually propagated in a nonstandard way, especially in a messaging architecture that is more sophisticated than a simple point-to-point topology. It's easy to see the *last* node that touched the message, but it's very hard to verify exactly who the original sender was, without needing to trust the body of the message (which any intermediate processor could have altered). If the message is a composite (made up of information from many different senders), our job gets even harder.

Since the application server and, consequently, the EJB container, potentially knows nothing about the true client who sent the message, if security is to be used, the container must be told what security role should be assigned to the client session for the message. This is done in the deployment descriptor using the `run-as` facility; each time a message is processed by the application server, the runtime session for the message will run as the identified security role (similar to the `setuid` or switch user capability in Unix). Therefore, any other beans called by a message-driven bean will think that they are being called by a principal in this `run-as` role.

The Message-Driven Bean Implementation

Lester's business has continued to grow, and he has added clients who will not be using his Java client program. Instead, they would like to create their own client and would like to post account changes to Lester's 401K system asynchronously using messages. Lester thinks this is great and has created an MDB to handle this messaging transaction.

The Client for the MDB

Lester has created a client for the MDB, which will take an account number and a balance amount, and construct and send a message requesting the account balance change. The code for this client application is shown next.

```
package book.ejb.moresecure.client;

import javax.naming.Context;
import javax.naming.InitialContext;
import javax.naming.NamingException;
import javax.jms.*;
import java.math.BigDecimal;

public class MDBeanClient {
  public static void main(String[] args) {
          String queueName = null;
          Context context = null;
          QueueConnectionFactory connectionFactory = null;
          QueueConnection con = null;
          QueueSession session = null;
          Queue queue = null;
          QueueSender sender = null;
```

```
MapMessage message = null;

if ((args.length < 1) || (args.length > 2)) {
      System.out.println(
        "Usage <account number> <new balance>");
      System.exit(1);
}
queueName = "java:comp/env/jms/MyQueue";
try {
      //
      // Use our initial context to get a
      // queue connection factory.
      //
      context = new InitialContext();
      connectionFactory = (QueueConnectionFactory)
            context.lookup(
              "java:comp/env/jms/MyConnectionFactory");
      queue = (Queue) context.lookup(queueName);
} catch (NamingException e) {
      e.printStackTrace();
      System.exit(1);
}

try {
        //
        // Connect to our message queue and create a session.
        //
      con = connectionFactory.createQueueConnection();
      session = con.createQueueSession(false,
                  Session.AUTO_ACKNOWLEDGE);
      sender = session.createSender(queue);
     //
     // Create a message to send.
     //
      message = session.createMapMessage();
      message.setString("AccountNumber",args[0]);
      message.setString("Balance",args[1]);
      sender.send(message);
} catch (JMSException e) {
      e.printStackTrace();
} finally {
      if (con != null) {
            try {
                  con.close();
```

```
                        } catch (Exception e) {}
                    }
                } // end finally

        }
}
```

Lester has created a test application to demonstrate to his clients how to access the message queue using Java. This application really knows nothing about the MDB and is merely posting a message to a JMS-compliant message queue. The application takes arguments for the account number and new balance, and creates a message containing those arguments. The application must then access the message queue and send the message.

In the main program block, the account number and balance are retrieved and stored in variables, and a JNDI initial context (`InitialContext`) is obtained. (This initial context connects to the naming service in the J2EE application server.) This initial context is used to create a queue connection factory, which is then used to create a queue session.

Now we need a message to populate. This message is obtained from the queue session object we have created, and we specifically request a map message allowing us to use Java collection facilities to reference the data in our message (which, in this case, is a Java `Map`). The message is populated with the account number and new balance, and then sent to the message queue.

The MDB Code

On the other end, at the application server, Lester's MDB will process incoming requests for account balance changes. This bean must read the message, access the account requested, and post the new balance to the account. The code for this MDB is shown next.

```
package book.ejb.moresecure.ejb;

import javax.jms.MessageListener;
import javax.jms.Message;
import javax.jms.MapMessage;
import javax.ejb.MessageDrivenBean;
import javax.ejb.EJBException;
import javax.ejb.MessageDrivenContext;
import javax.ejb.CreateException;
import javax.naming.Context;
import javax.naming.InitialContext;
import javax.rmi.PortableRemoteObject;
import java.math.BigDecimal;
public class MDBean implements MessageDrivenBean,
                               MessageListener {

  private MessageDrivenContext ctx;
```

```
  private AccountHome acctHome;
  public void ejbCreate() throws CreateException {
    acctHome = getAccountHome();
  }
  public void ejbRemove() {
  }

  public void setMessageDrivenContext(
              MessageDrivenContext messageDrivenContext) {
    ctx = messageDrivenContext;
  }

  public void onMessage(Message message) {
    if (message instanceof MapMessage) {
      MapMessage msg = (MapMessage) message;
      try {
        String accountNum = msg.getString("AccountNumber");
        BigDecimal balance = (BigDecimal) new
            BigDecimal(msg.getString("Balance"));

        Account a = acctHome.findByPrimaryKey(accountNum);
        a.setAccountBalance(balance);
        System.out.println("Set Acct balance to " + balance);
      } catch (Exception e) {
        // Consume the message and ignore it.
        System.out.println("Ignoring invalid message");
      }
    }
  }
    private AccountHome getAccountHome() {
      AccountHome retVal;
      try {
        Context c = new InitialContext();
        Object o = c.lookup("java:comp/env/ejb/AccountHome");
        retVal = (AccountHome)
            PortableRemoteObject.narrow(o,AccountHome.class);
      } catch (Exception e) {
        throw new EJBException("Trouble finding AccountHome",e);
      }

      return retVal;

  }
}
```

The MDB will read the message being sent and extract the account number and balance from the message. It will then access the home for the `AccountBean` entity bean and perform a lookup to find the account balance to change. Once the remote reference to the entity bean is obtained, the `setAccountBalance` method is called to change the account balance.

A Security Role for the MDB

In order to run the MDB within the application protection domain we have established, we must assign it a security role. This is where it becomes interesting. Since we do not have any direct connection to a client application, we do not truly have a principal associated with the message, and thus, we have no associated security role assignment. We need to create one using the `run-as` facility provided through the deployment descriptor. Using a `run-as` tag in the deployment descriptor, we assign a security role that will be associated with the MDB each time it is run, as shown next.

```
...
<message-driven>
      <display-name>MDBean</display-name>
      <ejb-name>MDBean</ejb-name>
      <ejb-class>book.ejb.moresecure.ejb.MDBean</ejb-class>
      <transaction-type>Container</transaction-type>
      <message-driven-destination>
        <destination-type>javax.jms.Queue</destination-type>
      </message-driven-destination>
      <ejb-local-ref>
        <ejb-ref-name>ejb/AccountHome</ejb-ref-name>
        <ejb-ref-type>Entity</ejb-ref-type>
        <local-home>book.ejb.moresecure.ejb.AccountHome</local-home>
        <local>book.ejb.moresecure.ejb.Account</local>
        <ejb-link>ejb-jar-ic.jar#AccountBean</ejb-link>
      </ejb-local-ref>
      <security-identity>
        <description></description>
        <run-as>
          <description></description>
          <role-name>admin</role-name>
        </run-as>
      </security-identity>
    </message-driven>
...
```

This example contains the entry for the MDB we have created, including the designation of a `run-as` security role. Now, every time a message is received for the message queue that is associated with this bean, the MDB will be run and assign a context that includes the `admin` security role.

Invalid Access to the Message Queue—Posting Malicious Messages

Popularity:	7
Simplicity:	3
Impact:	8
Risk rating:	**6**

What is most notable about MDBs from our perspective is their relative lack of security. In defense of message-oriented middleware (MOM), it did originate and is still used primarily behind the corporate firewall on closed, secure corporate networks. MOM vendors have also implemented various security mechanisms of their own. But Lester's application as shown is not secure. Any knowledgeable attacker with access to the message queue in the application server could post a malicious message. (Often message queues forward to other message queues, so there is the potential that an intermediate message queue could also be compromised.) As it stands, we currently have a sizeable security hole in our application.

Countermeasure: Digitally Signing Messages and Including a Serial Number

We must ensure that not just our message, but also its content has come from a trusted source and not from some unknown attacker. We know from previous chapters that digital signatures can be used to validate the source of a message, so that approach is an effective countermeasure for invalid message attacks.

The following code demonstrates the client adding a digital signature to the new account balance.

```
package book.ejb.moresecurewithjms.client;
import sun.misc.BASE64Encoder;

import javax.naming.Context;
import javax.naming.InitialContext;
import javax.naming.NamingException;
import javax.jms.*;
import java.math.BigDecimal;
import java.security.KeyStore;
import java.security.PrivateKey;
import java.security.Signature;
import java.io.FileInputStream;
```

```
import java.io.FileOutputStream;
import java.io.InputStream;
...
      message.setString("AccountNumber",args[0]);
      message.setString("Balance",args[1]);

      //
      // Add our serial number ...
      // In a real application, you'd store this in
      // a file and increment it with each message.
      //
      message.setInt("SerialNumber",serialNum);
      message.setString("CertName","lestersCert");
      //
      // Create our digital signature.
      //
      String signature = getSignature(args[0] +
             ":" + args[1] + ":" + serialNum++ +
             ":lestersCert");

      //
      // Add our signature.
      //
      message.setString("Signature",signature);
      //
      // Send the message.
      //
      sender.send(message);
      } catch (JMSException e) {
                  e.printStackTrace();
            } finally {
                  if (con != null) {
                        try {
                              con.close();
                        } catch (Exception e) {}
                  }
            } // end finally

      }
```

The only difference between the implementation of this main block and the one previously shown is the addition of the certificate name, the serial number, and the signature field in the message. The serial number can be used to track messages and can be stored on the server side for audit purposes. The serial number should be incremented each time a message is sent (not shown here), allowing the number and sequence of messages sent by a source to be tracked.

The `getSignature` method takes a string and generates a digital signature. In the case of this application, the string is constructed of the serial number, the account number, the balance, and the `CertName`, which is effectively the entire message. On the reverse side, at the message server, the same string will be created and the signature verified. If the signature matches the signature sent with the message, the recipient (our MDB) can be assured that the message was sent by the party we expected to send the message. With this assurance, the message can be processed. If the signatures do not match, the message will be rejected and will not be processed.

The `getSignature` method, shown next, performs the work necessary to generate a digital signature.

```
private static String getSignature(String infoToSign) {
  try {
    // Open and load the keystore.
    KeyStore ks = KeyStore.getInstance("JCEKS");
     //
     // Get the keystore from our classpath.
     //
    InputStream is =
 MDBeanClient.class.getClassLoader().getResourceAsStream("user.ks");
       //
       // We hardcode the keystore password for
       // demonstration purposes.
       //
      ks.load(is, "password".toCharArray());
      is.close();

      // Get the user's private key.
      // For simplicity we're assuming the
      // key does not have its own password.
      PrivateKey theKey = (PrivateKey)
           ks.getKey("lestersKey","password".toCharArray());

      // Initialize the signature.
      Signature s = Signature.getInstance("SHA1withRSA");
      s.initSign(theKey);

      // Generate the signature.
      s.update(infoToSign.getBytes("UTF-8"));
      byte[] sigBytes = s.sign();

      BASE64Encoder enc = new BASE64Encoder();
```

```
      return enc.encode(sigBytes);
    } catch (Exception e) {
        e.printStackTrace();
    }
    return null;
}
```

The method retrieves Lester's private key from the local keystore (in the classpath). We then initialize a signature using the key, generate the signature, and encode it using a base 64 encoder. The result is returned by the method.

The Server Implementation

On the server side, we must check the signature to determine whether it is a valid signature. It is valid if, using the public key corresponding to the private key the sender used, we can verify the signature the sender sent. This verifies that the owner of the sender's key was the actual entity that sent the message.

The onMessage method in our MDB contains the same code as shown previously, except for a small block that checks the signature, as shown next. Notice that the signature is tested with a concatenated string built with the account number, the balance to set, the serial number, and the certName. As you would expect, this is the same string used by the client to generate the signature.

```
...
 String checkString = accountNum + ":" +
                      msg.getString("Balance") + ":" +
                      msg.getInt("SerialNumber") + ":" + certName;

  if
    (!isSignatureOK(checkString,
                   msg.getString("Signature"), certName)) {
          System.out.println("Rejecting message");
          return;
        }
...
```

If the isSignatureOK method returns false, we assume the message is invalid, and the onMessage method returns at that point. Otherwise, processing continues and the account balance is changed as directed in the message.

The isSignatureOK method, shown next, performs the work required to verify the signature sent.

```
private static boolean isSignatureOK( String infoToCheck,
                                      String signature,
                                      String certName) {
    boolean retVal = false;
```

```
    try {
      // Open and load the keystore.
      KeyStore ks = KeyStore.getInstance("JCEKS");
      InputStream is =
       MDBean.class.getClassLoader().getResourceAsStream(
                 "admin.ks");
      ks.load(is, "password".toCharArray());
      is.close();

      // Get the user's RSA Cert.
      Certificate cert =  ks.getCertificate(certName);

      // Initialize the signature.
      Signature s = Signature.getInstance("SHA1withRSA");
      s.initVerify(cert);

      // Generate the signature based on what's in
      // the message.
      //
      s.update(infoToCheck.getBytes("UTF-8"));

      // Decode the signature sent with the message and
      // compare it to the signature we just generated.
      //
      BASE64Decoder dec = new BASE64Decoder();
      byte[] sigBytes = dec.decodeBuffer(signature);
       //
       // Compare the signature generated (s) to the one sent with
       // the message (sigBytes).
       //
      retVal = s.verify(sigBytes);

    } catch (Exception e) {
        e.printStackTrace();
    }
    System.out.println("Sig verifies " + retVal);
    return retVal;
  }
```

As you can see, the `isSignatureOK` method takes as arguments the string to check, the signature value as generated by the client, and the certificate name. It loads the keystore and retrieves the key for the certificate name passed into the method. (In this example, the keystore file is loaded from the classpath of the server.) This key is used to initialize the digital signature.

Once initialized, the digital signature is generated using the string passed into the method (`infoToCheck`). We then decode the signature sent with the message and passed into the method (`signature`), and compare it to the signature generated using the `verify` method. The value returned by this method (true if they match; false otherwise) is returned by the method.

The end result of Lester's efforts is an application that improves on some of the weaknesses of messaging systems. Using the techniques demonstrated here, Lester has added another layer of security to his application. When his server application accepts and processes messages, he can be assured that the message it is processing originated from a trusted user.

SUMMARY

Lester is comfortable now. He has learned, through these many chapters, that security is something that can't be ignored. Although Java is a secure language with many built-in security features, like seatbelts in cars, if they aren't used, they won't help you.

Lester learned that Java security is ever-present, a consistent architectural element of the language that is built into the basic design of the class loader and Java base classes. Using this architecture, developers can build Java protection domains to control application access to secure resources. Using policy files, Lester found that he could control how Java applications accessed secure system resources and create protection domains. But once again, the policy files must be written—the developer (in our case, Lester) must design and implement the application-level security, or it will not exist.

Java security was originally directed at access to system resources, but has been expanded with JAAS to include authentication and authorization of users by using pluggable modules. Lester found that he could use JAAS to authenticate users and also to perform authorization, allowing Java applications to create application-specific security domains.

The Internet is like an open book—anyone can read it. Lester was rightfully concerned about this until he learned that he could hide valuable information in plain sight using JCE to encipher the information. He found, as have many people, that there are a large number of cipher algorithms to choose from, but fortunately, he could focus on a few and use them to his advantage. In many cases, he found he did not need to encipher all of the data, but could get by with attaching a digital signature to allow the receiver to verify the sender's identity.

Using this valuable information on the basics of Java security, Lester then learned how to apply these techniques to J2EE applications. He progressed to securing client-server applications using JAAS and JCE, and securing RMI and Java servlets using similar techniques.

Lester thought web services were great, but then he found that, like many other nascent technologies, security for them is not yet complete. The Web in general, and Java servlets, also represent potential security risks. Lester, to his credit, learned and adapted.

Security is an imperfect science. Neither you nor Lester will ever be able to build a system that is totally secure. In this book, we have not presented many techniques that are theoretically "pure" or perfect, instead favoring techniques that will give you the most security "bang for your buck." Just as with your home, you want to apply a level of security that is appropriate for the assets you are attempting to protect. The most important aspect of making these security decisions is making *informed* decisions. The very fact that you have read this book and understand your options for security in a Java/J2EE environment will place you head and shoulders above many other developers in the industry today.

Good security is not a matter of making your system impenetrable; it's a matter of making your system less penetrable than your neighbor's system. Most people who choose to attack your system are not stupid. If potential attackers sense that the effort required to defeat your application is out of proportion to whatever gain they may realize by penetrating it, they'll move on to easier pickings (and there are plenty of them in production environments around the world).

Our main goal was to inform you of what is possible in a J2EE environment. From here, you can use your experience and common sense to apply the knowledge you've gained and put these techniques into practice.

So Lester is comfortable now, for the time being. He has learned all he can learn. But he is now aware that with security, it's not what you know, but what you *don't* know that will come back to haunt you.

INDEX

A

D

E

F

G

H

I

J

K

L

M

N

O

P

Q

R

S

T

U

V

W

X

INTERNATIONAL CONTACT INFORMATION

AUSTRALIA
McGraw-Hill Book Company Australia Pty. Ltd.
TEL +61-2-9415-9899
FAX +61-2-9415-5687
http://www.mcgraw-hill.com.au
books-it_sydney@mcgraw-hill.com

CANADA
McGraw-Hill Ryerson Ltd.
TEL +905-430-5000
FAX +905-430-5020
http://www.mcgrawhill.ca

GREECE, MIDDLE EAST, NORTHERN AFRICA
McGraw-Hill Hellas
TEL +30-1-656-0990-3-4
FAX +30-1-654-5525

MEXICO (Also serving Latin America)
McGraw-Hill Interamericana Editores S.A. de C.V.
TEL +525-117-1583
FAX +525-117-1589
http://www.mcgraw-hill.com.mx
fernando_castellanos@mcgraw-hill.com

SINGAPORE (Serving Asia)
McGraw-Hill Book Company
TEL +65-863-1580
FAX +65-862-3354
http://www.mcgraw-hill.com.sg
mghasia@mcgraw-hill.com

SOUTH AFRICA
McGraw-Hill South Africa
TEL +27-11-622-7512
FAX +27-11-622-9045
robyn_swanepoel@mcgraw-hill.com

UNITED KINGDOM & EUROPE (Excluding Southern Europe)
McGraw-Hill Education Europe
TEL +44-1-628-502500
FAX +44-1-628-770224
http://www.mcgraw-hill.co.uk
computing_neurope@mcgraw-hill.com

ALL OTHER INQUIRIES Contact:
Osborne/McGraw-Hill
TEL +1-510-549-6600
FAX +1-510-883-7600
http://www.osborne.com
omg_international@mcgraw-hill.com

www.ingramcontent.com/pod-product-compliance
Lightning Source LLC
Chambersburg PA
CBHW082108070326
40689CB00052B/3806

* 9 7 8 0 0 7 2 2 2 5 6 5 5 *